An Introduction to Silius Italicus and the *Punica*

Also available from Bloomsbury

A Guide to Reading Herodotus' Histories, Sean Sheehan
Hannibal, Robert Garland
Homer: A Guide for the Perplexed, Ahuvia Kahane

An Introduction to Silius Italicus and the *Punica*

John Jacobs

BLOOMSBURY ACADEMIC
LONDON • NEW YORK • OXFORD • NEW DELHI • SYDNEY

BLOOMSBURY ACADEMIC
Bloomsbury Publishing Plc
50 Bedford Square, London, WC1B 3DP, UK
1385 Broadway, New York, NY 10018, USA
29 Earlsfort Terrace, Dublin 2, Ireland

BLOOMSBURY, BLOOMSBURY ACADEMIC and the Diana logo are trademarks
of Bloomsbury Publishing Plc

First published in Great Britain 2021
This paperback edition published in 2022

Copyright © John Jacobs, 2021

John Jacobs has asserted his right under the Copyright, Designs and Patents Act, 1988,
to be identified as Author of this work.

For legal purposes the Acknowledgements on p. xii constitute an extension
of this copyright page.

Cover design: Terry Woodley
Cover image © John Trumbull, 1756–1843. *The Death of Paulus Aemilius at the
Battle of Cannae*. Yale University Art Gallery

All rights reserved. No part of this publication may be reproduced or transmitted in any
form or by any means, electronic or mechanical, including photocopying, recording,
or any information storage or retrieval system, without prior permission in writing
from the publishers.

Bloomsbury Publishing Plc does not have any control over, or responsibility for, any
third-party websites referred to or in this book. All internet addresses given in this book
were correct at the time of going to press. The author and publisher regret any
inconvenience caused if addresses have changed or sites have ceased to exist,
but can accept no responsibility for any such changes.

A catalogue record for this book is available from the British Library.

Library of Congress Cataloging-in-Publication Data

Names: Jacobs, John (Classicist), author.
Title: An introduction to Silius Italicus and the Punica / John Jacobs.
Description: London, UK ; New York, NY : Bloomsbury Academic, 2021. | Includes bibliographical references and index. | Summary: "In a much-needed comprehensive introduction to Silius Italicus and the Punica, Jacobs offers an invitation to students and scholars alike to read the epic as a thoughtful and considered treatment of Rome's past, present, and (perilous) future. The Second Punic War marked a turning point in world history: Rome faced her greatest external threat in the famous Carthaginian general Hannibal, and her victory led to her domination of the Mediterranean. Lingering memories of the conflict played a pivotal role in the city's transition from Republic to Empire, from foreign war to civil war. Looking back after the events of AD 69, the senator-poet Silius Italicus identified the Second Punic War as the turning point in Rome's history through his Punica. After introductory chapters for those new to the poet and his poem, Jacobs' close reading of the epic narrative guides students and scholars alike through the Punica. All Greek and Latin passages are translated to ensure accessibility for those reading in English. Far more than simply a retelling of Rome's greatest triumph, the Punica challenges its reader to make sense of the Second Punic War in light of its full impact on the subsequent course of the city's history"– Provided by publisher.
Identifiers: LCCN 2020024307 | ISBN 9781350071049 (hardcover) | ISBN 9781350071056 (ebook) | ISBN 9781350071063 (epub) Subjects: LCSH: Silius Italicus, Tiberius Catius. | Silius Italicus, Tiberius Catius. Punica. | Silius Italicus, Tiberius Catius—Themes, motives. | Punic War, 2nd, 218–201 B.C.–Literature and the war. | Epic poetry, Latin–History and criticism. | Rome–In literature. | Carthage (Extinct city)–In literature.
Classification: LCC PA6695 .J33 2021 | DDC 937/.04—dc23
LC record available at https://lccn.loc.gov/2020024307

ISBN:	HB:	978-1-3500-7104-9
	PB:	978-1-3501-9167-9
	ePDF:	978-1-3500-7105-6
	eBook:	978-1-3500-7106-3

Typeset by RefineCatch Limited, Bungay, Suffolk

To find out more about our authors and books visit www.bloomsbury.com
and sign up for our newsletters.

FILIO CARISSIMO

Contents

List of Maps	ix
Preface	x
Acknowledgments	xii
Note on Text/Translation	xiii
Note on Bibliography	xiv
List of Abbreviations	xv

	Introduction: Why Silius?	1
	1. Poggio and the Rediscovery of the *Punica*	1
	2. Who Is Silius Italicus, What Is the *Punica*, and What Is the *Punica* About?	3
	3. What Is the Place of Silius Italicus and the *Punica* in the Classics?	7
	4. How to Read the *Punica*	10
	5. About this Book	13
1	Who Is Tiberius Catius Asconius Silius Italicus?	17
	1. Introduction: The Julio-Claudians and the Flavians (31 BC–AD 96)	17
	2. Overview of the Testimonia for Tiberius Catius Asconius Silius Italicus	21
	3. Silius Italicus and Martial	26
	4. Silius Italicus and Pliny	32
	5. Conclusion: Pliny *Epistula* 3.7 as a Reading of the *Punica*	36
2	What Is the *Punica*?	41
	1. Introduction: The Punic Wars (264–146 BC)	41
	2. The *Punica* and the Second Punic War	45
	3. The *Punica* and the Historiographical Tradition	53
	4. The *Punica* and the Epic Tradition	56
	5. Conclusion: The Language and Style of the *Punica*	59
3	A Reading of *Punica* 1–10: From Saguntum to Cannae	63
	1. Introduction: The Structure of the *Punica*	63
	2. *Punica* 1.1–20: The Proem	68

	3. *Punica* 1–5: From Saguntum to Lake Trasimene	74
	4. *Punica* 6–10: From Lake Trasimene to Cannae	80
	5. *Punica* 10.657–8: The Turning Point	86
4	A Reading of *Punica* 11–17: From Cannae to Zama	91
	1. *Punica* 11.1–27: The Medial Proem	91
	2. *Punica* 11–15: From Cannae to the Metaurus River	94
	3. *Punica* 16–17: From the Metaurus River to Zama	101
	4. *Punica* 17.625–54: The (Beginning of the) End	104
	5. Conclusion: The Narrative of the *Punica*	108
5	Carthage and Rome in the *Punica*, Part 1	113
	1. Introduction: Cities and Heroes	113
	2. The Gigantomachy Theme	119
	3. The Fall of Troy Theme	126
	4. The Gallic Sack Theme	131
	5. Conclusion: Marcellus, Closure, and Counterfactual History	135
6	Carthage and Rome in the *Punica*, Part 2	141
	1. Introduction: From the Second Punic War to the Flavians	141
	2. The Curse of Dido Theme	146
	3. The *metus hostilis* Theme	149
	4. From Republic to Empire, from Foreign War to Civil War	153
	5. Conclusion: From the Triumph of Scipio to the Triumph of Domitian	162
Conclusion: Silius Italicus and the *Punica* in Classical Literature		165
	1. The Place of Silius Italicus and the *Punica* in Classical Literature	165
	2. The *Punica* and Earlier Literature: Livy and Vergil	167
	3. The *Punica* and Contemporary Literature: Lucan and Petronius	170
	4. The *Punica* and Later Literature: Florus, Ampelius, and the *De viris illustribus*	175
	5. Petrarch *Africa* and the Rediscovery of the *Punica*	181
Notes		183
Bibliography		209
Index		257

Maps

1 Italy: Third Century BC (Hoyos 2015: xiii) — xvi
2 North Africa during the Punic Wars (Hoyos 2015: xiv) — xvii
3 Spain: Third Century BC (Hoyos 2015: xv) — xviii
4 Eastern Mediterranean: Third Century BC (Hoyos 2015: xvi) — xix
5 Theaters and Major Battles of the Second Punic War (Gabriel 2008: 29) — xx
6 The Theatre of Civil War in AD 69 (Greenhalgh 1975: 141) — xxi

Preface

The present volume represents the first of two books on the Roman senator, consul, orator, and poet Silius Italicus and his Latin historical epic, the *Punica*, which I will be publishing with Bloomsbury Academic. In this book, I offer the first comprehensive introduction in any language to the poet and his poem; in the companion book, I will likewise offer the first comprehensive introduction in any language to their reception and their place in the Classical tradition. This first volume has its (distant) origins in my 2009 Ph.D. dissertation, but also reflects how my thinking about Silius and the *Punica* has (I hope) evolved over the course of the past decade. As Flavian literature and, in particular, Flavian epic continue to attract more and more attention among both students and scholars, there is a real need for an accessible overview of the poet and his poem. I hope that, in attempting to meet that need, I am at least able to garner the epic even more readers.

I have many students, colleagues, and friends to thank for their advice and support during the past two decades, especially from the many years spent with the *Punica*. First and foremost, I would like to thank my dissertation advisor at Yale, Chris Kraus, as well as my two readers, Kurt Freudenburg and Bob Cowan. More recently, I would like to thank the many students, parents, and colleagues at the Montclair Kimberley Academy who have sustained me as I completed this project over the past several years. In particular, I would like to thank my Headmaster, Tom Nammack, as well as my Upper School Head of Campus, Dave Flocco. Steve Valentine, Upper School Assistant Head of Campus, offered welcome advice and support at a number of critical junctures. Among other members of the MKA community, I would especially like to thank my colleagues David Hessler and Ron Wolfson; Ron, Carole, and David Reading; and my advisee, Luca Winters. I completed some of the research for this project, and much of the research for the second project, through the generous assistance provided by a PAMKA Faculty Trust Grant.

I would not have written this book if my first department chair, trusted colleague, and valued friend Fred Booth had not invited me to deliver the tenth annual Father Cotter Memorial Lecture at Seton Hall University in April 2016. Having the opportunity to speak about single combat in the *Punica* that afternoon rekindled my desire to write about the epic and to argue for its importance not only for Flavian literature but also for Classical literature as a whole. Around the same time, I happened to make contact with Alice Wright at Bloomsbury. She has supported both books enthusiastically from the beginning, and I would especially like to thank her, as well as Lily Mac Mahon and Georgina Leighton, for guiding me through the publishing process. I would also like to thank the anonymous readers for the press, as well as my copyeditor, Ben Harris, all of whom made a number of useful and helpful suggestions. Any remaining errors and infelicities are, of course, my own. I am deeply grateful to my friends (and first Latin teachers) Hartley and Susan Schearer, as well as to Steve Elgart, and to my family—to my brother, Michael, and, most of all, to my wife, Kerry—for their love, for their unflagging interest in my work, and for helping me to bring this project to fruition.

Acknowledgments

Maps 1–4 are reprinted from Hoyos 2015: xiii–xvi with permission of Oxford Publishing Limited through PLSclear.

Map 5 is reprinted from Gabriel 2008: 29 with permission of University of Nebraska Press.

Map 6 is reprinted from Greenhalgh 1975: 141. Every effort has been made to trace the copyright holders and obtain permission to reproduce this material.

Note on Text/Translation

All Greek and Latin texts are printed as in the relevant volume of the Bibliotheca Teubneriana or the Oxford Classical Texts unless otherwise noted, apart from minor changes in orthography. Likewise, all translations of these texts into English are my own unless otherwise noted.

Note on Bibliography

Throughout this book, I include references only to the essential scholarship in order to point the reader in the right direction and to keep the number and length of the footnotes to a minimum. I refer the reader to the bibliography at the end of the book for additional guidance. For a complete history of scholarship on Silius Italicus and the *Punica*, please consult the companion website.

Abbreviations

APh	*L'année philologique* (Paris, 1928–)
LSJ	H. G. Liddell, R. Scott, and H. S. Jones, eds., *A Greek–English Lexicon*, 9th ed., with a revised supplement (Oxford, 1996)
OCD[4]	S. Hornblower, A. Spawforth, and E. Eidinow, eds., *The Oxford Classical Dictionary*, 4th ed. (Oxford, 2012)
OLD	P. G. W. Glare, ed., *Oxford Latin Dictionary*, 2nd ed. (Oxford, 2012)

All abbreviations of Greek authors and titles are those found in LSJ; likewise, all abbreviations of Latin authors and titles are those found in *OLD*. All other abbreviations are those found either in *APh* or else in *OCD*[4]. I have, in a few cases, simply used the full title for a periodical.

1 Italy: Third Century BC (Hoyos 2015: xiii).

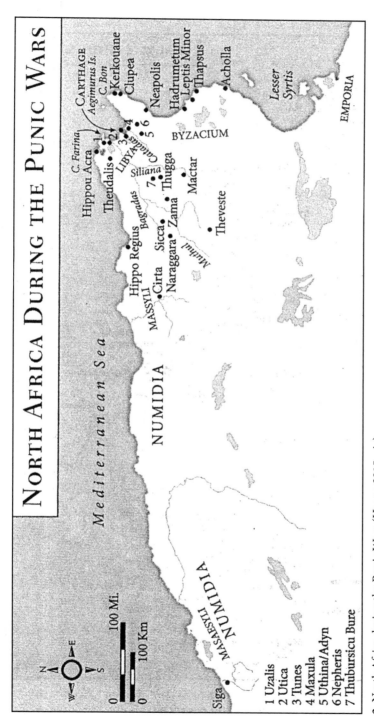

2 North Africa during the Punic Wars (Hoyos 2015: xiv).

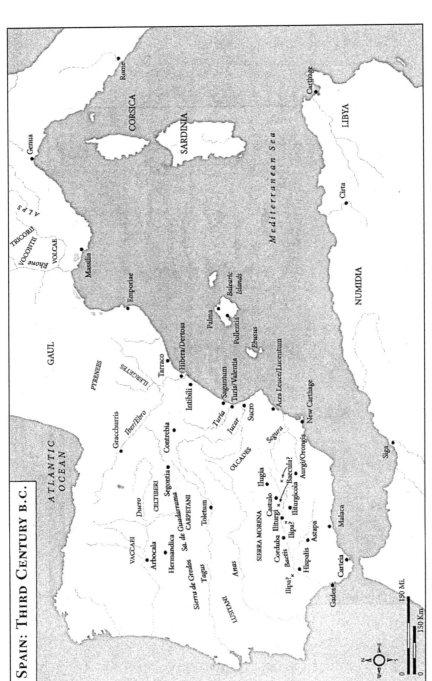

3 Spain: Third Century BC (Hoyos 2015: xv).

4 Eastern Mediterranean: Third Century BC (Hoyos 2015: xvi).

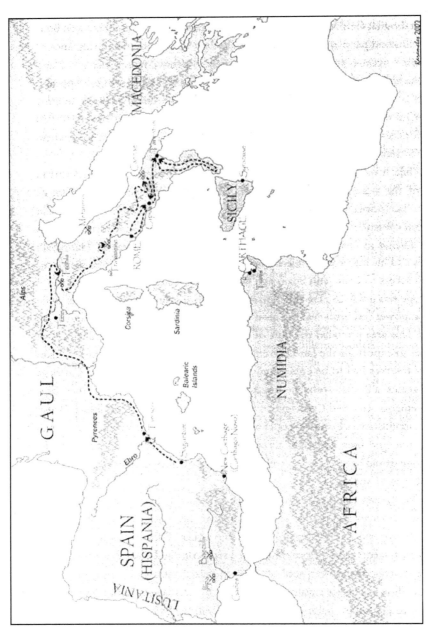

5 Theaters and Major Battles of the Second Punic War (Gabriel 2008: 29).

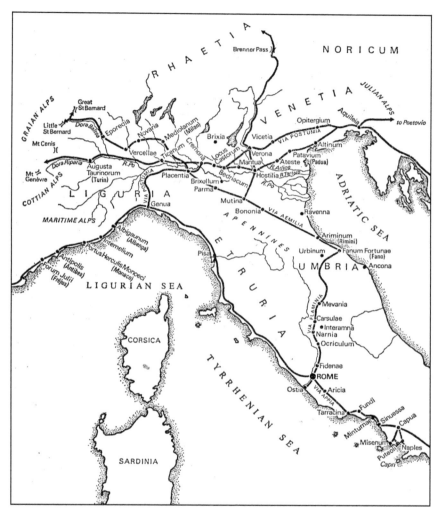

6 The Theatre of Civil War in AD 69 (Greenhalgh 1975: 141).

Introduction: Why Silius?

1. Poggio and the Rediscovery of the *Punica*

Just over six hundred years ago, the early Renaissance humanist Poggio Bracciolini (1380–1459) rediscovered a treasure trove of lost Classical Latin literature, including, perhaps most famously, Lucretius' *De rerum natura*, during his manuscript-hunting travels while serving as a member of the Roman Curia at the Council of Constance (1414–18).[1] In 1416 or 1417, perhaps at the Abbey Library of St. Gall, Poggio rediscovered a manuscript containing an historical epic about the Second Punic War (218–201 BC) called the *Punica*, by one Silius Italicus (c. AD 25–100), a Roman senator, consul, orator, and poet who flourished under Nero and the Flavians.[2] Although this early exemplar, now known as the codex Sangallensis, has again been lost, two copies of it appear to have been made, from which derive all of the thirty-two surviving manuscripts.[3] There is also indirect evidence for the existence of a second early exemplar, now known as the codex Coloniensis, at the Cologne Cathedral Library.[4] Louis Carrio (1547–95) and François Modius (1556–97) report various readings which they claim to have found in this latter manuscript, but, unfortunately, the original has yet again been lost.[5] In the initial decades following Poggio's rediscovery, the *Punica* attracted the attention of several prominent scholars at the Studium Urbis in Rome, including Pietro Odo (c. 1420–63), Pomponio Leto (1428–98), and, perhaps most importantly, Domizio Calderini (1446–78). After having been lost for more than a millennium, the epic was already well on its way to being rediscovered by critics as a worthy object of study.[6]

The *editio princeps* of the *Punica* was published in Rome on April 5, 1471, with a second Roman edition appearing only three weeks later, on April 26.[7] By the end of the century, at least seven more editions had been published, including that with the first complete commentary, by Pietro Marso (1442–1512).[8] Many more editions, with and without commentary, were published during the sixteenth and seventeenth centuries, including an Aldine in 1523, as well as the works of Daniel Heins (1580–1655) and Claude Dausque (1566–1644).[9] Thomas Ross (1620–75) brought the *Punica* to an even wider audience when he produced the first translation of the epic, into English, with a continuation (in three books, also in English) from the triumph of Scipio to the death of Hannibal.[10] The monumental editions of Christoph Keller (1638–1707) and Arnold Drakenborch (1684–1748), which gathered together the existing scholarship to date, marked the beginning of another new phase in the study of the poem at the turn of the eighteenth century.[11] Later that same century, Massimiliano Buzio (*fl.* 1750) rendered the entire *Punica* into Italian for the first time; thereafter, Jean-Baptiste Lefebvre de Villebrune (1732–1809) followed up with the first complete version in French.[12] Two more monumental editions marked the beginning of yet another new phase at the turn of the nineteenth century, namely, the important tomes by Johann Christian Gottlieb Ernesti (1756–1802) and Georg Alexander Ruperti (1758–1839).[13] Later that same century, Nicolas-Éloi Lemaire (1767–1832) published what remains to this day the last complete edition and commentary for the *Punica*, while Friedrich Heinrich Bothe (1771–1855) produced the first translation of the entire epic into German.[14] Ludwig Bauer, building on this now well-established tradition, as well as on the scholarly efforts of Georg Thilo and Hermann Blass, produced the first modern critical text of the poem at the turn of the twentieth century. Josef Delz subsequently produced the current standard critical text at the turn of the twenty-first century, around the same time as the appearance of both the Budé edition and the commentary of François Spaltenstein, the first such complete commentary since Lemaire.[15] Today, the *Punica* is available in a variety of modern translations, in English, French, Spanish, Italian, and German.[16] Together, these editions, translations, and commentaries, along with a host of other works, have all contributed to the establishment of a relatively stable and reliable modern critical text, as well as to the ongoing rediscovery of the poet and his poem by scholars of the Classics and in general.

In a sense, every age has rediscovered Silius Italicus and his *Punica* in its own way(s), but the dawn of the new millennium shows all the signs of marking the beginning of an *aetas Siliana*, as scholarship moves beyond the inveterate debate over positive and negative valuations of the poet and his poem to grapple with questions of greater interest and deeper significance.[17] This *aetas Siliana* has its roots, first and foremost, in the pioneering work of Onorato Occioni, an Italian scholar of the nineteenth century and the first true Silianist, as well as, more immediately, in a groundbreaking monograph published by Michael von Albrecht in 1964.[18] In the book, von Albrecht offered the first cogent analysis of the *Punica*'s structure, language, and themes, in the form of a generally optimistic reading of the poem as a celebration of Roman triumphalism. The work heralded the beginning of modern criticism on the epic and remains a touchstone for all of the scholarship which has followed in its wake. In a wide-ranging and thought-provoking 1986 article, Ahl, Davis, and Pomeroy proposed a more balanced interpretation which acknowledges both the optimistic and the pessimistic aspects of the *Punica*, and which accordingly accounts for its tragedy as well as its apparent triumphalism.[19] In a deceptively brief but profoundly impactful study published shortly thereafter, in 1993, Hardie advanced a sophisticated and nuanced reading of the post-Vergilian epics as a whole which reignited critical interest in Flavian epic, as well as in Flavian literature and the Flavians in general.[20] McGuire's 1997 monograph on the themes of civil war, tyranny, and suicide in the Flavian epics has proven particularly influential, especially in the past decade or so, as more and more scholars have come to listen for both the positive and the negative voices which speak so powerfully in and through these poems.[21] In another pivotal book, published in 2005, Marks argued for the immediate relevance of the *Punica* for its Flavian context and, more specifically, argued that Silius fashions the Roman hero Scipio as a role model for the emperor Domitian.[22] Tipping has complicated this attractive historicizing interpretation by examining both the positive and the negative aspects of the Carthaginian hero Hannibal and his Roman counterparts, Fabius and Scipio, while Stocks has offered a study devoted exclusively to Hannibal as an intentional counterweight to the focus on Scipio in Marks.[23] Last but certainly not least, a plethora of recent essay collections on both the *Punica* and Flavian epic as a whole has played a leading role in bringing all of these works to the attention of a much wider audience, especially the many volumes edited by Augoustakis.[24] In this book, I strive to demonstrate how a sustained engagement with this ever-growing body of scholarship can shape and inform our understanding of Silius Italicus and his *Punica* on their own terms and in their various contexts.[25]

2. Who Is Silius Italicus, What Is the *Punica*, and What Is the *Punica* About?

There are three essential questions which lay at the core of this scholarship and, accordingly, this book: who is Silius Italicus, what is the *Punica*, and what is the *Punica* about? As we will see below in more detail, Chapter 1 addresses the first of these three questions, Chapter 2 the second, and Chapters 3–6 the third. In what follows, however, I provide preliminary answers to all three questions in order to establish some common ground before digging any deeper into the place of the poet and his poem in the larger landscape of the Classics or into the theoretical foundation of the approach adopted for the reading of the epic elaborated over the course of this book.[26]

Tiberius Catius Asconius Silius Italicus was born c. AD 25, likely in northern Italy, and died c. AD 100, likely at one of his villas on the Bay of Naples.[27] Whereas many, if not most, Roman males under the Republic possessed the *tria nomina* ("three names," that is, *praenomen*, *nomen*, and *cognomen*) many Roman males under the Empire practiced polyonomy by adding *nomina* from elsewhere in their family trees. As his name indicates, Silius was a member of the *gens Catia*, *gens Asconia*, and *gens Silia*, all three of which were plebeian families of relatively modest fame: perhaps Silius added these *nomina* out of pride in his extended heritage; perhaps he did so simply to assert his status as a *novus homo*, a new member of the senatorial aristocracy. Silius lived during the final stages of the transition from the Republic to the Empire, from the middle of the reign of the Julio-Claudian emperors (31 BC–AD 68) to the Year of the Four Emperors (AD 68–9), and then, after that long year of civil war, from the reign of the Flavian emperors (AD 69–96) to the beginning of the reign of the Five Good Emperors (AD 96–180). This was undoubtedly one of the most tumultuous periods in Roman history and a time of great change in Rome, as well as in the Roman world at large. We actually know relatively little about Silius in detail, but the extant evidence (epigraphic, numismatic, and archeological, as well as, most importantly, literary) does at least enable us to reconstruct in outline the major milestones in his life. Indeed, the literary testimonia, which include passages from the works of Martial, Pliny the Younger, and Tacitus, all contemporaries or near contemporaries of Silius, provide us with the only information we have not only about his life as an orator but also about his life as a poet. Silius was born and raised during the reigns of Tiberius (r. 14–37) and Caligula (r. 37–41), entered the senate and held the consulship during the reigns of Claudius (r. 41–54) and Nero (r. 54–68), and played a pivotal role in the negotiations which brought the civil war of AD 68–9 to an end. He served as proconsul of Asia during the reign of Vespasian (r. 69–79) and afterwards returned to Rome as one of the leading men of the state during the reigns of Vespasian's two sons and successors, Titus (r. 79–81) and Domitian (r. 81–96). Thereafter, Silius retired to Campania to live out his days, intentionally absenting himself from Rome altogether during the transition to Nerva (r. 96–8) and then to Trajan (r. 98–117), before committing suicide by starvation in order to spare himself the incessant pain of an undiagnosed terminal illness. Remarkably, Silius held the dubious distinction of having been not only the last consul appointed by Nero, but also the last of the Neronian consulars to die. Essentially, for thirty years, he was a living ghost from the Julio-Claudian era who cast a pall over the civil war, the Flavians, and the Five Good Emperors.

At 12,204 verses in dactylic hexameter, Silius' epic, the *Punica*, is the longest surviving Latin poem.[28] The extant work spans seventeen books, but may have been originally composed or, at the very least, planned in eighteen. It is uncertain whether Silius left the poem incomplete at the time of his death, whether accidentally or intentionally, and it is also uncertain whether the poem suffered mutilation at some point(s) in its manuscript transmission, or whether both of these took place. The epic furnishes a selective account of the major action of the Second Punic War (218–201 BC), beginning with Hannibal's oath of eternal hatred against Rome and ending with Scipio's triumph in Rome after his victory at Zama. Between these twin narrative poles, Silius retells the fall of Saguntum (books 1–2); Hannibal's march from Spain to Italy, including his trek over the Alps (book 3); his victories over the Romans at the battles of the Ticinus River, the Trebia River, and Lake Trasimene (books 4–6); the stalemate between Hannibal and Fabius (book 7); the Roman disaster at the battle of Cannae (books 8–10); Hannibal's winter at Capua and subsequent failed march on Rome (books 11–12); the falls of Capua and Syracuse (books 13–14); the Roman victory at the battle of the Metaurus River (book 15); and Scipio's successful campaigns in Spain and Africa, culminating in his victories at the battles of Ilipa and Zama (books 16–17). Carthage and Rome clashed on three separate occasions between 264 and 146 BC, the First (264–241), Second (218–201), and Third (149–146) Punic Wars, but it was the Second Punic War, otherwise known as the Hannibalic War, which had the greatest impact on Roman history, Roman culture, and Roman literature, that is, literature about Rome written in both Greek and Latin. Indeed, the events of the Punic Wars play a prominent role throughout Roman literature, especially in historiography and epic, the highest genres of ancient prose and poetry. Silius thoughtfully and skillfully integrates his *Punica* into this tradition of historiography (especially Livy's history *Ab urbe condita*) and epic (especially Vergil's *Aeneid*), as well as many other genres. Even more particularly, he crafts his poem as the previously missing link between Vergil's *Aeneid* and Lucan's *Bellum civile*. The product of this literary engagement is perhaps the most intertextual, as well as the most intratextual, epic composed in the ancient world.

As we have seen, it is von Albrecht's seminal 1964 monograph which furnishes the foundation for all modern scholarship. According to von Albrecht, Silius presents the Second Punic War as a total war for hegemony in the Mediterranean Sea, a multigenerational cosmic conflict in which Rome proves its *virtus* in order to emerge victorious over Carthage.[29] Von Albrecht identifies "the walls of Rome" (*moenia Romae*) as the central theme and, in particular, Hannibal's mission to scale the walls and sack the city.[30] The specter of Hannibal looms large throughout the epic and remains ingrained in the Roman psyche forever after.[31] Eventually, however, Roman *fides* triumphs over Carthaginian *perfidia* in an affirmation of the existing order.[32] At its core, the *Punica* is about competing (re)constructions of collective memory, about the commemoration of the Second Punic War and its implications for the subsequent course of Roman history and Roman culture, especially for the fraught transition from Republic to Empire and the concomitant shift from foreign war (*bellum externum*) to civil war (*bellum internum*).[33] Silius "looks back" (*respicio*) to the fall of the Republic in order to make sense of the rise of the Empire, and, in doing so, he transforms his narrative of the Second Punic War into a totalizing vision of *Romanitas* which transcends the boundaries of space and time, of an *imperium sine fine* (Verg. Aen. 1.279), and yet also of an empire always on the brink of (self-)destruction.[34] Silius strives not simply to bridge the gap between the *Aeneid* and the *Bellum civile*, but even to outdo his predecessors in epic (as well as in historiography) by presenting the Second Punic War as a synecdoche for everything between the fall of Troy and the future fall of Rome. The *Punica* is about Flavian Rome as much as it is about the Second Punic War, and Silius stocks his narrative with characters drawn from all eras of Roman history.[35] Above and beyond that, the rise and fall of the Scipiones (Rome's Republican "dynasty") look ahead to the later rise and fall of the Julio-Claudians and the Flavians. By transforming the Second Punic War into this synecdoche for the idea of Rome as a whole, Silius makes the conflict and, in particular, the battle of Cannae, the defining moment in Roman history and Roman culture. The poet identifies Cannae as the turning point of both the war and the narrative, and the poet uses Cannae to connect the siege of Saguntum and the battle of Zama, as well as to connect the fates of Carthage and Rome. More generally, the *Punica* is about the relationship between the individual and the community, about the place of the individual in the family, the city, and even the cosmos. Silius invites the reader to contemplate the fate of all individuals and all communities by associating the falls of Carthage and Rome with various mythological and historical archetypes, as well as by problematizing the status of the epic's hero(es). Put simply, Silius challenges the reader to make sense of Rome's past, present, and future, and the *Punica* poses far more questions than it ever seeks to answer.

3. What Is the Place of Silius Italicus and the *Punica* in the Classics?

As we have seen, the *Punica* has found many willing readers in the six hundred years since the epic was first rediscovered in manuscript by Poggio, and this audience of supportive critics has diligently labored to reintegrate the poem into mainstream Classical scholarship. As we have also seen, Silius himself read quite voraciously, far beyond the generic boundaries of historiography and epic.[36] It is only fitting that he has, in turn, been read by a host of writers and artists beyond the disciplinary boundaries of the Classics: where scholars of an earlier generation might have referred to this phenomenon as Silius' place in the Classical "tradition," most scholars today would prefer to describe it as Silius' place in Classical "reception." (I myself see great value in retaining both terms, with "tradition" placing more emphasis on the role of the "source" and "reception" more emphasis on the role of the "target" in the shared construction of meaning.) In what follows, I briefly introduce three very different (and virtually unstudied) examples of this complex phenomenon which powerfully illustrate the profound and pervasive influence which Silius Italicus and his *Punica* have had in a variety of ways on literature and the arts in general.[37]

First and foremost, we find traces (and very often much more than traces) of the *Punica* throughout the epics of the Renaissance and Early Modern Europe, both those written in Latin and those written in the vernacular languages. One such epic, the *R(h)aeteis* (*c.* 1550), by Simon Lemm (*c.* 1511–50), was composed (in Latin) less than a century after the initial publication of the *Punica* and, interestingly enough, not far at all from St. Gall, where Poggio may have made his initial rediscovery of the epic.[38] The structure, language, and themes of the *R(h)aeteis* reflect a deep and meaningful engagement with those of the *Punica*, a clear indication that the *Punica* had already regained its rightful place in the canon. Like the *Punica*, the *R(h)aeteis* furnishes a selective account of the major events of a pivotal conflict: in this case, nine books on the Swiss or Swabian War of 1499 (fought between the Old Swiss Confederation and the Swabian League), from the outbreak of hostilities, inspired by Juno, to the Peace of Basel (September 22, 1499), when the Swiss effectively won their independence from the Holy Roman Empire.[39] On the one hand, Lemm grounds his narrative in that of the contemporary chronicles (much like Silius uses Livy); on the other, Lemm transforms history into epic by incorporating traditional elements like the extended description of the shield of the epic's hero, Benedikt Fontana (*c.* 1450–99), who sacrificed himself in order to ensure victory for his men at the climactic battle of Calven (May 22, 1499). In the only extended study of the poem's many sources, Michel rightly underscores the importance of the *Punica* and catalogs a number of parallel passages.⁴⁰ Nevertheless, much work remains to be done both in charting the obvious influence of the *Punica* on the *R(h)aeteis* and in analyzing why Lemm looks to Silius so often throughout his epic. Indeed, the *R(h)aeteis* offers compelling evidence for how later poets were able to transfer an optimistic reading of the *Punica* and, in particular, of Scipio to their own celebration of virtually any other ascendant hero in any other major (or even minor) conflict. As such, the *R(h)aeteis* instantiates a process of poetic reappropriation which plays out time and again elsewhere in the Neo-Latin historical epics written both before and after Lemm.⁴¹

The *Punica* has exerted an even more wide-ranging and long-lasting influence in Spain, especially on the literary tradition on the fall of Saguntum, the event which marked the beginning of the Second Punic War. Together with the accounts in the ancient historiographers, Silius' narrative of the tragic fall of Saguntum in *Punica* 1–2, by far the longest ancient account of the siege, has inspired several creative interpretations of this defining moment in the city's history over the course of the past five hundred years.⁴² Fittingly, amid the opulence and luxury of the Spanish Golden Age, the image of Saguntum lying in ruins served as a topos, especially in lyric poetry, for the mortality both of heroes and of the cities for which they stand and fall.⁴³ Two very different epics composed during this same era likewise attest to the prominence of the Saguntum theme. One, *La Saguntina* (1589), written in Spanish by Lorenzo de Zamora (d. 1614), consists of nineteen cantos on the siege which read very much like other Renaissance romance epics, with their elegant interweaving of the seemingly antithetical concepts of love and war.⁴⁴ The other, the *Saguntineida* (*c.* 1702), written in Latin by José Manuel Miñana (1671–1730), consists of a mere 415 verses in dactylic hexameter, suffused with the language and atmosphere of the *Punica*, in which we can discern the bare outline of the poem which might have been, if it had not been left unfinished at the time of its author's death.⁴⁵ Together with the many references in lyric, these two epics furnish intriguing evidence for how later poets were attracted not only to an optimistic reading of the *Punica*, but also to a pessimistic one, with its poignant emphasis on the common fate which awaits both the victors and the vanquished in the end. Indeed, two plays entitled *La destrucción de Sagunto* (one, by Gaspar Zavala y Zamora (b. 1762), premiered in 1787 and was later published in 1800; the other, by Enrique Palos y Navarro (1749–1814), was staged *c.* 1785 but only published in 2015) both read as if they had been written to commemorate the decline of Spain which inevitably followed the peak of the Golden Age.⁴⁶ The image of Saguntum lying in ruins, especially as depicted in the *Punica*, continued to hold the Spanish imagination, as we can see most vividly in two historical novels of the following century, *Las ruinas de Sagunto* (1845), by Isidoro Villarroya (1800–55), and *Sónnica la cortesana* (1901), by Vicente Blasco Ibáñez (1867–1928).⁴⁷ More recently, a scholar and a poet, Francisco Sánchez-Castañer and José María Pemán, collaborated on a new tragedy entitled *La destrucción de Sagunto* which was staged in the ruins of the ancient theater of Saguntum itself on June 8, 1954, long before the controversial restoration work of the 1980s and 1990s, and then published later that same year.⁴⁸ Through all these many iterations of the Saguntum theme, the narrative of the fall of the city in the *Punica* has figured prominently, imbued with the pathos of this climactic moment in history and myth.

The *Punica* has remained immediately relevant to literature and the arts in general even just in the last decade, but perhaps in something of an unexpected manifestation. In *La Seconda Guerra Tritonide* (2012), Salvatore Conte transforms the worldview of the *Punica* into a vision of a dystopian future in the form of a feminist science fantasy novel.⁴⁹ As its name implies, the term "science fantasy" refers to a mixed genre which combines elements of science fiction and fantasy, two genres which themselves can be difficult to distinguish from each other. Scholars have recently shown great interest in the reception of the Greek and Latin Classics in these two parent genres, but *La Seconda Guerra Tritonide* has, to my knowledge, not yet garnered any attention.⁵⁰ The novel depicts the final, desperate confrontation between a sterile and corrupt Earth of the not-too-distant future and the recrudescence of the (Jungian) feminine principle, the feminine *anima* to the masculine *animus*, incarnate in the three women who drive the action: Zenobia, Imilce, and Asbite, the latter two of whom (in Latin, Imilce and Asbyte) appear in the *Punica* and nowhere else in ancient literature. The back blurb explicitly describes *La Seconda Guerra Tritonide* as an epic novel inspired by the *Punica*, and scholars have, indeed, offered feminist readings of the ancient epic, making this an interesting case of scholarship and reception complementing each other.⁵¹ Furthermore, as we will see, Silius has a certain predilection for all types of virtual history, from counterfactual history to alternate history to future history, and so the *Punica*, perhaps surprisingly, lends itself well to such a treatment as science fantasy.⁵² As this final example makes especially clear, the *Punica* has found far more readers both inside and outside the Classics than most scholars have realized, and all of these readings contribute to our reading of the epic on its own, in its various contemporary contexts, and in its later reception.

4. How to Read the *Punica*

By this point, I hope that I have offered a convincing argument for why Silius Italicus and his *Punica* matter, why others have found the epic worth their time and energy, and why we should want to know the poet and his poem, too. In order to give some sense of what the experience of reading the *Punica* can be like, I want to begin with a thought experiment which is designed to illustrate how the epic might have been received among its contemporaries in Flavian Rome.[53]

Imagine a man born of a well-to-do but non-patrician family in New York City in 1938, right before Hitler's invasion of Poland on September 1, 1939 and the outbreak of World War II (1939–45). The man grows up during the war and its aftermath (that is, the beginning of the Cold War), goes on to college, earns his law degree, and is elected to the United States Senate during the turbulent year of 1968 at the earliest possible age of 30. Never a war hero (he was too young to have served in the Korean War (1950–3), too old to serve in Vietnam) the man commits himself instead to a life of politics, rising to the height of his power and prestige during the Watergate Affair (1972–4) and thereafter remaining in office until 1980. Not without scandals of his own, the man retires from politics in order to pursue a literary life and eventually leaves the turmoil of Washington, DC behind altogether for the self-indulgent pleasures of a well-appointed country retreat. The ex-senator becomes a committed writer in retirement and labors unremittingly for the next forty years or so on his magnum opus, an historical epic novel, in the manner of James Michener, about the American Revolutionary War (1775–83). Meanwhile, the rest of the country endeavors to navigate the troubled waters of the following two decades (including the supposed end of the Cold War), before suffering the devastating losses in the terrorist attacks of September 11, 2001 which set the course for the War on Terror, the defining conflict of the twenty-first century. After a long and celebrated life in politics and literature, the man dies in 2018 as the last surviving ex-senator who had been in office during Watergate. The man's novel, entitled *Britannica*, although left incomplete at the time of its author's death, is published to relatively little fanfare and meets with a tepid reception among critics. At one level, the ex-senator offers a traditional narrative of the conflict with the usual people, places, and events, albeit with a few surprises and a few idiosyncrasies, perhaps even a few real or apparent inconsistencies in comparison with historical records (themselves subject to debate, of course). At another level, he endows both the war and the narrative with a heightened significance by introducing God Himself into the novel as a direct participant in the affairs of mortals. At yet another level, the ex-senator transforms his account of the American Revolutionary War into an account of the entirety of the country's history (past, present, and future) by incorporating many references and allusions to the three English Civil Wars (1642–51) and the French and Indian War (1754–63), as well as to the War of 1812 (1812–15) and the American Civil War (1861–5), among other conflicts. Perhaps most intriguingly of all, the ex-senator devotes special attention to the three Yankee-Pennamite Wars (1769–99), fought between settlers from Connecticut (the "Yankees") and Pennsylvania (the "Pennamites"), even going so far as to make the infamous battle of Wyoming, fought on July 3, 1778 and the aftermath of the battle, on July 4, two years to the day after the signing of the Declaration of Independence, the turning point of the American Revolutionary War. In elaborating this totalizing interpretation of the war and its place in American history, the ex-senator appears to argue that the seeds of all future strife were sown at the time of the country's birth. The resulting product is a densely packed literary tour de force of extraordinary breadth and vision which makes great demands even on the ideal reader who possesses a complete mastery of American (and British) history, culture, and literature.

Now, I certainly do not intend to advance the claim that this thought experiment provides anything more than a rough approximation to the circumstances surrounding the composition, publication, and contemporary reception of the *Punica*, so far removed from us in both time and place, since both the times and the places have changed so much in the past two thousand years. I have not sought to map all of the details of the life of my imaginary author onto the details of the life of the real Silius Italicus (insofar as we think we know them), nor have I sought to represent the imaginary *Britannica* as some sort of translation or even adaptation of the *Punica*. Instead, I have sought to suggest a number of loose parallels between the two authors and their respective works in order to provide a new angle from which to approach a reading, especially a first-time reading, of the ancient epic. I have described the three narrative levels of the *Britannica* as such in order to give a better sense of the three comparable narrative levels of the *Punica*. So, at one level, Silius offers a traditional narrative of the Second Punic War with the usual people, places, and events, albeit with some apparent innovations on that existing tradition. At another level, he elevates the importance of both the war and the narrative by reintroducing the traditional divine machinery so crucial to the theology and theodicy of Vergil's *Aeneid*, but also so notably absent from Lucan's *Bellum civile* (perhaps replaced by Julius Caesar as the one true god). Finally, at yet another level, Silius transforms his account of the Second Punic War into an account of Rome *in toto* (Monarchy, Republic, and Empire) by incorporating many references and allusions to people, places, and events from across the entire breadth of the city's rich history, culture, and literature, from the civil wars between Marius (and his son) and Sulla (88–81 BC) and Caesar and Pompey (49–45 BC), to the civil war of AD 68–9 and the fall of Jerusalem in AD 70. Silius appears to construct this unique version, and unique vision, of the Second Punic War in order to argue for the centrality of the battle of Cannae as the turning point not only of the war and the narrative, but also of Roman history and Roman culture in general, as well as to argue for the importance of the subsequent fall of Carthage for the anticipated future fall of Rome through civil war. All of that can be frankly quite disorienting for a reader of the *Punica* to process, much less comprehend, especially a first-time reader, since the epic searches for an ideal reader even further removed from the here and now, one who possesses a complete mastery not of American (and British) but of ancient Roman (and Carthaginian, and Greek) history, culture, and literature.

So, then, how do we approach a reading, especially a first-time reading, of the *Punica* once we recognize and accept the reality of the spatial and temporal chasm which separates us from the circumstances of its composition, publication, and contemporary reception? On the one hand, whether we read the poem in the original Latin or in translation, we are more likely than not to read the work silently to ourselves, whereas we know for a fact that Silius gave public and private recitations of his work-in-progress in order to solicit feedback from friends and fellow poets.[54] On the other hand, even if we simulate the circumstances of this original performance (in many ways, the ancient equivalent of modern publication) by reading the poem aloud, we are likely to stumble at various points depending on our relative familiarity or lack thereof with the text on its own (that is, as Latin, if we are reading the original) and with the text in its various historical, cultural, and literary contexts.[55] Indeed, with each rereading of the *Punica*, the reader is bound to discover something new which is at least potentially relevant to an understanding and an appreciation of the work as a whole. This process of reading and rereading the *Punica*, as well as the rest of the ancient literary canon to which it belongs, entails grappling with the productive tension between tradition and originality. This tension between old and new lies at the very heart of contemporary literary theory about intratextuality, extratextuality, and intertextuality, and it will accordingly loom large in my close reading of the *Punica* across Chapters 3 and 4.[56] As the prefixes of these three terms imply, the first is concerned with what is inside the text, the second with what is outside the text, and the third with the relationship between two or more texts (for example, the relationship between the *Punica* and Livy's *Ab urbe condita* or Vergil's *Aeneid*). More broadly speaking, given its astute literary and historical self-consciousness, the *Punica* seemingly invites a close examination through the lens of New Historicism, Cultural Poetics, and Cultural Materialism, that is, a reading grounded in "the historicity of texts and the textuality of history."[57] Classicists have certainly made a number of contributions to this particular strand of theory, but much work remains to be done, especially in applying more recent developments in the theory to the evaluation of both historiographical texts and works in other major genres like epic, and so this theoretical framework will largely inform the extended treatment of the themes of the *Punica* which spans Chapters 5 and 6.[58] Ultimately, by applying this selected set of critical perspectives to Silius Italicus and his *Punica*, I hope to guide the reader, especially the first-time reader, of the epic through an informed and informative engagement with the poet and his poem.

5. About this Book

This book consists of the present introduction, six chapters, and a conclusion. I have written the volume to be read linearly from beginning to end, but there are certainly ways one might engage with its contents in a non-linear fashion. First and foremost, this introduction can be read as a stand-alone chapter which provides the reader with the essential information about Silius Italicus and his *Punica*. A reader already familiar with the poet and his poem can read this introduction along with the conclusion in order to understand how I approach my own reading of the epic and then see that process of reading and interpretation in action. I have written the six chapters which constitute the core of the book in three two-chapter pairs. Chapters 1 and 2 offer a more in-depth presentation of the essential information about Silius Italicus and his *Punica*; Chapters 3 and 4 present a linear reading of the epic itself book-by-book; Chapters 5 and 6 examine the thematic infrastructure of the text in its various historical, cultural, and literary contexts. A reader who is unfamiliar with the poet and his poem can profitably read the epic itself (whether in the original Latin or in translation) either before or after reading Chapters 3 and 4. I think of the conclusion as an invitation to read the *Punica* (preferably in Latin) and then to integrate that reading (and, I hope, subsequent rereadings) into an overall understanding and appreciation of the work's place in the Classical canon. To conclude this introduction, I outline in greater detail the contents of the six core chapters of the book in order to prepare the reader for the journey which lies ahead.

Chapters 1 and 2 tackle the interrelated questions "Who is Tiberius Catius Asconius Silius Italicus?" (Chapter 1) and "What is the *Punica*?" (Chapter 2). Both chapters are intended to offer the reader comprehensive presentations of the existing evidence in light of current trends in Classical scholarship, along with some new interpretive ideas and suggestions. In Chapter 1, I begin with an overview of the historical, cultural, and literary context for Silius Italicus, namely, the reigns of the Julio-Claudians and the Flavians (31 BC–AD 96), Rome's first two Imperial dynasties. I continue with an analysis of the various epigraphic, numismatic, and archeological, as well as literary, testimonia, with a special focus on the evidence in Martial, Pliny the Younger, and Tacitus. I conclude with a new reading of Pliny *Epistula* 3.7 (on the death of Silius Italicus) as itself a reading of the *Punica*, and, in particular, a reading of Silius Italicus as a Xerxes-like or Hannibal-like figure who outlived, and outlasted, his peers. In Chapter 2, I similarly begin with an overview of the historical, cultural, and literary context for the *Punica*, namely, the era of the three Punic Wars (264–146 BC), the defining conflicts of the Middle Republic. I continue with a discussion about the commemoration of the Second Punic War in Classical literature and, more specifically, about the relationship of the *Punica* to the historiographical and epic traditions about the conflict. I devote particular attention to the relationship between the *Punica* and Livy's *Ab urbe condita*, as well as to that between the *Punica* and Vergil's *Aeneid*. I conclude with a brief analysis of the language and style of the *Punica*, especially Silius' expert manipulation of sound and sense in service of structure and theme. Together, these two opening chapters equip a reader new to the poet and his poem with everything needed for a first-time reading of the epic.

Chapters 3 and 4 undertake a sustained close reading of the *Punica* book-by-book, with Chapter 3 covering the narrative of the war from the siege of Saguntum to the battle of Cannae (*Punica* 1–10), and chapter 4, the narrative from the aftermath of Cannae to the battle of Zama (*Punica* 11–17). In Chapter 3, I begin with an overview of the various structural models which scholars have proposed for the *Punica*, and I suggest a few new ways to group together the books of the poem. I continue with a close reading of the epic's proem (*Punica* 1.1–20) as an example for how to read and interpret the work as a whole. Thereafter, I proceed through *Punica* 1–5, the narrative from the siege of Saguntum to the battle of Lake Trasimene, and then through *Punica* 6–10, the narrative from the aftermath of Lake Trasimene to the battle of Cannae. For each book, I provide a detailed summary of its contents; then, for each group of books, I provide a sense of its place in the epic. I conclude with a close reading of the epic's famous turning point (*Punica* 10.657–8), a mere two verses which, in the eyes of many scholars, essentially summarize the work as a whole. In Chapter 4, I similarly begin with a close reading of the epic's medial proem (*Punica* 11.1–27) as an example for how to read and interpret the beginnings and ends of books in the poem, as well as for how to assess the thorny question of the poem's middle(s). Thereafter, I continue with the reading of *Punica* 11–15, from the aftermath of Cannae to the battle of the Metaurus River, followed by the reading of *Punica* 16–17, from the aftermath of the Metaurus River to the battle of Zama. In particular, I linger over the closing verses of the epic with a close reading of Scipio's triumph (*Punica* 17.625–54), in which I argue that Silius manipulates any sense of closure by transforming this climactic moment into the (apparent) end of both the war and the narrative, as well as, at the same time, the beginning of the end, the beginning of Rome's march from foreign war to civil war. I conclude with a brief narratological analysis of the *Punica* through which I strive to give the reader some idea of what the process of reading the epic is like.

Chapters 5 and 6 address the difficult, and ultimately unanswerable, question "What is the *Punica* about?" and, accordingly, build on the reading of the epic elaborated across Chapters 3 and 4. In Chapter 5, I begin with a contextualizing discussion about the fraught relationship in both history and myth between heroes and the cities for which they stand and fall, and I offer some initial thoughts on how this all plays out in the *Punica*. I explore how Silius interweaves the themes of single combat and decapitation across the arc of the poem, all in preparation for the long-anticipated single combat between Hannibal and Scipio ... which never happens. I then examine how Silius casts the Second Punic War as a new Gigantomachy, a new Trojan War, and a new Gallic sack, all in order to universalize his narrative of the conflict as well as to transform it into a broader meditation on the relationship between the fall of Carthage and the anticipated future fall of Rome. Thereafter, I conclude by considering the special case of Marcellus, the counterfactual hero who, had he not died prematurely, might have brought both the war and the narrative to a (different) close before Scipio's rise to power. In Chapter 6, I similarly begin with a contextualizing discussion about how Silius connects the era of the Second Punic War with that of the Flavians in the *Punica*. I then undertake an analysis of the epic's two major organizing themes, the curse of Dido and the *metus hostilis*, which together define the terms of the grand cultural narrative behind the transition from Republic to Empire, from foreign war to civil war, around the turning point of Cannae. I trace the evolution of the curse of Dido theme, and I argue that Silius seeks to "correct" the existing tradition by claiming that Hannibal does, indeed, fulfill the curse through his own suicide a generation after the end of the Second Punic War in 183 BC. I likewise trace the evolution of the *metus hostilis* theme, and I argue that Silius also seeks to "correct" the existing tradition by moving the turning point back from the fall of Carthage in 146 BC to the battle of Cannae in 216 BC. Thereafter, I explore how Silius ties these themes together in order to advance his overall claim about the role of the Second Punic War in the fraught transition from Republic to Empire, from foreign war to civil war, by presenting the conflict as a synecdoche for everything between the fall of Troy and the future fall of Rome. I conclude with a comparison between Scipio's triumph after his victory at Zama and three related events from the era of the Flavians: the fall of the Capitol and the destruction of the Temple of Jupiter Optimus Maximus during the civil war of AD 68–9; the fall of the Temple of Jerusalem and Titus' triumph in AD 70; and Domitian's triumphs over the Chatti in AD 83 and the Dacians in AD 86. Together, these two closing chapters provide both a balanced overview of existing readings of the *Punica* and a new reading aimed at pushing scholarship in a new direction through a more holistic interpretation of the epic.

1

Who Is Tiberius Catius Asconius Silius Italicus?

1. Introduction: The Julio-Claudians and the Flavians (31 BC–AD 96)

Tiberius Catius Asconius Silius Italicus[1] was born c. AD 25, likely in northern Italy, and died c. AD 100, likely at one of his villas on the Bay of Naples. Silius was a Roman senator, consul, orator, and poet who lived during the final stages of the fraught transition from the Republic to the Empire: from the middle of the reign of the Julio-Claudian emperors (31 BC–AD 68) to the Year of the Four Emperors (AD 68–9), and then, after that long year of civil war, from the reign of the Flavian emperors (AD 69–96) to the beginning of the reign of the Five Good Emperors (AD 96–180). This was undoubtedly one of the most tumultuous periods in Roman history and a time of great change in Rome, as well as in the Roman world at large. The violent and ultimately irrevocable transition from Republic to Empire manifested itself most visibly in the concomitant shift from foreign war (*bellum externum*) to civil war (*bellum internum*). Indeed, many later Romans, and many modern scholars, have located the beginning of this process in the end of the three Punic Wars (264–146 BC) and, specifically, in the fall of Carthage (as well as Corinth) in the fateful year of 146 BC. Rome's rise to hegemony over the Mediterranean put the city not only on the path to empire, but also on the path to Empire, the *imperium Romanum* in both senses of the term.[2] Various internal conflicts, from the agitations of the Gracchi (133–121 BC) to the Social War (91–88 BC), culminated in three rounds of full-scale civil war, between Marius (and his son) and Sulla (88–81 BC), Caesar and Pompey (49–45 BC), and Octavian (the future Augustus) and Mark Antony (42–31 BC). These three gladiatorial bouts between rival claimants to a nonexistent throne marked successive stages in the steady degradation of the consulship and the seemingly inevitable return to monarchy. Fittingly, Caesar's conquest of Gaul (58–50 BC) during this century of civil war likewise marked the last great foreign war of the Republic, when the

Romans exorcised their Gallic demons only to turn their swords against each other and then themselves in the suicide of civil war which followed Caesar across the Rubicon.

The assassination of Caesar on the Ides of March (March 15) in 44 BC inaugurated the final phase of this transition from Republic to Empire, culminating in Octavian's victory over Antony and Cleopatra at the battle of Actium in 31 BC. The transition from Caesar to Octavian functioned as a homology for the larger shift from Republic to Empire and laid the foundation for the dynastic principle in Rome.[3] Through the progressive consolidation of various traditional, and non-traditional, powers, Octavian gradually strengthened his position as the *princeps* (first citizen), rather than making any bold, and potentially unsuccessful, claim to outright supremacy. That said, by adopting the new name of Imperator Caesar Divi filius Augustus (Emperor Caesar son of the Divine [Julius Caesar] Augustus), he also transformed himself from a mere mortal into an abstract idea(l) and, ultimately, into a divine being (*divus*) in his own right.[4] By the time of his death in AD 14, Augustus had likewise transformed Rome and the rest of the Roman world by sparking a cultural revolution which, primarily through literature and the arts, radically redefined what it meant to be Roman and, in doing so, paved the way for the progressive consolidation of both the empire and, once again, the Empire.[5] The line of Julio-Claudian emperors, Rome's first imperial dynasty, thereafter continued with the reigns of Tiberius (r. 14–37), Caligula (r. 37–41), Claudius (r. 41–54), and Nero (r. 54–68). With each successive emperor, the Republic and, in particular, the circumstances surrounding the fall of the Republic faded further and further into the past, as the Empire became entrenched in every aspect of Roman culture. At the same time, the specters of Caesar and Augustus continued to loom large long after their *res gestae* (deeds and accomplishments) had made the fraught transition from history to memory. In many ways, the reign of Nero marked a return to the heady days of the reign of Augustus: like Augustus, Nero patronized literature and the arts in support of the ongoing cultural revolution.[6] All of this came to an abrupt end, however, when Nero, faced with growing opposition both in Rome and in the provinces, committed suicide in AD 68, thereby unleashing a new wave of civil strife. This was the world of Silius, who was born and raised during the reigns of Tiberius and Caligula, and who entered the Senate and held the consulship during the reigns of Claudius and Nero. In fact, Silius was the last consul appointed by Nero, and so there is no doubt that Nero's suicide had a profound impact on Silius and on the subsequent course of both his public and his private life.

The Year of the Four Emperors (AD 68–9) marked perhaps the most important turning point in the history of the Empire, when Rome faced a stark choice between seemingly incessant civil war and the apparent stability of monarchical rule.[7] In relatively quick succession, four rival claimants (Galba, Otho, Vitellius, and Vespasian) were proclaimed emperor, whether by their soldiers, the Senate, or both, and all, except Vespasian, marched on Rome to validate their claim. Galba was the first to be recognized as emperor, on June 9, 68: he ruled for seven months, until he was assassinated in the Roman Forum and then decapitated on January 15, 69 by supporters of Otho in the Praetorian Guard (the emperor's personal bodyguard). After a brief reign of only three months, Otho committed suicide on April 17, 69, following his loss to Vitellius' forces at the first battle of Bedriacum. Vitellius was subsequently recognized as emperor: he ruled for eight months, until he lost to Vespasian's forces under the command of M. Antonius Primus at the second battle of Bedriacum and was later assassinated (and perhaps decapitated) in Rome. A war-weary Senate hailed Vespasian as emperor on December 21, 69, although Vespasian himself backdated his accession to July 1, when he was initially proclaimed emperor by the legions in Egypt under Ti. Julius Alexander, followed soon thereafter by the legions in Judaea. Through it all, the events of AD 68–9 had left an indelible mark not only on the Roman psyche but also on the physical city. At the climax of the fighting between the supporters of Vitellius and those of Vespasian, the Capitol itself was set ablaze, and the Temple of Jupiter Optimus Maximus burned to the ground. The image of Roman soldiers trekking over the Alps into Italy, marching on the walls of their own city, and ascending the heights of the Capitol resurrected memories of the Gallic sack of 390 BC and of Hannibal's march(es) on Rome during the Second Punic War, not to mention the many marches on the city during the civil wars of the Late Republic. In a sense, the self-inflicted defeats of the civil wars subverted the hard-fought triumphs of the foreign wars. Silius himself witnessed all of the destruction firsthand, since he played a pivotal role in the negotiations which eventually brought the fighting to an end and evidently ingratiated himself with the new emperor, Vespasian, despite having been an ally of Vitellius earlier in the conflict.

Vespasian (r. 69–79) arrived in Rome the following year, in AD 70, and inaugurated a series of reforms aimed at restoring stability and improving public morals. In doing so, Vespasian intentionally cast himself in the mold of Augustus in order to establish what would later become Rome's second imperial dynasty.[8] That same year, his older son, Titus, captured Jerusalem after a lengthy siege and razed the Second Temple to the ground, marking a turning point in the Jewish

War (AD 66–74), the first of three such conflicts.[9] Titus subsequently entered Rome in triumph in AD 71, a moment commemorated by the construction of the Temple of Peace and, later, the Arch of Titus.[10] For Romans eager to put the Year of the Four Emperors behind them, the fall of Jerusalem and, especially, the fall of the Second Temple inspired hopes of other future conquests; in reality, however, the war continued until the fall of Masada through mass suicide in AD 73. Regardless, Vespasian wisely capitalized on the zeal for peace at home through war abroad by crafting the narrative of this new "Pax Flavia" in imitation of the earlier Pax Augusta. At his death in AD 79, Vespasian bestowed the Empire upon Titus. The brief reign of Titus (r. 79–81) was punctuated by two major events in Roman history: the eruption of Mt. Vesuvius in AD 79, which destroyed Pompeii, Herculaneum, and other settlements in the vicinity; and the opening of the Flavian Amphitheater, better known as the Colosseum, in AD 80, which, in many ways, became *the* symbol of the Roman Empire. At his death in AD 81, Titus was succeeded by his younger brother, Domitian, the third and final emperor of the dynasty. While Domitian (r. 81–96) continued many of the policies of his father and brother (both now *divi*), he also strengthened his grip on power by transforming the principate into a divine monarchy with himself at its head as (perhaps) *dominus et deus* (lord and god).[11] Accordingly, Domitian promoted the imperial cult and restored the Temple of Jupiter Optimus Maximus. In an attempt at recapturing the ancient glory of the Republic, Domitian embarked on a number of foreign military campaigns, against the Chatti, in Britain, and against the Dacians, but with varying levels of success. Much like Nero, the final Julio-Claudian emperor, Domitian patronized literature and the arts; also much like Nero, Domitian faced growing opposition to his rule, ultimately leading to his assassination.[12] Through it all, Silius continued to advance his remarkable career, serving as proconsul in Asia during the reign of Vespasian (probably AD 77/8) and afterwards returning to Rome as one of the city's leading senators. Around this time, if not before, Silius also began his career as a poet and became a regular fixture at *recitationes*, perhaps as a part of Domitian's cultural program.

Like the death of Nero, the death of Domitian marked another important turning point in the Early Empire, when Rome teetered on the brink of another round of civil war.[13] Accordingly, the Senate immediately declared the aged and childless Nerva (r. 96–8) emperor in an attempt at averting the threat of another relapse into internecine conflict by handing over the reins of power to someone who would rule with a steady hand. As the first of a series of rulers who would later be called the Five Good Emperors, Nerva established a new dynastic principle with his adoption of Trajan as his designated successor upon his (natural) death. Casting himself in the mold of Augustus and Vespasian, Trajan (r. 98–117), hailed as *optimus princeps* (best emperor) by the Senate, inaugurated an ambitious program in his domestic and foreign policy which brought the *imperium Romanum* to the height of its peace and prosperity. This complex process of expansion and consolidation, politically and economically, as well as socially and culturally, continued during the reigns of Hadrian (r. 117–38), Antoninus Pius (r. 138–61), and Marcus Aurelius (r. 161–80). Although the cycle of foreign war and civil war continued during this transition from the Early Empire to the High Empire (and, of course, beyond that), Rome was simply different after the death of Marcus Aurelius: the fraught transition from Republic to Empire, once a highly charged moment in Roman history, had essentially become a fixed memory, a faded piece of the larger cultural fabric. After a long and distinguished public life, Silius retired to Campania in the aftermath of the death of Domitian and did not return to Rome again; suffering from an unknown terminal illness, he committed suicide by starvation early in the reign of Trajan. Silius' passing marked the end of an era since, as the last of the Neronian consulars to die, he stood, Janus-like, poised between (Late) Republic and (High) Empire, looking both back to the Greek and Latin origins of Roman (literary) culture and ahead to Antonine archaism and the Second Sophistic.[14]

2. Overview of the Testimonia for Tiberius Catius Asconius Silius Italicus

The extant ancient testimonia for Silius and his epic, the *Punica*, include epigraphic, numismatic, and archeological material, as well as relatively abundant literary evidence in passages from the works of Martial, Pliny the Younger, and Tacitus, among others.[15] Taken together, the epigraphic, numismatic, and archeological testimonia provide important information about Silius' name, his consulship, and his proconsulship in Asia, while the literary testimonia round out the picture with interesting details about Silius' public and private life, including his checkered career as a poet. First and foremost, Silius appears as *consul ordinarius* (ordinary consul, i.e., a consul at the start of the year after whom the year was named) for the year AD 68, with P. Galerius Trachalus as his colleague, in a number of inscriptions. These inscriptions include the *fasti consulares* (official list of consuls) for AD 68,[16] as well as a number of other records in which Silius is named as a consul: the *fasti sodalium Augustalium Claudialium* (official acts of an Imperial priesthood) for AD 68 (*CIL* 6.1984 = *ILS* 5025); municipal *fasti* for that same year, in which Silius' name may have appeared in what is now a lacuna (*CIL* 10.5405 = *ILS* 6125); and a later military document dated to July 1, AD 94 (*CIL* 16, p. 146.12 = *ILS* 9059). In addition, a fragment of an amphora handle has been unearthed at Pompeii bearing the name of "T. Catius": perhaps simply an error for "Ti. Catius"?[17] A likewise fragmentary Greek inscription found just outside Aphrodisias (*MAMA* 8.76, no. 411 = *IAph2007* 13.609) records a decree promulgated by Silius during his proconsulship in which he appears to strengthen existing prohibitions regarding the sacred doves of Aphrodite, the city's titulary goddess.[18] Unlike the Latin inscriptions, which only record the name "Ti. Catius Silius Italicus" (or some portion thereof), the decree records what appears to be his true full name, "Ti. Catius Asconius Silius Italicus" (i.e., with the *nomen* "Asconius"). In addition, the name "Italicus" appears on the coinage of Blaundus, Dorylaeum, and Smyrna, all of which are likely to have been minted during Silius' proconsulship.[19] Finally, the "Silius Italicus" mentioned in a second-century AD sepulchral inscription for a slave named Crescens may refer either to *the* Silius Italicus or, perhaps, to a son (*CIL* 14.2653).[20] Either way, taken together, this inscriptional material confirms Silius' name and his tenure of the consulship and proconsulship, thereby establishing his status as a powerful and successful senator during very turbulent times.

All the same, Silius and his epic, the *Punica*, are perhaps best known to Classicists from various references in the epigrams of Martial, published during the reigns of Domitian, Nerva, and Trajan, as well as from the letter which Pliny the Younger addressed to Caninius Rufus shortly after Silius' death (3.7). Tacitus mentions Silius by name in the *Historiae* (3.65.2) and may allude to him in the *Annales* (4.33.4), both of which works were published during the early second century AD. From Martial and Pliny, as we will see in greater detail below, we learn much more about Silius' public and private life, about his relationships with the emperors and his literary ambitions, as well as about his two sons and the circumstances surrounding his death. From Tacitus' *Historiae*, we learn about Silius' pivotal role in bringing the civil war of AD 68–9 to an end: along with the historiographer Cluvius Rufus, Silius served as a witness to the agreement struck between Vitellius and Flavius Sabinus, Vespasian's older brother, at the Temple of Apollo Palatinus (3.65.2).[21] From his *Annales*, we learn about contemporary indifference (so Tacitus would have us believe) towards the competing memories of the Punic Wars (4.33.4):[22]

> tum quod antiquis scriptoribus rarus obtrectator, neque refert cuiusquam Punicas Romanasne acies laetius extuleris.

Then, there is the fact that virtually no one is a critic of ancient writers, nor does it matter to anyone whether you more happily praise the ranks of the Carthaginians or those of the Romans.

In the midst of his famous digression on writing historiography on Tiberius (4.32–3),[23] Tacitus contrasts his subject matter with that available to earlier historiographers. While Tacitus labors under the strain of a tedious body of material, ancient writers had the luxury of writing about grandiose topics of absorbing interest. Furthermore, while Tacitus runs the risk of offending the *princeps*, ancient writers enjoyed a far greater measure of freedom. At first glance, the reference to Carthaginians and Romans (i.e., the Punic Wars) recalls Livy and his expansive account of the Second Punic War in the third decade of his history *Ab urbe condita*. And yet, the relatively recent publication of the *Punica* (well known to Tacitus' close friend Pliny) makes it possible that Tacitus has the epic in mind, as well. Regardless, Tacitus' claim has profound implications for how we read the *Punica* and, in particular, for how we assess its contemporary reception. If we interpret Silius as offering praise and blame for both sides over the course of the epic, then, at least according to Tacitus, that was only to be expected, since the war had lost its ethical charge.

Outside of the works of Martial, Pliny, and Tacitus, Silius and his *Punica* make only a handful of appearances elsewhere in the literary record. The first testimonium comes from the *Dissertationes*, published not by its author, the Stoic philosopher Epictetus, but by his student Arrian, after his death, sometime during the early second century AD. In the passage (*Diss.* 3.8), Epictetus offers one of his usual exhortations to recognize the difference between the things we can and cannot change, and, thus, between the things for which we are and are not responsible. At the end of the diatribe, Epictetus uses himself as an example, recounting the hostile reception he received at the hands of one "Italicus" while speaking back in Rome (3.8.7). Although some scholars have been eager to identify this "Italicus" as Silius, others have been more hesitant to do so.[24] The fact that Silius appears as simply "Italicus" on his provincial coinage, as we saw above, at least renders plausible the identification of this "Italicus" as Silius. If we do equate them, this anecdote at least puts Silius in the company of an important and influential Stoic philosopher, if not offers evidence that Silius himself may have been highly regarded as a philosopher. The second testimonium comes from Charisius' *Ars grammatica* (fourth century AD) and appears to connect Silius with another contemporary Stoic, L. Annaeus Cornutus. In a note on *civitatium* (for *civitatum*), Charisius cites an example of the form from what appears to be a commentary on Vergil *Aeneid* 10 (?) addressed by Cornutus to one "Italicus" (*GLK* 1.125.16 = 157.27 Barwick):

> CIVITATIUM: Annaeus Cornutus ad Italicum de Vergilio libro X "namque exemplo tuo etiam principes civitatium, o poeta, incipient similia fingere."

> OF CITIES: Annaeus Cornutus [writes] to Italicus in his commentary on Vergil *Aeneid* 10 (?), "For, even the leading citizens of our cities, o poet, will begin to fashion exempla similar to yours."

Here, too, scholars have debated whether or not to identify this "Italicus" as Silius, although more scholars have been willing to see the presence of Silius in this passage than in the previous one.[25] Both the vocative *o poeta* and the reference to that poet's exemplum at least strengthen the identification of this "Italicus" as Silius, and indicate that, if we do equate them once again, Silius was deeply engaged in the study of the *Aeneid* long before composing his own epic.

Apart from these reasonably secure "Italicus" testimonia, the literary record includes four other works which may contain distant traces of Silius and his *Punica*. The so-called Colloquium Celtis (perhaps fourth century AD), a Greek–Latin bilingual text for ancient language learners, offers a charming and revealing glimpse of daily life at school (30–42) which includes a lengthy reading list in both languages (37–8).[26] Among such famous authors as Cicero and Vergil, the author refers, somewhat cryptically, to φωτίδιον <. . .>, δύο μάχη / *Lucanum, Statium, duo bella* ("Lucan, Statius, two wars," 38a–b). While the "two wars" in question could be those recounted by Lucan and Statius in their epics (or perhaps simply two different wars altogether), emending *Statium* to *Silium* would make it possible to interpret the "two wars" as the civil war between Caesar and Pompey, and the Second Punic War, an equally possible combination. Likewise, the *praefatio* to the second book of the *Disticha Catonis* (also perhaps fourth century AD) presents a reading list which begins with Vergil and includes a couplet which may conceal a reference to Silius: *si Romana cupis et Punica noscere bella, / Lucanum quaeres, qui Martis praelia dixit* ("If you want to learn about the Roman and the Punic wars, / then you will seek out Lucan, who has sung about the wars of Mars," *praef.* 2.4–5). Since Lucan did not write about the Punic Wars per se, although he did, of course, refer to them throughout his epic, scholars have emended *Punica* to *civica*.[27] If, however, we retain the reading *Punica*, then we may be able to discern a second garbled reference to Silius.[28] Sidonius Apollinaris (fifth century AD) incorporates yet another list of canonical authors which may contain a reference to Silius into a lengthy poem addressed to his boyhood friend Magnus Felix. The poem offers a negative priamel which covers all of the famous topics in Greek and Latin literature which Sidonius will *not* write about as a display of his profound knowledge of the Classics: *non Gaetulicus hic tibi legetur, / non Marsus, Pedo, Silius, Tibullus* ("Here, you will not read Gaetulicus, / nor Marsus, Pedo, Silius, or Tibullus," *carm.* 9.259–60). This passage clearly recalls a similar list of the canonical writers of epigram in Martial: *sic scribit Catullus, sic Marsus, sic Pedo, sic Gaetulicus, sic quicumque perlegitur* ("Thus writes Catullus, Marsus, Pedo, Gaetulicus, whoever is read," 1 *praef.* 10–12). Truth be told, however, Silius seems somewhat out of place in such a list: in fact, *Silius* is the vulgate reading for *Silvius* (the consensus reading of the manuscripts), and so perhaps we ought not to place too much hope in the idea that Sidonius refers to the *Punica* in this passage. Last but not least, Vibius Sequester (also fifth century AD) evidently relies on the *Punica* and, in particular, the relatively self-contained book 14, in a number of passages scattered across his geographical treatise *De fluminibus, fontibus, lacubus, nemoribus, paludibus, montibus, gentibus per litteras libellus* (15–18, 47–8, 82–5, 115, 124, 150–2, 174, 177, 186, 220). Bursian first mooted the idea that Vibius may have known the *Punica*, but few scholars have expressed much enthusiasm for the suggestion.[29] Nevertheless, Silius alone names seven of the rivers mentioned by Vibius in his substantial section on *flumina* (1–162), and so perhaps Vibius did know the *Punica*, or, at the very least, *Punica* 14, which could have circulated independently. Altogether, these four dubious testimonia may reflect, whether individually or collectively, a continued awareness of Silius and his epic long after his death, or they may simply create a mirage of continuity.

In the absence of any definitive evidence, scholars have long debated where Silius was born, with arguments based primarily on onomastic evidence.[30] The Renaissance *vitae* generally claim that Silius was born either in Italica (in Spain) or Corfinium (in Italy, which was renamed Italica during the Social War) because of his *cognomen* "Italicus." Modern scholars, however, have noted that, if Silius were from either of these two locales, then the form of the *cognomen* should be "Italicensis" rather than "Italicus."[31] Following the discovery of the inscription outside Aphrodisias, which added the *nomen* Asconius to Silius' name, scholars ventured the suggestion that he may have been born in Patavium, where, according to Silius himself (*Pun.* 12.212–52), the *gens Asconia* originated, or perhaps nearby.[32] Most recently, though, still other scholars have proposed that Silius may have been born in Capua, or perhaps elsewhere in Campania.[33] Each of these proposals reflects its own interpretation of Silius' life and, by extension, his epic. If Silius were from Italica, that would connect him with Scipio Africanus, who founded the city during the Second Punic War, in 206 BC, as well as with

Trajan, who was also born there. Silius would then join the ranks of the Spanish Latin writers, too, including both Senecas, Lucan, and Martial: scholars regularly note, however, that Martial says nothing about Silius being a fellow kinsman. If Silius were from Corfinium, that would associate him with the city which emerged as Rome's greatest rival in the Social War. If Silius were from Patavium, the most likely candidate, then he would share his birthplace with Livy, although it is curious that Pliny likewise says nothing about Silius being a fellow kinsman. If Silius were from Capua, that would associate him with the city which emerged as Rome's greatest rival, and Hannibal's greatest Italian ally, in the Second Punic War. In many ways, the debate about where Silius was born functions as a homology for the larger debate about the significance and the impact of his life and his epic, something of great concern both to Silius himself and to his contemporaries, especially Martial and Pliny.

3. Silius Italicus and Martial

Martial (c. AD 40–100) was born in Bilbilis, in the province of Hispania Tarraconensis, and emigrated to Rome during the reign of Nero in AD 64. His earliest extant work, the *Liber spectaculorum*, consisted of a collection of epigrams which commemorated the opening of the Colosseum in AD 80. Shortly thereafter, Martial published two collections of couplets meant to accompany Saturnalia gifts, the *Xenia* and the *Apophoreta*. He is best known, however, for the twelve books of epigrams on life in Rome which he produced between AD 85 and 101, during the reigns of Domitian, Nerva, and Trajan.[34] After living in the city for more than three decades, Martial returned to his native Bilbilis upon the death of Nerva in AD 98, just as Silius retired to Campania around the same time. (Indeed, Pliny includes a letter on the death of Martial, 3.21, in the very same book in which he writes about the death of Silius.) Martial refers to Silius some eight times and provides invaluable details about both his public and his private life.[35] Martial first mentions Silius in 4.14 (AD 88), early evidence that he was already at work on his epic:

> Sili, Castalidum decus sororum,
> qui periuria barbari furoris
> ingenti premis ore perfidosque
> astus Hannibalis levisque Poenos
> 5   magnis cedere cogis Africanis:
> paulum seposita severitate,

dum blanda vagus alea December
incertis sonat hinc et hinc fritillis
et ludit tropa nequiore talo,
10   nostris otia commoda Camenis.
nec torva lege fronte, sed remissa
lascivis madidos iocis libellos.
sic forsan tener ausus est Catullus
magno mittere Passerem Maroni.

Silius, glory of the Castalian sisters [Muses],
you who suppress the perjuries of barbarian fury
with your great eloquence, and you who force
the perfidious wiles of Hannibal and the faithless
5   Carthaginians to yield to the great Africani:
having put aside your severity for a little bit,
while December, inconstant with its pleasant gambling,
rings out here and there with its fickle dice boxes,
and plays games of chance with its naughty knucklebone,
10   accommodate your leisure to our Camenae [Muses].
And not with a grim expression, but with a carefree one
read my little books swimming with mischievous jokes.
In this way, perhaps, tender Catullus dared
to send his *Passer* to great Maro [Vergil].

While it is always a dangerous proposition to attempt to decipher Martial's tone, this particular epigram appears to entail a number of tonal shifts intended to disarm Silius and to convince him to partake in the fun and games of the Saturnalia (a festival held in honor of Saturn on December 17, and later extended until December 23). In the opening verses (1–5), Martial deftly imitates, and perhaps gently mocks, Silius' bombastic epic style in an extended apostrophe which clearly confirms that Silius had, indeed, already begun his lengthy poem on the Second Punic War. In the lines which follow (6–10), Martial offers Silius a hesitating invitation to put aside his work in order to join in the gambling legally permitted only during the Saturnalia. In the closing quatrain (11–14), Martial suggests that Silius get into the holiday mood by reading his epigrams, just as Catullus might have sent his *Passer* (whether poem 2 or else a collection beginning with poem 2) to Vergil as light reading while he was composing the *Aeneid*. The epigram ultimately hinges on this closing quatrain, in which Martial alludes to the practice of gift-giving, especially of literary works, during the Saturnalia and thereby evokes the more general idea of literary interactions in order both to celebrate Silius as a second Vergil and, of course, to celebrate himself as a second Catullus (cf. *Apophoreta* 195). A couple of years later, in 6.64 (AD 90–1), a moralizing satire in dactylic hexameters addressed to a carping critic, Martial makes a passing reference to Silius which subtly builds on this analogy between poets old and new. In response to the censures of the carping critic, Martial notes that the leading (literary) lights of the city, including Domitian himself, all esteem his *nugae* ("trifles," 7, 8), "which the scroll-cases of endless Silius deem worthy [of reading]" (*quas et perpetui dignantur scrinia Sili*, 10). By using the word *nugae* to describe his epigrams, Martial portrays himself as a second Catullus (cf. Catull. 1.4); likewise, by using the word *perpetuus*, he portrays Silius as a second Vergil, or, at the very least, another aspiring epic poet, perhaps not entirely favorably.[36] Shortly thereafter, in 7.63 (AD 92), Martial returns to "endless" Silius in an epigram addressed to the reader of the epic now taking shape:

> perpetui numquam moritura volumina Sili
>   qui legis et Latia carmina digna toga,
> Pierios tantum vati placuisse recessus
>   credis et Aoniae Bacchica serta comae?
> 5   sacra cothurnati non attigit ante Maronis
>   implevit magni quam Ciceronis opus:
> hunc miratur adhuc centum gravis hasta virorum,
>   hunc loquitur grato plurimus ore cliens.
> postquam bis senis ingentem fascibus annum
> 10   rexerat asserto qui sacer orbe fuit,
> emeritos Musis et Phoebo tradidit annos
>   proque suo celebrat nunc Helicona foro.

> You who read the volumes of endless Silius, destined never
>   to die, and his poems, worthy of the Latin toga,
> do you believe that Pierian haunts alone have given pleasure
>   to the bard, and Bacchic garlands to Aonian hair?
> 5   He did not touch the holy rites of Maro [Vergil] in his tragic boots,
>   before he had completely performed the work of great Cicero.
> The grave centumviral court still admires this man,
>   and many a client of his speaks about this man with grateful voice.
> After he had ruled with the twice-six fasces during the great year,
> 10   which was sacred because it was the year the world was set free,
> he handed over the years of his retirement to the Muses and to Phoebus,
>   and now, instead of the forum, he celebrates Helicon.

This epigram reveals a number of new important details regarding the circumstances of the epic's composition and, in doing so, casts Silius not only as a second Vergil but also as a second Cicero. In the first quatrain (1–4), Martial sets the stage for this comparison by asking whether readers of the epic realize that the poet has also had an illustrious career as an orator: the reference to the *perpetui . . . volumina Sili* (1), like the earlier reference to the *perpetui . . . scrinia Sili* (6.64.10), all but confirms that at least part of the *Punica* was already available in some form. Martial makes the comparison explicit in the next quatrain (5–8) when he mentions Vergil and Cicero by name and remarks on the great success which Silius enjoyed arguing before the centumviral court (a civil law court whose members were originally drawn from a pool of 100, in all likelihood). The final quatrain (9–12) cements this connection between Silius' two careers, first as an orator and then as a poet, by noting that Silius retired from public life after his consulship (AD 68) in order to devote himself to poetry, a tantalizingly vague declaration of political disengagement belied by his service as intermediary during the subsequent civil war and later as proconsul in Asia.

Indeed, Martial returns to the theme of Silius' lofty political aspirations in his very next book in an epigram, 8.66 (AD 93), which tells us more about the composition of his family:

>   Augusto pia tura victimasque
>   pro vestro date Silio, Camenae.
>   bis senos iubet en redire fasces,
>   nato consule, nobilique virga
> 5   vatis Castaliam domum sonare
>   rerum prima salus et una Caesar.
>   gaudenti superest adhuc quod optet,
>   felix purpura tertiusque consul.
>   Pompeio dederit licet senatus
> 10   et Caesar genero sacros honores,
>   quorum pacificus ter ampliavit
>   Ianus nomina: Silius frequentes
>   mavult sic numerare consulatus.

>   To Augustus, Camenae [Muses], give holy incense
>   and sacrificial victims, on behalf of your Silius.
>   Behold, Caesar orders that the twice-six fasces
>   return, with his son as consul, and that the Castalian home
> 5   of the poet ring out with the noble rod,
>   Caesar, the one and only savior of the state.

> Another wish still remains for the rejoicing [Silius],
> the lucky purple and a third consul [in his other son].
> Granted the Senate gave the sacred honors to Pompey,
> 10   and granted Caesar gave them to his son-in-law,
> whose names peace-making Janus ennobled
> three times: Silius prefers to number
> his successive consulships in this way.

Martial instructs the Muses to make an offering to Domitian because the emperor has named Silius' older son, L. Silius Decianus, to a suffect consulship for AD 94 (September–December, according to the *fasti Ostienses*).[37] Martial then notes that Silius entertains similar hopes for his younger son, Silius Severus, so that these Silii can attain to their third consulship, like Pompey and Augustus' son-in-law Agrippa, who each held three consulships on their own, and thereby ennoble the family. Unfortunately, however, the younger son passed away, apparently during that same year, because Martial hastily composes a funerary epigram, 9.86 (AD 94), in his honor:

> festinata sui gemeret quod fata Severi
>   Silius, Ausonio non semel ore potens,
> cum grege Pierio maestus Phoeboque querebar.
>   "ipse meum flevi" dixit Apollo "Linon";
> 5   respexitque suam quae stabat proxima fratri
>   Calliopen et ait: "tu quoque vulnus habes."
> aspice Tarpeium Palatinumque Tonantem:
>   ausa nefas Lachesis laesit utrumque Iovem.
> numina cum videas duris obnoxia Fatis,
> 10   invidia possis exonerare deos.

> Because Silius was lamenting the premature death of his dear Severus,
>   Silius, capable in not just one branch of Ausonian eloquence,
> I, in my grief, voiced my complaints with the Pierian flock and Phoebus.
>   "I myself wept," said Apollo, "for Linus";
> 5   and he looked back at Calliope, who was standing right next
>   to his brother [Orpheus], and he said, "You also have your wound."
> Behold the Tarpeian and the Palatine Thunderer:
>   Lachesis, daring to commit a sacrilege, harmed both Jupiters.
> When you see the gods themselves subject to the harsh Fates,
> 10   you can relieve the gods from the burden of envy.

Martial consoles Silius on the death of his son by once again praising him as a second Cicero and a second Vergil, then he directs his lament to Apollo and the

Muses (1–3); Apollo gently reminds Martial that he and the Muse Calliope lost their own sons Linus and Orpheus (4–6); Martial, in turn, gently reminds Silius that even Jupiter lost Sarpedon and even Domitian lost his young son, proof that even the gods are subject to the dictates of fate (7–10). The poem hinges on the literal and metaphorical implications of verse-initial *respexit* in line 5, which transforms the moment when Apollo gazes back upon Calliope into a reminiscence of the moment when Orpheus gazes back upon Eurydice, only to lose her forever. In this poignant meditation on the ineluctability of death, Martial skillfully balances praise and consolation on the heels of 8.66.

Across a series of poems in the later books of the epigrams, 11.48 and 11.50(49) (AD 96), as well as 12.67 (AD 101), Martial returns to the theme of Silius' literary status:

> Silius haec magni celebrat monumenta Maronis,
>   iugera facundi qui Ciceronis habet.
> heredem dominumque sui tumulive larisve
>   non alium mallet nec Maro nec Cicero.

> Silius celebrates these monuments of great Maro [Vergil],
>   he who has the fields of eloquent Cicero.
> Neither Maro [Vergil] nor Cicero could prefer any other
>   heir or guardian, whether of his tomb or of his Lar.

> iam prope desertos cineres et sancta Maronis
>   nomina qui coleret pauper et unus erat.
> Silius †optatae† succurrere censuit umbrae,
>   et vates vatem non minor ipse colit.

> Up to this point, there was but one poor man who cultivated
>   the deserted ashes and the holy name of Maro [Vergil].
> Silius determined to give help to the cherished shade,
>   and, no less a bard himself, he cultivates the bard.

> Maiae Mercurium creastis Idus,
> Augustis redit Idibus Diana,
> Octobres Maro consecravit Idus.
> Idus saepe colas et has et illas,
> 5   qui magni celebras Maronis Idus.

> Ides of May, you created Mercury,
> Diana returned on the Ides of August,
> Maro [Vergil] consecrated the Ides of October.
> May you often cultivate both these Ides and those,
> 5   you who celebrate the Ides of great Maro [Vergil].

Across these three poems, Martial appears to offer Silius undiluted praise as a second Cicero and a second Vergil, in recognition of his many accomplishments in both prose and poetry. In 11.48 and 11.50(49), Martial explicitly names Silius as custodian for the memory of his famous literary predecessors; in 12.67, while he does not name Silius explicitly, the linguistic resonance between 12.67.5 and 11.48.1 leaves the reader in no doubt as to the poem's addressee. Likewise, much of the language in these three later epigrams resonates with that of the references to Silius earlier in the collection(s), from the mentions of Maro, i.e., Vergil (4.14.14, 7.63.5, 11.48.1, 4, 11.50(49).1, 12.67.3, 5) and Cicero (7.63.6, 11.48.2, 4) to the repetition of relative clauses (4.14.2, 7.63.2, 11.48.2, 11.50(49).2, 12.67.5) and forms of key terms like *celebrare* (7.63.12, 11.48.1, 12.67.5). Taken together, these linguistic resonances furnish an illuminating example of a type of literary interaction which straddles the boundary between intratextuality and intertextuality, depending on whether we use the individual book of epigrams or the collection as a whole as our unit of measurement. Either way, through his references to Silius across these poems, Martial elaborates a clear and coherent image of a Roman senator, consul, orator, and poet who zealously followed in the footsteps of Cicero and Vergil in order to pursue his goal of literary fame and immortality.

4. Silius Italicus and Pliny

Pliny the Younger (*c.* AD 60–115) was born in Novum Comum, in the province of Gallia Cisalpina, and came to Rome as a teenager for his education. He was the biological nephew (and, later, the adopted son by will) of Pliny the Elder, who is likely best known for his encyclopedia, the *Historia naturalis*, and for his fatal heroics during the eruption of Mt. Vesuvius in AD 79. Pliny the Younger enjoyed a long and distinguished career during the reigns of Domitian, Nerva, and Trajan by adapting to the changing times, much like his close friend Tacitus. Pliny's extant writings include a *Panegyricus* addressed to Trajan and ten books of letters, including the two famous letters, 6.16 and 6.20, which he composed for Tacitus on the eruption of Mt. Vesuvius, as well as the correspondence with Trajan which constitutes the final book of the collection. In the third book (*c.* AD 100), Pliny includes *exitus* (death) letters for Silius (3.7) and Martial (3.21), along with related letters on T. Vestricius Spurinna (3.1) and Pliny the Elder (3.5).[38] As in his other obituaries, Pliny uses the missive as a means both of conveying the news to his addressee (here, Caninius Rufus) and of meditating on a related broader theme (here, the brevity of life):[39]

C. Plinius Caninio Rufo suo s.

1. modo nuntiatus est Silius Italicus in Neapolitano suo inedia finisse vitam. 2. causa mortis valetudo. erat illi natus insanabilis clavus, cuius taedio ad mortem inrevocabili constantia decucurrit usque ad supremum diem beatus et felix, nisi quod minorem ex liberis duobus amisit, sed maiorem melioremque florentem atque etiam consularem reliquit. 3. laeserat famam suam sub Nerone (credebatur sponte accusasse), sed in Vitelli amicitia sapienter se et comiter gesserat, ex proconsulatu Asiae gloriam reportaverat, maculam veteris industriae laudabili otio abluerat. 4. fuit inter principes civitatis sine potentia, sine invidia: salutabatur colebatur, multumque in lectulo iacens cubiculo semper, non ex fortuna frequenti, doctissimis sermonibus dies transigebat, cum a scribendo vacaret. 5. scribebat carmina maiore cura quam ingenio, non numquam iudicia hominum recitationibus experiebatur.

6. novissime ita suadentibus annis ab urbe secessit, seque in Campania tenuit, ac ne adventu quidem novi principis inde commotus est: 7. magna Caesaris laus sub quo hoc liberum fuit, magna illius qui hac libertate ausus est uti. 8. erat φιλόκαλος usque ad emacitatis reprehensionem. plures isdem in locis villas possidebat, adamatisque novis priores neglegebat. multum ubique librorum, multum statuarum, multum imaginum, quas non habebat modo, verum etiam venerabatur, Vergili ante omnes, cuius natalem religiosius quam suum celebrabat, Neapoli maxime, ubi monimentum eius adire ut templum solebat. 9. in hac tranquillitate annum quintum et septuagensimum excessit, delicato magis corpore quam infirmo; utque novissimus a Nerone factus est consul, ita postremus ex omnibus, quos Nero consules fecerat, decessit.

10. illud etiam notabile: ultimus ex Neronianis consularibus obiit, quo consule Nero periit. quod me recordantem fragilitatis humanae miseratio subit. 11. quid enim tam circumcisum tam breve quam hominis vita longissima? an non videtur tibi Nero modo modo fuisse? cum interim ex iis, qui sub illo gesserant consulatum, nemo iam superest. 12. quamquam quid hoc miror? nuper L. Piso, pater Pisonis illius, qui a Valerio Festo per summum facinus in Africa occisus est, dicere solebat neminem se videre in senatu, quem consul ipse sententiam rogavisset. 13. tam angustis terminis tantae multitudinis vivacitas ipsa concluditur, ut mihi non venia solum dignae, verum etiam laude videantur illae regiae lacrimae; nam ferunt Xersen, cum immensum exercitum oculis obisset, inlacrimasse, quod tot milibus tam brevis immineret occasus. 14. sed tanto magis hoc, quidquid est temporis futilis et caduci, si non datur factis (nam horum materia in aliena manu), certe studiis proferamus, et quatenus nobis denegatur diu vivere, relinquamus aliquid, quo nos vixisse testemur. 15. scio te stimulis non egere: me tamen tui caritas evocat, ut currentem quoque instigem, sicut tu soles me. ἀγαθὴ δ' ἔρις cum invicem se mutuis exhortationibus amici ad amorem immortalitatis exacuunt. vale.

Gaius Plinius sends greetings to his friend, Caninius Rufus.

1. The news has just arrived that Silius Italicus has starved himself to death at his villa near Naples. 2. The cause of his death was a chronic illness. He had developed a malignant tumor which caused him so much discomfort that he hastened to his death with a fixed resolve, blessed and fortunate until the very last day except for the fact that he had lost the younger of his two sons, even though he left behind the older and more successful son in the prime of his life and already of consular rank. 3. He had damaged his reputation under Nero (he was believed to have served as an informer), but he had conducted himself wisely and tactfully in his friendship with Vitellius, he had brought back glory when he returned from his proconsulship in Asia, and he had washed away the stain of his previous deeds by his praiseworthy retirement. 4. He took his place among the leading citizens without using excessive force or inciting envy: he was visited by clients and sought after, and, often lying on a couch, always in a room filled with friends of every rank, he spent entire days in very learned conversation, whenever he was able to take a break from his writing. 5. He wrote poetry with greater care than natural talent, and he routinely exposed his work to criticism at recitations.

6. Most recently, as he advanced in years, he retired from the city, and he established himself in Campania, and he was not stirred from there even by the arrival of the new emperor: 7. great is the praise for the emperor under whom one was free to do this, and great is the praise for Silius who dared to make use of this freedom. 8. He was a connoisseur of art to the point where he was criticized for his lavish purchases. He owned several villas in the same regions, and he often lost interest in the older ones when he fell in love with the newer ones. In all of these villas there were many books, many statues, and many portrait busts, which he not only owned but even worshipped, including that of Vergil before all of the others, whose birthday he celebrated more faithfully than his own, especially at Naples, where he would visit his tomb as if it were a temple. 9. Amidst this tranquility, he died during his seventy-fifth year, his body more weak than sickly; and, as he was the last consul appointed by Nero, so he was the last of all of those whom Nero had appointed as consul to die.

10. This is another remarkable fact: he was the last of the Neronian consulars to die, during whose consulship Nero himself perished. When I recall this, I feel pity for human frailty. 11. For what is so abrupt, so short, as the longest of human lives? Or does it not seem to you like Nero was alive just the other day? Meanwhile, no one is now left of those who had held the consulship under him. 12. And yet, why should this amaze me? Recently, L. Piso, the father of the Piso who was murdered in Africa through a very wicked crime by Valerius Festus, would say that he saw no one in the Senate whom he himself had called upon to speak when he was consul. 13. The vitality of such a great multitude is bounded

by such narrow limits that those famous royal tears seem worthy not only of forgiveness but even of praise; for, they say that Xerxes, when he had reviewed his massive army, began to weep, because such a swift fall loomed over so many thousands. 14. This is all the more reason why, if every passing moment is not given over to deeds (for, the opportunity for these lies in the hands of another), then let us at least advance in our studies, and, insofar as a long life is denied to us, let us at least leave something behind through which we may bear witness to the fact that we have lived. 15. I know that you do not need any goading: all the same, my affection for you prompts me to spur you on like a willing horse, just as you so often do for me. "Rivalry is good" when friends motivate each other through mutual encouragement to strive for immortal fame. Goodbye.

In terms of structure, the letter can be divided into three roughly equal sections: first, 3.7.1–5 announces Silius' suicide and recounts his life until his retirement from politics; then, 3.7.6–9 (introduced by the narrative transition *novissime*) covers his later years and death in Campania; finally, 3.7.10–15 relates Silius' recent passing to the larger subject of the transitory nature of human existence. The first two sections exhibit an elegant ring structure (especially 3.7.1–2 ~ 3.7.9), and this structural effect somewhat separates the narrative of Silius' life and death from the third and final section, in which Pliny reflects on his own mortality and then expounds the moral of his story. Throughout the letter, Pliny interweaves Silius' politics and poetry much like Martial does in his epigrams: generally speaking, scholars ascribe a positive tone to Martial's epigrams (apart from the slight jab in *perpetuus*) and a negative tone to Pliny's letter, but such a binary contrast ultimately breaks down. Even if lacking somewhat in specific detail, Pliny's letter offers a wealth of evidence for Silius' public and private life. Pliny confirms that Silius had two sons and that the older son held the consulship, while the younger died prematurely (3.7.2); Pliny likewise confirms that Silius enjoyed a long tenure of service which spanned the Julio-Claudians and the Flavians, although he also does not fail to pass along the rumor that Silius might have served as a *delator* (informer) under Nero (3.7.3).[40] According to Pliny, at least, Silius retired from politics in order to pursue a literary career after his governorship of Asia, and not, as a strict interpretation of Martial (7.63.9–12) would seem to imply, after his consulship (3.7.4–5).

Pliny also provides new details about Silius' final departure from Rome for Campania, including his momentous decision not to return to Rome for the accession of the new emperor, whether Nerva or, more likely, Trajan (3.7.6–7), as well as the vivid image of Silius as an artistic connoisseur hoarding his antiquarian wares in his many lavish villas and even worshipping at the tomb of Vergil

(3.7.8).⁴¹ Fittingly enough, it was at his Neapolitan villa where Silius, no longer able to bear the affliction of an unidentified *insanabilis clavus* (incurable tumor), committed suicide by starving himself to death at the age of 75, both the last consul appointed by Nero, and the last of the Neronian consulars to die (3.7.1–2, 9).⁴² Prompted to reflect on Silius' remarkable longevity, Pliny ends the letter with a meditation on the brevity of life (3.7.10–15). All readings of the letter ultimately hinge on Pliny's famous *bon mot* about Silius as a poet: *scribebat carmina maiore cura quam ingenio* ("He wrote poetry with greater care than natural talent," 3.7.5).⁴³ Most scholars have interpreted Pliny's remark as a clear condemnation of Silius' meager talent, while others have argued for a more neutral reading: interestingly enough, Pliny himself aspired to be a poet, and so perhaps we ought to interpret such remarks as an expression of literary rivalry.⁴⁴ In the same vein, there is something distinctly disingenuous about Pliny criticizing Silius for being a political chameleon given the course of his own career under the Flavians and thereafter: in this regard, at least, Tacitus speaks rather more openly and honestly at the beginning of his *Historiae* (1.1).⁴⁵ All in all, Pliny certainly provides the most complete and, therefore, the most important account of Silius' life, work, and death, but we are not necessarily constrained to agree with his assessment, nor should his verdict cast a pall over our own reading and interpretation of the epic.

5. Conclusion: Pliny *Epistula* 3.7 as a Reading of the *Punica*

Taken together, the extant ancient testimonia for Silius and his epic, the *Punica*, especially those passages from Martial, Pliny, and Tacitus, provide interesting and informative perspectives not only on the poet but also on his poem. Unfortunately, it is impossible to determine exactly what version of the epic any of these ancient witnesses may have read or, even more likely, heard at a *recitatio*, since it is impossible to determine exactly when Silius wrote, (inevitably) revised, and "published" his work, and especially since Silius appears to have left the *Punica* incomplete at the time of his death. Most scholars tend to claim that Silius began to compose his epic sometime during the reign of Titus and that he continued to labor on the poem until his death, while others have asserted that he began right after his consulship or perhaps even before that, under Nero.⁴⁶ Regardless, in their references to Silius and the *Punica*, Martial, Pliny, and Tacitus all prove themselves to be adept readers of both the poet and his poem; moreover, Pliny proves himself to be an adept reader of Martial, and

Tacitus proves himself to be an adept reader of both Martial and Pliny, all as part of an extended literary conversation both with and about one of the most important figures in Neronian, Flavian, and even post-Flavian Rome. So, for example, if Tacitus does have Silius in mind in the passage from the *Annales* (4.33.4) mentioned above, then perhaps his use of *extuleris* is intended to recall Silius' use of forms of *(at)tollere* in the same sense at various pivotal moments in the poem, beginning with the proem.[47] Martial and Pliny furnish even clearer evidence of direct knowledge of the epic. In lines written to accompany a gift of fine wine during the Saturnalia, *Xenia* 118, Martial quotes virtually an entire verse from the *Punica*:

Tarraconense

Tarraco, Campano tantum cessura Lyaeo,
   haec genuit Tuscis aemula vina cadis.

Tarragonese wine

Tarragon, yielding only to Campanian Lyaeus,
   produced these wines, rivaling Tuscan jars.

The first line here essentially repeats what Silius writes in the catalog of troops who march with Hannibal over the Alps: *dat Tarraco pubem / vitifera et Latio tantum cessura Lyaeo* ("Tarragon, vine-bearing / and yielding only to Latian Lyaeus, gives her young men," 3.369–70). Pliny cleverly tropes this complex literary dialogue in his letter about Silius' death when he alludes to Martial's many references to Silius at the tomb of Vergil, *cuius natalem religiosius quam suum celebrabat, Neapoli maxime, ubi monimentum eius adire ut templum solebat* (3.7.8). Indeed, the tomb serves as both a literal and a metaphorical locus for literary exchange, from Pliny's use of a relative clause (cf. Mart. 4.14.2, 7.63.2, 11.48.2, 11.50(49).2, 12.67.5) to his use of the key terms *celebrare* (cf. Mart. 7.63.12, 11.48.1, 12.67.5) and *monimentum* (cf. Mart. 11.48.1), and suggests that a dense web of allusions, quotations, and other phenomena remains to be explored further.

In the final third of his letter (3.7.10–15), Pliny relates Silius' death to the broader theme of the brevity of life. Pliny dwells on the fact that Nero died during Silius' consulship, and so the latter's passing truly marks the end of the Julio-Claudian era. Pliny turns this observation into a prompt for reflection on the brevity of even the longest of human lives and then juxtaposes a relatively recent exemplum with one from the (much) more distant past to illustrate his argument. The fraught choice of the L. Calpurnius Piso who, like Silius, held the consulship (AD 27) and then outlived the rest of his generation inevitably evokes memories of this man's father, the Cn. Calpurnius Piso (consul 7 BC) who, as governor of Syria, killed Germanicus by poisoning him (Tac. *Ann.* 2.43–84, 3.1–19), as well as of his son, the L. Calpurnius Piso (consul AD 57) who, as governor of Africa, was killed for his Vitellian sympathies by Valerius Festus in order to hand the province over to Vespasian (Tac. *Hist.* 4.48–50). Such a checkered family past complicates the import of the comparison with Silius, especially given his own charged relationship with both Vitellius and Vespasian. To this recent exemplum Pliny juxtaposes that of Xerxes, who broke into tears during his review of the forces assembled at Abydus as he contemplated how all of his men would be dead within a century (Hdt. 7.44–6). At one level, this image of Xerxes bears a strong superficial resemblance to that of Piso contemplating his own mortality and suggestively likens Silius to the Persian king.[48] At another level, however, this image also evokes other moments when great men (or else gods) break into tears upon recognizing their own (or else another's) imminent demise, from Scipio Aemilianus in tears at the fall of Carthage (Plb. 38.22.2, cited by D.S. 32.24; App. *Pun.* 132) to Hercules in tears at the fall of Saguntum in *Punica* 2.475–525.[49] Through this deft combination of exempla, Pliny tropes Silius' own approach to exemplarity (cf. the words of Cornutus cited by Charisius in *GLK* 1.125.16 = 157.27 Barwick mentioned above) in order to juxtapose past and present: more specifically, Pliny demonstrates his skill at forging connections between seemingly disparate exempla in order to suggest varying, even conflicting, interpretive trajectories, a literary move which Silius uses to great effect throughout his epic.

Fittingly enough, Pliny concludes his letter with an exhortation both to himself and to his addressee to continue to devote themselves to their literary labors in pursuit of (at least, literary) immortality. The Hesiodic *gnome* reads in full as ἀγαθὴ δ' ἔρις ἥδε βροτοῖσιν ("Rivalry is good, among mortals, at least," *Op.* 24) and perhaps alludes to Hannibal's invocation of *aemula virtus* ("rivaling manliness," *Pun.* 1.511) in his prayer to Hercules at the beginning of his single combat with Murrus before the walls of Saguntum.[50] Regardless, the accompanying specter of imminent death here at the letter's close brings the missive full circle by taking the reader back to the news about the death of Silius with which it opens. The fact that Silius dies by suicide and, more specifically, by starving himself to death could connect him with the tradition of Stoic suicides, including those of Seneca the Younger, Lucan, Petronius, and Thrasea Paetus (Tac. *Ann.* 15–16), though this could also be an example of an Epicurean suicide, considering how *un*theatrical an end Silius chose for himself, comparatively speaking. Either way, how we "read" Silius' death has profound implications for how we "read" his life, as well as how we "read" his epic. This is especially so if we read his death, his life, and his epic through the lens of Stoicism, as many (if not all) scholars do,[51] and if we consider contemporary Stoic attitudes towards Rome and the emperor, even the purported existence of a so-called Stoic opposition in the Roman Senate.[52] Suicide plays a major role in the *Punica* in a way which both reflects the existing traditions about the Second Punic War and yet also greatly amplifies its importance, perhaps as a reflection of contemporary concerns. Of the large number of individual and collective suicides (both real and imagined) which punctuate the narrative, two contrasting moments powerfully link suicide and food in a way which evokes the manner and the means of Silius' own demise: the famine which precedes the mass suicide at Saguntum in *Punica* 2, and the feasting which precedes the mass suicide at Capua in *Punica* 13. Perhaps most importantly of all, however, again and again over the course of the epic (2.696–707, 3.705–12, 13.874–5, 892–3), Silius looks ahead to the suicide of Hannibal, who died some twenty years after the war by ingesting poison, as if the poet were contemplating not only the general theme but perhaps even his own imminent death.[53]

2

What Is the *Punica*?

1. Introduction: The Punic Wars (264–146 BC)

The story of the rise and fall of Rome is inextricably linked with the story of the rise and fall of Carthage, her great nemesis and yet, at the same time, also her great sister city.¹ Both cities trace their origins back to a double foundation myth which connects a later "historical" legend with an earlier "mythical" legend dated to the era of the fall of Troy (traditionally, 1184 BC, for what it is worth). In the case of Rome, the double foundation myth links the exile of Aeneas from Troy with Romulus, Remus, and the "official" founding in 753 BC; in the case of Carthage, it links Azoros, Carchedon, and an early settlement before the Trojan War with the exile of Dido from Tyre and the "official" founding in 814 BC. Put simply, two of the greatest cities in the Western Mediterranean trace their roots back to two of the greatest cities in the Eastern Mediterranean, a powerful testament to the region's fraught interconnectedness in terms of history, culture, and literature. Indeed, it is precisely this fraught interconnectedness and, in particular, the complex relationship between Rome and Carthage which Livy and Vergil codify, and, at the same time, interrogate, in the *Ab urbe condita* and the *Aeneid*. As an indication of their growing power, the two cities are reported to have signed a number of treaties regarding their respective spheres of influence, beginning with an agreement dated to 509 BC, the first year of the Republic, but not all scholars support the historicity of these accords.² Ultimately, Carthage and Rome clashed on three separate occasions between 264 and 146 BC, the First (264–241), Second (218–201), and Third (149–146) Punic Wars, but it was the Second Punic War, otherwise known as the Hannibalic War, which had the greatest impact on Roman history, Roman culture, and Roman literature.³ The Punic Wars were the defining conflicts of the Middle Republic: in 264, Carthage was at her peak, and Rome was about to embark on her first overseas military expedition; in 146, Carthage was razed to the ground, and Rome was well on her way to establishing herself as the dominant Mediterranean superpower, and, in the process, transforming Republic into Empire.

The First Punic War (264–241 BC) was the longest of these three major conflicts, as well as one of the longest wars in the ancient world.[4] Most of the major battles were fought at sea as the two sides struggled to assert control over Sicily. The conflict began in 264 when a band of Italian mercenaries from Campania named the Mamertines, who occupied the city of Messana, called on the Romans for assistance against the combined forces of Hiero II of Syracuse and the Carthaginians, who controlled much of the island at the time. The Romans landed a fleet under App. Claudius Caudex, relieved Messana, and besieged Syracuse. Hiero II swiftly capitulated, abandoning his alliance with the Carthaginians and, instead, signing a treaty with the Romans. These events set the stage for the struggle between the Romans and the Carthaginians, including early Roman victories at the battle of Agrigentum (262) and the battle of Mylae (260), for which the admiral C. Duilius earned a triumph. Thereafter, the fighting remained inconclusive until the Romans decided upon a daring expedition into Africa itself to try to bring the conflict to an end. Following his victory at the battle of Ecnomus (256), M. Atilius Regulus landed in Africa and very nearly forced Carthage to capitulate, before being captured and killed himself. After another period of relatively inconclusive fighting, the Carthaginians scored a major victory over P. Claudius Pulcher and the Romans at the battle of Drepana (249). At this point, Hannibal's father, Hamilcar Barca, assumed command of the Carthaginian forces in Sicily and waged a successful guerilla campaign against the Romans, until a fleet under C. Lutatius Catulus won what proved to be the final engagement at the battle of the Aegates Islands (241). Hamilcar was thus forced to make peace with the Romans, as a part of which Carthage agreed to cede control over Sicily and to pay a massive indemnity. In the aftermath of the war, Carthage faced an internal insurrection among her (unpaid) mercenaries (241–237 BC).[5] Hamilcar eventually quelled the uprising, but not before Rome capitalized on the opportunity to seize Corsica and Sardinia in addition to Sicily and to impose an additional indemnity on her defeated enemy. This act of unchecked aggression rankled Hamilcar and his fellow Carthaginians, making a second conflict seem all but inevitable.

Fresh from this ignominious defeat, Hamilcar briefly returned to Carthage before setting out for Spain, ostensibly in order to reestablish Carthaginian control over the Iberian peninsula, but ultimately in order to challenge Roman hegemony. Prior to his departure, Hamilcar is said to have sworn his son, Hannibal, to an oath of eternal hatred against Rome, one of many moments in the conflict which could be said to elide the boundary between history and myth. Regardless of the oath's (dubious) historicity, Hannibal eventually succeeded his father as commander of the Carthaginian forces in Spain and shortly thereafter besieged Saguntum, whose fall marked the beginning of the Second Punic War (281–201 BC).[6] In time, the war was remembered not only as a clash of cultures (Carthaginian and Roman), but also as a clash of two transcendent leaders, the Carthaginian Hannibal and the Roman P. Cornelius Scipio (the future Africanus).[7] After the fall of Saguntum, Hannibal embarked on his famous march from Spain over the Alps into Italy,[8] where he conquered the Romans in three battles in quick succession, at the Ticinus River (218), the Trebia River (218), and Lake Trasimene (217). A panicked Senate back in Rome appointed Q. Fabius Maximus *dictator* to address the emergency, with M. Minucius Rufus as his *magister equitum* (master of the horse). Fabius was renowned for his policy of avoiding open combat with Hannibal in order to impede his progress, so much so that Fabius earned the moniker Cunctator (Delayer), a clever nickname with both positive and negative connotations. Eventually, however, Hannibal brought the Romans to battle at Cannae (216), where he scored his greatest victory in the entire war.[9] After the engagement, rather than press his advantage by marching on the city of Rome itself, Hannibal chose to celebrate a triumph of sorts in Capua, which had defected from its long-standing alliance with Rome. After a period of some five years of relatively inconclusive fighting, both in southern Italy and elsewhere in the Mediterranean, the Romans besieged Capua. Hannibal tried to draw the Romans away from the siege by belatedly making his long-delayed march on their own city, but ultimately to no avail, as Capua fell while Rome stood strong (211). Thereafter, the course of the war changed dramatically. Scipio assumed command of the Roman forces in Spain, captured Carthago Nova (209), and scored decisive victories at Baecula (208) and Ilipa (206). Meanwhile, back in Italy, the Romans defeated Hannibal's brother Hasdrubal at the Metaurus River (207). With the Carthaginians now reeling, Scipio invaded Africa, compelled Hannibal to return home to defend his fatherland, and brought the war to an end with his victory at Zama (202). According to the terms of the peace treaty, Carthage agreed to cede control over Spain and to pay yet another massive indemnity, as well as to severely limit the size of her armed forces, but Hannibal lived on after the war, and so the enmity between the two cities did, too.

    The events of the Second Punic War had forever changed both Carthage and Rome. Now that the Carthaginians had lost their hegemony over the Western Mediterranean, Rome pursued her imperial agenda with a renewed vigor in both the west and the east by waging wars across the Mediterranean world, from Spain to Asia Minor. Like Hannibal, Scipio survived the war and remained a fixture in Roman history, culture, and literature: fittingly, they both died in 183 BC, first Scipio, either through natural causes or else by suicide, and then Hannibal, by ingesting poison in order to elude capture. Their joint passing heralded the end of the era of the Second Punic War and the beginning of that of the Third Punic War (149–146 BC), the beginning of the end for Carthage. Indeed, the aged Roman senator M. Porcius Cato (Cato the Elder) insisted that, for the good of Rome, "Carthage must be destroyed" (*Carthago delenda est*), and ultimately he carried the day. Once again, a Roman fleet landed in Africa, and Scipio Aemilianus, the adoptive grandson of Scipio Africanus, eventually assumed command of the forces much like his adoptive grandfather before him during the previous conflict.[10] After a long siege, Carthage succumbed to the Roman onslaught and suffered complete destruction: the city itself is said to have burned for seventeen days; its inhabitants were either killed or sold into slavery; and, so the much later story goes, the city was sown with salt.[11] Without a doubt, this was a full-scale genocide.[12] Rome took control of the region and organized it as the province of Africa; meanwhile, the city of Carthage itself was settled as a Roman colony, first under C. Gracchus (*Colonia Iunonia*, in 122 BC) and then later under the future Augustus (*Colonia Iulia Carthago*, in 29 BC). By the first century AD, Carthage had in fact regained its status as the second city of the Western Mediterranean.

In the grandest of terms, like the Persian Wars, the Punic Wars represent an instantiation of the perennial conflict between East (Carthage) and West (Rome), notwithstanding the fact that Carthage actually lies further to the west than Rome. The two cities were interconnected at multiple levels (history, culture, and literature), and both sides wrestled with the fact that they recognized similarities as well as differences between themselves and their inveterate enemy. In many ways, just as Athenian culture and, in particular, Athenian literature flourished after the victory over the Persians at the battle of Salamis (480 BC), so, too, Roman culture and, in particular, Roman literature flourished after the victory over the Carthaginians at the battle of Zama (202 BC).[13] Indeed, the Second Punic War became and remained perhaps the single most important subject in Roman literature, especially in the high genres of historiography and epic.[14] Over time, memories of the Second Punic War inevitably changed, influencing narratives of the First Punic War and influenced by narratives, as well as the actual events, of the Third Punic War. Ultimately, recording for posterity what actually happened during the Punic Wars mattered far less than transforming these conflicts into moralizing exempla on such universal themes as the rise and fall of empires, and the merits and flaws of monarchical rule. While ancient authors acknowledged and respected the fact that there was a core of verifiable historical fact at the root of their divergent, sometimes outright conflicting, narratives, they evaluated any individual narrative for its degree of plausibility (not to say probability) along the spectrum from fact to fiction. As a result, we cannot use this material in order to reconstruct *the* Second Punic War: instead, we have to evaluate each account on its own terms in order to understand why the war and, in particular, the battle of Cannae emerged as *the* pivotal moment in the transition from Republic to Empire in Roman history, culture, and literature, especially in the *Punica*.

2. The *Punica* and the Second Punic War

Silius composed his *Punica*, at 12,204 verses in dactylic hexameter, the longest surviving Latin poem, under the Flavians, some three hundred years after the Second Punic War itself. The extant work spans seventeen books, but may have been originally composed or, at the very least, planned in eighteen. It is uncertain whether Silius left the poem incomplete at the time of his death, whether accidentally or intentionally, and it is also uncertain whether the poem suffered mutilation at some point(s) in its manuscript transmission, or whether both of these took place. The title of the epic is, in form, the neuter plural substantive adjective of a racial-ethnic identity group, i.e., *Punica* = "Punic (Carthaginian) / Phoenician things" ~ "ethnography of the Punics (Carthaginians) / Phoenicians" (where "ethnography" suggests a focus on culture above all else). As such, the title *Punica* not only stresses the link between the genres of epic and historiography, where this form of title is common, but also, more specifically, suggests that the poem will focus on the Carthaginian as much as, if not more than, the Roman perspective concerning the events of the Second Punic War and their impact on the two cultures.[15] Accordingly, the epic furnishes a selective account of the major action of the war, beginning with Hannibal's oath of eternal hatred against Rome and ending with Scipio's triumph in Rome after his victory at Zama. Between these twin narrative poles, Silius retells the fall of Saguntum (books 1–2); Hannibal's march from Spain to Italy, including his trek over the Alps (book 3); his victories over the Romans at the battles of the Ticinus River, the Trebia River, and Lake Trasimene (books 4–6); the stalemate between Hannibal and Fabius (book 7); the Roman disaster at the battle of Cannae (books 8–10);

Hannibal's winter at Capua and subsequent failed march on Rome (books 11–12); the falls of Capua and Syracuse (books 13–14); the Roman victory at the battle of the Metaurus River (book 15); and Scipio's successful campaigns in Spain and Africa, culminating in his victories at the battles of Ilipa and Zama (books 16–17). Over the course of the epic, Silius integrates allusions to the First and Third Punic Wars into this expansive narrative of the Second Punic War. Above and beyond that, as we will see in greater detail in the subsequent chapters of this book, Silius incorporates allusions to peoples, places, and events from throughout Roman culture, from the Trojan War to the Flavians, in order to transform the Second Punic War into a universal history. The following book-by-book summary provides an overview of the main content of the poem.[16]

Book 1: Following the proem (1–20), Silius recounts the rise of Hannibal, who swears an oath of eternal hatred against Rome in the Temple of Dido in Carthage, after which his father, Hamilcar, marches to Spain, where he soon dies in battle; following the death of his successor (Hasdrubal, son-in-law of Hamilcar and brother-in-law of Hannibal), Hannibal himself assumes command (21–270). Hannibal begins the siege of Saguntum, defeating the Saguntine Murrus in single combat, but then receiving a wound from Jupiter in his thigh which forces him to retreat from the fighting (271–583). Envoys sail from Saguntum to Rome, where they successfully plead for assistance from the Roman Senate (584–694).

Book 2: The siege of Saguntum continues, as envoys sail from Rome to Hannibal and then from Hannibal on to Carthage (1–55), the Saguntine Theron defeats the Amazon Asbyte in single combat and is then himself killed by Hannibal (56–269), and the envoys from Rome arrive at Carthage, where they are given a hostile reception by the Carthaginian Senate, and so Fabius formally declares war (270–390). Silius offers an ecphrasis on the shield of Hannibal (391–456); then, Hercules convinces Fides to descend from Mt. Olympus in order to ennoble the besieged Saguntines at their impending death (457–525); Juno, however, convinces the Fury Tisiphone to drive the Saguntines to mass suicide, delivering the city to Hannibal (526–707).

Book 3: After the fall of Saguntum, Hannibal travels to Gades in order to visit the Temple of Hercules, while his envoy Bostar travels to the Siwa Oasis in order to visit the Temple of Jupiter Ammon (1–60). Hannibal sends his wife, Imilce, and their infant son back to Carthage (61–

157); Mercury visits Hannibal in a dream (158–221); and Silius offers an extended catalog of the African and Spanish troops and their respective commanders (222–414). Hannibal marches over the Pyrenees, crosses the Rhône River and the Durance River, and scales the Alps (415–556). With Hannibal poised atop the Alps, Venus and Jupiter discuss the Second Punic War and its relationship to the rise of the Flavians (557–629). Hannibal descends the Alps and enters Italy, where he meets Bostar, who brings back his report from Jupiter Ammon (630–714).

Book 4: The Romans receive word that Hannibal has entered Italy and make immediate preparations to meet the invader (1–38). Hannibal defeats the Romans under the command of P. Cornelius Scipio, father of the future Africanus, at the battle of the Ticinus River (39–479). Soon thereafter, Hannibal defeats the Romans under the joint command of P. Cornelius Scipio and Ti. Sempronius Longus at the battle of the Trebia River (480–703). While the Romans, now under the command of C. Flaminius, march north, Hannibal, visited in a dream by Juno in disguise, marches over the Apennines towards Lake Trasimene (704–62). After Hannibal reaches his destination, envoys from Carthage arrive to ask whether he would be willing to sacrifice his infant son, but Hannibal refuses and instead promises another great victory over the Romans (763–829).

Book 5: Hannibal sets his ambush for Flaminius in the woods around Lake Trasimene (1–52); Flaminius receives a number of evil omens on the march, but ignores the warnings of Corvinus, choosing instead to prepare himself and his men for battle (53–185). Hannibal ambushes the Romans: among many other combatants, the Roman Appius kills the Cinyphian Isalcas, prospective son-in-law of Mago, in single combat and is then himself killed by Mago, but Mago is also wounded, and so Hannibal brings him to Synalus (186–375); among many more combatants, Flaminius kills the Carthaginian Sychaeus in single combat, and then Hannibal returns to the fray, where he learns about the death of Sychaeus and so seeks out Flaminius for a single combat, but Flaminius is killed by the Boian Ducarius, after which the Romans commit mass suicide to end the fighting (376–678).

Book 6: The next day, Hannibal and Mago revisit the battlefield in order to hunt down any remaining Romans amid the heaps of dead and dying warriors (1–61). Among the few survivors, Serranus, the son of Regulus, escapes to the humble abode of Marus, who had served under Regulus, near Perugia: Marus recognizes Serranus, welcomes him into his hut for the night, and tends to the wounded soldier (62–100). The next morning, Marus recounts the brave and noble deeds of Regulus during the First Punic War, culminating with his torture and death in Carthage (101–551). Serranus returns to Rome (552–99); Jupiter turns Hannibal away from Rome and instructs the Senate to name Q. Fabius Maximus *dictator* (600–40). Hannibal instead burns down a temple at Liternum (641–716).

Book 7: Hannibal learns about Fabius from Cilnius, an Etruscan captive (1–73), while the Romans offer propitiatory sacrifices at temples throughout the city (74–89). Fabius leads the army into the field, but he avoids battle with Hannibal, who retaliates by burning down the vineyards of Falernum (90–211); Fabius, in response, defends his policy of delay to his men, nearly traps Hannibal and his men, and then entrusts the army to his *magister equitum*, M. Minucius Rufus, so that he can return to Rome to fulfill a family religious obligation (212–408). The Nereids, terrified by the arrival of a Carthaginian fleet, consult Proteus, who tells them about Rome's ultimate victory over Carthage (409–93). After the Roman Senate divides the army between Fabius and Minucius, Minucius leads his men into battle against Hannibal at Gereonium; Fabius rescues the Romans from defeat; and Minucius hails Fabius as his savior (494–750).

Book 8: After his setback at Gereonium (1–24), Juno sends Anna down to Hannibal in a dream in order to encourage him to march to Cannae; Silius recounts the earlier history of Anna (Perenna) and Dido; and Anna completes her mission (25–241). With Hannibal on the march to Cannae, C. Terentius Varro, one of the two consuls for the year, rouses the Roman people against the invader, while Fabius advises L. Aemilius Paullus, the other of the two consuls, on how best to restrain his rash colleague in order to avert disaster (242–348); with the two consuls likewise on the march to Cannae, Silius offers an extended catalog of the Roman and Italian troops and their respective commanders (349–621). Once the Romans arrive at Cannae, they witness a host of evil omens and hear the dire predictions about the forthcoming engagement uttered by an unnamed soldier (622–76).

Book 9: After a minor skirmish in which several Romans fall, Paullus continues to strive, ultimately in vain, to dissuade Varro from leading the Romans into the field the next day (1–65). During the night before the climactic battle, the Italian Satricus is unwittingly killed by his son, Solymus, while unwittingly wearing the armor of his other son, Mancinus, who had been killed earlier that day, and then Solymus, realizing what he has done, commits suicide upon his corpse (66–177): morning reveals the evil omen, as Hannibal and Varro address their soldiers and line them up for battle (178–277). The engagement begins, on heaven and earth (278–410). Hannibal seeks out Varro for a single combat, but P. Cornelius Scipio, the future Africanus, turns the Carthaginian against himself, instead, until Mars and Pallas intervene to prevent the clash (411–569). While the Carthaginian elephants run amok (570–631), Paullus bitterly rebukes Varro for leading the Romans to their demise; Varro laments his fate before fleeing from the battlefield (632–57).

Book 10: Paullus seeks out Hannibal for a single combat, but Juno, first in the guise of L. Caecilius Metellus and then in the guise of Gelesta, intervenes to prevent the clash (1–91); instead, Hannibal slays Crista and his six sons, while Paullus wreaks havoc all across the field until he dies nobly in the fray (92–325). During the night after the climactic battle, Juno sends Somnus down to Hannibal in a dream in order to encourage him *not* to march on Rome (326–86). The surviving Romans gather at Canusium: the real Metellus advises his fellow soldiers to desert Rome, but Scipio storms in to compel everyone to swear an oath to defend their city (387–448). Instead of marching on Rome, Hannibal revisits the battlefield, where he honors the fallen Paullus (449–577). Back in Rome, Fabius exhorts the Roman people to stand strong, even as Varro makes his ignominious return (578–658).

Book 11: Silius offers an extended catalog of the Italian cities which defect from Rome to Hannibal after the battle of Cannae, culminating with Capua, the second city in Italy (1–54). Emboldened by their decision to defect, the Capuans send envoys to Rome in order to make the specious demand of a share in the consulship, and, as expected, the request is denied (55–121). Rejected by Rome, the Capuans invite Hannibal to enter their city in triumph, over the vociferous objections of Decius (122–266). After his triumph, Hannibal continues the celebration that night with a lavish banquet, during which the Capuan Pacuvius barely succeeds in dissuading his son, Perolla, from slaying Hannibal (267–368). With his brother Mago, as well as Decius, on the way back to Carthage, Hannibal and his men spend the winter at Capua, wasting away in luxury (369–482). Meanwhile, Mago returns to Carthage in triumph and convinces the Carthaginian Senate to send supplies (483–611).

Book 12: Enervated by their winter in Capua (1–26), Hannibal and his men unsuccessfully besiege Naples, Capua, and Puteoli (27–160), and so they attack Nola, where M. Claudius Marcellus wards off the Carthaginian assault and nearly kills Hannibal himself (161–294). The Romans rejoice at the news of the repulse of Hannibal, as well as the report back from the oracle of Apollo at Delphi (295–341). Silius then shifts the scene briefly to the war in Sardinia (342–419). Thereafter, Hannibal besieges Tarentum, until he is called back to defend Capua, which prompts him, in turn, to march on Rome (420–544). The terrified Romans prepare for an attack; Jupiter turns Hannibal away from the city for three days in a row, compelling him to abandon the siege; and the Romans rejoice at their good fortune (545–752).

Book 13: Hannibal learns about the Palladium, the sacred statue of Minerva which guards Rome, from Dasius Altinius, an Italian from Arpi allied with the Carthaginians: he gives up hope of capturing the city and plunders the Temple of Feronia (1–93). Meanwhile, Q. Fulvius Flaccus takes control of Capua, after Fides punishes the besieged Capuans for their faithlessness to the Romans by driving them to mass suicide (94–380). When he learns about the death of both his father and his uncle in Spain, Scipio decides to commune with the spirits of the dead in a traditional epic scene which combines a *nekyia* (the dead visit the living) and a *katabasis* (the living visit the dead): led by the Sibyl of Cumae, Scipio encounters App. Claudius Pulcher, tours the Underworld, and then converses with his mother, Pomponia, and with his father and uncle, P. and Cn. Cornelii Scipiones, as well as Paullus, before he receives a troubling vision of Rome's past and future (381–895).

Book 14: Silius digresses from the narrative about the rise and fall of Hannibal in order to recount the fall of Syracuse, beginning with an ecphrasis on the geography of the island of Sicily (1–78) and a brief account of the ongoing political turmoil in the city itself (79–109). After landing with his fleet at Messana, Marcellus swiftly captures the city of Leontini en route to Syracuse (110–77). While the Roman general surrounds the city, Silius offers an extended catalog of the Sicilian cities allied with the Romans, as well as those allied with the Carthaginians, including Syracuse itself (178–291). Archimedes, the famous Syracusan mathematician, contrives a number of mechanical devices to defend his native city; meanwhile, the Romans score a decisive victory over a fleet of reinforcements newly arrived from Carthage (292–579). A debilitating plague strikes first the Romans and then the Carthaginians; nevertheless, Marcellus presses his advantage and takes control of Syracuse, although he holds his men back from sacking the city (580–688).

Book 15: After the death of his father and uncle, Scipio first receives a vision in which he chooses Virtus over Voluptas and is then himself chosen by the Roman Senate to assume command of the forces in Spain (1–148). After sailing to Tarraco, Scipio swiftly captures the city of New Carthage (149–285). Silius then shifts the scene briefly to the war in Greece (286–319). Meanwhile, back in Italy, Fabius captures Tarentum (320–33), but Marcellus is ambushed and killed by Hannibal in Apulia (334–98). In Spain, Scipio defeats Hannibal's brother Hasdrubal at Baecula (399–492); Hasdrubal marches from Spain to the Alps and on into Italy in order to join forces with his brother (493–521). Visited in a dream by the goddess Italia, C. Claudius Nero races to the Metaurus River, where he joins forces with M. Livius Salinator, after which Hasdrubal makes a vain attempt at avoiding battle (522–657). Nero and Salinator defeat Hasdrubal at the Metaurus River, as Nero slays Hasdrubal in single combat by decapitating him (658–823).

Book 16: Broken by the defeat and the death of his brother, Hannibal retires to the lands of the Bruttii (1–22). In Spain, Scipio drives out Hannibal's brother Mago, captures Hanno after a surprise attack on his camp, and then defeats Hasdrubal Gisgo in battle at Ilipa, after which Masinissa changes sides from the Carthaginians to the Romans (23–169). Scipio and Hasdrubal Gisgo both sail to the court of Syphax in Africa, where they strive to gain the king as an ally (170–276).

After winning Syphax over to the Roman side, Scipio returns to Spain, where he holds funeral games in honor of his dead father and uncle, including a chariot race, a foot race, a gladiatorial fight, and a javelin throw (277–591). Having conquered Spain, Scipio returns to Rome in triumph and convinces the Roman Senate to send him with his army on to Africa, over the vociferous objections of Fabius (592–700).

Book 17: P. Cornelius Scipio Nasica, son of Cn. Scipio and cousin of the future Africanus, welcomes the Magna Mater into Rome on behalf of the city (1–47). Meanwhile, Scipio sails with his army to Africa, where he rebukes Syphax for changing sides from the Romans to the Carthaginians, and then defeats and captures the king at the battle of Campi Magni (48–148). Envoys sail from Carthage to Hannibal in order to instruct him to return home (149–200); Hannibal looks back at Italy as the ships set sail and then nearly dies during a storm at sea (201–90). While Hannibal and Scipio address their soldiers and line them up for battle, Jupiter and Juno discuss the outcome of the impending engagement (291–384). During the battle, when Scipio seeks out Hannibal for a single combat, Juno lures away the Carthaginian: ultimately, Hannibal flees from the battlefield, while his native city opens its gates to Scipio (385–624). Scipio returns to Rome in triumph (625–54).

As even this book-by-book summary of the epic well illustrates, Silius furnishes far more than a mere versified history of the Second Punic War. Rather, he crafts a version and a vision of the war which transforms historiography into epic, history into myth, and the Second Punic War into a new Trojan War, a defining conflict for Roman, as well as Carthaginian, identity. In doing so, Silius thoughtfully and skillfully integrates his *Punica* into the traditions of both historiography (especially Livy's history *Ab urbe condita*) and epic (especially Vergil's *Aeneid*), as well as many other genres. Even more particularly, he crafts his poem as the previously missing link between Vergil's *Aeneid* and Lucan's *Bellum civile*, historical epics which recount the rise of Rome from the ashes of Troy and then the fall of Rome into civil war at the end of the Republic. The product of this literary engagement is perhaps the most intertextual, as well as the most intratextual, epic composed in the ancient world. This literary engagement operates on three interconnected levels: first and foremost, Silius evinces a close and careful consideration of the existing traditions about the

Second Punic War in Roman literature; then, he incorporates literary elements from a host of other genres in order to universalize his narrative; finally, he argues for the pivotal importance of the war and, in particular, the battle of Cannae for Roman history, culture, and literature. As a result, the *Punica* simultaneously offers an archaizing narrative of the Second Punic War which reflects evolving memories of the conflict in the Roman imaginary and a modernizing narrative of the Year of the Four Emperors which reflects contemporary concerns about the recent descent into the madness of civil war and the subsequent rise of the Flavians. In essence, Silius achieves the virtually unthinkable: he transforms the narrative of a triumph from Rome's Republican past into the narrative of a tragedy from the city's Imperial present (and, perhaps, future, as well).[17]

3. The *Punica* and the Historiographical Tradition

While Silius demonstrates a profound direct knowledge of the Roman historiographical tradition (i.e., in both Greek and Latin), he primarily mediates his engagement with that tradition through his reading of Livy's own expansive narrative of the Second Punic War. Livy (64/59 BC–AD 12/17) was born in Patavium, in the province of Cisalpine Gaul (soon to become part of Italy), and perhaps emigrated to Rome around the beginning of the reign of Augustus. He is best known for his massive 142-book history of Rome "from the founding of the city" (*Ab urbe condita*), from Aeneas to Augustus, written to preserve "the memory of the deeds of the greatest nation in the world" (*rerum gestarum memoriae principis terrarum populi, praef.* 3). Unfortunately, most of this history has been lost, and so, apart from meager fragments, only books 1–10 and 21–45 are extant. The work is traditionally divided into groups of five or ten books (pentads or decades). In the third decade (i.e., books 21–30), Livy offers a remarkably well-researched, well-conceived, and well-executed account of the Second Punic War on a suitably grand scale: the first pentad (21–25) recounts the events from the fall of Saguntum to Hannibal's march on Rome, while the second (26–30) recounts the events from Hannibal's march on Rome to the battle of Zama.[18] By the time of Silius, Livy's history had established itself as a, if not the, canonical (re)presentation of *Romanitas*, especially in the narrative of the Second Punic War, which served as a metonymy for the work as a whole. Although Martial refers to an epitome of Livy in one of the couplets of the *Apophoreta* (14.190),[19] Silius undoubtedly read the third decade, if not the entire history, in its original full form, and nearly every verse of the *Punica* demonstrates Livy's deep and abiding influence on Silius' own (re)presentation of *Romanitas*. Accordingly, scholars have long studied the relationship between the two texts, primarily through the lens of Quellenforschung, but also, more recently, through that of intertextuality. In his engagement with Livy's third decade, Silius regularly expands and, far more often, contracts the narrative of events, rigorously simplifies the cast of characters, and, most importantly of all, universalizes the thematic import of the conflict for Rome's, as well as Carthage's, past, present, and future. Put simply, Silius transforms prose historiography into epic poetry. As a result, while the narrative of the Second Punic War in the *Punica* powerfully resonates with that in the third decade of the *Ab urbe condita*, Silius does not seek to slavishly versify Livy, nor does he confine himself to the third decade. Instead, as a part of his mission to transform his narrative of the war into a totalizing vision of *Romanitas*, Silius looks beyond the boundaries of the third decade to incorporate into his epic other key moments in Roman history and Roman culture from elsewhere in Livy's history, e.g., the narrative of the battle of the Allia River and the Gallic sack of Rome (traditionally, 390 BC) in book 5.

Through Livy, Silius engages with the rest of the rich historiographical tradition on the Second Punic War, indeed, with the Roman historiographical tradition in general, and scholars have long studied Silius' relationship to this tradition through a Livian lens.[20] The tradition on the Second Punic War, as well as the tradition on the three Punic Wars as a whole, itself plays a central role in the general tradition, as the era of the Punic Wars marks not only the beginning of Rome's history as a (ultimately, the) Mediterranean superpower, but also the beginning of the historiographical tradition about the city.[21] The Punic Wars, especially the Second Punic War, accordingly dominate in the first works written in both Greek and Latin, by Fabius Pictor and Cato the Elder, respectively, as well as in later works by various annalistic (year-by-year) writers, Coelius Antipater (who composed a monograph on the Second Punic War), the Greek historians Diodorus Siculus and Dionysius of Halicarnassus, and Velleius Paterculus.[22] Silius demonstrates his direct knowledge of this tradition at various points in the *Punica*, but he engages most often and most meaningfully with the narrative of the conflict in Polybius (*c.* 200–*c.* 118 BC). In his forty-book universal history, of which only books 1–5 are extant in their entirety, Polybius analyzes how Rome rose to prominence so swiftly and so decisively during the era of the Punic Wars (1.1, esp. 1.1.5–6); Silius likewise identifies this era as the turning point in the rise of the *imperium Romanum*.[23] Naturally, the Punic War tradition continues (long) after Silius in the works of the Greek historians Appian and Cassius Dio (epitomized by Xiphilinus and Zonaras), the Christian historians Augustine and Orosius, and, most importantly of all, the Livian tradition represented by Florus, Eutropius, Festus, and the *Periochae*. While it is quite difficult to precisely gauge the impact which the *Punica* had on the later tradition, especially given how much Silius draws on the earlier tradition (likely including material since lost to us), there is ample evidence for the sustained influence of the epic on the Livian epitome attributed to Florus (likely the L. Annaeus Florus who flourished during the reigns of Trajan and Hadrian). Above and beyond the Punic War tradition, scholars have identified various passages in the *Punica* in which Silius engages with other major authors and texts in both the Greek and the Latin historiographical traditions, from Herodotus and Thucydides to Caesar and Sallust.[24] In particular, Silius' Hannibal owes an obvious debt to Caesar's Vercingetorix, as well as to Sallust's Catiline and Jugurtha, all worthy adversaries of Rome and, in literary terms, truly three-dimensional characters. Scholars have also detected evidence of Silius' engagement with his contemporary Josephus, especially his *Bellum Judaicum*, as well as of his influence on his near contemporary Tacitus.[25] All in all, Silius qua senatorial historian not only evinces a profound knowledge of the existing tradition about the Second Punic War, but also strives to remake that tradition in the image of Flavian Rome.

Apart from historiography, Silius likewise draws on a wide range of authors and texts in other prose traditions, including geography, biography, and antiquarian literature, as well as rhetoric, philosophy, and oratory, even the ancient novel. Among the geographers, Strabo and Pomponius Mela appear to have been used by Silius as sources for his extensive material on the peoples and places of the Mediterranean and beyond, while Silius himself appears to have been used as a source by Pausanias and Vibius Sequester.[26] Likewise, various passages in the *Punica* resonate with various passages in biographies (not just of the major players in the Punic Wars) by Cornelius Nepos, Plutarch, and Suetonius, and especially the potted biographies in the *De viris illustribus*.[27] Silius displays an especially close affinity with the antiquarian tradition, drawing extensively on the works of Varro, Valerius Maximus, and Pliny the Elder, on the one hand, and perhaps reappearing in those of Aulus Gellius, Ampelius, and Solinus, on the other.[28] Indeed, this antiquarian literature, together with the Livian tradition, deserves particular attention because it affords us the opportunity to assess the scope, nature, and purpose of the version and the vision of the Second Punic War which a typical Roman senator like Silius would consider an accurate and authentic representation of Roman historical and cultural thinking, put simply, what an elite Roman would believe happened during the war, and what he would believe its impact was on the rise and fall of the *imperium Romanum*. Apart from Livy, Cicero (106–43 BC) exerts the most profound and most pervasive influence on Silius' engagement with the Roman historiographical tradition and, by extension, the prose tradition in general, especially in rhetoric, philosophy, and oratory, but also his engagement with the epic tradition.[29] Silius even goes so far as to include an encomium of Cicero in the midst of his catalog of Roman troops before the battle of Cannae (8.404–11; for similar encomia, see Vell. 2.66; Val. Max. 5.3.4; Sen. *Suas.* 6, esp. 26 [Cornelius Severus], 27 [Sextilius Ena]; Plin. *Nat.* 7.116–17).[30] Although he did not compose a sustained narrative of the Second Punic War, Cicero does make regular reference to key people, places, and events from the conflict across his oeuvre. Silius owes perhaps his greatest debt to the *Somnium Scipionis*, from book 6 of the fragmentarily preserved *De re publica*. Cicero recounts a (fictional) dream in which Scipio Africanus visits his adoptive grandson, Scipio Aemilianus, shortly before the latter captures Carthage at the end of the Third Punic War in 146 BC and provides him with a vision of Rome's (relatively insignificant) place in the world and in the universe. Elements of this dream resonate with various dreams in the *Punica* and, in particular, with Scipio's visit to the Underworld in book 13. During that visit, Scipio briefly converses with the ghost of Alexander the Great (13.762–77). In many ways, the evolving historical and cultural memory about the Macedonian world conqueror offers the best analogy for understanding Silius' approach to Hannibal, Scipio, and the Second Punic War in the *Punica*, especially the conflation of history and myth in the *Alexander Romance* tradition (e.g., Curtius Rufus and Julius Valerius).[31]

4. The *Punica* and the Epic Tradition

In transforming history into myth, Silius demonstrates an equally profound direct knowledge of the Roman epic tradition, indeed, the entire ancient epic tradition in both Greek and Latin, and mediates his engagement with that tradition through his reading of Rome's national epic, Vergil's *Aeneid*. Vergil (70–19 BC) was born in Andes, near Mantua, in Cisalpine Gaul, making him a compatriot of Livy, and, like Livy, subsequently emigrated to Rome. He is best known for his twelve-book epic on the origins of the city, from the fall of Troy and the exile of Aeneas to the rise of Rome and the reign of Augustus. The poem, extant in its entirety although lacking the *ultima manus*, is traditionally divided into groups of four or six books. In the tripartite division, books 1–4 recount Aeneas' travels from the fall of Troy to the death of Dido; books 5–8 concern

Aeneas' role in the future of Rome; and books 9–12 recount the war in Italy from the attack on the Trojan camp to the death of Turnus. In the bipartite division, books 1–6 cover Aeneas' journey from Troy to Italy, while books 7–12 cover the war in Italy: many scholars accordingly view the first half of the epic as Vergil's "*Odyssey*" and the second half as his "*Iliad*." Even during Vergil's lifetime, the *Aeneid* was already on its way to establishing itself as Rome's (new) national epic, supplanting Ennius' *Annales* (for which, see below), and so it remains to this day. In the poem, Vergil consistently casts Carthage as Rome's "Other."[32] As a part of his meditation on the fraught relationship between Dido and Aeneas, and, therefore, by extension, on that between Carthage and Rome, Vergil includes many references and allusions to the people, places, and events of the Punic Wars and, in particular, the Second Punic War, from Hannibal (*A.* 4.622–9, 10.11–15) to P. and Cn. Cornelii Scipiones (6.841–4), Fabius (6.845–6), and Marcellus (6.855–9), all in the Parade of Heroes during Aeneas' visit to the Underworld. Silius undoubtedly knew every verse of the *Aeneid* by heart, and scholars have again long studied the relationship between the two texts. Silius cues his debt to Vergil with an allusion to the poet himself in the midst of his catalog of Roman troops before the battle of Cannae (8.591–4), as well as by including Roman warriors named Maro (Vergil's *cognomen*) and Vergilius who slay their Carthaginian opponents in single combat during the battles of Baecula (15.447–9) and Zama (17.441–2), respectively. Above all else, however, Silius gestures toward Vergil in his choice of name for Marus (~ Maro), the aged veteran from the First Punic War who had served with Regulus and who recounts his great deeds to his son Serranus in book 6. In his engagement with the *Aeneid*, Silius incorporates elements of Vergilian plot, character, and theme in order to effect the transformation of prose historiography into epic poetry, especially the theme of single combat, culminating in that between Aeneas and Turnus, as the canonical expression of heroic (and, therefore, specifically Roman) masculinity.

Through Vergil, Silius engages with the rest of the epic tradition, and scholars have again long studied Silius' relationship to this tradition through a Vergilian lens.[33] First and foremost, of course, Silius directly engages with various passages from both the *Iliad* and the *Odyssey*, and, as elsewhere, he gestures towards this intertextual relationship by including Homer as a character in the *Punica*, during Scipio's visit to the Underworld (13.778–805).[34] Like the historiographical tradition, the Latin epic tradition emerges during the era of the Punic Wars against this Greek background, beginning with the (fragmentarily preserved) epics in the native Saturnian meter by Livius Andronicus (*Odusia*, a translation of the *Odyssey*) and Naevius (*Bellum Punicum*, from Aeneas to the First Punic

War). Together, these two epics not only distinguish the mythological and historical strands of the tradition, but also illustrate their inherent interconnectedness, forging a thematic link between the Trojan War and the Punic Wars.[35] Ennius' *Annales*, likewise only fragmentarily preserved, marks the next major phase in this interweaving of history and myth by recounting events from the fall of Troy through the aftermath of the Second Punic War across fifteen books (later expanded to eighteen); composed not in Saturnians but in the dactylic hexameter of the Homeric poems, the *Annales* quickly established itself as Rome's national epic. Silius yet again signals his debt by including Ennius as a character in the *Punica* (12.387–414): if we possessed more of the poem today, we would undoubtedly recognize the full extent of that debt.[36] Among the many epics written during the era of the transition from Republic to Empire, including many (lost) historical epics, Silius demonstrates his direct knowledge of Lucretius' *De rerum natura* and Catullus 64, both important influences on Vergil.[37] Apart from Vergil, Ovid (43 BC–AD 17/18) exerts the most profound and most pervasive influence on Silius' engagement with the epic tradition and, by extension, the poetic tradition in general, through his reception of Vergil in the *Metamorphoses*, a fifteen-book epic of transformations (mythological, historical, and cultural).[38] Among his (relative) contemporaries, Silius evinces a careful study of Lucan's *Bellum civile* (on the civil war between Caesar and Pompey),[39] as well as the other major Flavian epics, Valerius Flaccus' *Argonautica* (on Jason and the Golden Fleece) and Statius' *Thebaid* (on the civil war between Eteocles and Polynices), and perhaps even Domitian's (lost) *Bellum Capitolinum* (on the fall of the Capitol in AD 69).[40] Whereas it is difficult to gauge Silius' specific impact on the subsequent historiographical tradition, his impact on the epic tradition is all-pervasive, from the panegyrical epics of Claudian and Sidonius Apollinaris to the works of the North African poets Dracontius and Corippus (in the *Iohannis*),[41] from Prudentius' *Psychomachia* to Juvencus, Sedulius, and Arator, the Latin epic poets of the New Testament.[42] Scholars have even identified traces of the *Punica* in two medieval Latin epics, the *Waltharius* and the *Alexandreis*,[43] as well as in various Renaissance Latin epics written both before and after the rediscovery of the poem.

Apart from epic, Silius also draws on a wide range of authors and texts in other poetic traditions, including satire, lyric, and elegiac, but especially drama. Among the satirists, Lucilius, Horace, and Persius all leave their mark on Silius, and Silius, in turn, leaves his mark on Juvenal, e.g., in the famous apostrophe of Hannibal in 10.147–67 (cf. 6.170–1, 287–91, 7.158–66, 12.102–10).[44] Likewise, various passages in the *Punica* reflect Silius' engagement with the lyric poetry of

Catullus and Horace, e.g., the civil war *Epodes* 7 and 16, as well as *Odes* 3.5, the Regulus ode, and 4.4, with its verses on the battle of the Metaurus River. Among the elegiac poets, Silius draws on the work of Tibullus, Propertius, and, once again, Ovid, especially his *Fasti*, an (incomplete) poem in six books on the Roman calendar.[45] Above all else, Silius displays an especially close affinity with various types of Roman drama, from Plautine comedy to Senecan tragedy. Plautine comedy, with its stereotyped portrayal of Carthaginian identity (esp. in the *Poenulus*), offers an idea of contemporary Roman views about themselves vis-à-vis their foreign nemesis.[46] Senecan tragedy, with its sustained focus on the theme of multigenerational familial revenge, offers a roadmap for navigating the many twists and turns of the fraught ethical terrain of the *Punica*, including the relationships between Hannibal and his father, Hamilcar, on the one hand, and between Scipio and his father and uncle, P. and Cn. Cornelii Scipiones, on the other.[47] The *fabula praetexta* (Roman historical drama) tradition, which begins with (essentially lost) plays by Naevius and Ennius and continues into the Early Empire with the (extant) *Octavia*, may have also influenced Silius' approach to his material in the *Punica*, e.g., Ennius' *Scipio* (if it is a *fabula praetexta*, that is), but we simply do not have enough available evidence to assess the extent of that (possible) influence.[48] Regardless, it is clear that Silius engages not only with a great variety of authors and texts across an impressive array of literary traditions on the Second Punic War in both prose and poetry, but also with an equally broad range of cultural traditions on the conflict. As a result, the *Punica* functions as a pivotal contribution to the evolving collective memory of the war and, in particular, the battle of Cannae as *the* turning point in Roman history.

5. Conclusion: The Language and Style of the *Punica*

Scholarship on the language and style of the *Punica* has long concentrated on issues central to textual criticism, from the establishment of authoritative readings to the elucidation of obscure passages: only (relatively) recently has scholarship expanded its focus to embrace issues central to literary, historical, and other forms of criticism, as well.[49] Rightly so, textual criticism has long provided the foundation for study of the epic, beginning with the scholarship which culminated in the Teubner edited by Bauer at the end of the nineteenth century, followed by that which culminated in the Teubner edited by Delz at the end of the twentieth century, and continuing with the scholarship (today, using the tools of the Digital Humanities) which will undoubtedly lead to the establishment of an even more authoritative critical edition of the text in the current century. At the same time, as scholars have ventured into other forms of criticism, especially literary and historical, they have made several advances in the study of other aspects of the epic's language and style, from Silius' handling of the dactylic hexameter to the relationship between speech and narrative in the poem to various issues of morphology and syntax. Few scholars have offered a general assessment of the language and style of the *Punica*, but those who have done so have tended to conclude that Silius offers a unique mixture of prosaic and poetic features which renders some passages in the epic more (or less) successful than others.[50] Learned epithets serve as an example of a centrally important and yet surprisingly understudied feature not only of the *Punica* but also of Latin epic as a whole: such learned epithets pervade the historical epics of Vergil, Lucan, and Silius, and operate both within each poem and across the three poems as an integral part of each poet's exploration of Roman (and, therefore, non-Roman) identity. Some scholars have criticized Silius, in particular, for his seemingly excessive use of learned epithets,[51] while others have noted that each term captures a specific nuance with a specific set of historical, cultural, and literary resonances which often complicates the meaning of the epithet in context.[52]

Over the course of the epic, Silius uses dozens of different learned epithets which convey the meaning of "Trojan"/"Roman" or "Tyrian"/"Carthaginian" (the two most important of the many racial-ethnic groups mentioned in the poem). A host of terms evokes either people(s) or place(s) associated with Rome's Trojan and Italian origins, including three (the rare adjectives *Laomedonteus* and *Laomedontius*, as well as the equally rare patronymic *Laomedontiades*) which refer to Laomedon: son of Ilus and Eurydice, and grandson of Tros, the eponymous founder of Troy, Laomedon was a legendary king most famous for his treachery. According to the standard version of the myth,[53] Apollo and Poseidon came to Troy disguised as mortals and offered to build walls around the city for an agreed sum. After they completed their work, Laomedon reneged on his promise and refused to pay. In response, Apollo sent down a plague upon Troy, while Poseidon sent a sea monster to attack the city. Per the instructions of an oracle, Laomedon chained his own daughter, Hesione, to the cliffs overlooking the sea as a sacrificial offering to the sea monster. At this point, Heracles arrived and offered to save Hesione if Laomedon would give to him the horses which Zeus had given to the father of Ganymedes, whether Tros or even Laomedon himself, in compensation for taking the young prince up to Mt. Olympus. However, after Heracles killed the sea monster and saved Hesione, Laomedon reneged on his promise a second time. Heracles left, organized an expedition, and returned to lay siege to Troy: during the capture of the city, he killed Laomedon, gave Hesione over to his comrade Telamon, and handed the kingdom itself over to Laomedon's sole surviving son, Podarces, better known as Priam. It is Vergil who first alludes to this myth through his use of a learned epithet referring to Laomedon, in the passage from the end of *Georgics* 1 (498–514) in which he implores the Romans to put an end to their civil strife: *satis iam pridem sanguine nostro / Laomedonteae luimus periuria Troiae* ("We have already paid enough / with our blood for the false oaths of the Troy of Laomedon," 501–2). Here, Vergil powerfully connects the first fall of Troy with the potential fall of Rome: the poet pointedly identifies the current internecine conflict as a divinely ordained punishment meted out against the Romans as the descendants of the Trojans because of the faithlessness (*periuria*) of Laomedon towards Apollo, Poseidon, and Heracles.

Beyond this initial allusion to Laomedon in the *Georgics*, Vergil alludes to the king and his perfidy by using forms of *Laomedonteus*/*Laomedontius* and *Laomedontiades* six times in the *Aeneid*: 3.247–9 (*Laomedontiadae* [= Trojans], 248); 4.540–2 (*Laomedonteae ... gentis* [= Trojans], 542); 7.104–6 (*Laomedontia pubes* [= Trojans], 105); 8.18–21 (*Laomedontius heros* [= Aeneas], 18), 154–65 (*Laomedontiaden* [= Priam], 158, 162). In 4.540–2, in particular, Dido recalls the curse of the faithless king as she ironically rebukes herself for falling victim to another faithless Trojan in Aeneas: *nescis heu, perdita, necdum / Laomedonteae sentis periuria gentis?* ("Alas, lost soul, do you not know, not yet / do you perceive the false oaths of the clan of Laomedon?" 541–2). In this passage, in a stunning intertextual gesture, Dido's reference to the *Laomedonteae ... periuria gentis* deeply resonates with the initial reference to the *Laomedonteae ... periuria Troiae* in *Georgics* 1.502. It is as if Vergil were distancing himself from the otherwise dangerous attribution of faithlessness to the Trojans (and, thus, the Romans) by displacing the utterance from the narrative voice onto Dido. This displacement, however, strikes a note of irony since it is now a stereotypically "faithless" Carthaginian in Dido who attributes faithlessness to Aeneas and the Trojans (and, thus, the Romans).[54] While Lucan, surprisingly, does not develop the freighted meaning of these learned epithets referring to Laomedon by incorporating them into his narrative of the civil war between Caesar and Pompey, Silius clearly does recognize their interpretive potential for connecting the Second Punic War with the Trojan War by associating the Romans, especially in their capacity as descendants of the Trojans, with faithlessness, thus further destabilizing the purported opposition between Roman *fides* and Carthaginian *perfidia*. Accordingly, Silius likewise alludes to the king and his perfidy by using forms of *Laomedonteus* and *Laomedontiades* six times in the *Punica*: 1.541–7 (*Laomedonteae ... flammae* [= flame of the Vestal Virgins], 543); 7.437–42 (*Laomedonteus .../ pastor* [= Paris], 437–8); 8.171–2 (*Laomedonteae ... telluris* [= Troy], 172); 10.626–9 (*Laomedontiadum ... urbi* [= Rome], 629); 13.54–5 (*Laomedonteae ... Minervae* [= Trojan Minerva], 55); 17.1–4 (*Laomedonteae ... urbis* [= Rome], 4). In 10.626–9, in particular, Silius severely undercuts the positive message that Varro "did not lose hope" (*non desperaverit*, 629) when he fled ignominiously from Cannae by describing Rome as "the city of the descendants of Laomedon" (which suggests that the city may not ultimately avert disaster). As this single example powerfully illustrates, learned epithets play a pivotal role in the development of plot, character, and theme across Latin historical epic and, more particularly, introduce a wide variety of historical, cultural, and literary resonances, especially between the *Aeneid* and the *Punica*.

3

A Reading of *Punica* 1–10: From Saguntum to Cannae

1. Introduction: The Structure of the *Punica*

The extant manuscripts of the *Punica* transmit an epic which spans seventeen books, but which may have been originally composed or, at the very least, planned in eighteen. We simply do not know whether or not Silius completed the poem before his death, as well as whether or not any verses were subsequently lost in transmission. Accordingly, all analyses of the macrostructure of the *Punica* (the structure of the epic across all of its seventeen or eighteen books) as well as all analyses of its microstructure (the structure of the epic within each of its seventeen or eighteen books) remain, at least to some degree, provisional. Further complicating matters, the extant verses appear to include (at least?) two major lacunae. The first possible lacuna stands between those verses now numbered 8.143 and 8.224, a gap in the text which interrupts the narrative of Hannibal's dream before the battle of Cannae (8.25–241). Marso first identified the lacuna in the commentary to his 1483 edition of the poem, but it was not until 1508 that Giacomo Costanzi (1473–*c.* 1517) first published what he claimed were the recovered verses, those now numbered 144–223/224a.[1] Thereafter, Gian Francesco Torresano (d'Asola) (*c.* 1480–1546) included the supplement, in a slightly different version, in his 1523 Aldine edition of the poem, and so, since then, these contested verses have been known to scholars as the *additamentum Aldinum*.[2] The second possible lacuna stands either after the verse now numbered 17.290 or else after that now numbered 17.291, a gap in the text which interrupts the narrative of Hannibal's return to Africa and the seemingly abrupt transition to the battle of Zama.[3] In this instance, scholars have long debated whether or not there is a lacuna at this point in the epic and, if so, where to mark it, as well as how long it might be.[4] More recently, scholars have devoted considerable attention to the structural and thematic significance of how ancient works, especially large-scale productions like historiography and epic, begin, end, and mark (or not) their middle(s).[5] In the case of the *Punica*, the debate about the poem's middle, its περιπέτεια ("turning point"), generally centers on two possible candidates: Hannibal's decision not to march immediately on Rome after his victory at Cannae (book 10, 216 BC), or else his belated, and ultimately unsuccessful, march on the city five years later (book 12, 211 BC).[6] Scholars have proposed a number of (often quite elaborate) structural models in support of their respective arguments regarding the middle of the epic, as well as the relationship between that middle and both the beginning and the end of the poem.[7]

Bickel first mooted the idea that Silius may have originally composed or, at least, planned an epic in eighteen, rather than seventeen, books. He associated this proposal with the additional suggestion that Silius may have conceived of the *Punica* as consisting of three hexads or even six triads in imitation of the similar six-book structure of Ennius' *Annales* and Vergil's *Aeneid*.[8] A generation later, Martin developed this idea by identifying the Regulus episode in book 6, "die Peripetie" before the walls of Rome in book 12, and Scipio's triumph in book 17 (originally 18) as the pivot points in this hexadic structure: in particular, his recognition of Hannibal's march on Rome as "den Höhepunkt des ganzen Krieges" essentially initiated the debate about what event marks the "middle" of the poem.[9] A decade after that, Wallace offered a complementary analysis of the structure of the epic as consisting of two enneads, with the battle of Cannae marking the turning point across books 9 and 10.[10] Burck subsequently bolstered the argument in favor of the eighteen-book hypothesis, opting for Martin's hexads over Wallace's enneads, by examining the structural relationship between the *Punica* and the third decade of Livy's *Ab urbe condita*. Whereas Livy evenly divides his decade into two pentads, with one each focusing on Hannibal (21–5) and Scipio (26–30) as the central figure, Silius unevenly divides his material into three hexads, with two for Hannibal (1–6 and 7–12), but only one for Scipio (13–17, originally 18). As a result, although both Livy and Silius center their accounts of the war on Hannibal's failed march on Rome in 211 BC (the chronological midpoint in the war), only the historiographer correspondingly places that event at the midpoint in his narrative, while the poet places it at the two-thirds point in his.[11] In the same year, Kißel independently elaborated a much more complex hexadic model according to which he assigned the three phases of the epic to Hannibal (1–6), Fabius (7–12), and Scipio (13–17, originally 18): in particular, his recognition of Fabius as the central figure of the middle hexad represented a major innovation.[12] Most recently, Delarue sought to consolidate these various theories about the structure of an eighteen-book *Punica* into one comprehensive proposal by ascribing the enneads to "le plan divin" with nine books each for Juno (1–9) and Jupiter (10–17, originally 18) and the hexads to "le plan humain" with six books each once again for Hannibal (1–6), Fabius (7–12), and Scipio (13–17, originally 18).[13]

Not all scholars have embraced the eighteen-book hypothesis, of course, arguing instead for the integrity of the epic in its extant form. Niemann, who was the first to argue in favor of a seventeen-book *Punica*, discerned only two significant breaks in the narrative: the first between books 2 and 3, i.e., between the fall of Saguntum and Hannibal's march from Spain to Italy, and the second between books 10 and 11, i.e., between the battle of Cannae and Hannibal's triumph at Capua. As a result, Niemann divided the poem into three unequal phases spanning books 1–2 (Saguntum), 3–10 (the four battles of the Ticinus River, the Trebia River, Lake Trasimene, and Cannae), and 11–17 (Rome's resurgence). Furthermore, Niemann rejected the arguments in favor of identifying Hannibal's march on Rome as the "middle" of the epic in order to emphasize both the structural and the thematic centrality of Cannae.[14] A decade later, Ahl, Davis, and Pomeroy advanced a similar "battle-centered structure" with Cannae (books 8–10) as the focal point in a narrative parabola, much like Lucan's placement of the battle of Pharsalus in the *Bellum civile*.[15] In the same year, Küppers provided further support for Niemann's division of the poem through a book-by-book review of its contents.[16] Shortly thereafter, much like Delarue, Braun sought to harmonize these competing structural models by mapping Wallace's eighteen-book enneads onto Ahl, Davis, and Pomeroy's seventeen-book "battle-centered structure": in particular, he sought to identify Varro's flight from battle at the end of book 9 as the "Wendepunkt" in the epic.[17] Most recently, Fröhlich has propounded an elaborate seventeen-book structural model according to which the epic is arranged into three pentads (1–5, 7–11, and 13–17) interrupted by books 6 and 12: in an intriguing blend of epic and historiographical structures, Fröhlich likens these proposed pentads to the pentads in Livy's *Ab urbe condita*.[18] Nevertheless, Fröhlich's analysis of the poem actually bears a strong resemblance to Martin's scheme: where Martin had grouped the books by hexads according to the formula $(4 + 1 + 1) + (1 + 4 + 1) + (1 + 1 + 4)$, Fröhlich groups them by pentads according to the similar formula $5 + 1 + 5 + 1 + 5$. Ultimately, both models, despite their differences, underscore the pivotal nature of books 6 and 12, i.e., Hannibal's march(es) on Rome.

As scholars have rightly noted, no one analytical scheme can sufficiently account for all aspects of a long and complex poem like the *Punica*.[19] Accordingly,

I would like to propose two further structural models, neither of which is dependent on whether the epic originally consisted of seventeen or eighteen books: the first model combines various aspects of the division of the poem into hexads, while the second suggests a markedly simpler division into pentads. The first (hexadic) model divides the epic into groups of "siege books" and "battle books" as follows:

siege	books 1–2	Saguntum	books 13–14	Capua > Syracuse
battle	books 3–6	Ticinus River	book 15	New Carthage
		Trebia River		Baecula
		Lake Trasimene		Metaurus River
battle	books 7–10	Cannae	book 16	Ilipa
siege	books 11–12	Capua > Carthage	book(s) 17[–18]	Carthage (Zama)
		Nola > Rome		Rome

In this analysis, Hannibal once again dominates books 1–12, while Scipio dominates books 13–17[–18], but we also find a great many other resonances both within and between these two unequal halves of the epic. Each half forms the chiasmus siege–battle–battle–siege: across books 1–12, the fall of Saguntum (1–2) balances the triumphs in Capua and Carthage (11) followed by the unsuccessful sieges of Nola and Rome (12), while the battles of the Ticinus River, the Trebia River, and Lake Trasimene (3–6) balance the battle of Cannae (7–10); across books 13–17[–18], the falls of Capua and Syracuse (13–14) balance the battle of Zama (transformed by Silius into a narrative of the fall of Carthage: see 17.618-24) and the triumph back in Rome (17[–18]), while the fall of New Carthage (likewise transformed into a battle narrative) and the battles of Baecula and the Metaurus River (15) balance the battle of Ilipa (16). Between the two halves of the poem, the fall of Saguntum (1–2) balances those of Capua and Syracuse (13–14); the three engagements of books 3–6 balance those of book 15; the battle of Cannae balances that of Ilipa (16); and, most importantly of all, the triumphs in Capua and Carthage, followed by the unsuccessful sieges of Nola and Rome (11–12) balance (foreshadow) the fall of Carthage after the battle of Zama and the triumph back in Rome (17[–18]). A significant number of intratextual cues appear to support this particular structural analysis of the epic, especially the grouping together of books 3–6 and 7–10 (see, e.g., 1.45-54) and the overall demarcation between books 1–12 and 13–17[–18] (see, e.g., 1.125-39). In thematic terms, Silius casts the poem as a struggle between narrative delay and narrative speed, between the aging Hannibal, symbol of a decrepit Carthaginian empire on the decline, and the youthful Scipio, symbol of a precocious Roman empire on the rise.

The second (pentadic) model divides the epic into similar groups of books as follows:

books 1–5	books 6–10	books 11–15	books 16–17[–18]
	after Lake Trasimene	after Cannae	after Metaurus River
Saguntum		Capua > Carthage	
		Nola > Rome	
		Capua > Syracuse	
Ticinus River		New Carthage	
Trebia River		Baecula	
Lake Trasimene	Cannae	Metaurus River	Ilipa
			Carthage (Zama)
			Rome

In this analysis, which slightly reconfigures the correspondences outlined for the hexadic model proposed above, each of the three pentads culminates in a major engagement (Lake Trasimene, Cannae, and the Metaurus River) during which a, or the, commanding general of the losing side falls in combat (Flaminius, Paullus, and Hasdrubal) and after which Silius uses the aftermath of the battle to frame the next section of the poem. The dyad or triad which spans books 16–17[–18] culminates not in the battle of Ilipa but in the battle of Zama, prompting the reader to reflect on what will happen after Zama, after the fall of Carthage and the triumph back in Rome. Here, too, a significant number of intratextual cues appears to support this particular structural analysis, especially the themes of decapitation and burial (by Hannibal) which link Flaminius (5.132–9 ~ 644–78), Paullus (10.260–308, 503–77 ~ 12.212–67), and Hasdrubal (15.778–823), as well as Ti. Sempronius Gracchus (12.463–78) and Marcellus (15.334–98).[20] This pentadic model associates the *Punica* not only with Livy's *Ab urbe condita* but also with Ennius' *Annales*. In its original form, the epic spanned fifteen books, to which the poet later added three more, and so the three pentads and one triad of the *Annales* very well could have served as a template for the *Punica*, and this perhaps furnishes stronger evidence in support of an eighteen-book poem.[21] Because of its inherent clarity and simplicity, I adopt this pentadic structural model as the main organizing principle for the analysis of the epic elaborated across Chapters 3 and 4, but I use the hexadic structural model (and other earlier models, too) in the course of that sustained reading.

2. *Punica* 1.1–20: The Proem

    ordior arma, quibus caelo se gloria tollit
    Aeneadum patiturque ferox Oenotria iura
    Carthago. da, Musa, decus memorare laborum
    antiquae Hesperiae, quantosque ad bella crearit
5   et quot Roma viros, sacri cum perfida pacti
    gens Cadmea super regno certamina movit
    quaesitumque diu, qua tandem poneret arce
    terrarum Fortuna caput. ter Marte sinistro
    iuratumque Iovi foedus conventaque patrum
10 Sidonii fregere duces, atque impius ensis
    ter placitam suasit temerando rumpere pacem.
    sed medio finem bello excidiumque vicissim
    molitae gentes, propiusque fuere periclo,
    quis superare datum: reseravit Dardanus arces
15 ductor Agenoreas, obsessa Palatia vallo
    Poenorum, ac muris defendit Roma salutem.
    tantarum causas irarum odiumque perenni
    servatum studio et mandata nepotibus arma
    fas aperire mihi superasque recludere mentes.
20 iamque adeo magni repetam primordia motus.

    I begin my "arms," by which the glory of the Aeneadae raises itself
    to heaven and fierce Carthage endures Oenotrian [Italian] laws.
    Grant me, Muse, the power to remember the honor of the labors
    of ancient Hesperia [Italy], and how great and how many the men
5   whom Rome produced for the wars, when the Cadmean [Phoenician] race,
    faithless to the sacred pact, began the struggles for hegemony,
    and when for a long time it was uncertain on which citadel Fortune
    would finally place the capital of the world. Three times in ill-omened war
    the Sidonian [Phoenician] generals violated both a treaty sworn to Jupiter
10 and the agreements of the Senate, and the impious sword
    three times persuaded them to recklessly break an approved peace.
    But in the middle war the two nations strove in turn for the end
    and for the destruction of each other, and they were closer to danger,
    those to whom victory was granted: the Dardanian [Trojan] general opened up
15 the Agenorean [Tyrian] citadel, the Palatine was besieged by a rampart
    of Carthaginians, and Rome defended her safety with her walls.

> The causes of such great anger and the hatred preserved
> by unceasing zeal and the arms entrusted to descendants,
> these things it is right for me to reveal and to disclose the minds of the gods.
> 20 And now in this way I will trace the origins of this great conflict.

In *Punica* 1.1–20, as throughout the poem, Silius engages in a complex intertextual (as well as intergeneric) dialogue with the existing historiographical and epic traditions about the Second Punic War in order to define the structure and themes of his particular narrative of the conflict.[22] The passage can be divided into three major sections: first, the poet identifies the three Punic Wars as his general subject (1.1–11); then, he signals his specific interest in the Second Punic War (1.12–16); and, finally, he explains that he will begin his narrative with an investigation into the (ancient) causes of the conflict (1.17–20). Silius makes clear from the start his focus on the theme of "walls" (*muris*, 16) and "citadels" (*arces*, 14), as well as his commitment to presenting the Second Punic War as a moment of crisis and transition between the First and Third Wars (note especially *ter*, 8, 11 ~ *sed medio finem bello*, 12). As throughout the poem, Silius writes with one eye on Livy and the other on Vergil in order to weave together historiography and epic for his own original contribution to the rich literary tradition on the Second Punic War.

We begin with Livy's preface to books 21–30, the historiographical core of the *Punica*:

> 1. in parte operis mei licet mihi praefari, quod in principio summae totius professi plerique sunt rerum scriptores, bellum maxime omnium memorabile quae unquam gesta sint me scripturum, quod Hannibale duce Carthaginienses cum populo Romano gessere. 2. nam neque validiores opibus ullae inter se civitates gentesque contulerunt arma neque his ipsis tantum unquam virium aut roboris fuit; et haud ignotas belli artes inter sese sed expertas primo Punico conferebant bello, et adeo varia fortuna belli ancepsque Mars fuit ut propius periculum fuerint qui vicerunt. 3. odiis etiam prope maioribus certarunt quam viribus, Romanis indignantibus quod victoribus victi ultro inferrent arma, Poenis quod superbe avareque crederent imperitatum victis esse.

> 1. In this part of my work, it is fitting for me to say from the outset, what many writers have claimed at the beginning of every great undertaking, namely, that I am going to be writing about the most memorable war of all of the wars which have ever been fought, the war which the Carthaginians, with Hannibal as their leader, waged against the Roman people. 2. For no states or nations more blessed with resources ever bore arms against each other, nor did any have such great

strength and power as these; and they brought arts of war not unknown to each other, but instead tried and tested during the First Punic War, and so variable was the fortune of the war and so uncertain the outcome that those who won were closer to destruction. 3. Also, they strove against each other with hatreds almost greater than their strength, with the Romans indignant about the fact that the Carthaginians attacked them of their own accord, the conquered against the conquerors, and with the Carthaginians indignant about the fact that they believed that, as the conquered, they were ruled by the Romans with arrogance and greed.

Liv. 21.1.1–3

Livy opens the third decade of his *Ab urbe condita* with a candid acknowledgment of his use of the familiar, but, in this case, easily defensible, claim that he is embarking upon a narrative of "the most memorable war of all of the wars which have ever been fought" (*bellum maxime omnium memorabile quae unquam gesta sint*, 21.1.1). In describing the Second Punic War as such, Livy not only affirms the unique historical and cultural importance of the conflict, but also highlights its enduring impact on Roman collective memory. Ever the astute reader of Livy, Silius echoes this assessment of the war's significance when he calls upon the Muse to grant him the power "to remember" (*memorare*, *Pun.* 1.3) his own version of events in the *Punica*. More generally, Silius carefully structures his proem in response to Livy's preface, which can similarly be divided into three major sections: both texts begin by narrowing down their focus to the Second Punic War (*Pun.* 1.1–11 ~ Liv. 21.1.1); then, both explain why the Second Punic War was the greatest war ever fought (*Pun.* 1.12–16 ~ Liv. 21.1.2, esp. *sed*, *Pun.* 1.12 ~ *nam*, Liv. 21.1.2); and, finally, both end by tracing the origins of the current conflict back to the implacable hatred between the two cities (*Pun.* 1.17–20 ~ Liv. 21.1.3, esp. *odium*, *Pun.* 1.17 ~ *odiis*, Liv. 21.1.3). Both Livy and Silius place the blame for the outbreak of hostilities squarely on the Carthaginians: *bellum … quod Hannibale duce Carthaginienses cum populo Romano gessere* (Liv. 21.1.1) ~ *sacri cum perfida pacti / gens Cadmea super regno certamina movit* (*Pun.* 1.5–6). Both likewise stress the uncertainty of the outcome right up until the end of the war: *adeo varia fortuna belli ancepsque Mars fuit ut propius periculum fuerint qui vicerunt* (Liv. 21.1.2) ~ *quaesitumque diu, qua tandem poneret arce / terrarum Fortuna caput* and *propiusque fuere periclo, / quis superare datum* (*Pun.* 1.7–8, 13–14). Interestingly, however, whereas Livy explicitly identifies Hannibal as the leader of the Carthaginians (note especially the word order in *Hannibale duce Carthaginienses*, 21.1.1) and specifically locates the origins of the Second Punic War in the outcome of the First War (note especially *victoribus victi* and *victis*,

21.1.3), Silius transforms his narrative into a story of much wider significance by broadening his engagement with the existing tradition beyond the bounds of historiography to include epic.

We continue with Vergil's proem to the *Aeneid*, the epic core of the *Punica*:

> arma virumque cano, Troiae qui primus ab oris
> Italiam fato profugus Laviniaque venit
> litora, multum ille et terris iactatus et alto
> vi superum, saevae memorem Iunonis ob iram,
> 5 multa quoque et bello passus, dum conderet urbem
> inferretque deos Latio; genus unde Latinum
> Albanique patres atque altae moenia Romae.
> Musa, mihi causas memora, quo numine laeso
> quidve dolens regina deum tot volvere casus
> 10 insignem pietate virum, tot adire labores
> impulerit. tantaene animis caelestibus irae?

> I sing of arms and the man, who first from the shores of Troy
> exiled by fate came to Italy and the shores
> of Lavinium, that man having been much tossed about on land and by sea
> by the force of the gods, on account of the mindful anger of savage Juno,
> 5 that man also having suffered much in war, until he could found his city
> and bring his gods into Latium: whence the Latin race
> and the Alban fathers and the walls of lofty Rome.
> Muse, remind me about the reasons for this, because of what wounded divinity
> or grieving about what the queen of the gods compelled a man,
> 10 distinguished for his piety, to meet with so many misfortunes, to encounter
> so many labors. Do the minds of the gods have such great angers?
>   Verg. *Aen.* 1.1–11

Vergil famously begins his epic with a simple but yet powerful declaration of his theme (*arma virumque cano*, 1.1), followed by the itinerary for the poetic journey from the fall of Troy to the rise of Rome. By focusing on both war in general and one man, one hero, in particular, Vergil harkens back to the *Iliad* and the *Odyssey* as his prime exemplars. Silius likewise signals his debt to Vergil in his incipit (*ordior arma*, *Pun.* 1.1, which one might almost punctuate *ordior "arma"* and translate accordingly as "I begin my *Aeneid*").[23] More generally, Silius structures his proem in response to Vergil as much as in response to Livy: *Punica* 1.1–16, like *Aeneid* 1.1–7, announce the epic's theme, ending with a reference to the walls of Rome (*ac muris defendit Roma salutem*, *Pun.* 1.16 ~ *atque altae moenia Romae*,

Aen. 1.7); thereafter, *Punica* 1.17–20, like *Aeneid* 1.8–11, turn to an investigation into the (ancient) causes behind the war (*tantarum causas irarum, Pun.* 1.17 ~ *causas* and *tantaene ... irae, Aen.* 1.8, 11). Importantly, however, whereas Vergil celebrates the *labores* (*Aen.* 1.10) of one *vir* (1.1, 10), Aeneas, Silius celebrates the *decus ... laborum* (*Pun.* 1.3) of the many larger-than-life *viri* who fought for Rome in the three wars against Carthage (*quantosque ad bella crearit / et quot Roma viros*, 1.4–5). Both poets invoke the Muse (*Musa, Aen.* 1.8 and *Pun.* 1.3), but, while Vergil asks the Muse to sing on his behalf (*mihi ... memora, Aen.* 1.8), Silius asks the Muse to grant him the power to sing on his own behalf (*da ... memorare, Pun.* 1.3). Above all else, both poets deploy an elaborate system of learned epithets with (often esoteric) mythological, historical, and cultural resonances in order to transform their respective epics into grand cultural narratives which transcend time and space.

While Silius certainly grounds his poem in a thorough mastery of the existing tradition, especially Livy and Vergil, Silius also develops his own intratextual approach which structures his introspective interpretation of the Second Punic War and its pivotal role in the rise and fall of both Carthage and Rome. Here again, one example illustrates the overall idea. As we have seen, Silius opens his epic with a rather bold proclamation: *ordior arma, quibus caelo se gloria tollit / Aeneadum* ("I begin my 'arms,' by which the glory of the Aeneadae raises itself / to heaven," *Pun.* 1.1–2). The collocation (*at*)*tollere ... caelo / in caelum* is used in Latin both literally, to describe the raising of some concrete or abstract object up to heaven, as well as figuratively, to describe the raising of something mortal up to heaven, that is, to make something which is mortal immortal.[24] Across the arc of the *Punica*, Silius uses this collocation figuratively at several key thematic points in order to transform his narrative into a synecdoche for Roman history and Roman culture.[25] In doing so, Silius transforms Scipio into the ultimate synecdochic hero, a hero who simultaneously looks back to Aeneas and Romulus and ahead to the Julio-Claudians and the Flavians. During his conversation with Venus on Mt. Olympus while Hannibal stands atop the Alps in book 3, Jupiter begins his encomium of the Flavians (3.594–629) with a striking allusion to 1.1–2 which artfully incorporates the Flavians into the larger narrative: *exin se Curibus virtus caelestis ad astra / efferet* ("Then, heavenly virtue will raise itself up to the stars / from Cures," 594–5; cf. 601–2, 604–5, 625–9).[26] Later in book 12, during the fighting on Sardinia, Silius writes his epic predecessor Ennius into the story (12.387–419); Apollo intervenes to save the *vates* (409) from any harm and hails him as the first to use his poetic powers to immortalize Rome's heroes: *hic canet illustri primus bella Itala versu / attolletque duces caelo* ("This man will first sing about Italian wars in illustrious verse, / and will first raise generals up to heaven," 410-11). In the very next book, during his visit to the Underworld, Scipio has an interesting conversation with his mother, Pomponia, about the circumstances of his birth (13.615-49), at the beginning of which she exhorts him not to wait for any poet to do the job with his *dicta*, but instead to immortalize himself with his *facta*: *nec in caelum dubites te attollere factis* ("Do not hesitate to raise yourself into heaven by your deeds," 635). Later during the same visit, Scipio receives a vision of the civil wars to come in Rome's future (13.850-67), including a glimpse of the catasterism of Julius Caesar: *ille, deum gens, / stelligerum attollens apicem Troianus Iulo / Caesar avo* ("That man, of the race of the gods, / Trojan Caesar descended from Iulus raising up / his starry crown," 862-4). When read together, this series of passages not only associates the Flavians, Scipio, and Julius Caesar with each other as Aeneadae all in search of immortal(izing) glory through their deeds, but also powerfully links Silius with his predecessor Ennius as poets who claim to possess the ability to confer that immortality with their words. Indeed, in an elegant intertextual gesture which nicely complicates the intratextual system, all of these passages in the *Punica* draw their initial inspiration from a passage in the *Annales* in which Jupiter assures Mars that he will one day see his son Romulus made immortal: *unus erit quem tu tolles in caerula caeli / templa* ("There is one whom you will raise into the blue regions / of heaven," *Ann.* 54-5 Skutsch *ap.* Varr. *LL* 7.6). Ovid has Mars quote this promise back to Jupiter verbatim (minus *templa*, thus transforming *caerula* into a substantive) in both the *Metamorphoses* (14.814) and the *Fasti* (2.487).[27] By inserting himself into this (meta)poetic dialogue, Silius not only aspires to rank himself with the likes of Ennius and Ovid, but also adroitly unifies the narrative by making Scipio's quest for apotheosis the focal point of the Second Punic War and, in essence, the focal point of the larger synecdochic narrative of Roman history and Roman culture as a whole.[28]

In this close reading of *Punica* 1.1-20, we have seen how Silius lays great stress on the function of the Second Punic War as a moment of crisis and transition between the First and Third Wars. More broadly, the poet transforms the three Punic Wars into a powerful homology for the three eras of Roman history, namely, Monarchy, Republic, and Empire: according to this scheme, Regulus (whose name, fittingly enough, means "Little King") and the First Punic War parallel the Monarchy; Scipio Africanus and the Second Punic War parallel the Republic; and Scipio Aemilianus and the Third Punic War parallel the Empire.[29] Likewise, the period between the First and Second Wars recalls the transition from Monarchy to Republic, while the period between the Second and

Third Wars recalls the transition from Republic to Empire. The bond between the two Scipios reinforces the bond between the Second and Third Wars, and invites reflection upon the similar bond between Julius Caesar and Augustus. On a smaller scale, Silius adapts this tripartite framework to the three phases of the Early Empire as he knew it, namely, the Julio-Claudians, the Year of the Four Emperors, and the Flavians: according to this scheme, the poet recasts the narrative of the Second Punic War as a narrative of the civil war of the long year AD 69, a moment of crisis and transition which threatened the imminent collapse of the *imperium Romanum* much as the Hannibalic War had threatened the fall of Rome at the height of the Middle Republic. In a sense, therefore, the *Punica* defies categorization as either Neronian or Flavian epic, since it concerns itself with the theme of dynastic transition through internecine strife. That said, on the smallest scale, Silius also deftly crafts his narrative of the Second Punic War as a narrative of the rise (and fall) of the Flavians, highlighting both the similarities and the differences between Scipio Africanus, on the one hand, and Domitian, on the other. Above all else, I do not want to claim that Silius slavishly adheres to or rigidly applies the three schematic frameworks outlined above, but instead that he uses them as a template for exploring the nature of the complicated transition from Republic to Empire and the concomitant shift from *bellum externum* to *bellum internum*. Ultimately, by incorporating the events of both the First and Third Punic Wars into his narrative of the Second War, Silius transforms the Hannibalic War into a, if not the, story of *Romanitas* from beginning to end. Put simply, Silius asks the reader to join him in reflecting on the vicissitudes of the *res publica* from the Second Punic War to the Flavians, in the face of impending decline, moral and otherwise, leading one day to the fall of Rome itself.

3. *Punica* 1–5: From Saguntum to Lake Trasimene

Following the proem (**1.1–20**), Silius recounts the rise of Hannibal (**21–270**). Silius relates the history of Carthage from Dido to the First Punic War, ending with Juno's choice of Hannibal as the instrument of her vengeance; then, the goddess prophesies the major battles of the looming Second Punic War through Cannae; and, finally, Juno inspires Hannibal with dream visions of the Alps and the Capitol (21–69). Silius pairs this divine motivation for the conflict with an equally important human motivation: at the instigation of his father, Hamilcar, a member of the Barcid clan (which traces its lineage back to the exiles who accompanied Dido from Tyre), Hannibal swears an oath of eternal hatred against Rome in the Temple of Dido in Carthage and confirms the oath with a sacrifice, during which the presiding priestess utters a prophecy about events at and after Cannae until she is interrupted by Juno; shortly after this episode, Hamilcar marches to Spain, where he soon dies in battle (70–143). Following his death, his son-in-law Hasdrubal assumes control of the Iberian peninsula, but he rules like a tyrant until he is killed by the slave of a local noble named Tagus (144–81). At this pivotal moment, Hannibal himself assumes command of the Carthaginian forces in the region, and so Silius emphasizes the gravity of this change by inserting a catalog of the various African and Spanish contingents (182–238). Hannibal quickly secures his command by ingratiating himself with his men and by continuing his preparations for war against Rome (239–70). Hannibal initiates hostilities with his hated enemy by laying siege to Saguntum (**271–583**). Silius recounts the multicultural origins of the city (271–95); Hannibal leads the charge against the fortified walls of the settlement, slaying Caicus, the first named casualty of the siege, as well as the war (296–326); and the Saguntines valiantly shore up their crumbling defenses in the face of the Carthaginian onslaught (327–75). The Saguntine Murrus leads the countercharge against the Carthaginians, while Hannibal rages elsewhere in the battlefield: when the two warriors meet for the first single combat of the epic, Hannibal ultimately kills his overmatched foe (376–534); Jupiter descends from the heavens to hurl his thunderbolt against Hannibal, wounding him in the thigh, which prompts Juno to whisk her hero away from the fighting (535–55); and, after the Saguntines spend the night rebuilding their fortifications and dispatching envoys to Rome (556–75), the Carthaginians turn their attention away from the siege to their injured commander (576–83). Meanwhile, the Saguntine envoys complete their mission (**584–694**): following their difficult journey across rough seas (584–608), Silius offers an ecphrasis on the Roman Curia (609–29), and then Sicoris, the leader of the delegation, delivers an impassioned plea for assistance from the Roman Senate, which, despite the caution urged by Fabius, promptly dispatches a delegation to Hannibal (630–94).

The Roman envoys, led by Fabius and P. Valerius Flaccus (Liv. 21.6.8: Silius mentions a Publicola in 2.8 in order to allude to a more famous branch of the clan), sail on to Carthage after they are turned away from Saguntum by Hannibal, who tauntingly promises to see them in Rome soon (**2.1–55**). The Carthaginians resume the attack on Saguntum (**56–269**). The Amazon Asbyte enters the fray, narrowly avoids being killed by the Cretan archer Mopsus, and, in revenge, slays his two sons, Dorylas and Icarus, which prompts Mopsus to hurl himself in grief to his death from the battlements (56-147); the Saguntine Theron, priest of the Temple of Hercules, likewise enters the fray, mows down the enemy, and defeats Asbyte in single combat, decapitating her and then parading her head on a spear (148-207); and so Hannibal storms back into the field, hunts down Theron, and kills him in order to avenge the death of Asbyte, who receives an improvised burial (208-69). Meanwhile, the Roman envoys complete their mission (**270-390**): upon their arrival at Carthage, the anti-Barcid Hanno tries in vain to convince the Carthaginian Senate to turn Hannibal over to the Romans and avoid another war (270-326); the equally strident Gestar accuses Hanno of treason for suggesting that the Carthaginians capitulate to the Roman demands (327-77); and so, with a divided Carthaginian Senate unable to choose between war and peace, Fabius formally declares war (378-90). Back in Spain, Hannibal captures Saguntum (**391-707**). Silius offers an extended ecphrasis on the images which appear on the shield given to Hannibal by a local tribe: on the right side, Dido and Hamilcar, even Hannibal swearing his oath; on the left side, Xanthippus, the Spartan general who saved Carthage during the First Punic War, as well as Regulus in torment; on the boss, Saguntum under siege; and, on the rim, Hannibal crossing the Ebro River to formally break the existing treaty with Rome (391-456). As the siege wears on and the besieged suffer from famine (457-74), Hercules looks down in pity upon Saguntum and then beseeches Fides to descend from Mt. Olympus in order to ennoble the Saguntines at their impending death (475-92); Fides assures Hercules that Hannibal will one day pay the price for attacking the city and that she will, indeed, dignify the memory of the fallen (493-512), after which she flies down and inspires the besieged to prevent them from resorting to cannibalism (513-25). In response, Juno looks down in anger upon Saguntum and then orders the Fury Tisiphone to ascend from the Underworld in order to drive the Saguntines to mass suicide (526-42). Accompanied by her infernal entourage, Tisiphone assumes the guise of Tiburna, the grieving wife of the fallen Murrus, inspires the besieged to construct a massive funeral pyre and indulge in an orgy of mutual slaughter, and then, after the real Tiburna commits suicide upon her husband's tomb, returns in triumph to the Underworld (543-695). The book closes with a vision of Hannibal one day committing suicide himself, tortured by the souls of Saguntum (696-707).

After the fall of Saguntum, Hannibal travels to Gades in order to visit the Temple of Hercules, while his envoy Bostar travels to the Siwa Oasis in order to visit the Temple of Jupiter Ammon: Silius offers an ecphrasis on the Temple of Hercules, as well as a description of the tides of the Atlantic at Gades (**3.1-60**). Silius continues the account of the rise of Hannibal (**61-414**). In preparation for the march from Spain to Italy, Hannibal decides to send his wife, Imilce, and their infant son back home to Carthage: when he broaches the topic with her, however, Imilce rebukes Hannibal for underestimating her ability to endure the hardships of the campaign and implores him to restrain his ambition; Hannibal explains why he must forge ahead, puts his wife and child aboard a waiting ship, and holds her gaze until the ship crosses the horizon (61–157). That night, Mercury visits Hannibal in a dream: the god reproaches the Carthaginian for taking any rest in time of war, promises to guide him up to the very gates of Rome if only he will follow after him, and provides him with a frightening vision of the looming destruction of Italy; when he wakes, Hannibal thanks Mercury for the seemingly favorable omen with a sacrifice and orders his men to break camp (158–221). Silius once again emphasizes the gravity of the moment by inserting an extended catalog of the various African and Spanish contingents and their respective commanders, including the men from Carthage under Hannibal's brother Mago and those from Utica under Hasdrubal's son (and, therefore, Hannibal's nephew) Sychaeus (222–414). Hannibal marches from Spain to the Alps (**415–556**). First, he marches over the Pyrenees, the mountain range which separates Spain from Gaul (415–41); then, he crosses the Rhône River and the Durance River, both in Gaul (442–76); and, finally, he climbs up the Alps, avoiding the path trodden by Hercules and instead striking out on his own: after twelve days and twelve nights, the Carthaginians barely set up camp on the beetling cliffs of the mountain range which separates Gaul from Italy (477–556). With Hannibal poised atop the Alps, Venus and Jupiter discuss the Second Punic War and its relationship to the rise of the Flavians (**557–629**): frightened by the imminent Carthaginian invasion, Venus begs her father not to inflict any further punishment upon the Romans (557–69); in reply, Jupiter reassures his daughter by explaining how the Romans have sunk into indolence and by connecting the moral revitalization sparked by the Second Punic War with the later emergence of the Flavian dynasty, all culminating in the reign of Domitian (570–629). Meanwhile, Hannibal completes the march from Spain to Italy (**630–714**): climbing down the Alps with almost as much difficulty as when he had climbed up them (630–46), he pitches camp in the lands of the Taurini, where he meets Bostar, who brings back his report from Jupiter Ammon, including another prophecy of a Carthaginian victory at Cannae (647–714).

The Romans receive word that Hannibal has entered Italy and make immediate preparations to meet the invader: while some repair their weapons of war, others reinforce the fortifications (**4.1–38**). In the events leading up to the battle of the Ticinus River (**39–142**), the Romans under the command of the consul Scipio, father of the future Africanus, hasten from Gaul back to Italy when they learn of Hannibal's march over the Alps (39–55); Hannibal and Scipio both address their soldiers, march to the Ticinus River, and prepare for the engagement the next day (56–100); and then, once they have mustered in the field, the two sides witness the omen of the hawk, the doves, and the eagle: the Roman seer Liger interprets the omen as a bad sign for Hannibal, but the Carthaginian seer Bogus interprets it as a bad sign for the Romans and, hurling his spear, strikes down Catus, the first named casualty of the battle (101–42). During the battle itself (**143–479**), Scipio defeats the Boian Crixus in single combat and, before killing him, mocks him for boasting about his descent from Brennus, leader of the Gallic sack of 390 BC (143–310); seeing the Gallic forces falter, Mago and Hannibal charge into the fray in order to reinvigorate the Carthaginians (311–54); Roman (Virbius, Capys, and Albanus) and Spartan (Eumachus, Critias, and Xanthippus) triplets slay each other in single combat (355–400); and then, when Scipio finds himself surrounded, he is saved by his son, the future Africanus, and carried away from battle under the protection of Mars, ordered by Jupiter to escort the two of them from the field: the end of the day brings the end of the battle, the first of many victories for Hannibal (401–79). In the events leading up to the next engagement, the battle of the Trebia River (**480–524**), Scipio joins forces with his fellow consul, Longus (Liv. 21.50.7–51.7: Silius mentions a Gracchus in 4.495 in order to allude once again to a more famous branch of the clan) (480–97), after which Hannibal and Longus both address their soldiers (498–524). During the battle itself (**525–703**), Hannibal and Longus wreak havoc across the battlefield, inspiring the troops on both sides to kill countless of the enemy (525–53); together, Mago and Maharbal slay the Italian Allius, as the Carthaginians drive the Romans into the river itself (554–72); and then, at the behest of Juno, the Trebia swells beyond its banks in order to attack the Romans, even to swallow up a force of Carthaginian war elephants: Scipio fights back against the river in a μάχη παραποτάμιος which ends when he prays to Venus to send down Vulcan to parch the river dry and to compel it to return to its banks, leaving Hannibal victorious once again (573–703). In the events leading up to the third engagement, the battle of Lake Trasimene (**704–829**), the consul Flaminius marches to Etruria (704–21); Juno, in the guise of Lake Trasimene, visits Hannibal in a dream in order to encourage him to intercept Flaminius (722–38); Hannibal marches over the Apennines (739–62); and then, receiving a delegation from Carthage, Hannibal refuses to allow the sacrifice of his infant son, vowing to honor the gods with another victory instead (763–829).

In the continuation of the events leading up to the battle of Lake Trasimene (**5.1–185**), Hannibal sets his ambush for Flaminius in the woods around the lake (1–52); Flaminius and his men witness a number of unfavorable omens (53–76), followed by a foreboding prophecy uttered by one of the soldiers, Corvinus, in which he warns Flaminius to avoid the ambush and urges him to wait for his consular colleague, Cn. Servilius Geminus, but Flaminius rejects any delay (77–129); and then Flaminius prepares himself and his men for battle, donning the helmet which he had stripped from the Boian king Gergenus when he slew him in single combat, after which he addresses his soldiers (130–85). The battle itself consumes the rest of the day and the rest of the book (**186–678**). While Mars, Venus, and Apollo all turn away in horror, Juno takes her seat upon the Apennines and watches with delight as Hannibal leads the surprise attack and the war goddess Bellona herself spurs on the combatants (186–228). Amid the carnage, the Romans Lateranus and Lentulus team up to kill the Carthaginians Bagas and Syrticus; elsewhere in the field, Iertes slays Nerius, and Rullus, Volunx (229–67). The Roman Appius kills the Spaniard Atlas, decapitating him, before defeating the Cinyphian Isalcas, prospective son-in-law of Mago, in single combat (268–305). Mago himself avenges his future relative's death by killing Appius in return, but he is also wounded by him; the Roman standard-bearer Mamercus then falls amid a shower of enemy spears; and Hannibal escorts Mago from the field to receive treatment from the healer Synalus (306–75). With Hannibal temporarily away from the fighting, Flaminius storms back into the fray, killing Bogus, Bagasus, and the giant Othrys, while Hasdrubal's son Sychaeus kills Murranus, Tauranus, and several other opponents: when Flaminius and Sychaeus meet in single combat, the Roman easily dispatches the Carthaginian (376–529). Then, Mago and Hannibal return to battle, and Hannibal kills countless of the enemy; when Hannibal learns about the fate of Sychaeus, he vows to avenge the death by killing Flaminius: however, after a sudden earthquake puts the defeated Romans to flight, Flaminius tries in vain to turn the troops and falls amid a shower of spears hurled by Ducarius and his fellow Boii; the day, the battle, and the book end with the Romans committing mass suicide in order to create a tomb over their fallen general, and then Hannibal and Mago touring the battlefield to view the carnage (530–678).

Punica 1–5, the first pentad of the epic, provides a narrative of the events of the Second Punic War from the siege of Saguntum to the battle of Lake Trasimene. Across this first phase of the poem, Silius introduces his main character, Hannibal, describes Hannibal's victory over his first great enemy, Murrus, during the siege of Saguntum, and, after the capture of Saguntum, pits Hannibal against a series of Roman consuls at the battles of the Ticinus River, the Trebia River, and Lake Trasimene. By manipulating the pace of the narrative (speeding it up and, more often, slowing it down), Silius not only articulates his own, original, presentation of the Second Punic War, but also emphasizes the cumulative impact of that manipulation, especially the policy of delay, on the widening disjuncture between the pace of the narrative and the pace of the actual war. Accordingly, across books 1 and 2, Silius briskly relates events between Hannibal's oath of eternal hatred against the Romans and his later rise to power after the assassination of Hasdrubal, before grinding the narrative to a halt in order to develop the story of the fall of Saguntum and, in the process, outline both the theology and the theodicy of the epic. As a result, the account of the siege of Saguntum offers a template for all subsequent siege narratives, in *Punica* 11–12, 13–14, and 17[–18]. In book 3, Silius once again balances speed and delay, spending as much time on the preparations for the march from Spain to Italy as on the march itself, including the scene on Mt. Olympus at both the literal and the literary climax when Hannibal and his men have finally scaled the Alps. Across books 4 and 5 (and, indeed, according to the hexadic model, extending into book 6), Silius elaborates a tricolon crescens of battle narratives, each one longer than the preceding one(s): this progressive buildup from the Ticinus River to the Trebia River to Lake Trasimene underscores how one engagement leads naturally to the next (and prepares the reader for the ultimate engagement at Cannae in the next pentad). Especially when book 6 is included in the analysis, these three battles together offer a template for all subsequent battle narratives, in *Punica* 7–10, 15, and 16. Throughout this first pentad, memories of earlier conflicts invite the reader to look back to thematically similar moments in the (Roman) past, including the Gallic sack, the fall of Troy, and even mythical combats like the Titanomachy and the Gigantomachy.

4. *Punica* 6–10: From Lake Trasimene to Cannae

On the day after the engagement, Hannibal and Mago revisit the battlefield in order to hunt down any remaining Romans amid the heaps of dead and dying warriors: in particular, Silius recounts the gruesome fates of Laevinus and Tyres (**6.1–61**). Meanwhile, after a long digression with an extended flashback to the First Punic War, news of the disaster at Lake Trasimene reaches Rome (**62–640**). Among the few survivors, Serranus, the son of Regulus, escapes to the humble abode of Marus, who had served under Regulus, near Perugia: Marus recognizes

Serranus, welcomes him into his hut for the night, and tends to the wounded soldier (62–100). The next morning, Marus recounts the brave and noble deeds of Regulus during the First Punic War, culminating with his torture and death in Carthage: first, Serranus utters a lament for all of the Romans who have fallen since the beginning of the war, especially Flaminius; then, Marus reminisces about his service with Regulus, recounting the exploit of the Bagradas serpent, in which Marus helped Regulus to slay the monster after it devoured their comrades Aquinus and Avens; next, Serranus briefly resumes his lament, asserting that the Romans would never have suffered their recent defeats in battle at the hands of the Carthaginians if his father were still alive; and, finally, Marus reminisces further, recounting how Regulus was captured in Africa for the Carthaginians by the Spartan Xanthippus, how he was sent back home to Rome by the Carthaginian Senate in order to negotiate a hostage exchange, which he expressly instructed the Roman Senate to reject outright, and how he was consequently brought back to Africa, where he was tortured to death (101–551). As rumors of the ambush along the shores of Lake Trasimene reach Rome, the city descends into chaos amid fears of an imminent assault until the first waves of fugitives from the battle arrive at the city gates, including Serranus, who reunites with his mother, Marcia: then, faced with the prospect of filling the void left by the death of Flaminius, the Roman Senate convenes in order to appoint a new commander (552–99). Looking down from the Alban Mount, Jupiter himself hurls his thunderbolt four times in order to turn Hannibal away from Rome and then directs the Roman Senate to name Fabius *dictator*, after which Silius retells the story of the family, from their progenitor, Hercules, to the battle of the Cremera River (traditionally, 477 BC), when all but one member of the Fabian clan was killed (600–40). Turned away from Rome, Hannibal instead burns down a temple at Liternum, consigning the images of the First Punic War depicted on the temple murals to the destruction which he is unable to inflict upon the Romans (**641–716**).

Silius hails Fabius for his policy of delay; when word reaches the Carthaginians about the new commander, Hannibal learns from Cilnius, an Etruscan captive, about the *gens Fabia*, from Hercules to the Cremera River (**7.1–73**): meanwhile, the Romans offer propitiatory sacrifices at temples throughout the city (**74–89**). When Fabius leads his men out into the field, he avoids a direct engagement at all costs until he is recalled to Rome in order to fulfill a religious obligation (**90–408**). At the first sight of Roman forces, Hannibal addresses his soldiers and promises them a speedy victory, but Fabius frustrates that hope by not taking the bait and instead remaining in camp (90–130). Hannibal roams aimlessly around

Apulia before returning to Campania, where he retaliates against Fabius by burning down the vineyards of the ager Falernus (131–61). Silius then inserts a digression in which he offers an original etiology for the region's exceptional wine: the aged Falernus once welcomed Bacchus into his humble abode and offered him hospitality, for which the god rewarded the farmer by turning his water into wine and then cloaking the slopes of Mons Massicus with vines (162–211). After Hannibal ravages the Falernian fields, the Roman forces grow impatient of delay and pressure their commander to lead them out to battle, but Fabius addresses his soldiers with a stern rebuke in which he chides them for their restiveness and calms them in their frenzy by assuring them that the time for an engagement will eventually come (212–59). Hannibal attempts to turn the Romans against Fabius by sparing his fields the destruction wrought on the surrounding area, but to no avail; instead, Hannibal finds himself penned in by Fabius, and so he ventures a daring nighttime escape by attaching flaming torches to the horns of cattle, driving the cattle against the Roman sentries, and hurrying through the narrow defile when the Romans retreat (260–376). Called back to Rome, Fabius entrusts the army to his *magister equitum*, Minucius, first warning and then ordering Minucius not to engage with Hannibal under any circumstances (377–408). Meanwhile, the Nereids, terrified by the arrival of a Carthaginian fleet, consult Proteus, who tells them about Rome's ultimate victory over Carthage (**409–93**). In the events leading up to the battle of Gereonium (**494–566**), the Roman Senate divides the army between Fabius and Minucius after the latter appears to score a victory against Hannibal (494–518); while Minucius leads his men out to battle and Fabius prepares his men to save them, Hannibal addresses his soldiers (519–35); and then, when his son rejoices at the destruction awaiting Minucius, Fabius scolds him for his lack of patriotism and invokes the example of M. Furius Camillus, who returned from exile to save Rome after the Gallic sack (536–66). During the battle itself (**567–750**), Fabius charges into the fray, killing countless of the enemy (567–616), inspiring the younger men to follow his example (617–33); Brutus defeats Cleadas (634–60); Carmelus defeats Hampsicus (661–79); Cato kills the Moor Tunger, decapitating him (680–704); Fabius and his son save Minucius and his men by putting Hannibal to flight (705–29); and then, having been rescued from certain defeat, Minucius and his men all hail Fabius as their savior, celebrating their deliverance as a triumph (730–50).

After his setback at Gereonium (**8.1–24**), Juno sends Anna down to Hannibal in a dream in order to encourage him to march to Cannae (**25–241**): Juno summons Anna and gives her her orders (25–38); Anna agrees to comply (39–43);

Silius (along with a later interpolator, perhaps) inserts a digression in which he recounts the earlier history of Anna and Dido, including the story of how Anna came to Italy as an exile, was driven to suicide by Dido, and was transformed into the goddess Anna Perenna (44–201); and then, after Anna completes her mission, delivering the news that Fabius has now completed his term of office, Hannibal orders his men to break camp and head for Cannae (202–41). With Hannibal on the march to Cannae, Rome braces for the worst and prepares to march out for battle (**242–621**): Varro, one of the two consuls for the year, rouses the Roman people against the invader by pledging to dispense with the policy of delay and even boasting that he will soon lead Hannibal in chains through the streets of Rome when he returns home in triumph (242–77); Fabius advises Paullus, the other of the two consuls, on how best to restrain his rash colleague in order to avert disaster, after which Paullus vows to continue the policy of delay as well as he can and, failing that, to die in battle (278–348); and then, by inserting an extended catalog of the various Roman and Italian contingents and their respective commanders, Silius emphasizes the link between the looming battle and the siege of Saguntum, as well as that between the looming battle and Hannibal's march from Spain to Italy: the forces include the men from the various communities in Campania under Scipio, the future Africanus (349–621). In the events leading up to the battle of Cannae (**622–76**), once the Romans arrive at Cannae, they witness a host of evil omens (622–55), followed by the dire predictions uttered by an unnamed soldier about the flight of Varro and the death of Paullus soon to come (656–76).

In the continuation of the events leading up to the battle of Cannae (**9.1–277**), after a minor skirmish in which several Romans fall, the first of whom is a soldier named Mancinus, Paullus continues to strive, ultimately in vain, to dissuade Varro from leading the Romans into the field the next day (1–65). During the night before the climactic battle, the Italian Satricus, who had been captured by Xanthippus during the First Punic War and given in slavery to the king of the Autololes, and who had returned to Italy as a part of Hannibal's invasion and decided to try to flee back home, is unwittingly killed by his son, Solymus, while unwittingly wearing the armor of his other son, the Mancinus killed earlier that day: Solymus, realizing what he has done, commits suicide upon his corpse, writing on his shield in his own blood his father's warning to the Romans, FUGE PROELIA VARRO ("Flee the battle, Varro!") (66–177). The next morning, Hannibal addresses his soldiers, promising them that they will march victoriously from Cannae against the walls of Rome, and then lines them up for battle (178–243). Meanwhile, when the Roman soldiers stumble upon the evil omen and report it to Varro, he mockingly suggests that they instead report it to Paullus, and then lines them up for battle, too (244–77). The battle itself consumes the rest of the day and extends beyond book 9 into book 10 (**278–657**). In heaven and on earth, gods and mortals are locked in a cosmic fight as Mars himself spurs on the combatants (278–361). Amid the carnage, the Carthaginian Nealces slays the Roman Scaevola (362–400), after which the Carthaginian Symaethus likewise kills the Romans Marius and Caper (401–10). Scipio, the future Africanus, and Varro, among others, lead an effective countercharge, and so Hannibal seeks out Varro for a single combat, but Scipio turns the Carthaginian against himself, instead (411–37). Mars and Pallas intervene on behalf of Scipio and Hannibal, respectively, to prevent the clash: as Mars and Pallas prepare to face off, Jupiter sends down Iris to command Pallas to leave the battlefield (438–85). At the behest of Juno, the Vulturnus wind helps the Carthaginians and hurts the Romans, even attacking Mars: as Mars prepares to fight back, Jupiter sends down Iris to command him to leave the battlefield, too (486–555). Frustrated in his attempt at engaging with Scipio in a single combat, Hannibal recognizes Minucius in the fray and kills him, instead (556–69). While the Carthaginian elephants run amok (570–631), Paullus bitterly rebukes Varro for leading the Romans to their demise; Varro laments his fate before fleeing from the battlefield, choosing to return home in disgrace rather than to commit suicide (632–57).

The battle of Cannae continues (**10.1–325**). Paullus rescues Cato and then seeks out Hannibal for a single combat, but Juno intervenes twice to prevent the clash, first in the guise of Metellus in an ultimately unsuccessful attempt at turning away Paullus and then in the guise of Gelesta in an ultimately successful attempt at turning away Hannibal (1–91). Instead, whisked off to another corner of the battlefield, Hannibal slays the Umbrian warrior Crista along with his six sons (Lucas, Volso, Vesulus, Telesinus, Quercens, and Perusinus) (92–169). Meanwhile, Paullus kills countless of the enemy, including the giant Phorcys, as the Vulturnus wind grows more and more dangerous for the Romans: Viriathus kills Servilius; Paullus kills Viriathus; an unidentified assailant mortally wounds Paullus, who takes up a defensive position on a nearby rock; and then, when Hannibal joins the attack on Paullus, Piso defends his failing commander by throwing Hannibal from his horse, and so Hannibal kills Piso, instead (170–259). In flight from the battle, the wounded Cn. Cornelius Lentulus halts when he catches sight of Paullus on the rock and offers to escort him from the field: Paullus praises Lentulus for his bravery, gives him orders to bring back to Rome (that the gates of the city be closed and that Fabius be handed the reins of power), and fulfills his vow to die in battle, falling amid a shower of enemy spears, after which the engagement finally ends with a general rout of the Roman forces (260–325). That night, Juno sends Somnus down to Hannibal in a dream in order to encourage him *not* to march from Cannae against the walls of Rome: when the Carthaginian forces learn that they will not be attacking the city, Mago rebukes Hannibal for sacrificing so much in order to gain a victory over Varro alone and not Rome as a whole (**326–86**). Meanwhile, the surviving Romans gather at Canusium (**387–448**): as the wounded grieve both for themselves and for their lost comrades (387–414), first, the real Metellus advises his fellow soldiers to desert their city, to seek a new home far away from both Carthage and Rome (415–25), but, then, Scipio storms in to compel everyone to swear an oath to defend their city (426–48). And so, instead of marching on Rome, Hannibal revisits the battlefield (**449–577**): after he comes upon Cloelius gasping out his final breath beside his faithful steed, Hannibal learns from Cinna, who deserted the Romans to join the Carthaginians, about the story of his family and, in particular, about Cloelia, who swam across the Tiber River (449–502); the Carthaginians come upon the corpse of the fallen Paullus, whom Hannibal honors with a massive funeral pyre and a laudatory funeral oration (503–77). Back in Rome (**578–658**), while the city braces for an imminent attack (578–91), Fabius surprisingly exhorts the Roman to abandon the policy of delay which he had advocated for so strenuously up to that point in the war (592–604), even as Varro makes his ignominious return (605–39), after which the Roman Senate goes so far as to enlist slaves in order to fill out the ranks (640–58).

Punica 6–10, the second pentad of the epic, provides a narrative of the events of the Second Punic War from the battle of Lake Trasimene to the battle of Cannae. Across this second phase of the poem, Silius describes the aftermath of the battle of Lake Trasimene, pits Hannibal against his first true rival, Fabius, and provides an expansive narrative of the battle of Cannae. Once again, by manipulating the narrative pace, Silius emphasizes the structural and thematic significance of Cannae, as well as the growing disparity between the time and space allocated to events in the epic vis-à-vis the war itself. Accordingly, in book 6, Silius elegantly connects the Second Punic War with the First Punic War through the extended digression about the rise and fall of Regulus. In particular, this flashback prompts reflection upon a number of interrelated themes, including the fraught relationship between Carthage and Rome, the linear and cyclical nature of their, ultimately, three conflicts, and the endless complexities of heroic exemplarity. In book 7, the "Fabius book" (*Fabius*, 7.1), Silius formally introduces the Cunctator and his policy of delay as the first effective impediment to Hannibal's otherwise unchecked aggression against the Romans and their allies. While the discord between Fabius and Minucius clearly foreshadows that to come between Paullus and Varro, the outcome of the battle of Gereonium, where Fabius saves Minucius and his men, contrasts strongly with that of the battle of Cannae, where Paullus bravely fights to his death while Varro flees. Across books 8–10, Silius practices his own policy of (narrative) delay, as the extended account of the events before, during, and after the battle of Cannae represents the structural and thematic culmination of the trio of battles across books 4–6. Throughout this second pentad, memories of earlier conflicts continue to invite the reader to look back to thematically similar moments in the (Roman) past, including the Gallic sack, the fall of Troy, and the Titanomachy and the Gigantomachy, but also to even more ethically contentious moments from the more recent past, including Rome's various periods of civil war. References and allusions to all of these defining conflicts in Roman culture punctuate the narrative of the battle of Cannae, in particular, serving to transform that engagement into the ultimate expression of *Romanitas* and a, if not the, turning point in the war and so, by extension, in Roman history.

5. *Punica* 10.657–8: The Turning Point

640   at patres Fabiusque procul maerore remoto
        praecipitant curas. raptim delecta iuventa
        servitia armantur, nec claudit castra saluti
        postpositus pudor. infixum est Aeneia regna
        Parcarum in leges quacumque reducere dextra
645   proque arce et sceptris et libertatis honore
        vel famulas armare manus. primaeva suorum
        corpora praetexto spoliant velamine et armis
        insolitis cingunt. puerilis casside vultus
        clauditur atque hostis pubescere caede iubetur.
650   idem obsecrantes, captivum vulgus ut auro
        pensarent parvo (nec pauca fuere precantum
        milia) miranti durarunt prodere Poeno.
        cuncta adeo scelera et noxam superaverat omnem
        armatum potuisse capi. tunc terga dedisse
655   damnatis Siculas longe meritare per oras
        impositum, donec Latio decederet hostis.

> **haec tum Roma fuit. post te cui vertere mores**
> **si stabat fatis, potius, Carthago, maneres.**

640 But the senators and Fabius, having set aside their grief,
 put their plans into action. Slaves chosen for their youth
 were quickly armed, nor did shame, having given way to pride,
 close the camp to them. It was decided to bring the kingdom of Aeneas
 back under the laws of the Fates by whatever right hand was available
645 and to arm even the hands of slaves on behalf of the Capitol and empire
 and the honor of liberty. They despoil the tender bodies
 of their own children by taking off their *toga praetexta*,
 and they gird them with unfamiliar weapons. Their young face is hidden
 by the helmet and is ordered to grow up through the slaughter of the
  enemy.
650 When those same people begged, that they ransom the captured horde
 for a small amount of gold (nor were there only a few thousand praying
  for this),
 they persisted in not handing them over to the amazed Carthaginian
  [Hannibal].
 For an armed man to have been able to be captured had so completely
  surpassed
 all other evil deeds and every other crime. Then it was imposed upon
  those
655 who had been convicted of having fled to serve far away along the shores
 of Sicily, until the enemy retreated from Latium.
 This was Rome in those days. If it was fated for her to change her ways
 after your fall, Carthage, I would rather that you were still standing.

In *Punica* 10.640-58, Silius offers a somewhat different version for the events after the battle of Cannae compared to the rest of the tradition, especially when compared to the account in Livy (*Pun.* 10.326-658 ~ Liv. 22.50-61).[30] Perhaps most notably, Silius reintroduces Fabius into the narrative, elevating him to a level of visibility and importance far beyond his role in Livy (*Pun.* 10.578-658 ~ Liv. 22.54.7-61.15). In doing so, Silius invites the reader to compare the scene in Rome after Cannae (10.578-658) with that in the city after Lake Trasimene (6.62-640). In the aftermath of Lake Trasimene, with the death of Flaminius, Jupiter himself turned Hannibal away from Rome and directed the Roman Senate to name Fabius *dictator*; in the aftermath of Cannae, with the death of Paullus, Fabius once again emerges as a leading voice in Rome. These parallels between the two battles strengthen the characterization of Varro as a second Flaminius and, at the same time, that of Paullus as a second Fabius. More specifically, Silius also reinforces the link between Rome's staunch refusal to ransom the captives taken at Cannae (*Pun.* 10.650–4 ~ Liv. 22.58.1–61.10) and the refusal to ransom Regulus during the First Punic War (6.299–551). The couplet which closes book 10, 10.657–8, serves as an epigraph for the epic and marks this moment as a, if not the, turning point in the war and in the narrative.[31] Silius himself explicitly identifies Cannae as that turning point in his earlier invocation of the Muses at the beginning of the battle (9.340–53), including verses which powerfully resonate with those in 10.657–8:

> verum utinam posthac animo, Romane, secunda,
> quanto tunc adversa, feras! sitque hactenus, oro,
> nec libeat temptare deis, an Troia proles
> par bellum tolerare queat. tuque anxia fati
> 350   pone, precor, lacrimas et adora vulnera laudes
> perpetuas paritura tibi. nam tempore, Roma,
> nullo maior eris. mox sic labere secundis,
> ut sola cladum tuearis nomina fama.

> Truly, would that, o Roman, you later could endure the good times
> with as great a spirit as you then endured the bad! And, I beg, would that
> this were enough, and that it were not pleasing to the gods to see,
> whether the Trojan race were able to withstand another war. You, anxious
> 350   about your fate, do not weep, I pray, but bless those wounds which will bring
> you eternal glory. For, Rome, at no other time
> will you be greater. Soon you will succumb to your successes,
> such that you preserve your reputation through the fame of your defeats.

In these lines from that invocation of the Muses (9.346–53), Silius uses this familiar epic trope in order to transform history into myth and emphasize the gravity of the looming engagement, much as he had in another (also 14-line) invocation of the Muses during the battle of Lake Trasimene (5.420–33). In particular, Silius paradoxically celebrates the forthcoming disaster as both Rome's greatest defeat and the city's greatest victory: *nam tempore, Roma, / nullo maior eris* (351–2). This formulation captures the essence of the underlying idea that, in the *Punica*, a defeat can be a victory, and a victory, a defeat. Silius then expands on his claim that Cannae paradoxically marks Rome's concomitant shift from (military) defeat to (military) victory and from (moral) victory to (moral) defeat: *mox sic labere secundis, / ut sola cladum tuearis nomina fama* (352–3). Here, Silius asserts that the military defeat at Cannae represents a moral victory for Rome and, by extension, that the military victory later at Zama represents a moral defeat for the city. More broadly, the poet invites the reader both to look back and, after a first reading, to look ahead to other pivotal moments in the development of this theme. On the one hand, in book 3, during his conversation with Venus, Jupiter ominously predicts that "the time will one day come for you when Rome, the greatest city in the world, / will be more famous for her defeats" (*iamque tibi veniet tempus, quo maxima rerum / nobilior sit Roma malis*, 584–5). On the other, in book 15, after Scipio chooses Virtus over Voluptas, the rejected goddess (i.e., Venus herself) likewise predicts, "My time, my time will come one day, / when Rome, trained to my commands, will serve me / with great zeal, and I alone will be held in honor" (*venient, venient mea tempora quondam, / cum docilis nostris magno certamine Roma / serviet imperiis et honos mihi habebitur uni*, 125–7). Fittingly, both of these passages include wordplay which underscores the notion that Venus (i.e., luxury) will one day (soon) come to destroy Rome (Venus ~ *veniet / venient*).

All of these passages center on the closing couplet of book 10, where Silius sharpens the paradox of victory in defeat and defeat in victory in language which pointedly invites the reader to reflect on the arc of the war and the narrative across books 9 and 10, even across the poem as a whole: *haec tum Roma fuit. post te cui vertere mores / si stabat fatis, potius, Carthago, maneres* (10.657–8). Through the opposition between "then" and "now" in the chiasmus *posthac . . . / . . . tunc* (9.346–7) ~ *tum . . . post te* (10.657), Silius skillfully tropes the reversal of military victory and defeat vis-à-vis moral victory and defeat around the turning point of Cannae. The poet even goes so far as to cue this reversal through another chiasmus, of the consonants *r* and *m* in *Roma . . . mores*, and then to mark that chiasmus with the verb *vertere*, as if to say that Rome changed into her opposite when the city changed her ways after Cannae.[32] This particular wordplay on the consonants *r* and *m* pervades the epic and, in a sense, ties together many of the poem's essential themes. Silius engages with the *arma* (i.e., the *Aeneid*) of *Maro* (i.e., Vergil) in order to trace the rise of the city of *Roma* and its *maiores* ("ancestors") from its divine origins, *Amor* (i.e., Venus) and *Mars* (*Romulus* and *Remus*), as well as, after a long *mora* ("delay"), the decline and fall of the city's *mores* ("character"), leading to the decline and fall of its *muri* ("walls") and eventually to its *mors* ("death"), leaving behind only the *memoria* ("memory") of what was, including the memory of the three wars with the *Mauri* ("Carthaginians").[33] From the beginning of the epic (*ordior arma*, 1.1) to its end (*memorat . . . / . . . Roma*, 17.653–4), Silius returns time and again to this dense cluster of theme words in order to explore the fraught relationship between the rise and fall of Carthage and Rome, as well as the concomitant rise and fall of Hannibal and Scipio.

4

A Reading of *Punica* 11–17: From Cannae to Zama

1. *Punica* 11.1–27: The Medial Proem

    nunc age, quos clades insignis Iapyge campo
    verterit ad Libyam populos Sarranaque castra,
    expediam. stat nulla diu mortalibus usquam
    Fortuna titubante fides. adiungere dextras
5   certavere palam rumpenti foedera Poeno
    (heu nimium faciles lassis diffidere rebus!)
    saevior ante alios iras servasse repostas
    atque odium renovare ferox in tempore Samnis,
    mox levis et sero pensurus facta pudore
10 Bruttius, ambiguis fallax mox Apulus armis,
    tum gens Hirpini vana indocilisque quieti
    et rupisse indigna fidem, ceu dira per omnes
    manarent populos foedi contagia morbi.
    iamque Atella suas iamque et Calatia adegit
15 fas superante metu Poenorum in castra cohortes.
    inde Phalanteo levitas animosa Tarento
    Ausonium laxare iugum. patefecit amicas
    alta Croton portas Afrisque ad barbara iussa
    Thespiadum docuit summittere colla nepotes.
20 idem etiam Locros habuit furor. ora vadosi
    litoris, Argivos maior qua Graecia muros
    servat et Ionio alluitur curvata profundo,
    laetas res Libyae et fortunam in Marte secuta
    iuravit pavitans Tyrio sua proelia Marti.
25 iam vero, Eridani tumidissimus accola, Celtae
    incubuere malis Italum veteresque doloris
    tota se socios properarunt iungere mole.

>   Come now, I will recount which peoples the famous slaughter
>   in the Japygian [Apulian] field turned toward Libya
>   and the Tyrian camp. Nowhere does faith stay the same for long
>   for mortals when Fortune totters. They openly strove to join
> 5   right hands with the Phoenician [Hannibal] as he broke treaties,
>   (alas, too easy at losing their faith when affairs go poorly!)
>   the Samnites, more savage than all of the others to preserve their pent-up anger
>   and fiercer than all of the others to renew their hatred in time,
>   now the Bruttians, fickle and sure to weigh too late their actions
> 10 against their shame, now the Apulians, tricky with their deceitful weapons,
>   then the Hirpini, a vain tribe of people untrained to peace
>   and indignant at having broken their faith, as if the foul contagions
>   of the vile disease had spread throughout all peoples.
>   And now Atella, and now Calatia has led her cohorts
> 15 into the camp of the Phoenicians, as fear conquers their sense of right.
>   Then the spirited fickleness loosened the Ausonian [Italian] yoke
>   from Phalantean Tarentum. Lofty Croton laid bare
>   her friendly gates and taught the descendants of the Thespians
>   to lower their necks to the Africans to their barbarian commands.
> 20 The same fury also took hold of Locri. The shore of the low-lying coastline,
>   where greater Greece preserves Argive walls
>   and its curve is washed by the Ionian deep,
>   having followed the happy affairs and good fortune of Libya in war
>   swore an oath of loyalty out of fear for her own battles in a Tyrian war.
> 25 Now, indeed, the Celts, most arrogant inhabitants of the Po,
>   brooded over the evils of the Italians and ancient in their grief
>   they hastened to join themselves as allies with their full force.

In *Punica* 11.1–27, Silius marks the transition between books, between pentads, and between the two major phases of the Second Punic War (before and after Cannae) with a medial proem in the form of an extended catalog of the Italian cities which defect from Rome to Hannibal after the battle, culminating with an extended ecphrasis of Capua, the second city in Italy, in 11.28–54.[1] Once again, Silius offers a somewhat different version for the events after the battle of Cannae compared to the rest of the tradition, especially when compared to the account in Livy (*Pun.* 11 ~ Liv. 23.1–18). Perhaps most notably, in Livy, Hannibal marches from Cannae (in Apulia) into Samnium against the Hirpini and, from there, into Campania against Neapolis and then Capua; in Silius, however, while Hannibal still marches from Cannae into Samnium and, from there, into Campania, he acquires many more peoples and places as new allies along the way, including the Bruttians, the Apulians, and the Hirpini, as well as Atella and Calatia, Tarentum and Croton, the Locrians and the Celts, and, of course, Capua.² In cataloging these defectors, Silius not only emphasizes the gravity of the situation for the Romans, but also foreshadows many of the pivotal conflicts to come in both the war and the narrative, from events at Tarentum and Locri to those at Capua. Once again, Silius underscores the structural and thematic importance of *Punica* 11.1–27 for the epic as a whole through a deft intertextual gesture: *nunc age, quos clades insignis Iapyge campo / verterit ad Libyam populos Sarranaque castra, / expediam* (1–3), the opening sentence of the book, here recalls, but also significantly alters, the formulation which Vergil uses in his own medial proem in *Aeneid* 7.37–45, especially the opening sentence of the proem in 37–40:

> nunc age, qui reges, Erato, quae tempora, rerum
> quis Latio antiquo fuerit status, advena classem
> cum primum Ausoniis exercitus appulit oris,
> 40   expediam, et primae revocabo exordia pugnae.

> Come now, Erato, I will recount who were the kings,
> what were the times, and what was the state of affairs
> in ancient Latium, when the band of exiles first beached their fleet
> 40   upon the shores of Ausonia [Italy], and I will recall the origins of this first war.

Several intertextual resonances all but ensure that Silius intends the reader to compare *Punica* 11.1–3 with *Aeneid* 7.37–40: verse-initial *nunc age* (*Pun.* 11.1 ~ *Aen.* 7.37), the relative clause(s) which immediately follow (*Pun.* 11.1–2 ~ *Aen.* 7.37–8), and, most of all, the enjambment of verse-initial *expediam* (*Pun.* 11.3 ~ *Aen.* 7.40). These many linguistic similarities between the two texts point up the striking thematic similarity between them, as well. At this point in the *Aeneid*, Aeneas has just entered the Tiber and is sailing into Latium towards the future site of Rome, where he will soon wage the (proleptic) civil war which culminates in his victory over Turnus in single combat. At this point in the *Punica*, internecine conflict is likewise brewing, as Capua and others desert the Romans for the Carthaginians, transforming the Second Punic War into another (proleptic) civil war. On the small scale, Silius marks the transition between books 10 and 11 through the stark contrast between *haec tum* in 10.657 and *nunc age* in 11.1. On the medium scale, the poet marks the complementary transition between pentads, between books 1–5, 6–10, and 11–15, as well as the dyad/triad of books 16–17[–18], through the repetition of references to the

Bruttians at the beginning of books 6, 11, and 16: first, the reference to a certain Bruttius, a Roman eagle bearer who commits suicide after Lake Trasimene (6.14–40); then, the reference to the Bruttii in the catalog of Italian cities which defect from Rome to Hannibal after Cannae (11.9–10); and, finally, the reference to Hannibal venting his spleen in the land of the Bruttii after the Metaurus River (16.1–22). References to the Bruttii are otherwise infrequent in the *Punica* (8.568, 13.92–3, 17.179–80, 432–40) and consistently remind the reader that, like the Capuans, the Bruttians were among the first Italians to defect: as such, the references to this people at the beginning of books 6, 11, and 16 emphasize the thematic opposition throughout the epic between *fides* and *perfidia*. On the large scale, Silius uses his medial proem in 11.1–27 in order to mark the transition between the two major phases of the war (before and after Cannae), between the war against Hannibal, the foreign invader, and the war against the enemy within.

2. *Punica* 11–15: From Cannae to the Metaurus River

Silius recounts how the Capuans and other Italians desert the Romans for the Carthaginians after Cannae (**11.1–121**): following the catalog which serves as a medial proem (1–54), the Capuans send envoys to Rome in order to make the specious demand of a share in the consulship, at the instigation of Pacuvius Calavius, their chief magistrate (55–64); Vibius Virrius, the leader of the delegation, presents the proposal, which the Roman Senate unanimously rejects outright with a torrent of abuse (65–72); and the senators T. Manlius Torquatus, Fabius, Marcellus, and Fulvius offer especially harsh denunciations (73–121). Rejected by Rome, the Capuans turn to Hannibal (**122–482**). At the instigation of Virrius, the Capuans celebrate Hannibal's many successes thus far in the war and send envoys to him in order to propose an alliance (122–56). Decius Magius, the leader of the pro-Roman faction in Capua, speaks out against the proposed alliance, warning his fellow Capuans not to forget their ties with Rome; after Hannibal and the Capuans come to terms, the unsettling arrival of a large band of Autololes prompts Decius to make one final plea to his fellow Capuans not to allow Hannibal himself to enter the city (157–200). When Hannibal learns about the situation inside Capua, he orders his band of troops to take Decius into custody and to bring him to his camp outside the city, where Hannibal rebukes Decius for opposing him; upon entering the city himself, Hannibal again orders his troops to take Decius into custody, only this time he orders him to be thrown into chains and taken away for punishment: having removed Decius, Hannibal marches through the streets of Capua in triumph (201–66). That night, after his triumph, Hannibal continues the celebration with a lavish banquet, at first disapproving of but at last succumbing to the luxury of the feast, during which Teuthras plays and sings to the lyre, including a song on the founding of Capua: meanwhile, in the garden outside at the back of the house, Pacuvius barely succeeds in dissuading his son, Perolla, from killing and decapitating Hannibal by threatening to interpose himself between his son and his intended victim (267–368). The next day, with his brother Mago, as well as Decius, on the way back to Carthage (although Decius is subsequently driven off course to Cyrene, where he is granted asylum by Ptolemy IV), Hannibal and his men decide to spend the winter at Capua, wasting away in luxury: Venus sends down her Cupids to strike the Carthaginians with their arrows, causing them to burn with passion for wine, women, and song; above all else, Hannibal enjoys the performances by Teuthras, and so Teuthras sings of the bards Amphion, Arion, Chiron, and Orpheus, ending with the image of the decapitated head of Orpheus, still singing, floating out to sea (369–482). Meanwhile, Mago returns to Carthage (**483–611**): after entering the city in triumph (483–500), Mago addresses the Carthaginian Senate with a report about the victory at Cannae, as well as a request for supplies in order to bring the war to an end, and then rebukes Hanno for suggesting that Hannibal be turned over to the Romans (501–53); in reply, Hanno renews his call for peace, predicts that Rome will soon recover from Cannae, and rejects the request for supplies, but all to no avail (554–611).

Enervated by their winter in Capua (**12.1–26**), Hannibal and his men strike fear into the surrounding cities of Campania when they emerge from hibernation, but they discover that they lack their former strength and vigor (**27–160**): first, Hannibal attacks Naples, but he is repulsed from the walls of the city by a sudden counterattack (27–59); then, he threatens Cumae, but he is again repulsed, by a Roman garrison under the command of Ti. Sempronius Gracchus (60–107); finally, Hannibal unsuccessfully besieges Puteoli, and so he instead lays waste to the area around Mt. Gaurus (108–60). From there, Hannibal lays siege to Nola (**161–294**). Silius offers a brief ecphrasis on the city's topography and the Roman garrison stationed there under the command of Marcellus (161–6). When he catches sight of Hannibal approaching in the distance, Marcellus commands his soldiers to take up their arms and prepare to meet the assault, then he leads them out of the city against the Carthaginians: Marcellus seeks out Hannibal for a single combat, but Juno intervenes to prevent the clash; instead, Hannibal strives to rally his men (167–211). The Roman Pedianus kills the Carthaginian Cinyps, decapitating him and, in doing so, recovers the helmet and plume which

Hannibal had taken from Paullus and given to Cinyps (212–52). When Pedianus brings back this trophy, Marcellus praises him for his valor and then hurls his spear at Hannibal, narrowly missing him: the Carthaginians flee from the battlefield, leaving the Romans to hail Marcellus as their victor (253–80). As Marcellus returns to Nola in triumph, Hannibal addresses his soldiers and blames them, not himself, for their failure to take the city (281–94). The Romans rejoice at the news of the repulse of Hannibal (**295–341**): after punishing those who had shirked their responsibility towards the war effort, the people of Rome, rich and poor alike, pile up their private wealth as a contribution to the public coffers (295–319); meanwhile, envoys bring back their report from the oracle of Apollo at Delphi, including a prophecy about Rome's imminent victory in the war (320–41). Silius then shifts the scene briefly to the war in Sardinia (**342–419**): Silius relates how Torquatus leads the Romans against Hostus, son of Hampsagoras, who had earlier invited the Carthaginians to Sardinia (342–54), offers an ecphrasis on the history of the island (355–75), and recounts how Hostus and Hampsagoras meet their death (376–419). Thereafter, Hannibal lays siege to Tarentum and Capua (**420–544**): after capturing the cities of Acerrae, Nuceria, Casilinum, and Petelia in quick succession, Hannibal shifts his focus to Tarentum, where things stand at a stalemate (420–48); when word arrives that the Romans have besieged Capua, Hannibal hastens to relieve the city, along the way destroying armies under the command of M. Centenius Paenula and Cn. Fulvius Flaccus, and honoring Gracchus, who had been killed in an ambush by the Lucanians, with a proper burial (449–544). Finally, realizing that he is unable to defend Capua, Hannibal marches on Rome (**545–752**). The terrified Romans prepare for an attack (545–57). That night, Hannibal rides around the walls of Rome in order to inspect the fortifications (558–73). The next day, Hannibal addresses his soldiers and promises them a speedy victory, but the Romans frustrate that hope by charging out of the city against the Carthaginians (574–604). Jupiter turns Hannibal away from the city for three days in a row, until he sends Juno down to compel him to abandon the siege (605–732). The Romans rejoice at their good fortune once they realize that Hannibal has, indeed, marched away for good (733–52).

Hannibal learns about the Palladium, the sacred statue of Minerva which guards Rome, from Dasius Altinius, an Italian from Arpi allied with the Carthaginians: he gives up hope of capturing the city and plunders the Temple of Feronia (**13.1–93**). Meanwhile, Fulvius takes control of Capua (**94–380**). Fulvius addresses his soldiers and urges them to punish Capua for allying with Carthage (94–110). The Romans capture the white hind of Capua, a sacred animal raised by

Capys himself, the founder of the city, and then Fulvius sacrifices the hind to Diana (111–37). The Rutulian Ti. Claudius Asellus defeats the Capuan Cerrinus Vibellius Taurea in single combat, chasing him right through the city of Capua itself (138–78). Amid the carnage, Fulvius attacks Numitor, Laurens, and Taburnus, three brothers who guard the gates of the city, striking Numitor with his spear (179–212); Virrius leads the Capuans out of the city against the Romans, including Calenus, who slays Veliternus and Marius before falling himself to Scipio, the future Africanus (213–43); Volesus kills Ascanius, decapitating him, and then the Capuans flee back to their city (244–55). That night, while the Capuans await their imminent demise, Virrius laments his fate before gathering together his fellow senators for one last banquet: Fides punishes the besieged Capuans for their faithlessness to the Romans by driving them to mass suicide (256–98). The next day, the Romans enter Capua and, seeing the terrible conditions with their own eyes, restrain themselves from putting the city to fire and the sword (299–325). Silius explains that it is Pan who, sent down by Jupiter, holds back the Romans from destroying Capua (326–47). Instead, the Romans despoil the captured city: Fulvius hails Milo for being the first to scale the walls of Capua and then rebukes the captive Taurea when he commits suicide right in front of him rather than be punished by the Romans (348–80). After the fall of Capua, Silius recounts the rise of Scipio (**381–895**). When he learns about the death of both his father and his uncle in Spain (381–99), Scipio decides to commune with the spirits of the dead in a traditional epic scene which combines a *nekyia* and a *katabasis*, and so he seeks out the Sibyl Autonoe for instructions on the proper sacrifice (400–48). After completing the necessary rites, Scipio encounters the shade of App. Claudius Pulcher, who had been mortally wounded during the siege of Capua, and promises him a proper burial (449–87), then Autonoe introduces Scipio to the shade of the Sibyl Deiphobe: Deiphobe utters a prophecy about Scipio's future victories in Spain and Africa, but also about his later exile from Rome, and reluctantly leads him on a tour of the Underworld, including an ecphrasis of the ten gates which surround it (488–614). Thereafter, Scipio converses with his mother, Pomponia, who tells him that Jupiter is, in fact, his real father (615–49), and with his father and uncle, P. and Cn. Cornelii Scipiones, who both encourage him to exercise more caution than they did (650–704), as well as with Paullus (705–20), before he receives a troubling vision of Rome's past and future, including Hamilcar, Alexander the Great, Homer, a catalog of famous Roman women, the civil wars, and Hannibal himself (721–895).

Silius digresses from the narrative about the rise and fall of Hannibal in order to recount the fall of Syracuse. After an invocation of the Muses, Silius begins with an ecphrasis on the geography of the island of Sicily (**14.1–78**), as well as a succinct account of the ongoing political turmoil in the city itself: when Hiero III died after a long and peaceful reign, he was succeeded by his teenage grandson, Hieronymus, who unleashed a reign of terror until he was assassinated, leaving the Syracusans to fight it out among themselves over whether they should ally with the Carthaginians, the Romans, or neither of the two (**79–109**). This is the situation in Syracuse and in Sicily when Marcellus arrives on the island and swiftly captures the city of Leontini en route to Syracuse (**110–77**): after landing with his fleet at Messana (110–24), Marcellus storms into battle, leading the Roman attack against Leontini (125–47); during the fighting, Asilus spares the life of Beryas when the two face off in single combat and Asilus recognizes his opponent as the same man who had set him free after he had been captured at the battle of Lake Trasimene (148–77). Thereafter, Marcellus proceeds to the siege of Syracuse (**178–688**). While the Roman general surrounds the city (178–91), Silius offers an extended catalog of the Sicilian cities allied with the Romans (192–257), as well as those allied with the Carthaginians, including Syracuse itself (258–91). As Marcellus leads the Roman attack, Archimedes, the famous mathematician, contrives a number of mechanical devices to defend his native city (292–352). Meanwhile, the Romans score a decisive victory over a fleet of reinforcements newly arrived from Carthage by using one of their own innovations, the boarding bridge (*corvus*), in order to transform the naval battle into a land battle: among many others, the Roman ship commanded by Corbulo destroys the Carthaginian ship commanded by Himilco (353–579). A debilitating plague strikes first the Romans and then the Carthaginians, delaying the ultimately inevitable fall of the city (580–617); nevertheless, Marcellus presses his advantage and takes control of Syracuse (618–40): he marvels at the wealth and opulence of the homes and temples, although he holds his men back from sacking the city, with Archimedes as the most notable casualty (641–88).

Silius returns to the narrative of the rise and fall of Hannibal and, more specifically, to the narrative of the rise of Scipio (**15.1–148**): after the death of his father and uncle, Scipio seeks to avenge them (1–17); he first receives a vision in which he chooses Virtus over Voluptas (18–128) and is then himself chosen by the Roman Senate to assume command of the forces in Spain after Jupiter sends an omen (129–48). Scipio sets out for Spain immediately and swiftly captures the city of New Carthage (**149–285**). After sailing to Tarraco (149–79), Scipio is visited in a dream by his father, who instructs him to attack New Carthage, and vows funeral games after his future victory (180–213). As Scipio and his right-hand man, C. Laelius, lay siege to New Carthage by land and sea (214–19), Silius offers a brief ecphrasis on the city's topography (220-9). Scipio leads the Roman attack against the Carthaginian garrison stationed there under the command of Aris and, taking advantage of the tides, takes control of New Carthage the same day (230-50): the next day, the Romans celebrate their victory, and Laelius praises Scipio for his continence when he returns a captured virgin unharmed to her betrothed, the ruler of a local tribe (251-85). Silius then shifts the scene briefly to the war in Greece (**286-319**). Meanwhile, back in Italy, Fabius captures Tarentum (**320-33**), but Marcellus is ambushed and killed by Hannibal in Apulia (**334-98**): Silius laments the premature death of such a great hero (334-42); Marcellus and his fellow consul T. Quinctius Crispinus make the ill-fated choice to scout out a nearby hill between the camps of the Roman and Carthaginian armies (343-60); caught in the ambush, Marcellus rushes to his own death after he watches his son fall (361-80); and Hannibal honors the fallen Marcellus with a massive funeral pyre and a laudatory funeral oration (381-98). In Spain, Scipio defeats Hannibal's brother Hasdrubal at Baecula (**399-492**): after the swift capture of New Carthage, Hasdrubal, Mago, and Hasdrubal Gisgo, the three Carthaginian commanders in the peninsula, scramble to unite their forces against Scipio (399-409); Scipio attacks Hasdrubal, the nearest of the three commanders to him, as he celebrates a rite in honor of the founding of Carthage (410-40); Scipio leads the charge against the Carthaginians, striking down Sabbura, the first named casualty of the battle (441-50); Laelius kills Gala, Alabis, and Draces, the last of whom he decapitates (451-70); and Hasdrubal flees from the battlefield, leaving behind his camp for the Romans to plunder (471-92). Following in the footsteps of Hannibal (**493-521**), Hasdrubal marches from Spain to the Alps (493-506) and on into Italy in order to join forces with his brother (507-21). Visited in a dream by the goddess Italia, the consul C. Claudius Nero races to the Metaurus River (**522-76**); meanwhile, back in Rome, the city braces for the worst (**577-90**). In the events leading up to the battle of the Metaurus River (**591-657**), Nero reaches his destination, where he joins forces with his fellow consul, M. Livius Salinator (591-600); Hasdrubal makes a vain attempt at fleeing during the night (601-25); and so, the next day, after the Roman cavalry track down the Carthaginians (626-34), Hasdrubal (635-51) and Nero (652-7) both address their soldiers. During the battle itself (**658-808**), Salinator leads the charge against the Carthaginians, striking down Nabis, who has just slain Sabellus (658-91); Hasdrubal kills Arabus as he despoils the body of Nabis (692-9); Canthus defeats Rutilus in single combat (700-10); Salinator kills Mosa, decapitating him (711-34); and, after Hasdrubal wounds Salinator with his spear (735-77), Nero slays Hasdrubal himself in single combat by decapitating him (778–808). On the day after the engagement, Nero returns to his own camp in triumph, parading Hasdrubal's head on a spear for Hannibal to see from his camp (**809–23**).

Punica 11–15, the third and final pentad of the epic, provides a narrative of the events of the Second Punic War from the battle of Cannae to the battle of the Metaurus River. Across this third phase of the poem, Silius describes the aftermath of the battle of Cannae, charts the shift from Hannibal to Scipio, and provides an expansive narrative of the battle of the Metaurus River. By continuing to manipulate the narrative pace, Silius emphasizes the structural and thematic significance of the Metaurus River. Put simply, whereas Silius slows the narrative down across books 1–10, he speeds it up across books 11–15 (indeed, for the rest of the poem), all in order to reflect the impending fall of the Carthaginians and their leader, the aging Hannibal, as well as the concomitant rise of the Romans and their leader, the youthful Scipio. Accordingly, across books 11 and 12, Silius recounts a series of sieges which mark successive stages in this transition from Carthage to Rome, from Hannibal to Scipio, beginning with Hannibal's triumph at Capua, as well as his brother Mago's triumph at Carthage, and continuing with Hannibal's repulse from Nola, followed by his repulse from Rome. Across books 13 and 14, Silius recounts another series of sieges which likewise mark subsequent stages in this fraught transition from one superpower to the other, beginning with the fall of Capua to Fulvius and concluding with the fall of Syracuse to Marcellus. All of these siege narratives look back to the siege of Saguntum across books 1–2, and the fall of each city reflects and refracts elements of the falls of every other city in the epic. In book 15, Silius elegantly underscores the growing tension between Scipio and Rome: on the one hand, Scipio makes his dashing entrance into the war and the narrative with his victories at New Carthage (essentially a battle instead of a siege, since he captures the city the same day on which he attacks it) and Baecula; on the other, the Roman forces under the consuls Nero and Salinator garner their own monumental victory to conclude the book. The battle of the Metaurus River represents not only the structural and thematic culmination of this trio of battles, but also an intriguing climax to the pentad: the single combat between Nero and Hasdrubal, which ends with the death and decapitation of the defeated Carthaginian, represents a deft manipulation of closure, even a plausible end to the war and the narrative, were it not for the fact that Scipio must continue the conflict until he avenges the death of his father and uncle. Throughout this third pentad, memories of conflicts before and after the Second Punic War continue to punctuate the narrative. Above all else, however, Silius transforms Scipio into a truly epic hero, especially through his visit to the Underworld in book 13 and his choice of Virtus over Voluptas in book 15.

3. *Punica* 16–17: From the Metaurus River to Zama

Broken by the defeat and the death of his brother, Hannibal retires to the lands of the Bruttii, where he languishes until he is finally recalled to Africa in order to defend Carthage against the Roman invasion led by Scipio (**16.1–22**). In Spain, Scipio defeats the remaining Carthaginian forces at Ilipa (**23–169**). He drives out Hannibal's brother Mago (23–7) and captures Hanno after a surprise attack on his camp (28–43), during which L. Cornelius Scipio Asiaticus defeats the Cantabrian Larus in single combat (44–77). When word arrives that Hasdrubal Gisgo is on the march to join forces with Hanno, Scipio addresses his soldiers and urges them to seize the opportunity (78–93), and then he leads them to a final victory in Spain (94–114): after the battle, Masinissa, later to become the first king of Numidia, receives a favorable omen during the night (115–34), and so, the next day, he ventures into the Roman camp in order to meet with Scipio and change sides (135–69). Scipio and Hasdrubal Gisgo both sail to the court of Syphax in Africa, where they strive to gain the king as an ally (**170–276**): Silius offers an ecphrasis on the king and describes the arrival of the competing delegations (170–83); Syphax warmly receives both parties and encourages them to make peace, before offering them hospitality (184–228); and, the next day, Scipio ventures into the palace in order to convince Syphax to join the Romans (229–61), but the sacrifice to confirm the alliance goes awry, a grim harbinger of things to come (262–76). Scipio returns to Spain, where he holds funeral games in honor of his dead father and uncle (**277–591**). Scipio is hailed as "king" (*rex*), but he rejects the title as un-Roman and instead announces that he will celebrate the promised funeral games in seven days' time (277–302); on the appointed day, Scipio offers a sacrifice to his father and uncle, after which the games begin (303–11). The four-horse team led by Panchates and driven by Hiberus wins the chariot race (312–456); Eurytus wins the foot race (457–526); during the gladiatorial fights, twin brothers kill each other in single combat (527–56); and, finally, Burnus wins the javelin throw (557–74). At the conclusion of the games, Scipio Asiaticus and Laelius honor the dead, and then Scipio honors them, hurling his spear as a tribute to his father and uncle: the spear takes root in the ground and instantly grows into a tall oak tree, a favorable omen for the future (575–91). Scipio returns to Rome (**592–700**): after Scipio enters the city in triumph and is elected consul for the purpose of destroying Carthage (592–9), Fabius addresses the Roman Senate in order to advise them against allowing Scipio to invade Africa as long as Hannibal remains in Italy (600–44); in reply, Scipio rebukes Fabius for his policy of delay, predicts that he will meet with success, and, in the end, convinces the Roman Senate to send him with his army on to Sicily (645–700).

P. Cornelius Scipio Nasica, son of Cn. Scipio and cousin of the future Africanus, welcomes the Magna Mater into Rome on behalf of the city in order to drive Hannibal out of Italy: when the ship carrying the image of the goddess comes to a sudden halt, Claudia Quinta takes the rope and leads the ship up the Tiber (**17.1–47**). Scipio sets out for Africa immediately and swiftly defeats Syphax and Hasdrubal Gisgo at Campi Magni (**48–148**): Scipio sails with his army from Sicily to Africa (48–58); Silius offers an ecphrasis on Sophonisba, the daughter of Hasdrubal Gisgo and (new) wife of Syphax (59–75); Scipio rebukes Syphax for changing sides from the Romans to the Carthaginians (76–84); and, after Scipio attacks the enemy camp in the middle of the night (85–108), Syphax is defeated and taken captive, as Hasdrubal Gisgo flees back to Africa (109–48). Envoys sail from Carthage to Hannibal in order to complete their mission of instructing him to return home (**149–200**): following a three-day journey (149–59), the envoys arrive in Italy to find Hannibal tormented by dream visions of the countless Romans who have perished in the war, including Flaminius, Gracchus, and Paullus (160–9); the envoys deliver an impassioned plea for assistance (170–83); and Hannibal reluctantly agrees to depart from Italy (184–200). Hannibal finally returns home to Africa (**201–90**): he looks back at Italy as the ships set sail (201–17), and, in a fit of anger and madness, orders his men to turn around (218–35), but Neptune raises a terrible storm in order to drive the fleet on to Africa until Venus intervenes to plead with him to lessen the intensity of the storm (236–90). In the events leading up to the battle of Zama (**291–384**), Hannibal and Scipio march to the battlefield (291), and then Hannibal addresses his soldiers (292–337), but Scipio is unable to address his soldiers because they instead demand the signal for battle (338–40). Meanwhile, Jupiter and Juno discuss the outcome of the impending engagement: Jupiter reminds Juno that the time has now come for the end of the war; in acknowledging that, Juno requests that Hannibal be allowed to evade capture and that the walls of Carthage be allowed to stand; and, in accepting those terms, Jupiter reminds Juno that Carthage will one day be destroyed and stipulates that Hannibal never return to Italy (341–84). During the battle itself (**385–624**), Silius offers an ecphrasis of Hannibal and Scipio as they lead their respective armies into the field (385–405);

fierce fighting rages on both sides (406–43); and Hannibal (444–78) and Scipio (479–508) each kill countless of the enemy. Scipio seeks out Hannibal for a single combat, but Juno lures away the Carthaginian by assuming the guise first of Scipio himself and then of a shepherd, leaving the rest of the Carthaginians to flee from the battlefield (509–96): ultimately, Hannibal flees from the battlefield, too, after one final address in which he proclaims his immortality for his victory at Cannae (597–617), while his native city opens its gates to Scipio (618–24). Scipio returns to Rome in triumph (625–54).

Punica 16–17, or, perhaps, originally 16–18, making it either the closing dyad or perhaps the closing triad of the epic, provides a narrative of the events of the Second Punic War from the battle of the Metaurus River to the battle of Zama. Across this closing phase of the poem, Silius describes the aftermath of the battle of the Metaurus River, continues to chart the ongoing shift from Hannibal to Scipio, and provides an expansive narrative of the battle of Zama. The pace of the action reflects the stark contrast between the fall of the Carthaginians under Hannibal and the rise of the Romans under Scipio. In book 16, Silius continues to underscore the growing tension between Scipio and Rome: while Hannibal languishes in southern Italy, Scipio enjoys victory in Spain at the battle of Ilipa, acquires Masinissa and Syphax as allies for his future war in Africa, and celebrates funeral games in honor of his father and uncle, after which he returns to Rome in triumph. In book 17 or, perhaps, originally across books 17 and 18, Silius recounts a series of battles which essentially function as sieges because they involve the destruction of the enemy fortifications and which therefore mark the final stages in the transition from Carthage to Rome, beginning with the battle of Campi Magni and concluding with the battle of Zama. Throughout this closing phase, Silius completes the transformation of the *Punica* as a narrative of the Second Punic War into a narrative of the entirety of Roman history and Roman culture. At the end of the epic, Scipio Africanus enters Carthage in triumph before returning to Rome in triumph in order to foreshadow the end of the Third Punic War, when his adoptive grandson Scipio Aemilianus likewise presides over the destruction of Carthage before returning to Rome in triumph, as well.

4. *Punica* 17.625–54: The (Beginning of the) End

625 mansuri compos decoris per saecula rector
devictae referens primus cognomina terrae
securus sceptri repetit per caerula Romam
et patria invehitur sublimi tecta triumpho.
ante Syphax feretro residens captiva premebat
630 lumina, et auratae servabant colla catenae.
hinc Hannon clarique genus Phoenissa iuventus
et Macetum primi atque incocti corpora Mauri,
tum Nomades notusque sacro, cum lustrat harenas,
Hammoni Garamas et semper naufraga Syrtis.
635 mox victas tendens Carthago ad sidera palmas
ibat et effigies orae iam lenis Hiberae,
terrarum finis Gades ac laudibus olim
terminus Herculeis Calpe Baetesque lavare
solis equos dulci consuetus fluminis unda,
640 frondosumque apicem subigens ad sidera mater
bellorum fera Pyrene nec mitis Hiberus,
cum simul illidit ponto, quos attulit, amnes.
sed non ulla magis mentesque oculosque tenebat,
quam visa Hannibalis campis fugientis imago.
645 ipse adstans curru atque auro decoratus et ostro
Martia praebebat spectanda Quiritibus ora,
qualis odoratis descendens Liber ab Indis
egit pampineos frenata tigride currus,
aut cum Phlegraeis confecta mole Gigantum
650 incessit campis tangens Tirynthius astra.
salve, invicte parens, non concessure Quirino
laudibus ac meritis, non concessure Camillo.
nec vero, cum te memorat de stirpe deorum,
prolem Tarpei, mentitur Roma, Tonantis.

625 The leader [Scipio], having gained an honor which would remain
throughout the ages, as the first to bear the name of a conquered land,
now secure in his possession of the scepter, returns to Rome by sea
and is carried past the buildings of his fatherland in a lofty triumph.
Before [Scipio] Syphax, borne on a litter, was holding down
630 his captive eyes, and golden chains rested upon his neck.
Here, Hanno and the Carthaginian youth, noble by birth,
and the chief men of the Macedonians and the black-skinned Moors,

A Reading of Punica 11–17: From Cannae to Zama   105

then, the Numidians and the Garamantes, known to sacred Hammon,
when they survey the desert sands, and the Syrtes, always causing shipwrecks.
635   Soon, Carthage went by, lifting her conquered hands
to the sky, and the image of the shore of Spain, now calm,
Gades, the end of the earth, and Calpe, once the limit
for the praises of Hercules and the Baetis [River], accustomed
to wash the horses of the Sun in its sweet stream,
640   and fierce Pyrene, mother of wars lifting up her leafy crown
to the sky and Ebro [River], not gentle, when it beats on the sea
at the same time with the rivers which it has brought down with it.
But, no image held their minds and their eyes more,
than the image seen of Hannibal fleeing from the field.
645   He himself [Scipio], standing in his chariot and adorned with gold and purple,
put his warlike face on display for the Quirites,
just as Liber, coming down from scented India,
drove his chariot wreathed in vine, with a tiger wearing the bridle,
or just as the Tirynthian [Hercules] did, when, after finishing off
650   the mass of Giants, he strode forth in the Phlegraean Fields, touching the stars.
Hail, unconquered father, one not about to yield to Quirinus
in praises and merits, one not about to yield to Camillus.
Nor indeed does Rome lie, when she recalls that you are
from the race of the gods, the offspring of Tarpeian Tonans [Jupiter].

In *Punica* 17.625–54, Silius describes Scipio's triumphal return to Rome after his victory in Africa much as he had described his return to the city after his victory in Spain (16.592–9).³ The repetition of *repetit* (16.594, 17.627) unmistakably signals the link between the two scenes, while, at the same time, prompting reflection on both the similarities and the differences between these two moments in the war and in the narrative: Scipio returns from Spain as "the avenger of his country and family" (*ultor patriaeque domusque*, 16.593); he returns from Africa, however, as a *rector* (17.625), i.e., almost a *rex*, who clearly aspires for more than vengeance. The passage here at the end of the epic can be divided into three major sections: first, Scipio enters Rome in triumph endowed with his new *cognomen* Africanus to commemorate his victory (17.625–8); then, Silius describes the triumphal procession from Syphax in chains to the image of Hannibal in flight (17.629–44); and, finally, Scipio takes center stage dressed in the gold and purple of the *imperator* (17.645–54). On an initial reading, the passage offers an appropriately triumphant conclusion to both the war and the narrative. On a closer reading, however, grounded in the often complex intratextual and intertextual resonances, the passage suggests that Scipio's return to the city marks not only the end of the Second Punic War but also the beginning of the next phase of Roman history and Roman culture, the fraught transition from Republic to Empire through the equally fraught transition from victory in foreign war to self-inflicted defeat in civil war. So, for example, scholars have long debated whether Scipio returns to Rome *securus sceptri* (17.627) as simply a triumphant Republican general or, perhaps, as a proto-Imperial autocrat.[4] Likewise, the *pompa* (parade) which begins with Syphax, enumerates all of the conquered lands and peoples of Spain and Africa, and ends with Hannibal includes a number of equally unsettling resonances with passages earlier in the poem. On the one hand, Silius uses the language of "necks in chains" to describe Syphax (*auratae servabant colla catenae*, 17.630) just as Varro had boasted in the Senate before the march to Cannae that he would lead Hannibal back to Rome "bound with a chain upon his neck" (*devinctum colla catena*, 8.276; cf. 9.634, 11.117), and just as Aris "gave his conquered neck to chains" when Scipio captured New Carthage (*victa catenis / ... colla dedit*, 15.246-7).[5] On the other hand, Silius elsewhere uses the language of "necks in chains" to describe not only the captive Cilnius (7.32, 72), but also the captive Regulus (4.359, 6.505), and so Syphax in chains here at Scipio's triumph may serve as a substitute for Hannibal and as a new Regulus. In the same vein, the image of Hannibal in flight more obviously serves as a substitute for the man himself and evokes the description of Hasdrubal's head on a spear after the battle of the Metaurus River (15.809-23). Here again, the language of "images" (*imagines*, also, more specifically, "ancestor masks") looks back to several earlier moments in the epic, from the image of Hannibal returning home to Carthage (*redeuntis imago*, 4.773) and that of his father, Hamilcar (2.431), to those of the shades in the Underworld (13.444, 604, 662, 736, 751, the final two also of Hamilcar), from those of Saguntum (1.632), Capua (11.115), and Italy (15.546) to the false image of Scipio himself, created by Juno, fleeing from the battlefield (*campo fugiens ... imago*, 17.538). Through this procession of *imagines* leading up to the image of Hannibal in flight, Silius transforms not only Scipio's triumph but also the Second Punic War and, indeed, the entire *Punica* into a parade of heroes, simultaneously a *triumphus* and a *funus* for the Republic.[6]

This parade of heroes culminates with Scipio himself entering the city and scaling the Capitol in triumph. The stark juxtaposition with the *imago* of Hannibal in flight emphasizes the absence of the Carthaginian, and yet several startling intratextual resonances suggest that, even in his absence, Hannibal partakes in the celebration. When Silius describes Scipio as *ipse adstans curru* (17.645) with his *Martia ... ora* (17.646), the poet recalls not only the simile in which he likens Scipio to Mars during the fighting at Zama (17.486–90), but also that in which he likens Hannibal to Mars during the fighting at Saguntum (1.433–6). Likewise, when Silius describes Scipio as *auro decoratus et ostro*, the poet recalls, among many other leaders in the epic, both Roman and Carthaginian, Hannibal and Scipio dressed in purple as they lead their troops into battle at Zama (17.385–405, esp. 391, 395). That said, when Scipio enters Rome dressed in gold and purple, the triumphator looks most like Voluptas when she appeared to him "shining in her dress, / in which she had suffused Tyrian purple with tawny gold" (*veste refulgens, / ostrum qua fulvo Tyrium suffuderat auro*, 15.24–5, the only other collocation of *ostrum* and *aurum* in the poem). In essence, Scipio appears to fulfill the threat uttered by Voluptas in 15.121–8 when she promised that her time would come before she stormed off. In the simile which follows, Silius likens Scipio to the two canonical examples of heroic apotheosis, Bacchus and Hercules. In particular, Silius likens Scipio to Hercules "touching the stars" (*tangens ... astra*, 17.650) after the Gigantomachy, but the vagueness of this unusual turn of phrase could be read as a reference either to divinization or to theomachy. Accordingly, although Bassett long ago claimed that "Scipio's triumphal procession to the Capitol is his apotheosis, similar to that of Hercules on Mt. Oeta," it is Regulus whom Silius likens to Hercules in his suffering and death (6.452–7; cf. 3.43–4).[7] Finally, in the apostrophe which closes both the book and the epic, Silius hails Scipio as *invicte parens* (17.651); as the third founder of Rome (a title elsewhere awarded to C. Marius: Plut. *Mar.* 27.5) after Quirinus, the deified Romulus, and M. Furius Camillus; and even as the son of Jupiter himself. The use of *invictus* again recalls Hercules, and, in his *Scipio*, Ennius (*ap.* Cic. *Orat.* 45.152) had already hailed his honorand as *Scipio invicte*.[8] Earlier in the *Punica*, in the apostrophe of the fallen Saguntines and Hannibal in 2.696–707 which closes the book, Silius had hailed Hannibal as "the formerly unconquered warrior" (*invictus quondam ... bellator*, 706) who would one day commit suicide by ingesting poison (see also 3.692–714, 13.868–95). This leaves the reader to ponder whether Scipio will likewise one day become merely *invictus quondam* or remain *invictus* forever like Hercules (1.512) and Jupiter (12.672). Indeed, Silius complicates the tone of the apostrophe and, in particular, Scipio's claim to divine paternity in the closing verses of the epic through a deft intertextual gesture. In the closing verses of book 8 of his epic, Lucan, saddened by the death of Pompey, consoles himself with the thought that, one day, people will not believe the Egyptians when they claim to know the site of Pompey's tomb, just as people do not believe the Cretans when they claim to know the site of Jupiter's tomb (8.869–72). Silius marks his engagement with Lucan through his use of *Tonantis* (*Pun.* 17.654 ~ 8.872, verse-final and book-final in both): the Cretan story about the tomb of Jupiter (and, therefore, his mortality) is obviously a lie, and so, too, perhaps, is the story about Scipio's divine paternity (*mentitur, Pun.* 17.654 ~ *mendax*, 8.872), especially given the potentially ironic force of *vero* (*OLD* s.v. 3b).[9] As a result, Silius manipulates the sense of closure for both the war and the narrative by ending the epic on a note of indeterminacy, and by prompting the reader to reflect on the relative validity of claims to divine paternity made by other Romans before, during, and (long) after Scipio.

5. Conclusion: The Narrative of the *Punica*

Reading the *Punica*, especially for the first time, can make for a very demanding experience, as Silius transforms his narrative of the Second Punic War into a narrative of the entirety of Roman history and Roman culture through a sustained engagement with the entirety of Roman literature. The epic's incipit, *ordior*, functions as a metaliterary gesture toward this construction, as well as deconstruction, of a totalizing vision of *Romanitas* because of its origin as a weaving term (*OLD* s.v. 1): the poet weaves together history and myth by weaving together historiography and epic in order to transcend the boundaries of space and time. The narrative threads which comprise the resulting text include the standard epic type scenes, such as invocations of the Muses; catalogs, especially troop catalogs; digressions and ecphrases; similes; and night and dawn scenes; as well as other recurring plot elements like dreams, oracles, and prophecies; divine scenes; and scenes between fathers and sons.[10] Above all else, however, the *Punica* recounts the events of the Second Punic War itself through scenes of travel and diplomacy; single and group combat, including aristeiai; theomachy; and triumph. Accordingly, the hexadic model which divides the epic into groups of siege books and battle books provides perhaps the clearest guidance for a reading, especially a first-time reading, of the narrative within and across its 17 (or 18) books:

siege	books 1–2	Saguntum	books 13–14	Capua > Syracuse
battle	books 3–6	Ticinus River	book 15	New Carthage
		Trebia River		Baecula
		Lake Trasimene		Metaurus River
battle	books 7–10	Cannae	book 16	Ilipa

siege	books 11–12	Capua > Carthage	book(s) 17[–18]	Carthage (Zama)
		Nola > Rome		Rome

This particular schematic interpretation of the structure of the *Punica* invites a number of general observations which, upon closer inspection, reveal a number of interesting phenomena in the narrative, all of which involve groups of four. The siege books come in groups of two (1–2, 11–12, 13–14, and, if the epic originally consisted of 18 books, 17[–18]); the battle books first come in groups of four (3–6, 7–10) and then in single books which parallel these groups of four (15, 16). Within the siege books, major siege narratives span two days, and most major cities fall twice, for a total of four days; within the battle books, most of the battle narratives span one day, and so the four battles across books 3–10 and those across books 15–16 each likewise span four days in total. The normative pattern for a two-day siege narrative includes three elements: day 1, the initial assault on the city; night 1, the situation in the city under siege; and day 2, the fall of the city. Silius establishes this normative pattern in his narrative of the siege of Saguntum (books 1–2) and develops it further in his later accounts of the sieges of Capua and Rome (books 11–12, 13–14, and 17[–18]) by introducing various innovations on the normative pattern along the way:

	Saguntum, part 1	Saguntum, part 2	Capua, part 1	Capua, part 2
Day 1	1.271–555	2.1–269	11.1–266	13.94–255
Night 1	1.556–75	2.270–390	11.267–368	13.256–98
Day 2	1.576–694	2.391–707	11.369–611	13.299–380

	Saguntum, part 1	Saguntum, part 2	Rome, part 1	Rome, part 2
Day 1	1.271–555	2.1–269	12.605–47	12.682–752
Night 1	1.556–75	2.270–390		
Day 2	1.576–694	2.391–707	12.648–81	17.625–54

The narrative of the siege of Saguntum follows the normative pattern, except for the scene in the Carthaginian Senate in 2.270–390 which marks the passage of time instead of a night scene like that inside Saguntum earlier in 1.556–75. The narrative of the siege of Capua likewise follows the normative pattern, except for the fact that the city falls first to the Carthaginians, in book 11, and then to the Romans, in book 13. The narrative of the siege of Rome, however, presents the reader with a conundrum, whether Scipio's triumphal entrance into Rome in book 17 represents an inversion or perhaps a continuation of Hannibal's assault on the city earlier in book 12. In a comparable way, the one-day battle narratives function as a structural and thematic complement to the two-day siege narratives: the narrative of the Ticinus River, the Trebia River, and Lake Trasimene (books 3–6) culminates in that of Cannae (books 7–10), while the narrative of New Carthage, Baecula, and the Metaurus River (book 15) culminates in that of Ilipa (book 16).

Above and beyond this division of the *Punica* into siege books and battle books, each individual book in the poem plays a unique role in the development of the narrative. Book 3, in particular, with its account of Hannibal's march from Spain to Italy, offers a structural and thematic synecdoche for the narrative arc of the epic as a whole, especially the constant interplay between the rise and fall of empires and the tension between speed and delay.[11] Read in this way, Hannibal's march from the Pyrenees to the Alps parallels the events from Saguntum to Rome:

Punica 3	*Punica*
3.415–41 (the Pyrenees)	1–2 (Saguntum)
3.442–65 (Rhône River)	3–6 (Ticinus River, Trebia River, Lake Trasimene)
3.466–76 (Durance River)	7–10 (Cannae)
3.477–556 (Alps, part 1)	11–12 (Capua > Rome)
3.557–629 (Venus and Jupiter)	
3.630–714 (Alps, part 2)	13–17[–18] (Capua > Rome)

Structurally, the mountain crossings parallel sieges, and the river crossings parallel battles, while the conversation on Mt. Olympus between Venus and Jupiter tropes not only the turning point in Hannibal's ascent and descent of the Alps, but also, by extension, his rise and fall in both the war and the narrative. Thematically, Hannibal conquers nature in the very same way that he defeats his enemies, until, that is, he encounters the Alps as a prefigurement of the walls of Italy, even of the walls of Rome (Liv. 21.35.9; see also 30.5, as well as Plb. 3.54.2).[12] As in the correlation outlined above between the number of days and the number of books for both the siege and the battle narratives, Silius appears to have a similar correlation between days and books in mind here. Whereas Polybius (3.53.6) and Livy (21.35.4) agree that Hannibal took nine days to ascend the Alps, Silius (3.554–6) asserts that the ascent took twelve days, just as it takes Hannibal twelve books to reach the walls of Rome. More broadly, Polybius (3.47–56, esp. 56.3) claims that the crossing of the Alps took fifteen days in total; while Livy (21.29–38) offers an account which adds up to eighteen days, he also refers to the fifteen days cited by Polybius (3.56.3) at 21.38.1. Perhaps Silius alludes to this debate in his manipulation of closure in books 15 and 18 of the epic. Above all else, after his slow ascent of the Alps, Hannibal makes a rapid descent of the mountain range which prefigures his rapid decline after his failed march on Rome. Book 3 even ends with an allusion to Hannibal's victory at Cannae and its guarantee of his immortality after death which anticipates his own words at the end of the poem (3.700–12 ~ 17.605–17). Accordingly, like several other books in the epic, including 7, 14, and 15, book 3 functions as a mini-epic in tension with the surrounding narrative and, as a result, continues the transformation of the Second Punic War into a totalizing vision of *Romanitas*, from Troy to Carthage to Rome.

5

Carthage and Rome in the *Punica*, Part 1

1. Introduction: Cities and Heroes

As a part of his complete transformation of the Second Punic War into a synecdoche for the essence of *Romanitas*, Silius also (re)configures his narrative as a broader meditation on the rise and fall of cities and heroes in general. At one level, the poet skillfully transforms the Second Punic War into a new Gigantomachy, a new Trojan War, and a new Gallic sack, among other archetypal conflicts; at another level, he likewise transforms the Carthaginians, Romans, and others who populate his narrative into new versions of the heroes, both human and divine, who participate in those earlier struggles.[1] By presenting his narrative as a story which transcends the boundary between myth and history, Silius capitalizes on the familiar homology between the hero(ine) and the city for which (s)he stands and falls. In the *Iliad*, Hector's death foreshadows the fall of Troy; in the *Aeneid*, Dido's death foreshadows the fall of Carthage; and, in the *Punica*, Murrus' death in single combat with Hannibal foreshadows the fall of Saguntum, culminating with the suicide of Murrus' wife, Tiburna, by his own sword upon his own tomb. In all of these instances, the fall of the hero(ine) predicates the fall of the city. Elsewhere in Roman culture, however, heroes have the opportunity to consign themselves, as well as the enemy, to the gods of the Underworld in a ritual self-sacrifice (i.e., a ritual suicide) called the *devotio* whose express purpose is not to destroy but to save the city by offering the willing hero as a substitute victim.[2] Accordingly, with the fall of each hero in the epic, Silius reintroduces the tension between linear and cyclical time, as well as that between progressive and regressive repetition, by prompting the reader to question whether a given hero's fall hastens or averts the fall of his city.[3] Hercules plays an especially important role in the *Punica* as the chief heroic exemplum, although a complex one: he is both the founder and the destroyer of cities; he is both a hero and a villain; he is both mortal and immortal. Most importantly of all, Hercules' death (i.e., suicide) by immolation atop Mt. Oeta offers a challenging example for any other would-be

Hercules seeking to triumph in death in order to triumph over death through apotheosis. Above and beyond Hercules, Jupiter serves as another, perhaps unexpected, heroic exemplum, although he is certainly a fitting one for would-be kings both inside and outside the world of the epic, especially in his defense of Mt. Olympus against all challengers. In many ways, therefore, single combat provides the thematic key to the *Punica*, as the warrior who remains standing ensures that his city will remain standing, while the warrior who falls tropes the fall of the city for which he fights; furthermore, according to this homology, the decapitation of the fallen warrior tropes the fall of the citadel of the city for which he dies. Accordingly, across the narrative arc of the poem, as cities and heroes rise and fall, from Saguntum to Capua and Syracuse, to Carthage and Rome, as part of the overall transition from Republic to Empire, from *bellum externum* to *bellum civile*, Silius invites the reader to consider carefully both the similarities and the differences among all of these various case studies. In the end, of course, every city will fall, even Rome, the *urbs aeterna*, and every hero will fall, too: ineluctable fate joins conqueror (*victor*) and conquered (*victus*) in death, uniting all cities and all heroes in the suicide of civil war, where, simultaneously victorious and defeated, all sides can lay claim, like Hercules, to the title of "unconquered" (*invictus*). As a broader meditation on the life and death of cities and heroes, the triumphalist narrative of the *Punica* ultimately subverts itself by collapsing the vanishing boundary between Rome and Carthage, Romans and Carthaginians.

At various key thematic points throughout the poem, Silius (re)casts the Hannibalic War as a new Gigantomachy, a new Trojan War, and a new Gallic sack, and the poet correspondingly (re)casts his characters as heroes who straddle the boundary between myth and history. In doing so, Silius strikes a delicate balance between linear and cyclical time, progressive and regressive repetition, in order to underscore both the similarities and the differences between the events of the Second Punic War and the various narrative archetypes. Like the Seven Against Thebes and the Epigoni, these archetypes recount a multigenerational conflict for universal power, whether over the actual cosmos itself or a representative city qua cosmos. The Titanomachy, the battle between the Titans and the Olympians, is followed by the Gigantomachy, the battle between the Olympians and the Giants, which becomes, especially in Latin literature, a metaphor for civil war; the first Trojan War, when the city under King Laomedon falls to Hercules, is followed by the second, and much more famous, Trojan War, when the city under King Priam falls again to Hercules in the form of his bow wielded by Philoctetes; and, last but certainly not least in the Roman imagination, the first Gallic sack of Rome (traditionally dated to 390 BC) is followed by the ever-present threat of the second and, according to the paradigm, final fall of the city. The countless images of the "captured city" (*urbs capta*) in Latin literature, especially those of the "city raped, pillaged, and plundered" (*urbs direpta*), reflect the power and pervasiveness of Roman fears about their (perceived) impending doom.[4] That said, Romans also recognized that it was the fall of Troy which led to the rise of Rome in the first place, and so they had reason to hope that a new Rome might one day rise again like a phoenix from the ashes of the fallen city.

In the *Punica*, Silius constructs his literary cities as reflections and refractions of these archetypal abodes, as well as of one other, in order to explore the many sides of the relationship between the fall of Carthage and the future fall of Rome.[5] Put simply, just as the fall of a hero tropes the fall of the city for which he fights, so, too, the fall of any given city tropes the fall of every other city in the epic. That said, the poet still preserves the individuality of each city while highlighting the universality of the overall theme. Saguntum plays the role of an *altera Troia* in the poem, and yet the fall of Saguntum differs markedly from either of the two falls of Troy. Rather than succumb to Hannibal, the Saguntines commit mass suicide, thereby transforming the event from an act of foreign war into an act of civil war; importantly, however, Silius reassures the Saguntines that they will one day have their revenge, when Hannibal joins them in the Underworld after committing suicide himself (2.696–707). The fact that both the Saguntines and Hannibal die by suicide "unconquered" (2.613 ~ 2.706) establishes a grim precedent for the falls of all of the other cities and heroes to come in the narrative, and we are left to grapple with the question whether any given fall later in the *Punica* hastens or averts the fall of the next domino. The rise and fall of cities motif figures most prominently in the three marches on Rome at the end of the three hexads which span books 1–6, 7–12, and 13–17[–18]. On the first two occasions, at the end of books 6 and 12, Silius incorporates elements of all three of the narrative archetypes into his two accounts of the repulse of Hannibal from the walls of Rome; on the third and final occasion, at the end of the epic, Silius again invokes all three archetypes in his description of Scipio ascending the Capitol in triumph (17.645–54). With Scipio as an *alter Hannibal*, these closing verses leave it an open question whether he is triumphing in or over Rome, whether he is marching into the city in order to celebrate his victory in *bellum externum* or against the city in order to put it on the path to self-inflicted defeat in *bellum internum*, perhaps even both.[6]

Cities need their heroes, of course, and, while Silius packs his narrative with a host of characters, it is Hercules who looms largest in the background (and, sometimes, the foreground) as the chief heroic exemplum.[7] Hannibal, Scipio, and the rest of the would-be heroes in the epic all aspire to play the role of *alter Hercules*, but Silius nicely complicates matters by stressing the fact that Hercules himself provides no stable exemplum: rather, across the great divide from myth to history, from epic to historiography, Hercules remains an often uncomfortably liminal figure who simultaneously transgresses and transcends (sometimes violently) the purported boundaries between good and evil, creation and destruction, and, in his suicide qua apotheosis, even life and death. On yet a higher plane, Hannibal, Scipio, and some (but, importantly, not all) of the other would-be heroes also aspire to play the role of *alter Jupiter* in an attempt at supplanting the king of gods and men himself by seizing the Temple of Jupiter Optimus Maximus on the Capitol in a new Gigantomachy. Indeed, given that both "Barca" (Hannibal's "*cognomen*") and "Scipio" (etymologically related to *sceptrum*) connect the two greatest heroes of the *Punica* with the god's "thunderbolt," it is only fitting that they should square off against each other for the right to take on Jupiter.[8] That said, scholars have generally focused on Hannibal and Scipio to the exclusion of the many other heroes in the epic, and, as a result, scholars have generally offered a distorted picture of the heroic landscape. For von Albrecht, the *Punica* is essentially an "Epos der Fides" in which Roman collective virtue ultimately triumphs over the individual virtue of Hannibal.[9] There are, however, many problems with this optimistic presentation of the poem as the victory of the Roman many over the Carthaginian one, including the fact that the goddess Fides herself suffers defeat at the hands of the Fury Tisiphone (i.e., *furor* ~ mass suicide ~ civil war) in the fall of Saguntum (2.474–707). Most scholars since von Albrecht have focused on Hannibal, Fabius, and Scipio as a heroic triad, identifying either Hannibal or Scipio as the overall hero (or even as the overall antihero) of the epic.[10] As I will argue below, I believe that Marcellus ought to figure much more prominently in any study of the hero in the *Punica* given his special status as the last to win the *spolia opima*. For now, I simply want to stress that Silius offers the reader far more to think about (and think with) than a focus on Hannibal, Fabius, and Scipio alone might suggest.

Even a cursory review of the major players in the *Punica* demonstrates just how crowded this heroic landscape is. Among the Carthaginians, Hamilcar and his son-in-law Hasdrubal set the stage for the rise of Hamilcar's three sons, Hannibal, Hasdrubal, and Mago, but we also have Hanno and Hasdrubal Gisgo, as well as the two Numidians Masinissa and Syphax. Among the Romans, Regulus, the city's greatest hero during the First Punic War, looms large throughout the epic, especially after the lengthy flashback in book 6 which recounts his rise and fall, and offers a challenging heroic exemplum for all subsequent generals seeking to distinguish themselves in the ongoing struggle with Carthage. Across the arc of the *Punica*, we encounter a host of would-be heroes who succeed and/or fail to imitate Regulus (and, therefore, by extension, Hercules) during the action of the Second Punic War, including Flaminius, Paullus, and Marcellus, all of whom fall in battle, as well as Fabius and, of course, Scipio.[11] To complete the picture, Silius also gives us a glimpse of Scipio Aemilianus, the city's greatest hero during the Third Punic War. Scholars have organized these heroes into various groups, especially into heroic triads much like those which we find in Sallust and Lucan; some scholars have also ventured suggestions about possible links with the Flavians.[12] More generally, Silius explores the tension between the one, whether it be Hannibal, Scipio, or any other would-be hero, and the many, i.e., Rome.[13] In a sense, Regulus is a singular hero who recalls the one-man rule of the Monarchy, while Scipio Aemilianus is another singular hero who recalls the one-man rule of the Empire: between these two poles, Silius explores the tension between one and two, the hallmark of the transition from the Monarchy to the Republic, as well as the transition from the Republic to the Empire, through the competition between Fabius and Scipio, among others, to serve the state as the one true *primus inter pares*, whether as *consul*, *dictator*, *imperator*, or perhaps *rex*.

Silius tropes the overall transition from two to one, from the two consuls of the Republic to the one *princeps* of the Empire, in the transition from Scipio's father and uncle to Scipio himself. When the two generals (usually, but not always, the consuls) fight against each other, the Romans lose, as at Cannae (Paullus and Varro); when, however, the two generals fight together against the enemy, the Romans win, as at the Metaurus River (Claudius Nero and Livius Salinator). Put differently, when the consuls work together, Rome enjoys success in foreign war; when, however, the consuls fail to work together, Rome suffers defeat in civil war.[14] Above all else, heroes must make their choices, whether it be Paris choosing Venus over Juno and Minerva, or Hercules choosing Virtue over Vice, or, in the *Punica*, Scipio likewise choosing Virtue over Vice (15.1–148). When faced with the choice between fight and flight, heroes face the choice between life and death, between glory and infamy. The rise and fall of heroes motif figures most prominently in the choices between fight and flight made first by Paullus and Varro at the battle of Cannae, and then by Hannibal and Scipio at the battle of Zama, at the end of the two enneads which span books 1–9 and 10–17[–18]. At Cannae, Paullus confronts Varro on the battlefield, rebukes him for his cowardice, and then plunges back into the fray to meet his fate in the following book in a *devotio* worthy of Hercules, while Varro pauses to muse about his own plight, considers suicide, and then decides to flee the engagement (9.632–57). Later at Zama, likewise faced with the prospect of defeat, Hannibal pauses to muse about his own plight before similarly deciding to flee the engagement, thus depriving Scipio of the opportunity either to kill or spare him (17.597–617). Meanwhile, Scipio takes control of Carthage and then returns back to Rome for his triumph, but it is unclear whether he scales the Capitol as a would-be Hercules offering himself up as a sacrifice in order to merit apotheosis, a Republican hero dying for Rome in *bellum externum*, or as a would-be Jupiter asserting his divinity against the king of gods and men, a new type of Imperial hero putting the city on the path to *bellum internum* (17.618–54).

In many ways, single combats like those between Jupiter and the rivals to his throne provide the thematic key to the *Punica* as a whole.[15] Throughout the ancient Near East and the ancient Mediterranean, archetypal heroes like Gilgamesh and Hercules ranged far and wide in the course of their various exploits, ostensibly to impose order upon chaos, but, in reality, often simply to leave a trail of death and destruction in their wake. The single combat between hero and monster instantiated the cosmic clash between the forces of light and darkness, and the victorious hero represented the enduring triumph of civilization over barbarity. In time, however, heroes turned from killing monsters to killing each other: single combat was no longer a simple matter of right versus wrong; instead, heroes found themselves in an ethical quandary, no longer so certain of the justness of their cause. After all, with few exceptions, conqueror and conquered alike ultimately suffered the same fate of death, and even those rare heroes who were fortunate enough to earn immortality generally suffered a traumatic death of some kind in order to cleanse themselves of their humanness. The horrific death of Hercules by suicide atop Mt. Oeta serves as a powerful reminder of the punishment which awaits all conquerors and also serves, in the hands of poets, as a potent metaphor for the suicide of civil war which destroys all conquering nations in the end. Like the single combats of Gilgamesh and Hercules, the single combats of the *Iliad*, the *Aeneid*, and even the *Punica* straddle the evanescent dividing line between myth and history, making single combat an especially fruitful homology for such cosmic dyads as love and hate, war and peace, and life and death. The Roman tradition of winning the *spolia opima*, when the commanding general slew his opposing general in single combat and then stripped his enemy of all his armor, well demonstrates the lasting legacy of single combat, and it certainly comes as no surprise that the only three Romans ever to garner this distinction were all semi-mythical, semi-historical heroes.[16]

Over time, however, single combat degraded into nothing more than a mere gladiatorial bout, a spectacle of war and even a dehumanizing form of entertainment, yet another transition which tropes the overall transition from Republic to Empire, from *bellum externum* to *bellum civile*.[17] Given that it was Augustus who limited eligibility for the *spolia opima* (and the triumph[18]) to members of the Imperial family, it is tempting once again to ponder what Silius may have intended by resurrecting these memories of Republican military prowess in the context of the Imperial reality. Across the arc of the poem, Silius makes single combat the organizing theme of the entire narrative: if Hannibal is defeated and decapitated, then the walls and citadel of Carthage will fall; if Scipio is defeated and decapitated, then Rome will fall, instead.[19] Time and again, the poet delays the climactic single combat, eventually postponing it altogether, in a sense, denying closure to the narrative, if not to the war itself.[20] Indeed, by putting off the long-anticipated climax, Silius transforms himself into a "Fabius Cunctator" of sorts. Just as Fabius practices his policy of *cunctatio* in order to delay the war, so, too, Silius practices his policy of *cunctatio* in order to delay the narrative. Ultimately, Fabius can only hinder, but not derail, the progress of the war; Silius can only hinder, but not derail, the progress of the narrative. In the end, since neither Hannibal nor Scipio falls in battle, both will be able to lay claim to the title of "unconquered" (2.706 ~ 17.651), and both will share in the victory, as well as in the defeat.

2. The Gigantomachy Theme

At one level, Silius transforms the Second Punic War into a new theomachy, a new Titanomachy, and, most specifically of all, a new Gigantomachy, by troping the transition from one generation of the gods to the next through the transition from Carthage to Rome, from Hannibal to Scipio, as well as through the transition from Republic to Empire, from foreign war to civil war.[21] The Gigantomachy was traditionally fought at Phlegra, an ancient name for the peninsula of Pallene, but the site of the battle was later moved to the similarly named Campi Phlegraei in Campania:[22] Silius capitalizes on this geographical shift in order to transfer the myth from the Greek to the Roman context, cast the Hannibalic War as a new Gigantomachy (e.g., 4.275-6, 5.434-56, 8.536-45, 8.648-55, 17.647-50), and even envision the Capitol as a new Mt. Olympus.[23] Accordingly, when Jupiter makes his formal entry into the war and the narrative during the first day of the siege of Saguntum, he does so as Jupiter Tonans, hurling his thunderbolt in order to drive Hannibal away from the walls of the city and give the Saguntines a brief respite (1.535–55):[24]

> 535 hic subitus scisso densa inter nubila caelo
> erupit quatiens terram fragor, et super ipsas
> bis pater intonuit geminato fulmine pugnas.
> inde inter nubes ventorum turbine caeco
> ultrix iniusti vibrauit lancea belli
> 540 ac femine adverso librata cuspide sedit.
> Tarpeiae rupes superisque habitabile saxum
> et vos, virginea lucentes semper in ara
> Laomedonteae, Troiana altaria, flammae,
> heu quantum vobis fallacis imagine teli
> 545 promisere dei! propius si pressa furenti
> hasta foret, clausae starent mortalibus Alpes
> nec, Thrasymenne, tuis nunc Allia cederet undis.
> sed Iuno adspectans Pyrenes vertice celsae
> nava rudimenta et primos in Marte calores
> 550 ut videt impressum coniecta cuspide vulnus,
> advolat obscura circumdata nube per auras
> et validam duris evellit ab ossibus hastam.
> ille tegit clipeo fusum per membra cruorem
> tardaque paulatim et dubio vestigia nisu
> 555 alternata trahens aversus ab aggere cedit.

> 535 Now, suddenly, after the sky had been torn apart among the dense clouds,
> a splitting crash burst out, shaking the earth, and, above the battles themselves,
> the father [of the gods] thundered forth with his twice repeated bolt.
> Then, among the clouds in a blinding storm of winds
> the avenging lance of an unjust war flashed
> 540 and landed with its well-aimed spear tip right in his [Hannibal's] thigh.
> O Tarpeian rocks and stone inhabited by the gods
> and you, Laomedontean flames, Trojan fires,
> always shining upon the virgin altar,
> alas, how much the gods have promised you by the image
> 545 of a false weapon! If the spear had been pressed deeper into the man
> as he raged, the Alps would stand closed to mortals,
> nor would the Allia [River] now yield to your waves, [Lake] Trasimene.
> But Juno, looking down from the top of the lofty Pyrenees
> upon their eager undertakings and their first sweaty exertions in war,

550 when she saw the wound inflicted by the spear tip which had been hurled,
    she flew through the breezes, surrounded by a dark cloud,
    and drew the sturdy spear out of his tough bones.
    He [Hannibal] covers the gore pouring over his limbs with his shield,
    and, dragging his sluggish steps one after the other, little by little,
555 with uncertain effort, he moves back away from the rampart.

After defeating Murrus in single combat, Hannibal is prevented from despoiling his fallen enemy by a furious Saguntine counterattack, but he does not yield until Jupiter himself strikes him in the thigh with a spear like a thunderbolt (535–40), prompting Juno to rush down from the Pyrenees in order to draw the weapon out of the wound (548–52) so that Hannibal can limp back to camp to end the day's fighting (553–5).[25] Silius heightens the drama of the scene by interrupting the narrative at the very moment when Jupiter strikes Hannibal in the thigh for an apostrophe in which he laments the fact that the spear did not kill him (541–7). Ironically enough, the counterfactual actually ends up lessening the drama by giving away the ending (Hannibal survives): more to the point, Silius here associates this mini-Gigantomachy with the fall of Troy (541–5) and the Gallic sack (545–7), the two other major themes treated in detail later in this chapter. After narrowly averting death at Saguntum, Hannibal figuratively piles mountain on top of mountain as he scales the Pyrenees (3.415–41), the Alps (3.477–556, 630–46), and the Apennines (4.739–62) in the course of his Gigantomachic march from Saguntum to Cannae.[26]

As the Carthaginians and the Romans close for battle at Cannae, Silius again transforms the moment into a new Gigantomachy by having the gods themselves join the fight (9.287–309):

   nec vero fati tam saevo in turbine solum
   terrarum fuit ille labor. discordia demens
   intravit caelo superosque ad bella coegit.
290 hinc Mavors, hinc Gradivum comitatus Apollo
   et domitor tumidi pugnat maris, hinc Venus amens,
   hinc Vesta et captae stimulatus caede Sagunti
   Amphitryoniades, pariter veneranda Cybele
   Indigetesque dei Faunusque satorque Quirinus
295 alternusque animae mutato Castore Pollux.
   contra cincta latus ferro Saturnia Iuno
   et Pallas, Libycis Tritonidos edita lymphis,
   ac patrius flexis per tempora cornibus Hammon
   multaque praeterea divorum turba minorum.

300   quorum ubi mole simul venientum et gressibus alma
      intremuit tellus, pars implevere propinquos
      divisi montes, pars sedem nube sub alta
      ceperunt: vacuo descensum ad proelia caelo.
      tollitur immensus deserta ad sidera clamor,
305   Phlegraeis quantas effudit ad aethera voces
      terrigena in campis exercitus, aut sator aevi
      quanta Cyclopas nova fulmina voce poposcit
      Iuppiter, exstructis vidit cum montibus ire
      magnanimos raptum caelestia regna gigantas.

Nor indeed in such a savage storm of fate
was that struggle limited to the earth. Crazed discord
entered heaven and drove the gods to war.
290   Here, Mars fights, there, Apollo, accompanying him,
      and the master of the swollen sea [Neptune], here, Venus frantic,
      there, Vesta and the descendant of Amphitryon [Hercules], spurred on
      by the slaughter of captured Saguntum, along with venerable Cybele
      and the native gods of Italy and Faunus and father Quirinus
295   and Pollux, taking his turn at life from his brother, Castor.
      On the other side, Saturnian Juno, girt with a sword at her side,
      and Pallas, born from the Libyan waters of [Lake] Tritonis,
      and the native god Hammon with his horns curving around his temples
      and a great crowd of lesser gods, in addition.
300   When the nourishing earth rumbled at the weight and movement of
         them all
      coming at the same time, some of them divided up and filled
      the neighboring mountains, while others took their seat
      beneath a lofty cloud: the descent for battle left the sky empty.
      An immense shout was raised to the deserted stars,
305   voices as loud as those which the earthborn force poured out
      to the heavens in the Phlegraean Fields, or in a voice as loud as that
      in which the father of the universe, Jupiter, demanded new thunderbolts
      from the Cyclopes, when he saw the arrogant Giants go to seize
      the kingdom of heaven by piling mountain upon mountain.

At Lake Trasimene, the gods, apart from Juno, had turned their faces away from the fighting in sadness and grief (5.201–7); here at Cannae, however, they eagerly enter the fray (287–9): on the one side, Mars, Apollo, Neptune, Venus, Vesta, Hercules, Cybele, Faunus, Quirinus, and Castor and Pollux fight on behalf of the Romans (290–5); on the other side, Juno, Pallas, and Jupiter Ammon fight on behalf of the

Carthaginians (296–9). Silius vividly describes how the gods descend from the heavens (300–3), as well as how the mortal combatants raise a shout up to the heavens which rivals the loudness of the shouts raised both by the Giants and by Jupiter during the Gigantomachy (304–9). The simile at the end of the passage tropes the comparison between the Second Punic War and the Gigantomachy and, more specifically, foreshadows the single combat between Hannibal and Scipio which morphs into a single combat between Pallas and Mars in 9.411–555. After the long delay following his victory at Cannae, Hannibal brings his new Gigantomachy to its climax when he finally marches on Rome in order to sack the Capitol.

From the very beginning of both the war and the narrative, Silius identifies three stages in Hannibal's march on Rome, from scaling the Alps to scaling the walls of the city to scaling the Capitoline Hill (1.63–9, 134–9, 268–70). After his resounding victory at Lake Trasimene, Hannibal makes an initial abortive attempt at marching on Rome, but Jupiter himself, looking down from the Alban Mount, hurls his thunderbolt four times in order to turn Hannibal away from the city (6.600–18). After the winter in Capua, Hannibal resumes his Gigantomachy by visiting the Campi Phlegraei during the (ultimately unsuccessful) siege of Puteoli (12.108–60). This moment foreshadows not only the long-delayed march on Rome at the end of the book, but also Hannibal's ultimate failure: instead, Jupiter turns Hannibal away from the city for three days in a row, until he sends Juno down to compel him to abandon the siege (12.605–732). Fittingly, Silius transforms the climax of this new Gigantomachy into a complex reminiscence of another Gigantomachy, at the fall of Troy recounted by Aeneas (12.701–32 ~ Verg. *Aen.* 2.559–633):[27]

```
         his dictis grates agit ac turbata per auras
         devolat et prensa iuvenis Saturnia dextra
         "quo ruis, o vecors, maioraque bella capessis
         mortali quam ferre datum?" Iuno inquit et atram
705      dimovit nubem veroque apparuit ore.
         "non tibi cum Phrygio res Laurentive colono.
         en, age (namque oculis amota nube parumper
         cernere cuncta dabo) surgit qua celsus ad auras,
         adspice, montis apex, vocitata Palatia regi
710      Parrhasio plena tenet et resonante pharetra
         intenditque arcum et pugnas meditatur Apollo.
         at qua vicinis tollit se collibus altae
         molis Aventinus, viden ut Latonia virgo
         accensas quatiat Phlegethontis gurgite taedas
```

715   exsertos avide pugnae nudata lacertos?
       parte alia cerne, ut saevis Gradivus in armis
       implerit dictum proprio de nomine campum.
       hinc Ianus movet arma manu, movet inde Quirinus,
       quisque suo de colle deus. sed enim adspice, quantus
720   aegida commoveat nimbos flammasque vomentem
       Iuppiter et quantis pascat ferus ignibus iras.
       huc vultus flecte atque aude spectare Tonantem:
       quas hiemes, quantos concusso vertice cernis
       sub nutu tonitrus! oculis qui fulgurat ignis!
725   cede deis tandem et Titania desine bella."
       sic affata virum indocilem pacisque modique,
       mirantem superum vultus et flammea membra,
       abstrahit ac pacem terris caeloque reponit.
       respectans abit et castris avulsa moveri
730   signa iubet ductor remeaturumque minatur.
       redditur extemplo flagrantior aethere lampas,
       et tremula infuso resplendent caerula Phoebo.

After these words had been spoken, Saturnia [Juno] gives thanks and, troubled,
flies down through the breezes, and, having taken hold of the youth's right hand,
Juno says, "Where are you rushing to, o madman, and do you take up wars
greater than it has been granted to a mortal to bear?" And she moved away
705   the black cloud, and she revealed herself in her true form.
"Your business is not with a Phrygian [Trojan] or a Laurentian [Italian] colonist.
Behold, there (for, having removed the cloud from your eyes, for a little while
I will allow you to see everything), where the peak of the mountain rises
high toward the breezes, look, Apollo holds the Palatine, so called
710   by the Parrhasian king [Evander], with a full and rattling quiver,
and he stretches his bow, and he prepares for battle.
But, where the Aventine raises itself up to the lofty height
of the neighboring hills, do you see how the virgin Latonia [Diana]
brandishes the torches kindled in the stream of Phlegethon,
715   she naked with her outstretched arms in her eagerness for battle?
In another part, look how Gradivus [Mars] has filled the field
called after his own name [Campus Martius] with his fierce weapons.

>   From one side, Janus makes his move, from the other side, Quirinus does, too,
>   each god from his own hill [Janiculan and Quirinal]. But indeed, look,
> 720   how great Jupiter shakes the aegis as it spews forth storms and flames,
>   and with what great fires the savage god feeds his anger.
>   Turn your face in this direction and dare to look upon the Thunderer:
>   what snows, how great the thunderbolts you see when the heavens
>   ring out at his nod! What fire flashes in his eyes!
> 725   Yield to the gods at last and cease the Titanic wars [Gigantomachy]."
>   Thus having spoken she dragged the man away, unskilled
>   in peace and moderation, admiring the faces of the gods
>   and their flaming limbs, and she restored peace to earth and to heaven.
>   Looking back, he goes away, and the leader orders that the standards
> 730   be taken away from the camp, and he threatens that he will come back.
>   All of a sudden, the sun returns, burning even brighter in heaven,
>   and the blue skies sparkle with the pouring in of Phoebus.

Ordered by Jupiter to turn Hannibal away from Rome, Juno rushes down from Mt. Olympus, takes Hannibal by the hand, and calls upon him to abandon his Gigantomachy (701–5). Juno impresses this point upon Hannibal by granting him a vision of the gods themselves fighting on behalf of Rome, including Apollo, Diana, Mars, Janus, Quirinus, and, of course, Jupiter Tonans (706–28). Hannibal reluctantly orders his men to abandon the siege, and, as he departs, Jupiter signals his final victory in this new Gigantomachy by clearing away his storm clouds (729–32). Scholars have long recognized that, in this passage, Silius recalls a similar scene from the fall of Troy in *Aeneid* 2, when Venus likewise tries to bring Aeneas to his senses (2.559–633): however, whereas Hannibal stands outside the walls of Rome trying in vain to attack his enemy city when Juno appears to him in order to show him how the gods strive to save it, Aeneas stands inside the walls of Troy trying in vain to defend his own city when Venus appears to him in order to show him how the gods (here, Neptune, Juno, Pallas, and Jupiter) strive to destroy it. Silius calls the reader's attention to this replay of Troy at Rome through a number of intertextual resonances: Venus and Juno "take" Aeneas and Hannibal, respectively, "by the hand" (*dextraque prehensum, Aen.* 2.592 ~ *prensa iuvenis ... dextra, Pun.* 12.702); both goddesses call their mortal heroes back from their reckless battle fury (*quid furis, Aen.* 2.595 ~ *quo ruis, Pun.* 12.703); and both deities also call on their warriors to "look" when they reveal the gods fighting all around them (*aspice, Aen.* 2.604; *respice,* 2.615 ~ *adspice, Pun.* 12.709, 719). Most of all, just as Venus warns Aeneas to yield to the gods and not mistake them for a mortal foe like Helen or Paris, so, too, Juno warns Hannibal (in a clever intertextual gesture) to yield to the gods and not mistake them for a mortal foe like Aeneas (*non tibi* ..., *Aen.* 2.601 ~ *non tibi* ..., *Pun.* 12.706). Altogether, these intertextual resonances transform Hannibal's assault on Rome not only into a new Gigantomachy, but also, more specifically, into a new Gigantomachy which itself "looks back" to a similar moment at Troy.

3. The Fall of Troy Theme

At another level, Silius transforms the Second Punic War into a new Trojan War, as the fall of each city in the epic, from Saguntum to Rome, tropes the fall of Troy.[28] While neither Homeric poem includes a narrative of the second and final fall of Troy, they both incorporate references to the event into their narratives of the war before and after this climactic moment. In particular, the single combat between Achilles and Hector functions as a homology for the entire conflict, and the fall of Hector accordingly foreshadows the future fall of Troy. Above and beyond the *Iliad* and the *Odyssey*, the Epic Cycle, although only extant in fragments and summaries, provided a fuller narrative of the war from beginning to end, including a two-book epic on the fall of Troy called the *Iliou persis*.[29] Vergil looks back to the *Iliou persis* in his narrative of the fall of Troy which fittingly concludes in book 2 of the *Aeneid*, and Silius likewise looks back to Vergil and, through him, to the *Iliou persis* in his narrative of the fall of Saguntum which concludes in book 2 of the *Punica*, thereby transforming Saguntum into an *altera Troia*, a model for all other cities in the epic, as well as, more specifically, a proleptic *altera Roma* (1.339–40, 384–6, 389–90, 479).[30] This transformation of Saguntum into a new Troy likewise transforms the single combat between Hannibal and Murrus in 1.376–555 into a new iteration of the single combat between Achilles and Hector. Silius confirms the connection through a complex intertextual gesture when he has Hannibal hail Murrus as *Romani Murrus belli mora* ("Murrus, the delay of the Roman war," 1.479). The name "Murrus" effectively equals *murus* ("wall"), and the phrase *belli mora* also appears elsewhere as a description of none other than Hector (Arbon. fr. 2 ap. Sen. *suas.* 2.19–20: the name "Hector" itself means "he who stays [the battle]"), and, interestingly, of the triumvir Crassus, *sola futuri / ... belli medius mora* ("in the middle, the only delay of the future war [between Caesar and Pompey]," Lucan. 1.99–100).[31] At the climax of their single combat, Hannibal and Murrus both utter a prayer to Hercules, Murrus to Hercules as the founder and preserver of cities, Hannibal to Hercules as the sacker and destroyer of cities (1.502–17):[32]

> conclamant utrimque acies, ceu tota Saguntos
> igne micet. trahit instanti languentia leto
> membra pavens Murrus supremaque vota capessit:
> 505 "conditor Alcide, cuius vestigia sacra
> incolimus terra, minitantem averte procellam,
> si tua non segni defenso moenia dextra."
> dumque orat caeloque attollit lumina supplex –
> "cerne," ait "an nostris longe Tirynthius ausis
> 510 iustius affuerit. ni displicet aemula virtus,
> haud me dissimilem, Alcide, primoribus annis
> agnosces, invicte, tuis. fer numen amicum
> et, Troiae quondam primis memorate ruinis,
> dexter ades Phrygiae delenti stirpis alumnos."
> 515 sic Poenus pressumque ira simul exigit ensem,
> qua capuli statuere morae, teloque relato
> horrida labentis perfunditur arma cruore.

> The battle lines raise a shout on both sides, as if all of Saguntum
> were ablaze with fire. In fear, Murrus drags his sluggish limbs,
> with death looming, and he begins to utter his final prayers:
> 505 "Founder Alcides, whose tracks we inhabit
> in this sacred land, turn away the threatening storm cloud,
> if I defend your walls with a right hand not slow to act."
> And while he prays and lifts his eyes up to heaven in supplication –
> he [Hannibal] says, "Consider whether the Tirynthian will not far more justly
> 510 give support to our bold ventures. Unless rival valor be displeasing,
> you will recognize me, Alcides, as one little different from yourself
> in your earliest years, unconquered one. Bring your divinity to my aid,
> and, as one remembered for the first fall of Troy long ago,
> be propitious and give support to me as I destroy the sons of the Phrygian stock."
> 515 Thus the Carthaginian [speaks], and, at the same time, he drives home the sword,
> pressed in by wrath, until the hilt caused it to stop, and, after the weapon had been
> drawn out, the dread armor is drenched with the gore of the dying man.

Both the Carthaginians and the Saguntines raise a shout as if the city of Saguntum itself were about to fall, albeit for different reasons, when they see Murrus, on the verge of losing his single combat with Hannibal, pray to Hercules to help him save both himself and his city (502–7). Hannibal likewise prays to Hercules to help him destroy Murrus and Saguntum, and then slays his enemy, sealing the city's fate (508–17). In his prayer to Hercules, Murrus hails the god as *conditor* (505), both the canonical founder of cities and, specifically, the founder of Saguntum (1.273–95), and then he links his fate with the fate of his city's *moenia* (507). In his prayer, Hannibal hails the god as *invicte* (512), famous for his sack of Troy (*Troiae quondam primis memorate ruinis*, 513), and calls upon him to recognize him for his *aemula virtus* (510), for his desire to replay the fall of Troy in the fall of Saguntum and, ultimately, the fall of Rome. By having both warriors address Hercules as *Alcide* (505 ~ 511), Silius emphasizes the god's status as both creator and destroyer, an irresolvable paradox. Ultimately, Hercules presides over the fall of Murrus and, later, Saguntum, just as he had presided over its foundation (2.457–707).

When Silius transforms Hannibal's departure from Saguntum into a replay of Aeneas' departure from Troy (*postquam, Pun.* 3.1 ~ *postquam,* Verg. *Aen.* 3.1), the equation between the two cities becomes complete.[33] After the fall of Saguntum, Hannibal marches from Spain to Italy in order to replay the fall of Troy a second time in the fall of Rome, but his long-delayed march on the city ultimately fails when Jupiter himself turns Hannibal away from its walls. Instead, Silius transforms Hannibal's retreat into a complex reminiscence of another moment at the fall of Troy as recounted by Aeneas, the Greek flight to Tenedos (12.733–52 ~ Verg. *Aen.* 2.1–249):[34]

```
         at procul e muris videre ut signa revelli
         Aeneadae versumque ducem, tacita ora vicissim
735      ostentant nutuque docent, quod credere magno
         non audent haerente metu; nec abire volentis,
         sed fraudem insidiasque putant et Punica corda,
         ac tacitae natis infigunt oscula matres,
         donec procedens oculis sese abstulit agmen
740      suspectosque dolos dempto terrore resolvit.
         tum vero passim sacra in Capitolia pergunt
         inque vicem amplexi permixta voce triumphum
         Tarpeii clamant Iovis ac delubra coronant.
         iamque omnes pandunt portas. ruit undique laetum
745      non sperata petens dudum sibi gaudia vulgus.
```

>   hi spectant, quo fixa loco tentoria regis
>   adstiterint, hi, qua celsus de sede vocatas
>   affatus fuerit turmas, ubi belliger Astur
>   atque ubi atrox Garamas saevusque tetenderit Hammon.
> 750 corpora nunc viva sparguntur gurgitis unda,
>   nunc Anienicolis statuunt altaria nymphis.
>   tum festam repetunt lustratis moenibus urbem.

> But, when from their walls the Aeneadae saw the standards
> being taken up and the leader [Hannibal] turning to leave, in turn they exchange
> 735 silent glances, and with a nod they relate something which they did not dare
> to believe while the great fear remained; they believe that he is not going away
> willingly, but that it is a fraud and a plot and Punic perfidy,
> and, staying silent, mothers plant kisses on their children,
> until the army, marching forth, went away before their eyes
> 740 and, taking away their fear, released them from their suspicions of treachery.
> Then, truly, they flock from every quarter to the sacred Capitol,
> and, embracing one other in turn, they proclaim with mixed voices
> the triumph of Tarpeian Jupiter and deck the shrines with garlands.
> And now they open all of the city gates. The happy people rush around
> 745 from every quarter, seeking pleasures they had not hoped to enjoy.
> Some look, where the king's [Hannibal's] tent stood fixed in the ground,
> while others look, where, seated on his lofty throne, he called together
> his squadrons and addressed them, where the warlike Asturian and where
> the savage Garamantian and where the fierce Ammonian pitched their tents.
> 750 Now, they sprinkle their bodies with the running water of a stream,
> now, they set up altars for the nymphs who dwell in the Anio [River].
> Then, having purified their walls, they return to their festive city.

At first, the cautious Romans, fearing Punic treachery, cannot believe their eyes as they watch Hannibal lift the siege and recede into the distance: only when they see his army follow suit do they realize that they are truly free; in their unbounded joy, they rush to the Temple of Capitoline Jupiter in a throng and celebrate their triumph (733–43). Then, opening up their own city gates, they emerge from within their walls in order to explore the battlefield and perform a lustration; having completed these duties, the Romans reenter the city and resume the festivities (744–52). As above, scholars have long recognized that, in this passage, Silius recalls a similar scene from the fall of Troy in *Aeneid* 2, when the Greeks likewise depart from Troy, ostensibly for home, but, in reality, for the nearby island of Tenedos, and leave behind the Trojan Horse (2.1–249). While the Greeks return to sack Troy after the Trojans unwisely bring the Trojan Horse into their city, Hannibal will not, in fact, see Rome ever again. And yet, in another deft manipulation of closure, Silius appears to suggest that the city may still be poised to fall, as the closing verses of *Punica* 12 recall the closing verses of the Vergilian intertext, lines which describe the celebration at Troy on the night before its fall: *nos delubra deum miseri, quibus ultimus esset / ille dies, festa velamus fronde per urbem* ("We, however, wretched, for whom that day would be our last, / cover the shrines of the gods with festive garlands throughout the city," Verg. *Aen.* 2.248–9). Through the echo of *festa . . . fronde per urbem* (2.249) in *festam . . . urbem* (12.752), Silius links the fates of Troy and Rome. In addition, he recalls his only other use of the collocation *festa . . . urbs* in the entire *Punica*, in the description of Hannibal's triumph earlier at Capua: *instituunt de more epulas festamque per urbem / regifice exstructis celebrant convivia mensis* ("They set up a banquet according to their custom, and, throughout the festive city, / they celebrate a feast with tables piled high fit for a king," 11.270–1). Given that Capua falls not long after this triumph, Silius appears to suggest that Rome may actually have been better off with *Hannibal ad portas*.

Just as Silius uses the transition from book 2 to 3 in order to complete the transformation of Saguntum into an *altera Troia*, so, too, he uses that from book 12 to 13, as well as a long delay between books 12 and 17, in order to do the same for Rome. While the narrative of the march on Rome in book 12 does not include a new Trojan Horse, Silius does not simply omit this essential feature of the fall of Troy narrative. On the one hand, book 13 opens with Hannibal looking back at Rome as he reluctantly retreats, already planning his return to the city, until he learns about the Palladium (13.1–93). This cult image of Pallas Athena (~ Minerva) protected Troy from capture until Odysseus and Diomedes stole it so that the Greeks could take the city; after the Trojan War, Diomedes brought the Palladium with him to Italy, where he returned it to Aeneas: ultimately, the cult image was installed inside the Temple of Vesta in the Roman Forum, where it likewise guarded Rome from capture. On the other hand, book 17 opens with the Romans welcoming the cult image of the Magna Mater into Rome in order to drive Hannibal out of Italy once and for all (17.1–47). This cult image was brought in from Pessinus, not far from Troy, and installed in the Temple of Victory on the Palatine after an oracle was discovered in the Sibylline Books which declared that, if a foreign enemy had invaded Italy and the Romans wanted to drive him out of the peninsula, they should import the goddess. Livy 29.10.4–11.8, 14.5–14 provides the most complete narrative, and Ovid provides an equally important account in *Fasti* 4.247–348: Silius makes use of both authors, but he also innovates on the existing tradition by transforming the cult image of the Magna Mater into something of an anti-Palladium, even a new Trojan Horse. First and foremost, Silius links together the cult images of Pallas Athena and the Magna Mater through the repetition of the loaded adjective *Laomedonteus* (13.55 ~ 17.4), suggesting that the Romans will ultimately not be able to escape their Trojan past. Both cult images are essentially brought from Troy to Rome: however, whereas the Palladium must be taken out of Rome for the city to fall, Silius appears to suggest that, by bringing in the cult image of the Magna Mater, the Romans may have paradoxically freed themselves from Hannibal *and* put themselves on the path to (self-)destruction. In his description of the entrance of the cult image of the Magna Mater into Rome, Silius draws on the description of the entrance of the Trojan Horse into Troy, turning the ship on which the cult image travels into another wooden horse and, at the same time, turning the wooden horse itself into a ship (*Pun.* 17.13–25 ~ *Aen.* 2.234–49): both vessels even come to the same ominous "stop" before entering the city (*substitit, Pun.* 17.24 ~ *substitit, Aen.* 2.243, both verse-initial). As the Magna Mater makes her grand entrance, she is accompanied by her eunuch priests called *galli*, whose name suggests not only a possible Mesopotamian origin (cf. *gala* in Sumerian and *kalû* in Akkadian), but also, more immediately, another band of *Galli*, the Gauls.

4. The Gallic Sack Theme

At still another level, Silius transforms the Second Punic War into a new Gallic War and, more specifically, into a replay of the Gallic sack of 390 BC.[35] For centuries, the Romans and Gauls waged intermittent war with each other, from the Gallic victories at the battles of the Cremera River (traditionally, July 18, 477 BC), when all but one male member of the *gens Fabia* fell in combat, and the Allia River (traditionally, July 18, 390 BC), when the Gauls marched on Rome and took control of the city, if not of the Capitol itself, to the later Roman victory at the battle of Clastidium (222 BC), when Marcellus slew the Gallic king Viridomarus in single combat, one of many (semi-)legendary engagements between Roman and Gallic heroes. Throughout the epic, Silius recalls these and other moments from their various conflicts, but he dwells most of all on the events of 390, not only on how the Gallic Senones under the command of Brennus invaded Italy and how they scored an easy victory over the Romans in battle and just as easily captured their city, but also on how the Romans paid a ransom in gold for the Gauls to leave and how the disgraced general M. Furius Camillus returned from exile in time to halt the payment and avenge the loss by annihilating the Gauls. Silius transforms Hannibal's march over the Alps, his victory at Cannae, and his long-delayed march on Rome into a new, if significantly different, version of the Gallic march over the Alps, their victory at the Allia River, and their immediate march on the city, especially as recounted most famously in Livy 5.32–55. Later, in his analysis of the battle of Cannae at 22.50.1–3, Livy explicitly compares and contrasts Cannae with the Allia River, and he implicitly suggests a number of other significant similarities and differences. Silius follows suit: besides directly comparing Lake Trasimene (1.547, 6.555–6) and Cannae (8.647) to the Allia River, the poet transforms much of the action in books 1–12 into a replay of earlier conflicts with the Gauls and, in particular, the march on Rome in book 12 into a replay of the events of 390.

Hannibal himself invokes the memory of the Gallic sack in his rebuke of the Roman embassy on the shores of Spain near Saguntum during the early stages of the siege (2.25–35):[36]

25	hic alto Poenus fundentem vela carinam
	incessens dextra: "nostrum, pro Iuppiter!" inquit
	"nostrum ferre caput parat illa per aequora puppis.
	heu caecae mentes tumefactaque corda secundis!
	armatum Hannibalem poenae petit impia tellus!
30	ne deposce, adero; dabitur tibi copia nostri
	ante exspectatum, portisque focisque timebis,
	quae nunc externos defendis, Roma, penates.
	Tarpeios iterum scopulos praeruptaque saxa
	scandatis licet et celsam migretis in arcem,
35	nullo iam capti vitam pensabitis auro."
25	Here, the Phoenician [Hannibal], shaking his right hand at the ship as it spreads out its sails upon the deep, said: "By Jupiter! That ship prepares to carry my very head across the seas. Alas, minds blinded by and hearts swollen with successes! That impious land seeks Hannibal, armed, for punishment!
30	Do not bother with your demands, I will be there; you will have plenty of me to deal with before you know it, and you will fear for your gates and hearths,

>   Rome, you who now defend the household gods of others.
>   Although you may again climb up the Tarpeian rocks and
>   sharp stones, and although you may again retreat to your lofty citadel,
> 35 once captured you will not ransom your lives for any amount of gold."

While the Roman envoys, led by Fabius and Valerius Flaccus, sail on to Carthage after they are turned away from Saguntum, Hannibal tauntingly promises to see them in Rome soon when he marches on the city. In threatening a repetition (*iterum*, 33) of the Gallic sack, however, Hannibal vows that, unlike Brennus, he will not allow the Romans to ransom their lives. Furthermore, he imparts a religious tone to his threat by using the verb *scandatis* (34), the *terminus technicus* for scaling the Capitoline (e.g., Hor. *Carm.* 3.30.8–9). Elsewhere, Silius uses forms of *scando* for "scaling" the walls of a city (1.495, 15.231; cf. 11.444, 14.310), as well as the Alps (3.111; cf. 4.747), the walls of Rome (12.46), and the Capitol (1.385, 4.72, 12.339), even for "scaling" up to heaven in a Gigantomachy (12.71). (Interestingly, Vergil uses the verb only twice in the entire *Aeneid*, both times in connection with the Trojan Horse: *scandit*, 2.237; *scandunt*, 2.401). After the fall of Saguntum, Gauls make frequent, if perhaps unexpected, appearances at all three of the battles leading up to Cannae.[37] The narrative of the fighting at the Ticinus River begins with the single combat between Scipio (father of the future Africanus) and the Boian Crixus, who boasts about his descent from Brennus: when Scipio slays his opponent and puts the Gauls to flight, he not only exacts vengeance for Brennus' earlier victory, but also demonstrates that Hannibal will need more than a mere repetition of the Gallic sack in order to scale the Capitol (4.143–310). Soon thereafter, during the fighting at the Trebia River, Mago and Maharbal metaphorically put the memory of the Gallic sack to rest when they team up to dispatch an Italian warrior by the name of Allius (4.554–72). Nevertheless, the Gauls live on, as Ducarius and the Boii exact vengeance of their own against Flaminius for his earlier victory over them by killing him to bring the fighting at Lake Trasimene to an end (5.632–78; cf. 4.704–7). Ironically, despite his claim to the contrary at Saguntum, Hannibal actually does accept a ransom of sorts at Cannae when he collects the gold signet rings from the bodies of the fallen Romans and sends them back home to Carthage with his brother Mago as evidence of the great victory (11.532–5; cf. 8.674–6).

After Cannae, Hannibal famously delays, choosing not to march immediately on Rome, whereas Brennus had chosen to march on the city immediately after the Allia River, only to find it virtually undefended. When Hannibal does finally decide to attack, he mistakenly believes that he can still follow in the footsteps of

Brennus, and so he exhorts his men to envision their assault as a replay of the Gallic sack, including the eerie scene of the elder statesmen awaiting death as they dressed themselves in their official robes and sat upon their chairs of state (12.574–86):

>   atque ubi nox depulsa polo primaque rubescit
> 575   lampade Neptunus revocatque Aurora labores,
>   effundit rupto persultans agmina vallo
>   et, quantum clamare valet: "per plurima nostra,
>   o socii, decora et sacratas sanguine dextras,
>   vobis ite pares et tantum audete sub armis,
> 580   quantum Roma timet. reliquam hanc exscindite molem:
>   nil quod vincatis toto restabit in orbe.
>   neu populi vos Martigenae tardarit origo;
>   intratam Senonum capietis milibus urbem
>   adsuetamque capi. fortasse curulibus altis
> 585   iam vos exemplo proavorum ad nobile letum
>   exspectant de more senes mortique parantur."

>   And now, when the night is banished from the sky and the sea
> 575   grows red with the first light of day and Aurora [Dawn] calls back her labors,
>   he [Hannibal] pours out his marching columns, riding along the broken rampart,
>   and, as loud as he is able to shout, he says: "By our very many
>   great deeds, o comrades, and by our right hands consecrated in blood,
>   go forth equal to your former selves and dare to do in battle things as great,
> 580   as the fear Rome feels for you. Destroy this one remaining obstacle:
>   nothing else will remain in the entire world for you to conquer.
>   Nor will the origin of this people descended from Mars delay your assault;
>   you will capture a city formerly entered by thousands of Senones
>   and accustomed to be captured. Perhaps the elders, following the example
> 585   of their forefathers, are already seated upon their lofty curule chairs,
>   waiting for you to repeat the famous slaughter and ready for death."

Through this allusion to the Gallic sack, as well as through the narrative of what follows inside Rome in 12.587–604, Silius appears to suggest that Hannibal has simply lost his grip on reality and that he squandered his opportunity to capture Rome when he failed to march on the city after Cannae, whereas Brennus had captured the city by making his march after the Allia River. In the aftermath of the climactic events of book 12, Hannibal qua Brennus recedes into the background, and Scipio qua Camillus emerges into the foreground. Apart from a passing mention of Camillus in the ecphrasis of the doors of the Roman Curia in 1.609–29, the redeemed hero makes his first significant appearance in the epic in book 7, when Fabius reminds his son how Camillus returned from exile to save Rome from the Gauls and forgave the Romans for their harsh treatment of him (7.547–66). Later, Scipio sees Camillus in the Underworld (13.722), a moment which elegantly anticipates the simile at the end of the epic when Silius compares Scipio to Quirinus, the deified Romulus, and Camillus (17.651–2), perhaps to point up the contrast between Camillus, who returned from exile to save Rome from one great nemesis, and Scipio, who famously died in exile at Liternum after saving Rome from another, just as his enemy Hannibal died in exile, too.

5. Conclusion: Marcellus, Closure, and Counterfactual History

The *Punica* is a long, dense, and totalizing historical epic which challenges the abilities of even the most skilled "full-knowing reader"[38] to tease out the sense of every literary allusion, cultural reference, and learned epithet. The poem requires a deep familiarity with each and every aspect of *Romanitas*, the full breadth and depth of the Roman experience. That said, the epic is well worth the time and effort, and the fundamental themes which Silius explores remain as relevant today as they were at the time of the poem's original composition. As we have seen, the *Punica* is an important work for our understanding of both the Second Punic War itself and, equally so, of the memory of the war, especially during the Early Empire, if we can even identify this or any war as an ontological entity separable from its commemoration (and I would argue that we cannot). As we have also seen, Silius universalizes his narrative of the war by casting it as a new version of the Gigantomachy, the Trojan War, and the Gallic sack in order to present the story of the rise and fall of Carthage and Rome as a broader meditation on the rise and fall of cities and heroes in general. But the story does not end there, far from it. By way of conclusion, I would like to take a brief look at how Silius integrates Marcellus into the *Punica* and, in particular, how he uses the rise and fall of Marcellus to manipulate the closure of both the war and the narrative through a powerful example of counterfactual history which (could have) changed everything.

Over the course of the poem, Silius transforms his version of Marcellus into the ultimate counterfactual synecdochic hero, a larger-than-life soldier-general who uncomfortably straddles the vanishing divide between Republican and Imperial *imperatores*, and whose premature death marks the ultimate counterfactual turning point in both the war and the narrative. Throughout the epic, but especially in his presentation of the death of Marcellus in 15.334–98, Silius engages with his literary predecessors in order to elaborate a counterfactual version of events according to which it was Marcellus, and not Scipio, who would have, could have, and should have led Rome to victory over Hannibal in the Second Punic War, if only he had not died prematurely in the ambush. At its core, the death of Marcellus enacts the poem's root irony of defeat in victory and victory in defeat, while, at the same time, absolving the Roman through his death from any responsibility for the final outcome. In preparation for the pathos of the death scene in book 15, Silius reminds the reader at several points throughout the epic (1.132–3, 3.587, 8.254–5) that it was Marcellus, and not Scipio, who was famed as Rome's quintessential soldier-general at the outset of the conflict, most notably for slaying the Gallic chieftain Viridomarus in single combat at the battle of Clastidium in 222 BC and thereby earning (for the third and final time in Roman history) the *spolia opima*. Furthermore, it was Marcellus, and not Scipio, who gave Rome her first "victory" in the war by successfully defending Nola against Hannibal's onslaught, a victory which Silius explicitly sets above his winning the *spolia opima* (12.161–294, esp. 278–80; cf. 295–319, 420–2). Silius even isolates book 14, the narrative of the Sicilian campaign culminating in the fall of Syracuse, from the rest of the poem in order to cast the book as a miniature anti-epic in tension with the *Scipiad* which occupies books 13–17 and, therefore, in order to pit Marcellus against Scipio in a literary, if not historical, battle to take on Hannibal. This is the foundation upon which Silius constructs his unique version of the death scene itself.

The death of Marcellus marked an important turning point in Roman history and, not surprisingly, left an indelible stain on Roman historical memory both before and after Silius.[39] While there was lingering debate among the varying and ultimately irreconcilable traditions about the fate of Marcellus' fellow consul T. Quinctius Crispinus and about the fate of his own corpse, there was virtually no debate about Marcellus' culpable lack of *prudentia*, especially given his advanced age and extensive experience, and there was also virtually no debate about the irreparable harm which Marcellus' demise did to his reputation as Rome's greatest and grandest hero. In his reimagining of the death scene, Silius dramatically instantiates the contested nature of historical memory by transforming the narrative into a series of essential topoi framed by two competing eulogies for the fallen Marcellus, the first in the voice of the narrator and the second in the voice of the narrator's alter ego, Hannibal, all in order for Silius to encourage the reader to question the "historical" foundations of the entire war as recounted in the *Punica*.[40]

The narrative of the death of Marcellus in 15.334–98 begins, in a sense, at the end, with a proleptic lament for the (soon-to-be) fallen commander which culminates with the haunting image of the consul already lying dead on the battlefield before Silius has even begun his account of the circumstances surrounding the ambush. In 15.334–42, the narrator eulogizes Marcellus in suitably heroic language as a mass of a man who died gloriously in combat, but who, had he lived, might have enjoyed even more glory for bringing both the war and the narrative to an end and thereby earning the title of Africanus, for, that is, becoming an *alter Scipio*: *iacet campis Carthaginis horror / forsan Scipiadae confecti nomina belli / rapturus, si quis paulum deus adderet aevo* ("He lies dead in the fields, the terror of Carthage, / perhaps on the verge of seizing the title for finishing the war [Africanus] / away from Scipio, if some god added even only a little bit to his life span," 15.340–2). In a pointed rejection of Lucretius (*Scipiadas, belli fulmen, Carthaginis horror*, 3.1034), Silius suggests that it was Marcellus, and not Scipio, who was the real *Carthaginis horror* and who might have led Rome to victory at Zama in an act of individual heroism redolent of the one vs. many theme which facilitates the transition from Republic to Empire, although Silius also softens that claim with the wistful *forsan* in 15.341. Fortunately for Marcellus, however, as the epitaphic *iacet* in 15.340 makes clear, he was lucky enough to die in battle before having to make the impossible choice between Republic and Empire; instead, per the homology between the hero and the city for which he stands and falls, the death of Marcellus represents not only the death of the "one man" left who might have delayed, if not ultimately prevented, Scipio's emergence as a new kind of *imperator*, but also, more to the point, the death of one of the few remaining pillars of the Republic (Fabius Cunctator notwithstanding). In a radical departure from the rest of the tradition surrounding the death of Marcellus, Silius defies the expectations of the full-knowing reader and transforms a memory of catastrophic shame and ignominy elsewhere in the tradition (both before and after him) into a meditation on the final defeat of Rome through victory and the final victory of Carthage through defeat, via the dramatic fall of Marcellus and the concomitant rise of Scipio.

In 15.381–98, Hannibal eulogizes Marcellus in language which strikingly recalls that which the narrator had used earlier: *iacet exitiabile nomen, / Ausonii columen regni* ("The death-dealing name lies dead, / the pillar of the Ausonian kingdom," 15.384–5): note especially the repetition of *iacet* in 15.384 to stress the fact that Marcellus really is dead and gone. In typical epic fashion, Hannibal orders the construction of a massive funeral pyre appropriate for the last rites of a worthy enemy and then, setting fire to the offering, celebrates his fallen foe: *Marcellum abstulimus Latio. deponere forsan / gens Italum tandem arma velit* ("We have taken Marcellus away from Latium. Perhaps the nation / of Italians may finally wish to put down their arms," 15.393–4): note *forsan* in 15.393 (with another *forsan* in 15.375, by far the densest cluster of examples in the epic). Hannibal evidently honored and respected Marcellus because he was, like Hannibal himself, a vestige of a bygone era, while both the war and the narrative continued the inexorable march from Republic to Empire. In burying Marcellus as he had buried Paullus and Gracchus before him, Hannibal believed that he was, in essence, burying the Republic (cf. V. Max. 1.6.6): indeed he was, but he was also preparing himself for burial in the process by helping to clear the path for Scipio and for the Empire. By imitating the positive exemplum of Marcellus and Crispinus and by avoiding the negative exemplum of Paullus and Varro, Nero and Salinator were able to defeat Hasdrubal at the Metaurus River and thereby exact Republican revenge for the defeat at Cannae in a closing act of collective heroism, but this victory was, in reality, insufficient to stem the tide. By this point, only Scipio could exact Imperial revenge for the losses suffered in Apulia and emerge as a new kind of *imperator* by defeating Hannibal himself at Zama, although without, of course, winning the *spolia opima*.

The specter of Marcellus looms large long after his death in book 15. In particular, his removal from the narrative marks a moment of false closure for both the war and the narrative, appropriately commemorated by Hannibal with a *laudatio* which subtly anticipates the *laudatio* for himself which he pronounces later in 17.605–17. In reality, of course, the narrative of book 15 continues with Scipio's victory in Spain at Baecula and Hasdrubal's subsequent flight over the Pyrenees and the Alps in order to join forces in Italy with Hannibal. At this point, it is actually another Claudian, Claudius Nero, who comes to the rescue and who, in collaboration with Livius Salinator, repels Hasdrubal's invasion, even winning the *spolia opima* by defeating Hasdrubal in single combat and decapitating him. In a clever wordplay on an etymology of the *nomen* Claudius (~ *claudo*, "to close"), Silius uses the progression from one Claudius to another in order to manipulate this sense of closure which dominates book 15. More generally, the focus on the interplay between single combat and closure manifests itself most clearly in the deployment of the collocation *proelium poscere* at three critical junctures (see also 4.271, 7.249–50, 17.128): first, during the single combat between Hannibal and Murrus at Saguntum (1.420, 483); then, during the siege of Nola, when Marcellus calls for single combat with Hannibal (12.198), but Juno intervenes to put off the climactic combat; and, finally, during the battle of Zama, when Scipio likewise calls for single combat with Hannibal (17.521), but Juno once again intervenes, transforming even the end of the epic into a moment of tantalizingly false closure. Silius incorporates the death of Marcellus and other moments of counterfactual history into his narrative in order to issue his ultimate challenge to the reader, that of deciding whether the *Punica* memorializes the war as "fact," "fiction," or some uncomfortable mixture of the two.

6

Carthage and Rome in the *Punica*, Part 2

1. Introduction: From the Second Punic War to the Flavians

By transforming the Second Punic War into a new Gigantomachy, a new Trojan War, and a new Gallic sack, Silius looks back not only to what comes before the conflict in Roman history and Roman culture, but also to what comes after it, Rome's ultimate victory in the Third Punic War and the fall of Carthage in 146 BC, the long period of internal strife from the Gracchi to the rise of Octavian/Augustus (133–31 BC), and the relapse into civil war during the Year of the Four Emperors in AD 69, as well as the subsequent rise and fall of the Flavians (AD 69–96). The world of the Flavians initially enters into the world of the Second Punic War in the epic's first simile (1.324–6),[1] when Hannibal casts poison arrows during the assault on Saguntum "like a Dacian along the weapons-bearing coasts of the Getic land" (*Dacus ut armiferis Geticae telluris in oris*, 324). As the first simile of the poem, we could even read this passage as a metaliterary gesture on the part of the poet, as an intimation that we should read the entire epic as a simile comparing the world of the Second Punic War with the world of the Flavians. Silius formally introduces all three Flavian emperors, Vespasian and his sons, Titus and Domitian, in the famous encomium uttered by Jupiter during his conversation with Venus on Mt. Olympus (3.594–629):[2]

> "exin se Curibus virtus caelestis ad astra
> 595 efferet, et sacris augebit nomen Iulis
> bellatrix gens bacifero nutrita Sabino.
> hinc pater ignotam denabit vincere Thylen
> inque Caledonios primus trahet agmina lucos,
> compescet ripis Rhenum, reget impiger Afros
> 600 palmiferamque senex bello domitabit Idymen.
> nec Stygis ille lacus viduataque lumine regna,
> sed superum sedem nostrosque tenebit honores.
> tum iuvenis magno praecellens robore mentis

	excipiet patriam molem celsusque feretur
605	aequatum imperio tollens caput. hic fera gentis
	bella Palestinae primo delebit in aevo.
	at tu transcendes, Germanice, facta tuorum,
	iam puer auricomo praeformidate Batavo.
	nec te terruerint Tarpei culminis ignes;
610	sacrilegas inter flammas servabere terris.
	nam te longa manent nostri consortia mundi.
	huic laxos arcus olim Gangetica pubes
	summittet vacuasque ostendent Bactra pharetras.
	hic et ab Arctoo currus aget axe per urbem,
615	ducet et Eoos Baccho cedente triumphos.
	idem indignantem tramittere Dardana signa
	Sarmaticis victor compescet sedibus Histrum.
	quin et Romuleos superabit voce nepotes,
	quis erit eloquio partum decus. huic sua Musae
620	sacra ferent, meliorque lyra, cui substitit Hebrus
	et venit Rhodope, Phoebo miranda loquetur.
	ille etiam, qua prisca, vides, stat regia nobis,
	aurea Tarpeia ponet Capitolia rupe
	et iunget nostro templorum culmina caelo.
625	tunc, o nate deum divosque dature, beatas
	imperio terras patrio rege. tarda senectam
	hospitia excipient caeli, solioque Quirinus
	concedet, mediumque parens fraterque locabunt;
	siderei iuxta radiabunt tempora nati."

	"Then, heavenly virtue will raise itself up to the stars
595	from Cures, and a warlike family nourished by the Sabine olive
	will increase the fame of the sacred Julians.
	From here the father [Vespasian] will sail to conquer unknown Thule
	and will be the first to lead columns of troops into the groves of Caledonia,
	will contain the Rhine [River] within its banks, will zealously rule the Africans,
600	and, as an old man, will subdue palm-bearing Idumea in war.
	Nor will that man hold the pools of the Styx and the kingdom deprived of light,
	but he will instead hold the realm of the gods and the same honors as us.
	Then, the young man [Titus], excelling in the great strength of his mind,
	will take up his father's burden and will be borne aloft,
605	raising up his head to equal his authority. This man will bring an end

> to the fierce wars of the people of Palestine at the very beginning of his youth.
> But you, Germanicus [Domitian], will transcend the deeds of your family, still only a boy but feared by the golden-haired Batavian.
> Nor will the flames of the Tarpeian peak terrify you;
> 610 you will be saved amid the sacrilegious flames for the peoples of these lands.
> For the comforts of our world will wait for you for a long time.
> One day, the youth of the Ganges [River] will lay down their loosened bows for this man, and Bactra will show its quivers empty of arrows.
> This man will drive his chariot through the city from the North,
> 615 and he will lead triumphs from the East, as Bacchus yields to him.
> This same man, victorious, will restrain the Danube [River] within the lands
> of the Sarmatians, disdaining to allow Dardan [Trojan] standards to cross over it.
> What is more, he will surpass the descendants of Romulus in speaking, those who have gained glory for their eloquence. To this man the Muses
> 620 will bring their offerings, and, better at the lyre than he [Orpheus] for whom
> the Hebrus [River] stood still and Mt. Rhodope was moved, he will sing songs
> wondrous to Phoebus. Where, as you see, my ancient palace now stands, that man will also put the golden Capitoline upon the Tarpeian Rock and will join the peak of the temple to our abode in heaven.
> 625 Then, o son of the gods and father of future divinities, rule the blessed lands of the earth with the authority of your father.
> The comforts of heaven at last will take you up in your old age, and Quirinus
> will yield his throne, and your father and brother will place you between them;
> next to you the temples of your deified son will send forth rays of light."

When Hannibal finally reaches the peaks of the Alps after a dozen days of arduous climbing, Silius deftly transfers the scene of the action from that range to the heights of Mt. Olympus (3.557–629). Venus frantically asks of her father, Jupiter, whether he will permit a repetition of the fall of Troy (and, more recently, the fall of Saguntum) in the fall of Rome (557–69); in his reply, Jupiter first reassures her that, despite the fact that Rome will one day be more famous for her defeats, Paullus, Fabius, Marcellus, and, of course, Scipio will prove their *virtus* and lead the Romans to victory (570–93); and Jupiter then connects the Republican past with the Imperial present through the encomium of Vespasian, Titus, and Domitian (594–629). Scholars have long recognized that, in this passage, Silius recalls two similar divine scenes at climactic moments in the *Aeneid*, the conversation on Mt. Olympus, also between Venus and Jupiter, when Aeneas first arrives at Carthage (1.223–304), and the *concilium deorum* ("council of the gods"), also held on Mt. Olympus, when Jupiter instructs his fellow divinities not to interfere in the war between the Trojans and the Latins, but instead to wait for a future war between the Carthaginians and the Romans, i.e., the Second Punic War (10.1–117). Most scholars offer generally positive readings of the encomium as a celebration of the Flavian triad (along with the passing reference to the son of Domitian who died in infancy and was proclaimed *divus* like his uncle and grandfather). That said, other scholars have read the passage in a far less positive light, especially the lines in praise of Domitian, because they contain a number of references to less-than-flattering moments before, during, and, perhaps, after his reign. After all, given that Silius lived and wrote before, during, and after the Flavian dynasty, we simply do not know when he originally wrote the encomium, much less whether he revised it (and, if so, when). It matters very much for our understanding of the passage and, indeed, our understanding of the epic as a whole whether the extant verses were composed (much less heard and/or read) before or after Domitian's death. Either way, through the encomium as a whole, Silius forges a link between the Second Punic War and the Flavians, as well as, more specifically, a link between Scipio and Domitian, as we will see in detail below.

Roman culture identifies two driving forces behind the city's transition from victory in foreign war, the hallmark of the Republican era and its climax in the Second Punic War, to self-inflicted defeat in civil war, the hallmark of the Imperial era and, for Silius, its climax in the chaos of AD 69. On the one hand, we have the curse of Dido theme, the mythological pillar of the Roman worldview; on the other, we have the *metus hostilis* theme, its historical pillar. Over the course of the *Punica*, Silius interweaves these two major themes in order to underscore the symbiotic relationship between Carthage and Rome, two cities which, as we will see in detail below, are fated either to stand or to fall together, as well as to elaborate something of a grand unified theory for the transition from Republic to Empire, from *bellum externum* to *bellum civile*, around the turning point of Cannae. In (re)constructing this model for explaining Rome's rise and future fall, Silius strikes a delicate balance between linear and cyclical time, between a conception of the past, present, and future which recognizes a beginning, a middle, and an end, a rise and a fall, and a conception which recognizes the creative powers of destruction, a rebirth after a death.[3] In terms of Stoic cosmology, Silius envisions a *palingenesis* (rebirth) after an *ekpyrosis* (death by fire) or a *kataklysmos* (death by water), and he accordingly reintroduces the divine machinery, present in the *Aeneid* but absent from the *Bellum civile*, in order to emphasize the controlling power of fate and fortune.[4] That said, by associating Republic and Empire with *bellum externum* and *bellum internum*, respectively, Silius also invites his reader to reflect on the tension between progressive repetition and regressive repetition, the tension between a repetition which conquers the past and a repetition which is conquered by it. Romans famously associated both the rise and the fall of their city with internal strife, since they and only they were able to defeat themselves in war. Over the course of his epic, Silius prompts the reader to consider the special role of the Second Punic War in this process and, in particular, the pivotal role of Cannae.

As we have seen in detail in the sustained reading of the poem across Chapters 3 and 4, Silius posits an inverse relationship between military success and moral success. Before Cannae, the Carthaginians enjoy military success after military success, but they suffer a moral failure along the way; the Romans, meanwhile, suffer military defeat after military defeat, but they enjoy a moral triumph.[5] After Cannae, the Carthaginians begin to suffer military defeat *because* of their prior military success and the consequent moral failure; the Romans, in contrast, begin to enjoy military success *because* of their prior military defeat and the consequent moral triumph: having proved their *virtus*, they now find themselves in essentially the same position as the Carthaginians at the start of the epic. This dynamic relationship between military success and moral success not only cements the unbreakable bond between Carthage and Rome, but also instantiates the tension between linear and cyclical time, as well as that between progressive and regressive repetition. Silius encourages his reader to consider carefully both the similarities and the differences between the Carthaginians and the Romans, as well as to reflect on the impact of Cannae on both civilizations. Will the Carthaginians, like the Romans before Cannae, now enjoy a moral regeneration in the face of military defeat after the fateful battle has been won, and will such a moral regeneration one day bring renewed military success? Will the Romans, like the Carthaginians before Cannae, now suffer a moral degeneration in the face of military success after the fateful battle has been lost, and will such a moral degeneration one day bring renewed military defeat? Put simply, if victory at Cannae eventually leads to the fall of Carthage at the end of the Third Punic War, does defeat at Cannae eventually lead to the fall of Rome, too, or will Rome successfully avert this fate through the fall of Carthage as its sacrificial substitute?[6] If (when?) Rome falls, will the city rise again? These are the fundamental questions which Silius poses through his integration of the curse of Dido and *metus hostilis* themes in order to account for the looming threat of self-defeat through civil war in the aftermath of victory in foreign war.

2. The Curse of Dido Theme

We begin with the curse of Dido theme. Dido utters her famous imprecation as Aeneas prepares to set sail from Carthage in order to continue his journey on to Italy. She calls upon her fellow Tyrians to wage ceaseless war against the Trojans, and, in particular, she envisions the rise of a descendant who will punish the descendants of Aeneas for his perfidy (Verg. *Aen.* 4.622–9):[7]

>   "tum vos, o Tyrii, stirpem et genus omne futurum
>   exercete odiis, cinerique haec mittite nostro
>   munera. nullus amor populis nec foedera sunto.
> 625   exoriare aliquis nostris ex ossibus ultor
>   qui face Dardanios ferroque sequare colonos,
>   nunc, olim, quocumque dabunt se tempore vires.
>   litora litoribus contraria, fluctibus undas
>   imprecor, arma armis: pugnent ipsique nepotesque."

>   "Then, you, o Tyrians, wear down every future stock and race
>   in your hatred, and send these funeral offerings
>   to my ashes. Let there be no love and no peace for these peoples.
> 625   Let someone arise from my bones as an avenger,
>   you who may pursue the Dardanian [Trojan] colonists with fire and the sword,
>   now, one day in the future, whenever you have the strength.
>   I pray that our shores be opposed to their shores, our waves to their waves,
>   our arms to their arms: let them and their descendants remain at war."

In a nod to the future repetition of this curse in the oath of Hannibal, as well as to its future fulfillment at Cannae, Dido instructs her aptly named nurse, Barce, to go and fetch her sister, Anna (4.630–41): the name connects the nurse with the Barcids, the family of Hamilcar and Hannibal, and suggests that Hannibal will play the role of avenger. Immediately thereafter, the queen of Carthage scales her funeral pyre, utters her final words against Aeneas, and buries his sword in her chest. Vergil likens the lamentation for Dido to the lamentation for an imagined fall of Carthage or Tyre (4.642-71, esp. 669-71). During the *concilium deorum* on Mt. Olympus in book 10, Jupiter himself all but identifies the *ultor* with Hannibal, as he looks ahead to the time *cum fera Karthago Romanis arcibus olim / exitium magnum atque Alpis immittet apertas* ("when fierce Carthage will one day bring great destruction / and the opening up of the Alps against the Roman citadel," *Aen.* 10.12-13).[8] In the end, however, while Hannibal will succeed in "opening up" the Alps, he will not succeed in "opening up" the walls of Rome, where he will have to content himself with standing "at the gates"; instead, it will be a Roman, Scipio, who scales the walls (and the Capitol) at his triumph and thereby puts Rome on the path to civil war.

In the *Punica*, the curse of Dido plays an especially important thematic role in the events at Saguntum, Cannae, and Zama.[9] Immediately after the proem (1.1-20), Hannibal, driven by Juno and by his father, Hamilcar, swears his famous oath of vengeance at a shrine dedicated to Dido herself (according to Silius), indeed at the very spot where the queen had pronounced her original curse and then committed suicide: the topographical repetition tropes the thematic repetition of the curse in the oath (1.21-139, esp. the ecphrasis of the shrine in 81-98). Hannibal cements this link with Dido by identifying himself as the instrument of her revenge (1.114-19):

> "Romanos terra atque undis, ubi competet aetas,
> 115 ferro ignique sequar Rhoeteaque fata revolvam.
> non superi mihi, non Martem cohibentia pacta,
> non celsae obstiterint Alpes Tarpeiaque saxa.
> hanc mentem iuro nostri per numina Martis,
> per manes, regina, tuos."

> "I will pursue the Romans on land and by sea, as long as my life will last,
> 115 with fire and the sword, and I will unroll Rhoetean [Trojan] fates.
> The gods will not stand in my way, nor the peace agreements
> forbidding war, nor the lofty Alps and the Tarpeian rocks.
> I swear this oath by the divine authority of our Mars,
> by your spirit, o queen."

Silius frames the oath of Hannibal with visions of the coming war uttered first by Juno (1.38-55) and then by a Massylian priestess (1.123-39), both of which identify Hannibal's victory at Cannae as the fulfillment of the curse, as well as of the oath. From the ecphrasis of his shield during the siege of Saguntum (2.391-456), we see that Hannibal carries on his shoulders a constant reminder of his obligation to avenge both his queen and his father. Later in the epic, to begin the lengthy narrative of Cannae across books 8–10, Juno sends Anna, Dido's sister, to Hannibal in a dream so that she can share the story of her own exile and death in order to spur the Carthaginian to battle: Hannibal welcomes the dream as an omen of his impending victory and vows to consecrate a shrine to Anna back in Carthage (8.25–241).[10] Finally, faced with the choice of fight or flight at Zama, Hannibal utters a prophecy of his own in which he identifies his victory at Cannae as his crowning glory before receding into the shadows, both literally and figuratively, no longer a mere mortal, but instead now a disembodied cultural icon who will live forever in the Roman imagination, long after his later suicide in exile, like Dido (17.605–17):

> 605 iamque propinquabant hostes tumuloque subibant,
> cum secum Poenus: "caelum licet omne soluta
> in caput hoc compage ruat terraeque dehiscant,
> non ullo Cannas abolebis, Iuppiter, aevo,
> decedesque prius regnis, quam nomina gentes
> 610 aut facta Hannibalis sileant. nec deinde relinquo
> securam te, Roma, mei, patriaeque superstes
> ad spes armorum vivam tibi. †nam modo pugna
> praecellis, resident hostes† mihi satque superque,
> ut me Dardaniae matres atque Itala tellus,
> 615 dum vivam, exspectent nec pacem pectore norint."
> sic rapitur paucis fugientum mixtus et altos
> inde petit retro montes tutasque latebras.

> 605 And now the enemy were approaching and drawing closer to the hill,
> when the Phoenician [Hannibal] [said] to himself: "Even though the whole sky,
> loosened from its bonds, may fall down upon this head, and the lands of the earth
> may gape open, you, Jupiter, will not abolish the memory of Cannae in any age,
> and you will descend from your kingdom before the peoples of the earth
> 610 stop talking about the fame or the deeds of Hannibal. Nor, then, do I leave
> you, Rome, free from the fear of me, and, outliving my own country,
> I will live for the hope of waging war on you. For you have defeated me
> only in this battle, the enemy lie low: for me [it is] enough and more than enough,
> that Dardanian [Trojan] mothers and the land of Italy, while I live,

615 wait for me to return and do not know peace in their hearts."
Thus he is ushered away, mixed in with a few of the fugitives, and, from there,
he heads back for the lofty mountains and safe hiding places.

As the Romans close in on him, Hannibal contemplates his legacy. Even if the heavens should fall to the earth, the fame of Cannae will ensure his immortality, exactly as Juno (1.50–4) and the Massylian priestess (1.125–6) prophesied, and exactly as Juno instructed Somnus to tell Hannibal in a dream the night after his momentous victory (10.326–86, esp. 333–6, 366–8; cf. 8.25–7). Before vanishing into the hills, Hannibal rightly claims that the Romans will not know peace as long as he lives (*vivam*, 17.612, 617). As we will see in detail below, however, the Romans may actually have been better off with Hannibal at least alive, if not *ad portas*.

3. The *metus hostilis* Theme

We continue with the *metus hostilis* theme.[11] The notion that Rome benefited from the collective fear of a strong external enemy enjoyed deep roots in ancient political theory, as well as in ancient conceptions about the rise and fall of states (e.g., Plb. 6.57.1–9), evolving into a dominant cultural idea(l) at least by the time of the Punic Wars.[12] Romans identified countless iterations of the phenomenon, from the *metus Etruscus* to the *metus Gallicus* and *metus Punicus* to the *metus Parthicus* (Cic. *fam.* 2.17.1), *metus Germanicus*, and *metus Gothicus*, among others. In the debate in the Roman Senate between M. Porcius Cato and P. Scipio Nasica over the fate of Carthage before the outbreak of the Third Punic War, Cato is said to have argued that the city "must be destroyed" (*Carthago delenda est*), while Scipio is said to have countered that the city "must be saved" (*Carthago servanda est*).[13] In reality, this debate concerned the fate of both cities, since the point at issue was whether Rome needed to destroy or to save Carthage in order to preserve her own existence: like the curse of Dido, the *metus hostilis* dictates that both cities must either stand or fall together. This law of reciprocity is itself reflected in the inherent grammatical ambivalence of the phrase *metus hostilis*, since the adjective bears both an active and a passive sense. This is evidenced by Aulus Gellius' explanation of the subjective and objective uses of the genitive in the grammatically equivalent phrase *metus hostium*: nam "*metus hostium*" recte dicitur, et cum timent hostes et cum timentur ("For, *metus hostium* ['fear of the enemies'] is correctly said, both when the enemies fear and when they are feared," 9.12.13; cf. 9.12.13–16 in general for the grammatical concept). Ultimately, of course, Cato convinced his fellow Romans that Carthage had to be destroyed, and the city fell to end the Third Punic War.

A century later, Sallust codifies the *metus hostilis* as the driving force in the history, as well as in the historiography, of the *imperium Romanum*, in a series of passages which span all three of his major works, including the *Catiline* (6–13), the *Jugurtha* (41–2), and the *Histories* (1.11–16 Maurenbrecher = 1.9–14 McGushin).[14] In his trenchant analysis of the rise and fall of Rome, Sallust traces the city's descent from *virtus* into *luxuria* and directly associates this moral and political decline with the fall of Carthage at the end of the Third Punic War. Indeed, in all three passages, Sallust famously identifies this moment as the turning point in the history (and, again, in the historiography) of the *res publica*. In assigning the fall of Carthage this honor, he artfully capitalizes on the fundamental paradox that it is Rome's victory over Carthage in *bellum externum* which put her on the path to self-inflicted defeat in *bellum internum*: *postquam remoto metu Punico simultates exercere vacuom fuit, plurumae turbae, seditiones et ad postremum bella civilia orta sunt* ("Afterwards, once the fear of the Carthaginians had been taken away, there was a void for exercising rivalries, and so there arose many disturbances, uprisings, and, finally, civil wars," *Hist.* 1.12 Maurenbrecher = 1.12 McGushin). Sallust's presentation of the *metus hostilis* plays a central role in all subsequent historiography about the rise and fall of Rome, including Velleius Paterculus, who divides his two-book history of Rome at 146 BC (1.12.2–7 ~ 2.1–3) and adopts a similar model of moral and political decline, and Florus, who likewise divides his two-book history of Rome's wars into *bella externa* (book 1) and *bella civilia* (book 2), and also adopts a similar model of decline (1.47).[15] In an interesting and, apparently, overlooked passage in his *Facta et dicta memorabilia*, Valerius Maximus associates the *metus hostilis* and the seeds of Roman decline not with the end of the Third Punic War, but with that of the Second. During the debate in the Roman Senate over the terms of peace at the end of the war, Q. Caecilius Metellus "averred that, after the defeat of Carthage, he did not know whether that victory would bring more good or evil to the state" (*devicta Carthagine nescire se illa victoria bonine plus an mali rei publicae attulisset adseveravit*, 7.2.3), since Hannibal's presence in Italy had kept the Romans in a constant state of readiness. Appian, who also reports the debate (*Lib.* 62.290–1), does not assign this opinion to Metellus specifically; instead, he simply comments that such a sentiment was in the air. That said, Appian does claim that Cato the Elder later attributed the notion to none other than Scipio

Africanus. In a very similar way, Silius identifies Cannae, not simply the end of the Second Punic War, as the turning point for both Carthage and Rome, and Silius identifies this turning point as the beginning of Rome's decline from virtue to vice.

Perhaps surprisingly (or perhaps not), civil wars are relatively more common, have higher death tolls on average, and generally last longer than foreign wars.[16] Without a doubt, civil strife pervades the annals of both Greek and Roman history, and this brand of conflict defines not only the transition from Republic to Empire, but also (the equally contested collective memory of) the transition from Monarchy to Republic, sparked by the suicide of Lucretia.[17] In Rome as in other societies ancient and modern, the transition from *bellum externum* to *bellum internum* predicates the parallel transition from killing the "Other" (i.e., homicide) to killing the "Self" (i.e., suicide) via various forms of intrafamilial slaughter, especially patricide and fratricide. Sadly, just as civil wars outnumber foreign wars, so, too, suicides outnumber homicides.[18] The confusion, if not the conflation, of "Self" and "Other" beautifully, if tragically, captures the essence of civil war as the ultimate manifestation of *furor* (fury, rage, anger, madness, insanity). Lucan memorably portrays civil war as an act of suicide in the proem to his *Bellum civile* (1.1–7, along with *quis furor?*, 8), and the twin themes of civil war and suicide play a prominent role in Flavian epic, including the *Punica*.[19] The Romans notoriously associated civil war not only with the destruction, but also with the foundation of their city through the death of Remus.[20] Livy 1.6.3–7.3 offers two versions of the death of Remus, in the first of which Remus falls during the fighting over the augury of the vultures, and in the second of which Romulus slays his brother in single combat (1.7.2–3):

> volgatior fama est ludibrio fratris Remum novos transiluisse muros; inde ab irato Romulo, cum verbis quoque increpitans adiecisset, "sic deinde, quicumque alius transiliet moenia mea," interfectum. 3. ita solus potitus imperio Romulus; condita urbs conditoris nomine appellata.
>
> The more common story is that Remus crossed over the new walls as a joke on his brother; then, he was killed by Romulus in a rage, after he had verbally rebuked him, adding, "So I will kill him, whoever crosses over my walls." 3. Thus Romulus took sole power; a city was founded and called "Rome" after its founder.

From the moment of its first foundation, Rome is a city obsessed with the status of its walls, as evidenced by the wordplay *Remum . . . muros . . . Romulo*. From the moment of its first foundation, Rome is also a city marred by the original sin of internecine conflict, all throughout its history, but especially during the transition from Republic to Empire. Horace ruminates on this Roman proclivity for civil war in *Epodes* 7 and 16, where he laments the recent transition from *bellum externum* to *bellum internum*, and specifically identifies the curse of Remus as the force behind the shift (7.17–20).[21] Vergil explores the theme of civil war by transforming the narrative of the war between the Trojans and the Latins (albeit that the Trojans do claim Italian origins) across *Aeneid* 7–12 from a foreign war into a (proleptic) civil war between (future) Romans culminating in the fratricidal single combat between Aeneas and Turnus.[22] Building on this theme, Silius goes one step further, transforming his narrative, at one and the same time, into a narrative of Rome's greatest foreign war, the Second Punic War, and Rome's greatest civil war, the events of AD 69, thus pitting the *Punica* against both the *Aeneid* and the *Bellum civile* as Rome's one true epic.

Just as Silius transforms the Second Punic War into a synecdoche for Roman history and Roman culture as a whole, so, too, he transforms the battle of Cannae into a synecdoche for the Second Punic War, the turning point of both the war and his narrative, and even the "singularity" for his totalizing vision of *Romanitas*. In his account of the war in the third decade of his history *Ab urbe condita*, Livy makes Hannibal's march on Rome in 211 BC, approximately halfway through the conflict, the climax of both the war and his narrative. Silius, however, reserves this honor for the battle of Cannae much earlier in 216 BC, approximately one quarter of the way through the conflict. In doing so, as we will see in the conclusion, Silius aligns his narrative not with Livy and (the rest of?) the annalistic tradition, but instead with an alternate tradition which we find before and after the *Punica*. This alternate tradition shifts the midpoint of the war from the march on Rome back to the battle of Cannae and then balances Hannibal's four victories at the battles of the Ticinus River, the Trebia River, Lake Trasimene, and Cannae (four *clades* for Rome) with four stages of Roman vengeance for those earlier defeats. Across the narrative arc of the *Punica*, Silius develops his version of this alternate tradition in order to place even greater emphasis on the significance of the battle of Cannae for the Second Punic War and, indeed, for the entire course of Roman and Carthaginian history. By yoking together the curse of Dido and *metus hostilis* themes, Silius strives to develop a model which integrates myth and history into a grand cultural narrative which accounts for the rise and fall of both Carthage and Rome.

Accordingly, like the curse of Dido, the *metus hostilis* plays an equally important role throughout the *Punica*.[23] We have seen how Silius introduces the *metus hostilis* theme into the conversation between Venus and Jupiter on Mt. Olympus (3.557–629). During a complementary exchange between Cymodoce, the eldest of the Nereids, and Proteus, the Old Man of the Sea, after the sudden arrival of a Carthaginian fleet at Caieta, Silius elegantly reinforces the bond between the Second Punic War and the Flavians by subtly patterning this later conversation after the earlier one between Venus and Jupiter (7.409–93). In response to her frantic questions (7.409–34 ~ 3.557–69), Proteus likewise reassures Cymodoce that, in the end, Rome will surely triumph over Carthage. In the first half of his speech (7.435–78 ~ 3.570–93), Proteus retells the tale of the choice of Paris in order to demonstrate how the fall of Troy led to the rise of Rome; in the second half (7.479–93 ~ 3.594–629), something of an encomium of the Scipiones to match the earlier encomium of the Flavians, Proteus counsels the Nereids to avoid Cannae and, instead, to wait patiently for revenge at the Metaurus River and, of course, Zama, where Scipio will lead Rome to victory in preparation for the future fall of Carthage to another Scipio, Scipio Aemilianus, at the end of the Third Punic War. In two pivotal passages, one from the beginning (9.340–53) and the other from the end (10.657–8) of his narrative of the battle of Cannae, Silius definitively identifies Cannae as the turning point and explicitly describes this turning point as the beginning of Rome's transition from military defeat to military success, but also from moral triumph to moral failure. Accordingly, when Scipio celebrates his triumph at the end of the war and the narrative (17.625–54), Silius prompts his reader to reflect on the impact of this military victory on Rome's moral decline, on the way to the future fall of the city through civil war. Put simply, it is the battle of Cannae which unites the curse of Dido and *metus hostilis* themes in Silius' all-encompassing vision of Roman history and Roman culture, and it is the same battle of Cannae which enacts the transformation from Republic to Empire by collapsing the purported boundary between *bellum externum* and *bellum civile*. Indeed, by casting the battle of Cannae in this role, Silius poses his most challenging question to his reader: is the *Punica* about the Second Punic War or the events of AD 69, or perhaps both at one and the same time?

4. From Republic to Empire, from Foreign War to Civil War

After the Roman and Carthaginian forces reach Cannae, *Punica* 9 begins with a minor skirmish in which several Romans fall, the first of whom is a soldier named Mancinus (1–65). That night, the Italian Satricus, who had been captured by Xanthippus during the First Punic War and given in slavery to the king of the Autololes, and who had returned to Italy as a part of Hannibal's invasion and decided to try to flee back home, is unwittingly killed by his son, Solymus, while unwittingly wearing the armor of his other son, the Mancinus killed earlier that day. Solymus, realizing what he has done, commits suicide upon his corpse, writing on his shield in his own blood his father's warning to the Romans, FUGE PROELIA VARRO ("Flee the battle, Varro!") (66–177). Long ago, Occioni recognized the literary merits of this purple passage, including a key intertext in Tacitus' *Historiae*.[24] But there is far more to the episode than simply its literary merits, and I would go so far as to assert that, through this intricate example of mistaken identity, Silius skillfully conflates patricide, fratricide, and suicide into one sweeping condemnation of the Second Punic War as a whole, as well as into one sweeping condemnation of the events of AD 69, by effectively transforming the battle of Cannae into a (proleptic) civil war engagement:[25]

necnon et noctem sceleratus polluit error.
Xanthippo captus Libycis tolerarat in oris
servitium Satricus, mox inter praemia regi
Autololum dono datus ob virtutis honorem.
70 huic domus et gemini fuerant Sulmone relicti
matris in uberibus nati, Mancinus et una
nomine Rhoeteo Solymus. nam Dardana origo
et Phrygio genus a proavo, qui sceptra secutus
Aeneae claram muris fundaverat urbem
75 ex sese dictam Solymon. celebrata colonis
mox Italis paulatim attrito nomine Sulmo.
at tum barbaricis Satricus cum rege catervis
advectus, quo non spretum, si posceret usus,
noscere Gaetulis Latias interprete voces,
80 postquam posse datum Paeligna revisere tecta
et patrium sperare larem, ad conamina noctem
advocat ac furtim castris evadit iniquis.
sed fuga nuda viri. sumpto nam prodere coepta
vitabat clipeo et dextra remeabat inermi.
85 exuvias igitur prostrataque corpora campo
lustrat et exutis Mancini cingitur armis.
iamque metus levior. verum, cui dempta ferebat
exsangui spolia et cuius nudaverat artus,
natus erat, paulo ante Mace prostratus ab hoste.
90 ecce sub adventum noctis primumque soporem
alter natorum, Solymus, vestigia vallo
Ausonio vigil extulerat, dum sorte vicissim

alternat portae excubias, fratrisque petebat
Mancini stratum sparsa inter funera corpus,
95 furtiva cupiens miserum componere terra.
nec longum celerarat iter, cum tendere in armis
aggere Sidonio venientem conspicit hostem,
quodque dabat fors in subitis necopina, sepulcro
Aetoli condit membra occultata Thoantis.
100 inde, ubi nulla sequi propius pone arma virumque
incomitata videt vestigia ferre per umbras,
prosiliens tumulo contorquet nuda parentis
in terga haud frustra iaculum, Tyriamque sequentum
Satricus esse manum et Sidonia vulnera credens
105 auctorem caeci trepidus circumspicit ictus.
verum ubi victorem iuvenili robore cursus
attulit et notis fulsit lux tristis ab armis
fraternusque procul luna prodente retexit
ante oculos sese et radiavit comminus umbo,
110 exclamat iuvenis subita flammatus ab ira:
"non sim equidem Sulmone satus tua, Satrice, proles
nec frater, Mancine, tuus fatearque nepotem
Pergameo indignum Solymo, si evadere detur
huic nostras impune manus. tu nobile gestes
115 germani spolium ante oculos referasque superba
me spirante domus Paelignae perfidus arma?
haec tibi, cara parens Acca, ad solacia luctus
dona feram, nati ut figas aeterna sepulcro."
talia vociferans stricto mucrone ruebat.
120 ast illi iam tela manu iamque arma fluebant
audita patria natisque et coniuge et armis,
ac membra et sensus gelidus stupefecerat horror.
tum vox semanimi miseranda effunditur ore:
"parce, precor, dextrae, non ut mihi vita supersit
125 (quippe nefas hac velle frui), sed sanguine nostro
ne damnes, o nate, manus. Carthaginis ille
captivus, patrias nunc primum advectus in oras,
ille ego sum Satricus, Solymi genus. haud tua, nate,
fraus ulla est. iaceres in me cum fervidus hastam,
130 Poenus eram. verum castris elapsus acerbis
ad vos et carae properabam coniugis ora.
hunc rapui exanimi clipeum. sed iam unice nobis

haec fratris tumulis arma excusata reporta.
curarum tibi prima tamen sit, nate, referre
135 ductori monitus Paulo: producere bellum
nitatur Poenoque neget certamina Martis.
augurio exsultat divum immensamque propinqua
stragem acie sperat. quaeso, cohibete furentem
Varronem; namque hunc fama est impellere signa.
140 sat magnum hoc miserae fuerit mihi cardine vitae
solamen, cavisse meis. nunc ultima, nate,
invento simul atque amisso redde parenti
oscula." sic fatus galeam exuit atque rigentis
invadit nati tremebundis colla lacertis,
145 attonitoque timens verbis sanare pudorem
vulneris impressi <et> telum excusare laborat:
"quis testis nostris, quis conscius affuit actis?
non nox errorem nigranti condidit umbra?
cur trepidas? da, nate, magis, da iungere pectus.
150 absolvo pater ipse manum, atque in fine laborum
hac condas oculos dextra, precor." at miser imo
pectore suspirans iuvenis non verba vicesque
alloquio vocemve refert, sed sanguinis atri
sistere festinat cursum laceroque ligare
155 ocius illacrimans altum velamine vulnus.
tandem inter gemitus miserae erupere querelae:
"sicine te nobis, genitor, Fortuna reducit
in patriam? sic te nato natumque parenti
impia restituit? felix o terque quaterque
160 frater, cui fatis genitorem agnoscere ademptum.
ast ego, Sidoniis imperditus, ecce, parentem
vulnere cognosco. saltem hoc, Fortuna, fuisset
solamen culpae, dubia ut mihi signa dedisses
infausti generis. verum linquetur iniquis
165 non ultra superis nostros celare labores."
haec dum amens queritur, iam deficiente cruore
in vacuas senior vitam disperserat auras.
tum iuvenis maestum attollens ad sidera vultum
"pollutae dextrae et facti Titania testis
170 infandi, quae nocturno mea lumine tela
derigis in patrium corpus, non amplius" inquit
"his oculis et damnato violabere visu."

```
        haec memorat, simul ense fodit praecordia et atrum
        sustentans vulnus mananti sanguine signat
175     in clipeo mandata patris FUGE PROELIA VARRO,
        ac summi tegimen suspendit cuspide teli
        defletumque super prosternit membra parentem.
```

A wicked crime committed in error polluted the night, as well.
Captured by Xanthippus, Satricus had endured slavery
along the shores of Libya, then had been given as a gift
among other rewards to the king of the Autololes in honor of his virtue.

70 This man had left behind in Sulmo his home and his two sons
at their mother's breast, Mancinus and along with him
Solymus, the Trojan name for Sulmo. For, their origin [was] Dardanian [Trojan]
and their race [came] from a Phrygian [Trojan] forefather, who, following
the scepter of Aeneas, had founded a city famous for its walls

75 called Solymus after his own name. Then, after this name was shortened
little by little to Sulmo, the city was thronged with Italian colonists.
But then, Satricus, who had arrived with the king among his barbarian hordes,
and whom the Gaetulians [Autololes] had not, when the occasion called for it,
spurned to use as an interpreter in order to understand speech in Latin,

80 after he was given the opportunity to be able to visit his Paelignian haunts
and to hope to see the household gods of his country, calls upon the night
to aid his enterprise and secretly flees from the enemy camp.
But the man fled unarmed. For, if he had taken up a shield, then he might have
betrayed his undertaking, and so he returned home with no sword in hand.

85 Therefore, he scans the armor and the bodies strewn across the battlefield,
and he arms himself with the weapons stripped from the body of Mancinus.
Now his fear was lesser than before. However, the bloodless corpse, from whom
he had taken the spoils which he was carrying and whose limbs he had stripped,
was his son, who had been laid low by the Libyan enemy a little while before.

90 Look, around the beginning of the night and the first time for sleep,
the other of his sons, Solymus, watchful, had ventured

out of the Ausonian [Italian] camp, when it was his turn again by lot
to stand guard outside the gate, and he was looking for the corpse
of his brother, Mancinus, laid low among the scattered bodies,
95 wishing to bury his wretched brother in a secret plot of earth.
He had hurried along his way not very far, when he caught sight of an enemy
coming towards him from the Sidonian [Carthaginian] camp to contend in arms,
and, because this is what unexpected chance gave him in his exigency,
he hid himself in secret beside the tomb of the Aetolian Thoas.
100 From there, when he [Solymus] saw no weapons following close behind
and the man [Satricus] venturing through the shadows all alone,
jumping out from beside the tomb he hurls a javelin true to its mark
against the undefended back of his father, and Satricus, believing
that it was a band of Tyrians following him and that his wounds were Sidonian,
105 looks around trembling to catch sight of the author of the surprise attack.
But when his running, with its youthful energy, brought the victor [Solymus]
into view, and a gloomy light shone forth from weapons he knew well,
and, with the moon betraying the deed from afar, the boss of his brother's shield
revealed itself before his very eyes and gleamed right in front of him,
110 then the young man, enraged with a sudden anger, shouts:
"I would be no true son of your native Sulmo, Satricus,
nor your true brother, Mancinus, and I would confess that
I was a descendant unworthy of Pergamene [Trojan] Solymus, if this man
were allowed to escape my hands unpunished. Could you wear
115 the noble armor of my brother before my very eyes, and could you, faithless man,
carry back the proud weapons of our Paelignian house while I still breathe?
I will bring these gifts to you, my dear mother, Acca, as a solace
for your grief, so that you may fix them forever upon the tomb of your son."
Uttering words such as these, he attacked with his sword drawn.
120 But already that man [Satricus] was losing his grip on his sword and shield
after he had heard the names of his home and children and wife and arms,
and a chilly fear had stunned his limbs and senses.

Then a pitiable voice poured forth from his half-dead mouth:
"Spare your right hand, I beg you, not so that I may live
125 (indeed, it would not be right for me to wish to remain in this life),
but so that you may not condemn, my son, your hands with my blood.
I am that man, the prisoner of Carthage, who has now arrived for the first time
at the shores of his country, Satricus, of the race of Solymus. The crime
is hardly yours, my son. When you hurled your spear in anger against me,
130 I was a Phoenician [Carthaginian]. But, having slipped out of the enemy camp,
I was hurrying to see you, my two sons, and the face of my dear wife.
I grabbed this shield from a lifeless body. But now, only son left to me,
carry back these weapons, freed from guilt, to the tomb of your brother.
However, let the first of your concerns, my son, be to report
135 this warning to the general Paullus: let him strive to draw out the war,
and let him deny the Phoenician [Hannibal] the opportunity for battle.
He [Hannibal] rejoices in the augury of the gods and hopes for
an immense slaughter at an upcoming engagement. I beg you, hold back
Varro in his fury; for, the rumor is that this man urges the standards forward.
140 This great thing will be solace enough for me at the end of my wretched life,
to have issued this warning to my countrymen. Now, my son,
give a final kiss to the father whom you have found and lost
at the same time." Having spoken thus, he took off his helmet
and wrapped his trembling arms around the neck of his motionless son,
145 and, fearing for him in his shock, he strives with words to lessen the shame
of the wound inflicted upon him and to free his weapon from guilt:
"Who was a witness to what we have done, who was aware of it?
Has the night not hidden our error in a dark shadow?
Why do you tremble? Give me more, my son, give me another embrace.
150 As your father I absolve your hand from this crime, and, at the end of my labors,
I beg that you close my eyes with this right hand of yours." But, wretched,
the young man, breathing deeply from the bottom of his chest, does not reply
with any words or mumbling response or even a sound, but he hurries
to stop the coursing of his black blood and, as his tears fall more quickly,
155 to bind the deep wound with a piece of fabric torn from his garment.

Finally, wretched complaints burst forth among his groans:
"Is this how, dear father, Fortune leads you back to your country
to us? Is this how she faithlessly restores you to your son
and your son to his father? O three times and four times blessed,
160 my brother, deprived of the opportunity to recognize his father by the
    fates.
But I, unharmed by the Sidonians [Carthaginians], look, I recognize
my father by his wound. At least this could have been a solace for my guilt,
Fortune, that you could have given me unclear indications
of our unlucky race. But it will no longer remain possible
165 for the cruel gods to conceal our labors."
While he utters these complaints in his frenzy, as the gore begins to slow
    its pace,
his aged father had already scattered his life among the empty breezes.
Then, the young man, lifting up his gloomy face to the heavens, said:
"Titan goddess [Luna], witness to my polluted right hand and my
170 unspeakable deed, you who guide my weapons into the body
of my father by your nocturnal light, no longer will you be violated
by these cursed eyes and this cursed sight."
He recounts these things, and, at the same time, he buries his sword in his
    gut
and, holding back his black wound, he traces in his own flowing blood
175 upon his shield the command of his father FLEE THE BATTLE,
    VARRO,
and then he suspends the targe upon the topmost point of his weapon
and spreads out his limbs over his lamented father.

This scene, which is original to the *Punica*, powerfully resonates with other civil war moments throughout the epic, especially the numerous intrafamilial killings during the fall of Saguntum in 2.457–707, but also the near-exemplum of Pacuvius and Perolla during Hannibal's triumphal banquet in Capua in 11.267–368 and the anti-exemplum of Asilus and Beryas during the attack on Leontini in 14.148–77. At the same time, Silius may very well have remembered that both Polybius (18.28.9) and Livy (22.46.4) reported that the Carthaginians marched into battle at Cannae arrayed in arms taken from the Romans themselves after the engagements at the Trebia and Lake Trasimene, especially when Satricus tries to console his son Solymus by reminding him that *iaceres in me cum fervidus hastam, / Poenus eram* (9.129–30). Most of all, however, Silius recalls a number of similar episodes from the civil wars of the Late Republic, as well as one specific episode from the civil war of AD 68–9, later recorded by Tacitus towards the end of his narrative of the second battle fought between Bedriacum and Cremona (*Hist.* 3.25.2–3):

> 2. eo notabilior caedes fuit, quia filius patrem interfecit; rem nominaque auctore Vipstano Messalla tradam. Iulius Mansuetus ex Hispania, Rapaci legioni additus, impubem filium domi liquerat. is mox adultus, inter septimanos a Galba conscriptus, oblatum forte patrem et vulnere stratum dum semianimem scrutatur, agnitus agnoscensque et exsanguem amplexus, voce flebili precabatur piatos patris manis, neve se ut parricidam aversarentur: publicum id facinus; et unum militem quotam civilium armorum partem? 3. simul attollere corpus, aperire humum, supremo erga parentem officio fungi. advertere proximi, deinde plures; hinc per omnem aciem miraculum et questus et saevissimi belli exsecratio. nec eo segnius propinquos, adfinis, fratres trucidant, spoliant: factum esse scelus loquuntur faciuntque.

> 2. This slaughter was all the more notable, because a son killed his father; I relate the deed and the names of those involved on the authority of Vipstanus Messalla. Julius Mansuetus from Spain, enrolled in the Rapax legion, had left his young son at home. He later grew up, was called up for service by Galba among the soldiers of the Seventh legion, encountered his father in battle by chance and laid him low with a wound; while he looked at his half-dead body, his father recognized him and he recognized his father, and, embracing his now lifeless body, he prayed in a voice choked with tears that his father's spirits be appeased and that they not shun him as a parricide: his deed had been a public one, and what small part of the civil war was one single soldier? 3. At the same time, he lifted up the body, opened up the earth, and performed the last rites owed to a father. Those soldiers nearby noticed what had happened, then more and more of them took note; from here along the entire battle line there was wonder and complaint and the cursing of this cruelest of wars. Nevertheless, they killed and despoiled their friends, relatives, and brothers with no less ferocity: they said that a crime had been committed, and then proceeded to commit the very same crime themselves.

As a careful reading of the two passages immediately suggests, Tacitus evidently shapes his version of this civil war exemplum in the image of that elaborated by Silius in *Punica* 9. And yet, since the story circulated by word of mouth long before Tacitus wrote it down, Silius may very well have shaped his account of Satricus, Solymus, and Mancinus after what he had heard about Julius Mansuetus and his son. Perhaps most tellingly of all, despite the grim omen of internecine killing, the fighting continues in both Silius and Tacitus, a sign of the endlessness of civil war.[26]

5. Conclusion: From the Triumph of Scipio to the Triumph of Domitian

The conflation of foreign war and civil war reaches its climax in Tacitus' *Historiae* in the image of Romans scaling the heights of the Capitol and burning down their most sacred site, the Temple of Jupiter Optimus Maximus.[27] Over the course of the city's lengthy history, the Romans witnessed several such assaults, first at the hands of foreign foes, then, beginning with Marius and Sulla, at the hands of domestic invaders. Tacitus recounts in vivid detail the ruination of the Capitol during the internecine fighting between the Flavians and the Vitellians (*Hist.* 3.72.1–2):[28]

> id facinus post conditam urbem luctuosissimum foedissimumque rei publicae populi Romani accidit, nullo externo hoste, propitiis, si per mores nostros liceret, deis, sedem Iovis Optimi Maximi auspicato a maioribus pignus imperii conditam, quam non Porsenna dedita urbe neque Galli capta temerare potuissent, furore principum exscindi. 2. arserat et ante Capitolium civili bello, sed fraude privata; nunc palam obsessum, palam incensum, quibus armorum causis, quo tantae cladis pretio? stetit profecto dum pro patria bellavimus?
>
> This turned out to be the most lamentable and despicable crime for the republic of the Roman people since the founding of the city: although there was no foreign enemy, although the gods were favorable, if we could claim as much according to our customs, the Temple of Jupiter Optimus Maximus, founded under good auspices by our forefathers as the symbol of our empire, which neither Porsenna at the surrender of the city nor the Gauls at its capture had been able to desecrate, was now destroyed because of the fury of our leaders. 2. The Capitolium had already burnt down during an earlier civil war, but by a private act of arson; now it was openly besieged, openly set on fire, but for what military reasons, and at what cost for such a great disaster? Did it not stand so long as we fought on behalf of our country?

In the midst of the chaos atop the Capitol during the fighting, some of the Flavians resort to a disguise in order to escape the carnage, including the young Domitian himself (*Hist.* 3.74.1–2):[29]

> Domitianus prima inruptione apud aedituum occultatus, sollertia liberti lineo amictu turbae sacricolarum immixtus ignoratusque, apud Cornelium Primum paternum clientem iuxta Velabrum delituit. 2. ac potiente rerum patre, disiecto aeditui contubernio, modicum sacellum Iovi Conservatori aramque posuit casus suos in marmore expressam; mox imperium adeptus Iovi Custodi templum ingens seque in sinu dei sacravit.

Domitian, after the first assault, had hidden himself at the house of the temple attendant, and then, at the wise suggestion of a freedman, donning a linen garment he mixed himself in among the crowd of celebrants and, undetected, he lay low at the house of Cornelius Primus, one of his father's clients, near the Velabrum. 2. And, when his father assumed control of affairs, having knocked down the temple attendant's hut, he set up a small sanctuary for Jupiter the Preserver and an altar engraved in marble with his own misadventures. Later, after having acquired control over the empire, he consecrated a large temple to Jupiter the Guardian and a statue of himself on the god's lap.

Tacitus provides a superficially neutral, if not positive, account of what must have been one of the most embarrassing moments of the war for the new royal family, but I find it hard to believe that Domitian would have been especially proud of his inglorious actions or interested in seeing them preserved for posterity. Perhaps Tacitus tips his hand when he attributes the dubious idea of Domitian donning the disguise to *sollertia liberti* (3.74.1), especially since neither Josephus (*BJ* 4.645–9) nor Suetonius (*Dom.* 1.2) nor Cassius Dio (64.17) includes this detail in his version of the episode. In the course of Jupiter's encomium in *Punica* 3.594–629, Silius highlights this unflattering moment towards the beginning of the section purportedly in praise of Domitian: *nec te terruerint Tarpei culminis ignes; / sacrilegas inter flammas servabere terris. / nam te longa manent nostri consortia mundi* (609–11). The poet seemingly lauds Domitian for escaping the fall of the Capitol in order to live out his allotted time as emperor, but the rhetoric of the passage militates strongly against any straightforward reading of the encomium as unvarnished praise. Likewise, when Silius hails Domitian as *Germanice* (607), the poet prompts the reader to reflect on how Domitian's triumphs over the Chatti and the Dacians in AD 83 and 86, respectively, for which he claimed the honorific title of Germanicus, compare to the far more deserved triumph of Titus (and Vespasian) over the Jews after the fall of Jerusalem in AD 70.[30] Tacitus (*Germ.* 37; *Agr.* 39) and Suetonius (*Dom.* 6.1, 13.3) condemn Domitian for claiming a false triumph in no uncertain terms, whereas Martial (2.2) and Statius (*Silv.* 4.2), like Silius, leave it to the reader to decide whether they intend to praise or blame the emperor for his supposed victories.[31] Perhaps most of all, Silius invites the reader to juxtapose the images of Domitian qua Germanicus and Scipio qua Africanus scaling the Capitol, to recognize both the similarities and the differences between the two triumphant *imperatores*, and to realize that it was, indeed, Rome's victory in the Second Punic War which put the city on the path to its later fall through the suicide of civil war.

Conclusion: Silius Italicus and the *Punica* in Classical Literature

1. The Place of Silius Italicus and the *Punica* in Classical Literature

By constructing his unique version, and unique vision, of the Second Punic War in the *Punica*, as a dual narrative of victory in *bellum externum* and defeat in *bellum internum*, Silius secures his place in Classical literature. At the same time, his transformation of the conflict into a new Gigantomachy, a new Trojan War, and a new Gallic sack reflects a contemporary obsession with the theme of Rome's decline and fall, especially after the fall of the Capitol. In his *epicedion in patrem suum* ("lament for his father," *Silv.* 5.3), Statius describes the tumultuous period between Nero and the Flavians in a manner which powerfully resonates with the manner in which Silius describes the Second Punic War, as a new iteration of these archetypal conflicts (195–204):[1]

> 195 talia dum celebras, subitam civilis Erinys
> Tarpeio de monte facem Phlegraeaque movit
> proelia. sacrilegis lucent Capitolia taedis
> et Senonum furias Latiae sumpsere cohortes.
> vix requies flammae necdum rogus ille deorum
> 200 siderat, excisis cum tu solacia templis
> impiger et multum facibus velocior ipsis
> concinis ore pio captivaque fulmina defles.
> mirantur Latii proceres ultorque deorum
> Caesar, et e medio divum pater adnuit igni.

> 195 While you were celebrating such things, the Fury of civil war
> suddenly hurled her torch down from the Tarpeian Rock and sparked
> a Gigantomachy. The Capitol blazed with sacrilegious fires
> and the Latin cohorts took up the furies of the Gauls.

>   Scarcely had the flames died down, and not yet had the pyre of the gods
> 200 grown cold, when you in your eagerness to outstrip those torches
>   sang of solace for the temples which had been destroyed
>   in pious tones, and you mourned the thunderbolts taken captive.
>   The Latin nobles and Caesar, the avenger of the gods, stood in amazement,
>   and the father of the gods gave his consent from the midst of the fire.

Like Silius over the course of the *Punica*, Statius here imagines the *furor* of civil war bringing destruction to the Capitol in a replay of the Gigantomachy and the Gallic sack (195–8), after which Statius' father composed a poem (with similar language and imagery?) which met with approval from the Roman Senate, Domitian, and even Jupiter himself (199–204). Interestingly enough, poet and *princeps* merge into one here, since Domitian composed an epic on the fall of the Capitol, the lost *Bellum Capitolinum* (cf. the *Fall of Troy* composed by Nero at the time of the great fire of AD 64: Tac. *Ann.* 15.39.3; Suet. *Nero* 38.2).[2] In an epigram written to celebrate the formal publication of the poem, Martial compares the work to the *Aeneid* "of tragic Vergil" (*cothurnati* ... *Maronis*, 5.5.8), a collocation which he uses only once elsewhere, to compare the *Punica* to Rome's national epic (7.63.5).[3] By associating these two particular poems, the *Bellum Capitolinum* and the *Punica*, with the (tragic elements of the) *Aeneid*, Martial suggests that both contained tragic elements of their own, that both owed a great debt to the *Aeneid*, and, perhaps, that Silius composed his epic (especially the verses on Domitian?) with Domitian's epic in mind.

A generation later, Florus likewise casts the civil war between Marius and Sulla as a new Gigantomachy and a new Gallic sack, and even as a new Second Punic War (*Epit.* 2.9.7):

> ipse quoque iaculatus incendia viam fecit arcemque Capitolii, quae Poenos quoque, Gallos etiam Senones evaserat, quasi captivam victor insedit.

> He himself [Sulla], made his way by hurling firebrands and seized the Capitol, which had escaped capture at the hands of the Carthaginians and the Gallic Senones, as if he were a victor taking it captive.

During his first march on Rome in 88 BC, Sulla accomplishes what no foreign foe had yet been able to do: he seizes the Capitol. The rhetoric of the passage recalls that of the descriptions of the fall of the Capitol in AD 69 in Statius and Tacitus, and, at the same time, transforms the Second Punic War into another archetypal conflict. More broadly, throughout his history, Florus evinces a close and careful engagement with the *Punica* which informs not only his own approach to the arc of Roman history and Roman culture through the transition from Republic to Empire, from *bellum externum* to *bellum civile*, but also, as we will see, his narrative of the Second Punic War.

Across the six chapters which constitute the core of this book, I have sought to address three essential (and, as we have seen, interrelated) questions: who is Silius Italicus, what is the *Punica*, and what is the *Punica* about? In Chapters 1 and 2, we studied how both the poet and his poem are very much a product of their age, the tumultuous transition from the Julio-Claudians to the Flavians (in contrast to the remarkably smooth transition from the Flavians to the Five Good Emperors). In Chapters 3 and 4, we examined the narrative of the *Punica* book by book, as well as representative passages from throughout the work which provide some sense of what the epic as a whole has to offer. In Chapters 5 and 6, we considered how and why Silius transforms his narrative of the Second Punic War into a totalizing vision of *Romanitas*. Throughout, we have seen how Silius engages with a great variety of authors and texts across an impressive array of literary traditions on the Second Punic War (and beyond) in both prose and poetry, but especially with Livy and the historiographical tradition, on the one hand, and Vergil and the epic tradition, on the other. In this conclusion, I offer a series of three close readings which explores the place of Silius Italicus and the *Punica* in Classical literature, but especially in historiography and epic, in order to illustrate various facets of that literary engagement in greater detail. Ultimately, this series of close readings will bring us back to where we began in the introduction to this book, with the loss and later rediscovery of Silius Italicus and his *Punica* during the Renaissance.[4]

2. The *Punica* and Earlier Literature: Livy and Vergil

On the march from Spain to Italy, from Saguntum to Cannae and, eventually, Rome, Hannibal is guided by his dreams, especially those sent by Juno, every step of the way.[5] It is Juno who fills his head with thoughts of crossing the Alps and scaling the Capitol (1.64–5), Juno who inspires him to set the ambush along the shores of Lake Trasimene (4.722–38), Juno who sends Anna to prompt him to march to Cannae (8.202–41), and, of course, Juno who sends Somnus to prompt him *not* to march on Rome after his momentous victory (10.326–86). In book 3, however, after the fall of Saguntum and the triumph at Gades, it is not Juno but Jupiter who dispatches Mercury to visit Hannibal in a dream (3.158–221).[6] After sending his wife, Imilce, and their infant son back to Carthage, Hannibal returns to Gades, where he succumbs to the need for sleep after his many travails (158–62); as a test of Roman *virtus*, Jupiter sends Mercury down to Hannibal in a dream so that he can rebuke him for resting after the fall of Saguntum instead of continuing on to Rome (163–82). Mercury ends his rebuke with the surprising promise that Hannibal will stand victorious before the walls of the city, but he must not "look back" along the way (179–82):

> "en age, si quid inest animo par fortibus ausis,
> 180 fer gressus agiles mecum et comitare vocantem.
> respexisse veto; monet hoc pater ille deorum.
> victorem ante altae statuam te moenia Romae."

> "Come on, if you have a spirit inside you equal to these bold adventures,
> 180 hurry along with me and follow after me as I call to you.
> I forbid you from looking back; the father of the gods issues this warning.
> You will stand before the walls of lofty Rome in victory: I guarantee it."

Hannibal then dreams that Mercury takes him by the hand and leads him on to Italy: startled by a sudden din, Hannibal, forgetting the god's instruction, looks back, sees a massive serpent leaving a large swathe of destruction in its wake, and asks the god what the monster portends (183–202). Mercury explains how the serpent represents Hannibal himself and the terrible destruction soon to be wrought by him as he storms over the Alps, invades Italy, and threatens Rome (203–13):

> cui gelidis almae Cyllenes editus antris:
> "bella vides optata tibi. te maxima bella,
> 205 te strages nemorum, te moto turbida caelo
> tempestas caedesque virum magnaeque ruinae
> Idaei generis lacrimosaque fata sequuntur.
> quantus per campos populatis montibus actas
> contorquet silvas squalenti tergore serpens
> 210 et late umectat terras spumante veneno,
> tantus perdomitis decurrens Alpibus atro
> involves bello Italiam tantoque fragore
> eruta convulsis prosternes oppida muris."

> To him the god born in the chilly caves of nourishing Mt. Cyllene [said]:
> "You see the wars which you desire. The greatest wars follow after you,
> 205 the devastation of forests and groves, a swirling storm created by
> the moving clouds and the slaughter of men and the great fall
> of the race of Mt. Ida [Trojans, i.e., Romans] and their sorrowful fate.

> As great as the serpent with its scaly back which rolls through the plains
> the trees dragged down from the denuded mountains
> 210 and stains the earth far and wide with its frothy venom,
> so great will you, rushing down from the conquered Alps,
> embroil Italy in black war and with such a great din
> will you lay low the settlements torn up from their toppled walls."

With that, Mercury departs, leaving Hannibal to wake up in a cold sweat: after reflecting on the dream, Hannibal offers a sacrifice to Jupiter, Mars, and Mercury, and orders his men to prepare themselves for the march from Spain to Italy (214–21). On the one hand, Silius draws on the various versions of this story preserved by Livy (21.22.5-9), Cicero (*Div.* 1.24.49), and Valerius Maximus (1.7.ext.1), all of whom include the injunction not to "look back" as well as Hannibal's unwitting backward glance. On the other hand, Silius also draws on another dream scene, in the *Aeneid*, when Jupiter sends Mercury down to Aeneas in order to rebuke him for remaining at Carthage instead of continuing on to Italy (Verg. *Aen.* 4.219-78, cf. 556-70). Silius cues his engagement with Vergil through his use of the learned epithet *Cyllenius*, which refers to the site of Mercury's birth, Mt. Cyllene. Vergil uses forms of *Cyllenius* in the *Aeneid* only in this passage (252, 258, 276; cf. 8.138-9), and Silius likewise uses forms of the word twice in Hannibal's dream (168, 219; cf. 8.111, 13.630, 16.500). However, whereas Mercury, on behalf of Jupiter, instructs Hannibal *not* to "look back" (*respexisse veto*, 181), the messenger of the gods, once again on behalf of Jupiter, instructs Aeneas to do the exact opposite, to "look back" upon (~ remember) his promised future and that of his son, Ascanius, in Italy (*respice*, 275; cf. 225, 236).

By weaving together these disparate threads of the historiographical and epic traditions, Silius transforms Hannibal's backward glance here and elsewhere in the *Punica* into a complex (meta)literary and (meta)historical gesture which functions as a homology for a whole series of other backwards glances in myth and history before, during, and after the Second Punic War.[7] In the myth of Orpheus and Eurydice, the bard loses his wife for a second and final time when he fails to heed the injunction not to look back at her while leading her out of the Underworld. In his version of the story in the *Georgics*, Vergil accordingly emphasizes how Orpheus "looked back" (*respexit*, 4.191) and lost his wife forever, and later authors followed suit, from Ovid (*Met.* 10.57 *flexit* ... *oculos*, 11.66 *respicit*) to Seneca (*Her. F.* 585 *respice*; cf. *Her. O.* 1085 *respicit*), even to Boethius (*Cons.* 3 *metrum* 12.49-58, esp. *respicit*, 52 ~ *lumina flexerit*, 56). In the *Aeneid*, Vergil himself elegantly connects this backward glance with Aeneas and his wife,

Creusa, whom he lost at the fall of Troy when, by his own later admission, he did *not* "look back" (*respexi*, 2.741) to see whether she was still with him before making it out of the living hell of the city burning to the ground all around them. When Aeneas sets sail from Carthage, "looking back at the walls" of that city (*moenia respiciens*, 5.3), he sees what he later learns are the flames of Dido's funeral pyre, a proleptic image of the future fall of Carthage itself. (Tibullus later likewise describes the moment when Aeneas "looked back" [*respiceret*, 2.5.22] at Troy in flames.) In Livy, Hannibal is said "to have looked back" at Italy just like a man leaving his homeland to go into exile rather than like an enemy leaving a foreign country when he left the peninsula in order to sail back to Africa (30.20.7, esp. *respexisse*).[8] Across all of these examples, looking back, or, in the case of Creusa, at least, *not* looking back, entails the irrevocable loss of one's own family and/or city. Across the narrative arc of the *Punica*, Silius capitalizes on the freighted significance of the backward glance as both a physical and a psychological gesture in order to trace the rise and fall of Hannibal. After his dream at Gades, Hannibal encounters so many grave challenges during his arduous climb up the Alps that he has no opportunity "to have looked back" on how far he has come (*respexisse*, 3.532); later at Rome, however, he reluctantly retreats, "looking back again and again" as he marches off, never to return to the city (*respectans*, 12.729; cf. *respectantem*, 7.403; *respectans*, 12.106). And yet, as Hannibal looks back at Rome, like a new Orpheus or a new Aeneas (cf. *Culex* 157–201 ~ 268–95), he appears to consign the city to its fate and fulfill Mercury's promise of "the devastation of Italy" (*vastitas Italiae*: Liv. 21.22.9; Cic. *Div.* 1.24.49; V. Max. 1.7.ext.1), if not through the Second Punic War,[9] then through the later civil wars.[10]

3. The *Punica* and Contemporary Literature: Lucan and Petronius

Lucan's epic treatment of the civil war between Caesar and Pompey casts a long shadow over Flavian epic and complicates the reception of both Vergil and Ovid, especially as later authors like Valerius Flaccus, Statius, and, of course, Silius explored the theme of civil war in Roman history and Roman culture, from Monarchy to Republic to Empire. Across the narrative arc of the *Bellum civile*, Lucan essentially offers the inverse of what Silius offers in the *Punica*. Where Silius transforms a foreign war into a civil war, Lucan transforms a civil war into a foreign war; in particular, where Lucan casts Julius Caesar in the mold of

Hannibal, Silius casts Hannibal in the mold of Julius Caesar.[11] Ultimately, Lucan and Silius juxtapose (conflate) *bellum externum* and *bellum internum* in order to highlight both the similarities and the differences between the fight against the foreign foe and that against the enemy within. Accordingly, like Silius, Lucan uses the backwards glance at several key points in the narrative as a way of transforming his epic into a reflection, a refraction, even a diffraction, of the competing memories about the fall of the Republic and the rise of the Empire. In the closing verses of the extant (unfinished?) *Bellum civile*, if not the closing verses which Lucan intended to write, Julius Caesar "looks back" in a gesture which homologizes this fraught process of competitive memorialization (10.534–46):[12]

>   molis in exiguae spatio stipantibus armis
> 535 dum parat in vacuas Martem transferre carinas,
>   dux Latius tota subitus formidine belli
>   cingitur: hinc densae praetexunt litora classes,
>   hinc tergo insultant pedites. via nulla salutis,
>   non fuga, non virtus; vix spes quoque mortis honestae.
> 540 non acie fusa nec magnae stragis acervis
>   vincendus tum Caesar erat sed sanguine nullo.
>   captus sorte loci pendet; dubiusque timeret
>   optaretne mori respexit in agmine denso
>   Scaevam perpetuae meritum iam nomina famae
> 545 ad campos, Epidamne, tuos, ubi solus apertis
>   obsedit muris calcantem moenia Magnum.

>   As the soldiers throng around him in the narrow space of the mole,
> 535 while he prepares to shift the fight onto the empty boats,
>   the Latin leader [Caesar] is suddenly surrounded by an overwhelming fear
>   of battle: on this side the densely packed fleets gather along the shores,
>   on that side the infantry soldiers press from behind. There is no road to safety,
>   not by flight, not by fighting; there is barely any hope for an honorable death.
> 540 Caesar was not then to be conquered after seeing his army defeated in battle
>   or after seeing heaps of his men in great slaughter, but without drawing any blood.
>   Trapped by the circumstances of his position, he hesitates; and uncertain whether

>   he should fear or desire death, he looked back in the densely packed
>   column
>   at Scaeva, who had already earned a reputation for eternal glory
> 545 in your fields, Epidamnus, where he alone
>   beneath the open walls withstood the onslaught of Magnus [Pompey].

Trapped on the mole which connects Pharos (the famous lighthouse) with Alexandria, in Egypt, Caesar is stricken by the sudden fear that he faces imminent defeat without the opportunity to die heroically in combat (534–41). As he hesitates between fearing and desiring to die, Caesar "looks back" upon (~ remembers) his centurion Scaeva, who bravely fought and fell during the siege of Dyrrhachium (542–6, esp. *respexit*, 543). Silius appears to have had the passage in mind when composing Hannibal's parting words in 17.597–617. As the enemy closes in, both men, seated upon a natural eminence, realize that they are in a perilous position and then reflect on a turning point in their respective wars which put them in their current predicament. In the case of Caesar, he looks back to Dyrrhachium, his greatest defeat; in the case of Hannibal, he looks back to Cannae, his greatest victory. Just as Mercury issues the injunction against "looking back" during Hannibal's dream at Gades, so Caesar issues a similar injunction of his own earlier in the narrative during his *adhortatio* before the climactic battle at Pharsalus (7.308–10):[13]

>   vestri cura movet; nam me secura manebit
>   sors quaesita manu: fodientem viscera cernet
> 310 me mea qui nondum victo respexerit hoste.
>
>   It is my concern for you which moves me; for the secure fate
>   sought by my hand will wait for me: anyone who looks back
> 310 before defeating his foe will see me ripping out my own guts.

Caesar expresses his concern over the coming engagement and, in particular, the fate of his men: at the same time, he warns them that, if anyone of them "looks back" (*respexerit*, 310) before the battle is won, he will see Caesar committing suicide. The image of Caesar driving his sword into his entrails recalls both the epic's proem, in which Lucan describes the civil war in general in the same terms (1.1–7), and the later suicide of Cato the Younger, which may have been the intended ending of the poem. When Caesar violates his own injunction against "looking back" at the end of the (again, extant) epic, he sends the reader back to an important turning point, perhaps even the middle of a planned 12-book poem, when the centurion Scaeva single-handedly defends the Roman camp at

Dyrrhachium against a vigorous Pompeian attack until he falls under a hail of spears (6.138–262).[14] Scholars have long debated about the positive and the negative aspects of this *exemplum virtutis*: in particular, scholars have remarked on how (like Murrus at Saguntum in the *Punica*),[15] Scaeva initially stands and ultimately falls for the wall of the Roman camp. At the pivotal moment in his (anti-)*aristeia*, Scaeva "looks back" in order to kill a foe (6.180–5):

> 180 ut primum cumulo crescente cadavera murum
>   admovere solo, non segnior extulit illum
>   saltus et in medias iecit super arma catervas,
>   quam per summa rapit celerem venabula pardum.
>   tunc densos inter cuneos conpressus et omni
> 185 vallatus bello vincit, quem respicit, hostem.

> 180 As soon as the growing pile of corpses knocked
>   the wall off its foundation, no less eager a leap carried him over it,
>   and threw him into the middle of the fray on top of their weapons,
>   than the leap which snatches the swift panther away from the hunter's javelins.
>   Then, trapped among the densely packed ranks and surrounded
> 185 by the fighting on all sides, he defeats the enemy whom he looks back to see.

In the verses which immediately follow, Scaeva loses his momentum and, after a long struggle, finally falls in death: at the very moment when he "looks back" (*respicit*, 185), Scaeva seals his fate. Moreover, when Caesar "looks back" upon (~ remembers) Scaeva's backward glance, in violation of Caesar's own injunction not to "look back" until victory is attained, Lucan appears to direct the reader's glance both backwards, through this prism of earlier moments in the epic, and forwards, ahead to the death of Cato the Younger and, perhaps, even that of Caesar himself.

Above and beyond the theme of the backwards glance, Lucan and Silius evince their shared concern with the transition from Republic to Empire, from *bellum externum* to *bellum civile*, by exploring the fraught relationship between Hannibal and Caesar as enemies of Rome who cross the Alps, invade Italy, and threaten the city itself with destruction. Where Silius posits a link between the cosmic disturbance caused by Hannibal and that later caused by Caesar and Pompey (1.36–7 ~ 13.861–7),[16] Lucan goes so far as to have Caesar himself compare his own invasion to that of Rome's most hated foreign enemy in an address to his men (1.303–5):[17]

> non secus ingenti bellorum Roma tumultu
> concutitur, quam si Poenus transcenderit Alpes
> 305   Hannibal.
>
> Rome is shaken to its core by the great tumult of war
> no less than if the Phoenician had crossed the Alps,
> 305   Hannibal himself.

This simile once again elides the boundary between Republic and Empire, foreign war and civil war. More broadly, it reflects the totalizing approach to Roman literature, Roman history, and Roman culture which Lucan and Silius, among many others, adopt in an ultimately vain attempt at making sense of Rome's descent into the suicidal *furor* of *bellum civile*. Petronius captures the essence of this totalizing approach to the descent into civil war in the prefatory remarks on the stereotypical orator-turned-poet (e.g., Silius Italicus?) offered by the hack Eumolpus before he recites his own (unfinished) epyllion on the civil war between Caesar and Pompey (118).[18] At the end of those remarks, Eumolpus warns against taking on the theme of civil war (118.6):

> ecce belli civilis ingens opus quisquis attigerit nisi plenus litteris, sub onere labetur. Non enim res gestae versibus comprehendendae sunt, quod longe melius historici faciunt, sed per ambages deorumque ministeria et fabulosum sententiarum tormentum praecipitandus est liber spiritus, ut potius furentis animi vaticinatio appareat quam religiosae orationis sub testibus fides.
>
> Behold, the endless theme of civil war: whoever ventures upon this topic, unless he is steeped in literature, will falter under its weight. For, great deeds must not be confined to verse, since historians handle them far better, but a free spirit must be hurled head over heels into plots and interventions of the gods and the story-like twists and turns of aphorisms, so that it may appear to be more like the prophecy of a raging spirit than the faithful account of a sacred speech before witnesses.

The reference to the *belli civilis ingens opus* immediately recalls Vergil's *maius opus* (*Aen.* 7.45), the (proleptic) civil war which occupies the narrative of the second half of Rome's national epic, and perhaps playfully acknowledges that the unfinished epyllion cannot possibly do justice to the grandeur of the theme. In the extended description of his climb up the Alps (122–3, esp. verses 144–208), Caesar trod both literally and metaphorically in the footsteps of Hercules, the Gauls, and Hannibal (cf. esp. *Pun.* 3.477–556), perhaps against the backdrop of the events of AD 69. At the climax of this part of the poem, Caesar is likened to

Hercules and then to Jupiter himself, standing atop Mt. Olympus and hurling his thunderbolt against the Giants (123, verses 205-8):

> 205 qualis Caucasea decurrens arduus arce
> Amphitryoniades, aut torvo Iuppiter ore,
> cum se verticibus magni demisit Olympi
> et periturorum deiecit tela Gigantum.

> 205 Just like the son of Amphitryon [Hercules], rushing down in full force
> from the peaks of the Caucasus, or Jupiter with his terrible gaze,
> when he took himself down from the heights of great Mt. Olympus
> and hurled the weapons of the very Giants who were going to be killed.

Above and beyond the resonance between this simile and the narrative transition from the Alps to Mt. Olympus in *Punica* 3, the simile itself likens Caesar to Hercules and then to Jupiter just as the simile at *Punica* 17.647-50 likens Scipio to Bacchus and then to Hercules after his victory in the Gigantomachy. Regardless of whether Silius wrote with an eye on Petronius or vice versa, the two similes, read together, complicate the relationship between Caesar and Hannibal, as well as the conflation of *bellum externum* and *bellum internum*, by adding Scipio to the equation.[19]

4. The *Punica* and Later Literature: Florus, Ampelius, and the *De viris illustribus*

In their groundbreaking study of the *Punica*, Ahl, Davis, and Pomeroy offer the following ruminations on the structure of the epic and, in particular, the pivotal importance of Cannae:[20]

> In making Cannae the pivotal battle and assigning it the central position in his epic, Silius is, as we have noted, breaking with traditional, historical techniques....
> It is reasonable to conclude that Silius' decision to focus his epic on Cannae and to devote three of his seventeen books to the battle and to the events immediately preceding and following it was not based on any prior tradition of the second Punic War. Further, neither Homer nor Vergil provided a clear precedent for setting the major military conflict in the middle of the epic. Silius' most obvious exemplar is Lucan, whose epic reaches its climax with the battle in Pharsalia 7.

While Silius certainly does owe a great debt to Lucan in this respect, as in many others, Silius also certainly owes an equal debt to the rich existing tradition on the Second Punic War itself. Despite its extraordinary length, the *Punica* actually offers a rather simplified narrative of the conflict compared to the wealth of detail preserved elsewhere in the tradition and especially by Polybius and Livy.[21] This tradition appears to include evidence of a popular memory of the war which reduced the long string of battles to a series of four victories for Hannibal, culminating with Cannae, and a series of four revenge victories for the Romans, culminating with Zama. This model radically distorts the narrative chronology of the war by identifying its turning point not with Hannibal's march on Rome in 211 BC, but with his victory at Cannae in 216 BC, a mere five years into the 20-year conflict. This chronological distortion, in turn, prompts both a narrative compression, as the victory at Cannae and the march on Rome eventually merge into one event (e.g., Ampel. 45.2 and Zos. 1.1.1), and a narrative simplification, as most of the events after Cannae and the march on Rome eventually fall out of the later tradition altogether, as well as a narrative displacement, as the events of the war are rearranged to fit the scheme. In the end, the only consistent element which survives intact is the list of Hannibal's four victories: the battles of the Ticinus River, the Trebia River, Lake Trasimene, and Cannae. The major evidence for this popular memory of the war includes Florus' narrative of the Second Punic War in his *Epitome* (*Epit.* 1.22), Ampelius' biography of Hannibal (28.4) and narrative of the Second Punic War (46.4–6) in his *Liber memorialis*, and the biography of Hannibal in the *De viris illustribus* (42), often wrongly attributed to Sex. Aurelius Victor. All of these sources postdate the *Punica* but may very well preserve later versions of an epitomizing tradition which predates the epic and may already surface at various points in Cornelius Nepos' biography of Hannibal in his *Vitae*.[22]

In his abbreviated account of the Second Punic War in *Epit.* 1.22, Florus provides ample evidence for this complex process of narrative compression, simplification, and displacement. He begins with Hannibal's oath of eternal hatred against Rome (1–2) and continues with the fall of Saguntum (3–8). Thereafter, Hannibal marches from Spain to Italy (9), where he then defeats the Romans in four consecutive battles: the Ticinus River, the Trebia River, Lake Trasimene, and Cannae (10–18). Following Cannae, Hannibal marches to Capua to celebrate his victory instead of continuing on to Rome (19–22). For Florus, this disastrous decision *not* to march immediately on Rome marks the turning point in the war, since Hannibal and his men are soon conquered by Campanian *luxuria*: Florus goes so far as to quote Livy for the idea that "Capua was Hannibal's Cannae" (*Capuam Hannibali Cannas fuisse*, 21 = Liv. 23.45.4). At this pivotal moment in the conflict, the Romans seize the initiative and begin the long march back to victory (23–6). The Romans exact vengeance for their four earlier defeats in Italy by scoring victories of their own over the Carthaginians in all four theaters of combat: Italy (27–32), Sicily (33–4), Sardinia (35), and Spain (36–40). In a noticeable departure from the usual chronology, Fabius enters the fray not before but *after* the battle of Cannae (27–8), and New Carthage falls to Scipio not after but *before* Hannibal's march on Rome (39–40). Following this awkward enumeration of Roman successes, Florus returns to Italy, where Hannibal finally makes his long-delayed, and ultimately fruitless, march on the city (41–8). Florus then concludes his narrative with the Roman victories at the battles of the Metaurus River (49–53) and Zama (54–61). In a telling comment on Rome's moral transformation during the course of the conflict, Florus observes how "then, with Scipio in command, the Roman people, turning their entire force against Africa herself, began to imitate Hannibal and to avenge the disasters of their native Italy on Africa" (*duce igitur Scipione in ipsam Africam tota mole conversus imitari coepit Hannibalem et Italiae suae clades in Africam vindicare*, 55).[23] Whereas Hannibal had inflicted *clades* upon *clades* in Italy at the beginning of the conflict, the Roman people now do the same in Africa at its end. At Zama, Hannibal simply "withdrew" (*cessit*, 61) from the battlefield just as he "withdrew" (*cessit*, 46) from the walls of Rome earlier in the war; perhaps surprisingly, Florus ends his narrative not with the image of Scipio returning to Rome in triumph but instead with that of Hannibal in flight, a decision which Florus explicitly claims put Rome on the path to becoming *the* superpower (61). This version and, once again, vision of the Second Punic War may very well have been what (elite) Romans learned at school and considered the "standard" account, and, I would claim, may very well reflect how Silius and his contemporaries remembered the conflict, as well as its place in Roman history and Roman culture, especially the pivotal importance of the battle of Cannae.

Later generations subjected this popular memory of the Second Punic War to even more narrative compression, simplification, and displacement, ultimately whittling down a full decade of Livy's *Ab urbe condita* to a mere list of major engagements. Writing perhaps sometime in the early third century AD, Ampelius offers, essentially, a handbook of Roman history and Roman culture in his *Liber memorialis*, including many references to all three of the Punic Wars. In two different passages, the first from a biography of Hannibal (28.4) and the second from a summary of the Second Punic War (46.4–6), he reduces the narrative of the conflict to its barest outline. In Chapter 28, Ampelius compiles a list of famous enemies with whom the Romans waged war: *Populus Romanus cum quibus gentibus bella conseruit et quibus de causis* ("The nations with which the

Roman people waged war and the reasons for which they did so"). After recounting the wars waged by the seven kings (1), the Roman defeat at the battle of the Caudine Forks (2), and the war against Pyrrhus of Epirus (3), Ampelius concludes the list with Hannibal (4):

> Hannibal qui novem annorum patrem in Hispaniam secutus, minor annorum XXV imperator factus triennio in Hispania vicit, et <cum> eversione Sagunti rupto foedere per Pyrenaeum et Alpes in Italiam venisset, Scipionem <aput> Ticinum Tiberium Claudium aput Trebiam Flaminium aput Trasimennum Paulum et Varronem aput Cannas Gracchum in Lucania Marcellum in Campania superavit. ***

> Hannibal who, at the age of 9, followed his father into Spain; who, at an age less than 25, was made general and was victorious in Spain within three years; and who, when he had come through the Pyrenees and the Alps into Italy after the destruction of Saguntum and the dissolution of the treaty, defeated Scipio along the Ticinus, Tiberius Claudius along the Trebia, Flaminius along the shores of Trasimene, Paullus and Varro near Cannae, Gracchus in Lucania, Marcellus in Campania. ***

In this condensed biography of Hannibal which doubles as a truncated summary of the Second Punic War, Ampelius provides further evidence for the ongoing process of transforming history into memory, for deciding what does and does not make the cut as Roman history, culture, and literature become objects of memorialization. Like Florus, Ampelius mentions Hannibal's oath of eternal hatred against Rome, the fall of Saguntum, and the march from Spain to Italy, where he then defeats the Romans in the same four battles at the Ticinus River, the Trebia River, Lake Trasimene, and Cannae. However, whereas Florus continues with the march to Capua (instead of Rome), Ampelius extends the list to include Hannibal's victories against "Gracchus in Lucania" (cf. *Pun.* 12.473–8) and "Marcellus in Campania" (cf. *Pun.* 15.334–98). Here, Ampelius may have conflated Marcellus' victory over Hannibal at Nola (in Campania) with Hannibal's later victory over Marcellus in the ambush between Venusia and Bantia (in Apulia), but there may also simply be something wrong or missing in the text. Textual issues likewise obscure the end of Chapter 46, in which Ampelius offers a second account of the conflict as part of a broader narrative *De tribus Punicis bellis* ("On the three Punic Wars"). In between very brief summaries of the First (1–3) and Third (7) wars, Ampelius provides a relatively fuller account of the Second in which he divides the war into four victories for Hannibal and then four for the Romans (4–6):

4. secundum Punicum bellum longe omnium cruentissimum fuit. causa quod Hannibal contra foedus Saguntum evertisset. 5. prima cladis huius belli aput Ticinum vulnerato patre Scipione quem Publius Scipio nondum pubes protexit ac liberavit; secunda clades aput Trebiam vulnerato Flacco consule; tertia aput Trasimenum vastato Flamini exercitu; quarta aput Cannas deletis duobus exercitibus Pauli consulis morte Terenti fuga Varronis. 6. postea vero quattuor duces Punici belli gloriam sibi vindicant: Fabius [sibi] Cunctator qui imminentem urbis excidio Hannibalem mora fregit; Marcellus qui primus Hannibali aput Nolam restitit et inclinata<m> eius aciem penitus trucidavit; Claudius Nero qui venientem ab Hispania Hasdrubalem cum ingentibus copiis priusquam se Hannibali iungeret excepit et ingenti proelio vicit; <Scipio Africanus qui ***>.

4. The Second Punic War was by far the bloodiest of all of our wars. The cause of the war was because Hannibal had sacked Saguntum contrary to our treaty. 5. The first disaster of this war took place along the Ticinus, when the elder Scipio was wounded and Publius Scipio, not yet a young man, protected him and freed him; the second disaster was along the Trebia, when the consul Flaccus was wounded; the third was along the shores of Trasimene, when the army of Flaminius was demolished; and the fourth was near Cannae, when two armies were destroyed by the death of the consul Paullus and the flight of Terentius Varro. 6. Thereafter, indeed, four Roman generals secured the glory of the Punic war for themselves: Fabius Cunctator, who broke Hannibal by delay as he threatened the destruction of the city; Marcellus, who first opposed Hannibal near Nola and completely butchered his retiring battle line; Claudius Nero, who intercepted Hasdrubal and defeated him in a great battle as he came from Spain with great forces, before he could join up with Hannibal; and Scipio Africanus, who . . . .

Ampelius pares the memory of the Second Punic War down to the absolute minimum and, in particular, to the intertwined themes of rise and fall around the turning point of Cannae, as first Hannibal individually scores four victories over the Romans and then four different Roman generals collectively score four victories over Hannibal. Although the text breaks off with the battle of the Metaurus River, there can be no doubt that Ampelius concluded his narrative with the battle of Zama as the fourth and final Roman victory. By cutting out the oath of Hannibal and the march from Spain to Italy, as well as the march to Capua after Cannae and the later march on Rome, Ampelius divides the Second Punic War into two phases: the first comprises Hannibal's victories through Cannae, and the second comprises Rome's victories through Zama. In doing so, he distills the conflict down to its moral essence: Hannibal will fall, and Rome will rise (again).

The popular memory of the Second Punic War continues to (d)evolve in the various lives of the key players, both Roman and Carthaginian, included in the *De viris illustribus*, which was compiled during the first half of the fourth century AD. The biography of Hannibal (42) offers a narrative of the conflict which bears a striking resemblance to those in Florus and Ampelius and, at the same time, offers a slightly but significantly different account of the events after Cannae:[24]

> 1. Hannibal, Hamilcaris filius, novem annos natus, a patre aris admotus odium in Romanos perenne iuravit. 2. exinde socius et miles in castris patri fuit. mortuo eo causam belli quaerens Saguntum Romanis foederatam intra sex menses evertit. tum Alpibus patefactis in Italiam traiecit. 3. P. Scipionem apud Ticinum, Sempronium Longum apud Trebiam, Flaminium apud Trasimenum, Paullum et Varronem apud Cannas superavit. 4. cumque urbem capere posset, in Campaniam devertit, cuius deliciis elanguit. 5. et cum ad tertium ab urbe lapidem castra posuisset, tempestatibus repulsus. primum a Fabio Maximo frustratus, deinde a Valerio Flacco repulsus, a Graccho et Marcello fugatus, in Africam revocatus, a Scipione superatus, ad Antiochum regem Syriae confugit eumque hostem Romanis fecit.
>
> 1. Hannibal, the son of Hamilcar, when he was 9 years old, was brought by his father to the altar and swore an oath of eternal hatred against the Romans. 2. Then, he was an ally and soldier for his father in camp. When Hamilcar died, Hannibal, seeking a cause for war, sacked Saguntum, an ally for the Romans by treaty, within six months. Then, after laying bare the Alps, he crossed over into Italy. 3. He defeated Publius Scipio along the Ticinus, Sempronius Longus along the Trebia, Flaminius along the shores of Trasimene, and Paullus and Varro near Cannae. 4. And when he could have seized the city of Rome itself, he turned aside into Campania, because of whose delights he grew weak. 5. And when he had pitched camp near the third milestone from the city, he was driven off by storms. First hampered by Fabius Maximus, then driven off by Valerius Flaccus, then put to flight by Gracchus and Marcellus, then called back into Africa, then defeated by Scipio, he fled to Antiochus, king of Syria, and made him an enemy to the Romans.

The biography once again begins with the oath of Hannibal (1) and continues with the fall of Saguntum followed by the march from Spain to Italy (2). Thereafter, the biography rehearses the canonical list of victories for Hannibal (3) and then recounts the march to Capua instead of Rome after Cannae (4). When Hannibal does finally march on Rome, he is easily repulsed: at this point in the narrative, the biographer reduces the description of the events after Cannae to a long string of participial phrases which includes a list of four victories for the Romans (different from those in Florus and Ampelius) and culminates with Hannibal's flight from Carthage several years after the war had ended (5). All in all, the moral purpose of the narrative here remains the same as that in the earlier texts, to commemorate Hannibal's rise and fall (*superavit*, 3 ~ *superatus*, 5) and to emphasize the significance of the events after Cannae for Rome's subsequent recovery. When read together, this evidence from Florus, Ampelius, and the *De viris illustribus* for the popular memory of the Second Punic War provides a glimpse of why and how the war became a defining conflict in Roman history and Roman culture, especially as a part of the fraught transition from Republic to Empire, from *bellum externum* to *bellum civile*. Accordingly, the notion that it was Silius who transformed Cannae into the turning point of the Second Punic War, whether inspired by Lucan or not, strains credulity when it is just as possible, if not eminently plausible, that he was engaging with an earlier stage of this evolving popular memory of the conflict. The fact that the narratives in Silius and Florus, in particular, bear such a striking resemblance to each other in structure, language, and theme suggests that they reflect a, if not the, standard version and vision of the Second Punic War (and perhaps of the Republic as a whole) during the Early Empire.

5. Petrarch *Africa* and the Rediscovery of the *Punica*

Although the *Punica* appears to have been lost for nearly a millennium before its rediscovery by Poggio in the early fifteenth century, the epic's memorialization of the Second Punic War clearly exerted a meaningful and lasting impact on later memorializations in Roman history, Roman culture, and Roman literature.[25] Composed less than a century before the rediscovery of the *Punica*, Petrarch's *Africa*, also a Latin epic poem in dactylic hexameter, recounts not the entire Second Punic War but instead only Scipio's campaigns in Spain and Africa, culminating in his victory at Zama and triumph back in Rome.[26] (Petrarch covers much the same material in prose in the *Vita Scipionis* included in his *De viris illustribus*.)[27] Scholars have long debated and, barring any new evidence, will long continue to debate whether or not Petrarch somehow read Silius, in whole or in part.[28] One editor and translator, Lefebvre de Villebrune, believing that Petrarch had, in fact, read Silius, not only accused Petrarch of plagiarizing *Africa* 6.885–918, but even went so far as to "restore" these verses to their rightful place by inserting them between *Punica* 16.27 and 16.28.[29] A generation later, Ugo Foscolo rebutted this baseless charge of plagiarism in his *Essays on Petrarch*.[30]

If nothing else, this scholarly kerfuffle reflects the underlying fact that Silius and Petrarch composed their respective epics within a shared linguistic and literary tradition against a shared historical and cultural backdrop. As a result, any perceived similarity between the *Punica* and the *Africa* in structure, language, and theme may be the result of direct contact or else simply the result of that common origin. Like Silius, Petrarch looks to Vergil's *Aeneid* and Livy's *Ab urbe condita* for his main literary inspiration; like Silius, Petrarch transforms history into epic and Scipio into the epic's (albeit complex) hero; and, most of all, like Silius, Petrarch transfers his reading of the Second Punic War and, in particular, of Scipio to contemporary events. In many ways, therefore, whether or not Petrarch read Silius, the *Africa* marks the beginning of the modern reception of the *Punica* and the reintroduction of the lost epic into Classical literature.

Notes

Introduction: Why Silius?

1. Harth 1984–7 presents the critical edition of Poggio's letters (in Latin) documenting these finds; Goodhart Gordon 1974 provides an English translation of the voluminous correspondence between Poggio and Niccolò de' Niccoli (1364–1437); Greenblatt 2011 recounts the rediscovery of the *De rerum natura* and its impact on the rise of the modern West. For Poggio in general, Walser 1914 remains the most complete and authoritative account of his life and works.
2. The CESG (Codices Electronici Sangallenses) project provides an online digital collection of the existing manuscripts in the Abbey Library: visit http://www.cesg.unifr.ch/.
3. For an overview of the manuscripts of the *Punica*, as well as of the early editions, translations, and commentaries, see Delz 1966; Bassett, Delz, and Dunston 1976; Reeve 1983; McGushin 1985; Delz 1987: v–lxxviii; Muecke 2011.
4. The CEEC (Codices Electronici Ecclesiae Coloniensis) project likewise provides a collection of the existing manuscripts in the Cathedral Library: visit http://www.ceec.uni-koeln.de/.
5. Carrio 1583; Modius 1584.
6. For the *Punica* in Italy during the early Renaissance, see Muecke 2005a–b; Muecke 2010. Muecke and Dunston 2011 publishes Calderini's previously lost commentary on the epic.
7. Bussi 1471 (April 5); Leto 1471 (April 26). In a forthcoming companion volume to this book, I explore the history of the editions, translations, and commentaries for the *Punica* in more detail.
8. Marso 1483. For Marso in general, see Dykmans 1988, esp. 11, 19–20, 29–30, 71–2, 98–9.
9. Heins 1600–1 (also, Heins 1646); Dausque 1615/18.
10. Ross 1661/72. For this translation, see Vander Motten and Daemen-de Gelder 2004; Daemen-de Gelder and Vander Motten 2008; Bond 2009; von Contzen 2013; Augoustakis 2018.
11. Keller 1695; Drakenborch 1717.
12. Buzio 1765; Lefebvre de Villebrune 1781a–b.
13. Ernesti 1791–2; Ruperti 1795–8.
14. Lemaire 1823; Bothe 1855–7.

15 Bauer 1890-2; Delz 1987; Budé: Miniconi and Devallet 1979; Volpilhac, Miniconi, and Devallet 1981; Volpilhac-Léntheric, Martin, Miniconi, and Devallet 1984; Martin and Devallet 1992; Spaltenstein 1986-90.
16 English: Kline 2018; Augoustakis and Bernstein: forthcoming; French: Budé; Spanish: Villalba Álvarez 2005; Italian: Vinchesi 2001; German: Rupprecht 1991; Stürner: forthcoming.
17 For an overview of recent scholarship, see Ariemma 2000; Dominik 2010; Augoustakis 2016.
18 Occioni 1869[1]/71[2]; Occioni 1878; Occioni 1889; Occioni 1891; von Albrecht 1964. For Occioni, see also Gentile 1962; Piras 2013; Sacerdoti 2014. Other early monographs include Casale 1954; Romano 1969.
19 Ahl, Davis, and Pomeroy 1986.
20 Hardie 1993a.
21 McGuire 1997.
22 Marks 2005.
23 Tipping 2010; Stocks 2014.
24 Augoustakis 2010a; Augoustakis 2013; Augoustakis 2014a; Augoustakis 2016; Augoustakis and Littlewood 2019; Augoustakis, Buckley, and Stocks 2019.
25 The most recent scholarship includes Syré 2017 and Haselmann 2018. Dissertations completed during the past twenty years, mostly unpublished, include Marks 1999; Abdel Baky 2000; Augoustakis 2001; Chhana 2005; Klaassen Kennedy 2005; Ronet 2008; Jacobs 2009; Gajderowicz 2011; Yue 2011; García Amutxastegi 2015a; Montes Mérida 2015; van der Keur 2015; Hamvas 2016; Zaia 2016; Dibbern 2017; Conner 2018; Roumpou 2018; Siepe 2019.
26 In looking ahead to the substance of these six chapters, I provide bibliographical references for the major critical perspectives which I apply to Silius Italicus and his *Punica* in the course of this study, but I do not privilege any one theory over another. Instead, I adopt an eclectic approach to theory throughout the volume, and I see value in continuing to grapple even with outmoded ideas like authorial intention (for which, see Farrell 2017, a welcome reappraisal). For the application of theory to the Classics, especially Classical literature, see Hexter and Selden 1992; de Jong and Sullivan 1994; Harrison 2001; Heath 2002; Schmitz 2002 ≈ Schmitz 2007; Hitchcock 2008.
27 For the relevant bibliography, see below in Chapter 1.
28 For the relevant bibliography, see below in Chapter 2.
29 Von Albrecht 1964: 16-24, esp. 16-19.
30 Von Albrecht 1964: 24-46. Hardie 1989: 15 helpfully elaborates on this idea: "Von Albrecht sees the unifying theme of the *Punica* as Hannibal at the walls of Rome ... ; it would be more correct to say that there are two unifying themes, Hannibal at the walls *and* Hannibal's attempt to climb the Capitol" (italics in original). See also Hardie 1993a: 14-16.

31 Von Albrecht 1964: 47–55.
32 Von Albrecht 1964: 55–86.
33 For collective memory and collective amnesia in general, see Halbwachs 1925; Halbwachs 1950 ≈ Halbwachs 1980 ≈ Halbwachs 1992; Yates 1966; Connerton 1989; Assmann 1992; Ricoeur 2000 ≈ Ricoeur 2004; Erll 2005 ≈ Erll 2011; Connerton 2009; Berger and Niven 2014; Corning and Schuman 2015; Barash 2016; Reiff 2016. For collective memory and collective amnesia in the Roman world, see Hölkeskamp 1987; Flower 1996; Hölkeskamp 2004; Walter 2004; Flower 2006; Galinsky 2014; Galinsky 2016; Galinsky and Lapatin 2016.
34 I use the term *Romanitas* advisedly, given its near absence from Classical Latin: Adams 2003. For looking back to the Republic during the Empire, especially the transition through civil war from the Late Republic to the Early Empire, see Gowing 2005; Gallia 2012; Wilkinson 2012.
35 For analysis of this dauntingly complex, but crucially important, process of transhistoricizing (as well as translocalizing) throughout the epic, see Ahl, Davis, and Pomeroy 1986; McGuire 1995; Mezzanotte 1995 ≈ Mezzanotte 2016; McGuire 1997; Hartmann 2004; Marks 2005a. For the manipulation of time and space in narrative in general, see Bakhtin 1981: 84–258; Ricoeur 1980; Ricoeur 1983–5 ≈ Ricoeur 1984–8; with Collington 2001.
36 In the conclusion to this book, I offer a series of close readings which explores the place of Silius Italicus and the *Punica* in Classical literature, but especially in historiography and epic.
37 In the forthcoming companion volume, I explore the place of both the poet and his poem in the Classical tradition / Classical reception in greater depth, including the following three examples.
38 Plattner 1874 provides the only critical text; Plattner 1882, the only translation (into German).
39 Scott 2017: 30–44 provides a succinct overview of the war in its historical context.
40 Michel 1912–13 *passim*.
41 For the Neo-Latin historical epics of fifteenth-century northern Italy, see Lippincott 1989.
42 The following survey discusses selected major works in Spanish, but this is actually an Iberian phenomenon, including literature in Catalan, Galician, and Basque, as well as in Portuguese: Pérez Mostazo 2017; Pérez Mostazo 2018. Elsewhere, Philip Frowde (d. 1738) composed a tragedy entitled *The fall of Saguntum*, which was acted at Lincoln's Inn Fields in London and then published in 1727: an anonymous "A. B." (Frowde himself?) wrote a supplementary volume called *The history of Saguntum, and its destruction by Hannibal* (1727) which makes clear Frowde's debt to Silius through a detailed analysis of the play. Both of these works have recently been reprinted and translated into Spanish: for *The fall of Saguntum*,

see Rodríguez and Martín 1995; for *The history of Saguntum*, see Rodríguez and Martín 1992.

43 Rodríguez and Martín 1988: 325–48 collects many of these references to Saguntum.
44 Rodríguez and Martín 1988 provides the only critical text, along with an ample introduction (pp. xi–cxi) which offers a full discussion of the poem's many sources, including the *Punica* (pp. lxiv–lxxviii). For de Zamora in general, see López López 2015.
45 Pérez i Durà and Estellés i González 1991: 359–403 provides the only critical text and translation (into Spanish), along with an introduction (pp. 361–74) which treats the relationship between the *Saguntineida* and the *Punica*: see also Pérez i Durà 1993; Pérez Vilatela 2002.
46 Gaspar Zavala y Zamora: Rodríguez Cuadros 1996 provides the only critical text, along with an ample introduction; Enrique Palos y Navarro: Millón Villena 2015 publishes a transcription and facsimile of the only manuscript, recently rediscovered in the Archivo Histórico Nacional.
47 Bernstein 2017: xliii briefly remarks on the relationship between *Sónnica la cortesana* and the *Punica*, but he does not mention any of the other works discussed here.
48 María Pemán and Sánchez-Castañer 1954.
49 Conte 2012.
50 For the Classics and science fiction, see Rogers and Stevens 2015. For the Classics and modern fantasy, see Rogers and Stevens 2017. For both, see also Rogers and Stevens 2018.
51 La Penna 1981; Reitz 1993; Keith 2000; Augoustakis 2001; Vinchesi 2005; Uccellini 2006; García Amutxastegi 2009; Augoustakis 2010b; García Amutxastegi 2010; Augoustakis 2012; Keith 2013; Sharrock 2015.
52 Hawthorn 1991; Hellekson 2001; Tetlock, Lebow, and Parker 2006; Singles 2013; Gallagher 2018. As this branch of scholarship well illustrates, "fake news" is nothing new at all: today's "fake news" has become tomorrow's "fake history" for millennia. For counterfactual history in ancient epic, see Nesselrath 1992; for the *Punica*, see Cowan 2010. For alternate history and the Classics, see Grandazzi and Queyrel-Bottineau 2018, esp. the many essays on ancient epic.
53 I intend this thought experiment as a conscious nod to the *Columbiad* (1807), by Joel Barlow (1754–1812), like the *Punica*, a long-forgotten and much-maligned attempt at a national epic: Blakemore 2007 offers the only modern reading of that epic in its literary and historical contexts.
54 For the performance culture of the *recitatio*, see Starr 1991; Markus 2000; Johnson and Parker 2009; Winsbury 2009; Roller 2018a. For Imperial Rome as a (mostly silent) reading culture, especially under the Five Good Emperors, see Johnson 2010; Howley 2018. For the debate about silent reading in general, see also Knox 1968; Gilliard 1993; Gavrilov 1997; Burnyeat 1997; Saenger 1997; Johnson 2000.

55 For the origins and subsequent development of reader-response criticism, a branch of literary theory which focuses more on the work's impact on the reader than the intention of its author, see Jauß 1970; Iser 1972 ≈ Iser 1974; Iser 1976 ≈ Iser 1978; Jauss 1982a–b; Iser 1989.

56 For the tortuous path which leads from the original coining of the term *intertextualité* by Julia Kristeva to its current understanding among Classicists, see Kristeva 1969: 143–73; Genette 1982 ≈ Genette 1997; Pasco 1994; Fowler 1997a; Hinds 1998; Pucci 1998; Edmunds 2001; Damon 2010; Pelling 2013; Conte 2014; Conte 2017. For the complementary idea of intratextuality, see Sharrock and Morales 2000; Edmunds 2004; Harrison, Frangoulidis, and Papanghelis 2018.

57 For the origins and subsequent development of New Historicism, see White 1973; White 1978; Greenblatt 1980; White 1987; Hunt 1989; Veeser 1989; Thomas 1991; Veeser 1994. For recent overviews, see Ryan 1996; Brannigan 1998; Asdal and Jordheim 2018. Like all theoretical systems, New Historicism, Cultural Poetics, and Cultural Materialism have come in for their fair share of criticism: see, e.g., Felperin 1992; Maza 2004. The quotation which concludes the sentence and which serves, in many ways, as the mantra of New Historicism comes from Montrose 1989: 20.

58 For New Historicism and the Classics, see Wiseman 1979; Gabba 1981; Plass 1988; Woodman 1989; Momigliano 1990; Wiseman 1994; Kraus 1999; Potter 1999; Foucher 2000; Pelling 2000; Feldherr 2009; Manuwald 2014; see also the collections of articles in Levene and Nelis 2002; Miller and Woodman 2010.

1 Who Is Tiberius Catius Asconius Silius Italicus?

1 For the name, see *TLL Onom.* II. 264.46–266.6, as well as Schulze 1904: 76, 231–2, 347, 423, 424–5; Kajanto 1965: 180; Solin and Salomies 1988: 23, 50, 171, 346; Salomies 1992: 000–000, with Salomies 2014: 513, 515 n. 8, 516.

2 Perhaps most notably among modern scholars, Scullard 1959 begins his account of the Late Republic and Early Empire with 133 BC and traces the course of Roman history through to the death of Nero in AD 68. More recently, see also Mackay 2009; Flower 2010; Osgood 2018.

3 Syme 1939 remains the classic treatment. More recently, see also Osgood 2006; Alston 2015.

4 Raaflaub and Toher 1993; Zanker 1987 ≈ Zanker 1988; Galinsky 2012; Koortbojian 2013; as well as Weinstock 1971.

5 Galinsky 1996 offers the standard introduction to Augustan culture; for the cultural revolution and its lasting impact throughout the Roman world, see Wallace-Hadrill 2008; Spawforth 2012.

6 Griffin 1984; Sullivan 1985; Rudich 1993; Rudich 1997; Champlin 2003; Malitz 1999 ≈ Malitz 2005; Buckley and Dinter 2013; Bartsch, Freudenburg, and Littlewood 2017; Drinkwater 2019.
7 Henderson 1908; Grassl 1973; Greenhalgh 1975; Wellesley 1975; Murison 1993; Morgan 2006.
8 Briessmann 1955; Evans 1974; Nicols 1978; Bengtson 1979; Lana 1980; Darwall-Smith 1996; Boyle and Dominik 2003; Pfeiffer 2009; Kramer and Reitz 2010; Suess 2011; Zissos 2016.
9 Mason 2016 provides a magisterial study of the war; see also Rudich 2015.
10 Temple of Peace: Tucci 2017. Arch of Titus: Pfanner 1983.
11 Jones 1992; Southern 1997; Gering 2012.
12 Coleman 1986; Franchet d'Espèrey 1986; Leberl 2004. For a *synkrisis* of Nero and Domitian, see Bönisch-Meyer, Cordes, Schulz, Wolsfeld, and Ziegert 2014; Cordes 2017.
13 Grainger 2003; Morelli 2014.
14 Russell 1990; Anderson 1993; Swain 1996; Whitmarsh 2001; Whitmarsh 2005; Richter and Johnson 2017; König and Whitton 2018.
15 Bassett, Delz, and Dunston 1976, esp. 342–60, provides an authoritative treatment of these testimonia. Other discussions, primarily about the passages from Martial and Pliny, include Klotz 1927; Groag 1927a–b; Smallwood 1967: 1–8 (esp. 6), 50, cf. 142; Eck 1974; Vessey 1974; McDermott and Orentzel 1977: 24–7, 31–4; Laudizi 1989: 9–26; Matier 1981; Matier 1989b. For the derivative Renaissance *vitae*, see Bassett, Delz, and Dunston 1976: 361–4. In addition to these Renaissance *vitae*, see also Blumenröder 1694; Heister 1734; Stefani 1893. Silius almost certainly did *not* write the *Ilias Latina* attributed to one "Baebius Italicus": Buecheler 1880: 390–1; Stefani 1893: 11–25; Bassett, Delz, and Dunston 1976: 398.
16 Degrassi 1947: 332–4; Degrassi 1952: 000–000; with Gallivan 1974: 292–3, 295, 311.
17 Della Corte 1919: 236; Deane 1921: 91.
18 Calder 1935; Calder and Cormack 1962 [= *MAMA* 8]: 76, no. 411; Reynolds 1982: 46; also visit http://insaph.kcl.ac.uk/iaph2007/iAph130609.html.
19 Burnett, Amandry, and Carradice 1999: 1.3, 119, 156–9, 204–5, 216, 2.000–000.
20 de Rossi 1882.
21 See also Suet. *Vit.* 15 and D.C. 65.16–18, neither of whom mentions Silius.
22 Woodman 2009: 37; Gibson 2010: 37; Gibson 2013: 76–9; Woodman 2018: 185 *ad* 4.33.4.
23 Moles 1998 remains the standard treatment of this justly famous passage.
24 Buecheler 1880: 391; Schinkel 1884: 12–16; von Albrecht 1964: 64; Bassett 1966: 263 n. 19; von Albrecht 1973: 181; Bassett, Delz, and Dunston 1976: 343; McDermott and Orentzel 1977: 26 n. 11; Laudizi 1989: 16; Rocca-Serra 1990: 382; Cotta Ramosino 1999: 94.

25 Buecheler 1880: 390; Bassett 1966: 263 n. 19; von Albrecht 1973: 181; Bassett, Delz, and Dunston 1976: 343; Laudizi 1989: 16–17; Most 1989: 2057–9; Pomeroy 1989: 121–2; Rocca-Serra 1990: 382–3; Takács 1998: 133–5; Takács 2002; Takács 2004; Takács 2018.
26 Dickey 2012–15: 2.173–8, esp. 175–6; as well as Dionisotti 1982.
27 Blass 1876: 133 n. 1; Ussani 1918. More recently, see Connolly 2010.
28 This same error may occur much later in a 1410/12 list of codices donated by Amplonius Ratinck of Rheinberg to the University of Erfurt: Bassett, Delz, and Dunston 1976: 348.
29 Bursian 1867: iii–ix; Blass 1876; Pueschel 1907: 34–7; Nicol 1936: 172–3; Gelsomino 1967: xlvii, 63; Bassett, Delz, and Dunston 1976: 344.
30 Likewise based on this onomastic evidence, Salomies 1992: 95–6 (see also Syme 1983: 111), argues that, in addition to his two biological sons, Silius either adopted Ti. Catius Caesius Fronto or else was his uncle. Fronto was one of the suffect consuls for AD 96 (September–December, according to the *fasti Ostienses*) when Domitian was assassinated: Degrassi 1947: 223–4; Degrassi 1952: 000–000; Vidman 1982: 45, 89; with Gallivan 1981: 192, 218.
31 Blumenröder 1694: 5–11; Hübner 1875: 58.
32 Calder 1935: 217; Campbell 1936; Chilver 1941: 109–11; Syme 1958: 1.88 n. 7; Bassett, Delz, and Dunston 1976: 342; McDermott and Orentzel 1977: 24; Laudizi 1989: 11–14; Pomeroy 1989: 132–3; Cotta Ramosino 1999: 93; Dominik 2010: 428–31.
33 Watts 1971: 94–5, 97–8, 100–1; Vessey 1984; McGuire 1985: 30 n. 5; Laudizi 1989: 11–14.
34 For the most recent discussion of these dates, see Nauta 2002: 441–2.
35 In addition to the scholarship in n. 15, see Szelest 1959.
36 Henderson 2002: 116. Any use of *perpetuus* after Ovid also inevitably recalls the proem of the *Metamorphoses*, in which the poet calls upon the Muses to strike a balance between a *carmen perpetuum* and a *carmen deductum*: *ad mea perpetuum deducite tempora carmen* ("Lead my endless song down to my own times," *Met.* 1.4; cf. Hor. *Carm.* 1.7.6; Stat. *Theb.* 7.289).
37 Degrassi 1947: 222–3; Degrassi 1952: 000–000; Vidman 1982: 45, 87; with Gallivan 1981: 191, 194, 218.
38 Gibson and Morello 2012: 104–35.
39 In addition to the scholarship in n. 15, see Sherwin-White 1966 *ad loc.*; Lefèvre 1989: 118–23 ≈ Lefèvre 2009: 142–5; Gagliardi 1990; Henderson 2002: 102–24.
40 Rutledge 2001, esp. 25–6, 47–9, 51–2, 125 n. 69 (on p. 361), 268–9, 298.
41 Joseph Wright of Derby (1734–97) incorporates Silius into his cycle of paintings of the tomb of Vergil: Trapp 1984: 3, 11, 13–14, 16–17, 26; see also Trapp 1987; Hendrix 2018; Laird 2018; Peirano Garrison 2018, esp. 266, 269–80; Smiles 2018, esp. 301–6.

42 Bolaffi 1960: 160–1; Laudizi 1989: 16.
43 Pliny renders a similarly harsh judgment on Martial as a poet in the letter about his death later in the very same book: *at non erunt aeterna quae scripsit: non erunt fortasse, ille tamen scripsit tamquam essent futura* ("But, the poems which he wrote will not last forever: I should say, perhaps they will not last forever, even though he wrote them as if they would," 3.21.6).
44 Hershkowitz 1995, esp. p. 177 and n. 23 (on p. 181).
45 In general, see Geisthardt 2015.
46 Buchwald 1886: 3–22; Cartault 1887; Bickel 1911; Wistrand 1956; Bassett, Delz, and Dunston 1976: 343; McDermott and Orentzel 1977: 24–5, 32–3; Laudizi 1989: 27–54; Wilson 2013.
47 *Pun.* 1.1, 3.164, 7.94, 12.319, 411, 13.635, among many other passages.
48 Bridges 2015: 163–70 makes brief mention of the connection between Herodotus and Pliny in the course of a discussion about Xerxes as an exemplum, but does not link Xerxes with Silius.
49 In general, see Hagen 2017; Vekselius 2018.
50 The collocation *aemula virtus*, along with similar collocations, appears elsewhere in Latin literature in related contexts, including Luc. 1.120 and V.F. 5.86 (both also verse-final). In Hannibal's case, he compares himself, perhaps unwisely, to Hercules at the (first) fall of Troy.
51 Mendell 1924: 100–2; von Albrecht 1964: 82, 87–8; Bassett 1966: 262–4; Billerbeck 1985; Colish 1985: 1.281–9; Billerbeck 1986: 3134–43; Neri 1986: 2026–46; Danesi Marioni 1989; Matier 1990; Cotta Ramosino 1999; Auhagen 2006 ≈ Auhagen 2011; Baier 2006: 296–305 ≈ Baier 2011: 284–93; Dominik 2010: 429–30.
52 Dixon 1973; Brunt 1975; Malitz 1985.
53 Kißel 1979: 60 n. 178; McGuire 1989: 24; McGuire 1997: 188–9. See also Stoffel 2017.

2 What Is the *Punica*?

1 Standard accounts of Carthage include Kahrstedt and Meltzer 1879–1913; Gsell 1913–28; Huß 1985; Lancel 1992 ≈ Lancel 1995; Ameling 1993; Hoyos 2010; Miles 2010. For a recent collection of articles on Carthage and Rome before, during, and (long) after the Punic Wars, see *CPh* 112.3 (2017), especially Feeney 2017. See also Manz 2017; Sebastian 2017. Kneale 2017 offers a brisk account of seven epoch-making falls of Rome from the Gauls to the Nazis.
2 Mantel 1991; Palmer 1997; Gerhold 2002; Serrati 2006; Eckstein 2010.
3 Standard histories include Caven 1980; Bagnall 1990; Goldsworthy 2000. See also Hoyos 1998; Hoyos 2003; Hoyos 2011; Hoyos 2015; as well as Vogt 1943.
4 In addition to the scholarship in n. 3, see Lazenby 1996.

5 Hoyos 2007 offers the only modern account of this conflict.
6 In addition to the scholarship in n. 3, see Lazenby 1978; Cornell, Rankov, and Sabin 1996; Fronda 2010.
7 Hannibal: most recently, Hoyos 2008; Gabriel 2011; MacDonald 2015; Hunt 2017. Scipio: most recently, Acimovic 2007; Gabriel 2008.
8 Scholars have engaged in endless, and relatively fruitless, debate about the exact course of Hannibal's march. Most recently, see Prevas 1998; Mahaney 2008a–b; Mahaney, Kapran, and Tricart 2008; Mahaney et al. 2010; Kuhle and Kuhle 2012; Mahaney 2013; Kuhle and Kuhle 2015; Mahaney 2016; Kubler 2018: 133–77; as well as Bona 1996 ≈ Bona 1998: 95–110.
9 Goldsworthy 2001; Daly 2002; O'Connell 2010; Miething 2011; Brizzi 2016.
10 Scipio Aemilianus: Astin 1967.
11 Ridley 1986; Stevens 1988; Visonà 1988; Warmington 1988.
12 Kiernan 2004.
13 Porcius Licinus recognizes this relationship between Rome's victory in the Second Punic War and the rise of "modern" Roman literature in a famous couplet written in the aftermath of the fall of Carthage in 146 BC: *Poenico bello secundo Musa pinnato gradu / intulit se bellicosam in Romuli gentem feram* ("At the time of the Second Punic War the Muse with her winged step / brought herself, warlike, against the fierce tribe of Romulus," *fr.* 1 *ap.* Gel. 17.21.45; cf. Hor. *Ep.* 2.1.156–63, for which see Courtney 1993: 83–6, who also cites Cic. *Tusc.* 1.3).
14 Dessau 1916; Mineo 2011; Kubler 2018, esp. 55–132.
15 For the relationship between the terms "Phoenician" and "Carthaginian" in Latin, see Franko 1994; Prag 2006. Neuter plural titles are common for novels, as well, e.g., Petronius *Satyrica*.
16 Maps 1–6 on pp. xvi–xxi provide basic geographical orientation for the summary which follows.
17 In the conclusion, I present a series of case studies which illustrate various facets of this literary engagement in greater detail: in what follows, I simply strive to provide an overview.
18 For books 21–30, see Hoffmann 1942; Burck 1950; Paratore 1970; Walsh 1982; Ridley 2000; Levene 2010.
19 Begbie 1967 examines the place of this (lost) epitome in the Livian tradition outlined below. For the Livian epitomators in general, see Galdi 1934.
20 Cosack 1844; Wezel 1873; Heynacher 1874; Heynacher 1877; Bauer 1881; Kerer 1881; Schlichtheisen 1881; Bauer 1883; Klotz 1933; Nicol 1936; Sechi 1951; Venini 1972a–b; Taisne 1994; Villalba Álvarez 2008; Pomeroy 2010b; Billot 2014. For the (relatively) recent debate about the extent to which Silius draws on the existing tradition on the Second Punic War, see Nesselrath 1986; Spaltenstein 1986; Lucarini 2004; Spaltenstein 2006.

21 Badian 1966; Timpe 1972.
22 Fabius Pictor: Heynacher 1874; Heynacher 1877. Cato the Elder: Biliński 1937. Silius honors Cato by including him as a character in the *Punica*, giving him a victory in single combat over the Moor Tunger at the battle of Gereonium (7.680–704), a brief cameo at the battle of Cannae (10.13–16), and (perhaps) another brief cameo at the battle of the Metaurus River (15.730–4).
23 Karakasis 2018. Generally speaking, Silius mediates his reading of Polybius through Livy, but he also clearly evinces an engagement with how Polybius handles such fraught moments as the deaths of Regulus and Marcellus, both of whom Polybius condemns in the harshest of terms.
24 Sallust: Wezel 1873: 101–3; Neumann 1897: 313–14; Jacobs 2010.
25 Josephus: Rupprecht 1995; Hulls 2018. Tacitus: Mendell 1924: 94, 102; Manolaraki and Augoustakis 2012; Buckley 2018. See also Noè 1984.
26 Pausanias: Woodruff 1910: 386–9. Vibius Sequester: Bursian 1867: iii–ix; Blass 1876; Pueschel 1907: 34–7; Nicol 1936: 172–3; Gelsomino 1967: xlvii, 63; Bassett, Delz, and Dunston 1976: 344.
27 This biographical tradition, especially for the era of the Punic Wars, owes at least something to the Scipionic *elogia*, the *elogia* of the forum of Augustus, and similar inscriptions, as well as to the individual and family histories elaborated over the centuries in the oral tradition.
28 Silius likewise displays a close affinity with the general anecdotal tradition, especially the *strategemata* literature represented by his contemporary Frontinus and, later, Polyaenus. Frontinus: Gallia 2012: 178–216; König 2018.
29 Wezel 1873: 47–70; Bassett 1963: 76–80; Heck 1970; Pomeroy 1989: 132–5; Ripoll 2000b.
30 Keeline 2018, esp. 80, 119. Silius honors Cicero by creating an ancestor for him named Tullius among the commanders at Cannae and then associating that Tullius with his famous descendant.
31 Toohey 1992: 224–9 discusses ancient epic and the ancient novel, but he does not mention the *Punica*. For epic and the novel in general, see Bakhtin 1981: 3–40.
32 Giusti 2018, esp. 22–147. For Carthage in Roman history, Roman culture, and Roman literature in general, see also Burck 1943; Bonnet 2005; Ciocârlie 2006–8; Ciocarlie 2008.
33 Groesst 1887; Baudnik 1906; Wood 1933; von Albrecht 1964: 144–84; Cowherd 1972, esp. 150–2; von Albrecht 1973: 182–8; Lorenzo 1978; Kißel 1979: 197–208; Ahl, Davis, and Pomeroy 1986: 2493–501; Barnes 1995; Buckingham 1996; Pomeroy 1989: 127–9; Pomeroy 2000: 152–61; Ripoll 2000a, c; Villalba Álvarez 2004; Klaassen 2005; Schrijvers 2005; Ariemma 2007; Stocks 2014: 61–7; Dibbern 2017.
34 von Albrecht 1964: 144–54; Juhnke 1972; Ripoll 2001; Ripoll 2006; Fucecchi 2014; Karakasis 2014; Littlewood 2014; van der Keur 2014; Pomeroy 2016.

35 For historical epic in general, see Kroll 1916; Clinard 1967; Häußler 1976–8. For the relationship between history and epic in general, see Konstan and Raaflaub 2010; for the fraught relationship between epic, especially historical epic, and empire, see Quint 1989a. In many ways, the *Bellum Punicum* serves as the direct model for the *Punica* as an epic on a war with Carthage.

36 Cosack 1844: 17–18; Wezel 1873: 17–47; Woodruff 1906 ≈ Woodruff 1910; Fürstenau 1916; Mendell 1924, esp. 97–100; von Albrecht 1964: 21–2, 161–4; Häußler 1976–8: 2.148–61; Bettini 1977; Runchina 1982; Matier 1991.

37 Lucretius: Wezel 1873: 98–101; Bassett 1963: 74–6.

38 Wezel 1873: 86–9; Bruère 1958; Bruère 1959; von Albrecht 1964: 154–61; Wilson 2004; Bernstein 2016b.

39 Wezel 1873: 89–95; Steele 1922: 326–30; Meyer 1924; Hadas 1936, esp. 154–5; von Albrecht 1964: 164–6; Häußler 1976–8: 2.161–7; Brouwers 1982; Ahl, Davis, and Pomeroy 1986: 2501–4; Laudizi 1989: 148–52; Fucecchi 1999; Ariemma 2007; Marks 2010; Esposito 2012.

40 Valerius and Statius: Wezel 1873: 95–8; Mendell 1924, esp. 92–4, 96, 102–4; Steele 1930; Cousin 1939; Bolaffi 1959; Mozley 1963–4; Schönberger 1965; Burck 1966–81; Gossage 1969; McDonald 1971; Sturt 1977; Burck 1978; Thuile 1980; La Penna 1981; Vessey 1982a; Tandoi 1985; Cristóbal 1988; Hardie 1989; McGuire 1989; Toohey 1992: 186–210; Hardie 1993a; McGuire 1997; Ripoll 1998; Cowan 2003; Paschalis 2005; Franchet d'Espèrey 2006; Bernstein 2008; Augoustakis 2010b; Vidal 2010; Augoustakis 2013; Manuwald and Voigt 2013; Augoustakis 2014a; Walter 2014; Augoustakis 2016; Bernstein 2016a; Hamvas 2016; Manioti 2016; Ginsberg and Krasne 2018; Augoustakis and Littlewood 2019; Coffee, Forstall, Galli Milić, and Nelis 2020; Ferenczi and Zissos: forthcoming; Fratantuono and Stark: forthcoming; Papaioannou and Marinis: forthcoming. Valerius: Frank 1974; Ripoll 1999; Ripoll 2003; Augoustakis 2014c; Stocks 2014: 70–3. Statius: Helm 1892: 156–70; Legras 1905; Lorenz 1968; Venini 1969; Santini 1992; Delarue 1995; Vinchesi 1999; Morzadec 2009; Agri 2010; Lovatt 2010; Sacerdoti 2011; Marks 2013b; Marks 2014; Stocks 2014: 73–5; Ripoll 2015; Ripoll 2017; Agri 2020. For Flavian literature in general, see also Coffee 1953–4; Huxley 1954; Huxley 1968; Dudley 1972; Nauta 2002; Gasti and Mazzoli 2005; Nauta, van Dam, and Smolenaars 2006; Bonadeo and Romano 2007; Bonadeo, Canobbio, and Gasti 2011; Baier 2012; Baertschi 2013; Bessone and Fucecchi 2017.

41 Claudian: Prenner 2002. Sidonius Apollinaris: Brolli 2004. Corippus: Delattre 2011.

42 Green 2006, esp. 331–2. For the influence of the *Punica* on, among many examples from early Christian Latin poetry, Venantius Fortunatus *Vita Sancti Martini*, see Kay 2020 *passim*.

43 *Waltharius*: Zwierlein 1970: 000–000, 000–000, 000–000 ≈ Zwierlein 2004: 522–000, 534–5, 547–8; Schieffer 1975; Önnerfors 1979: 26–7, 34–7, 45–6; Önnerfors 1988: 19 n. 28. *Alexandreis*: Christensen 1905: 69 n. 13, 95 n. 1, 209–11.

44 Horace: Martin 1990; Cowan 2006; Jourdan 2008.
45 Tibullus: e.g., *Pun.* 7.68 ~ Tib. 1.3.42 (cf. Luc. 6.398). Propertius: e.g., *Pun.* 14.93–5, 15.291–2 ~ Prop. 4.11.39–40.
46 Augoustakis 2014b.
47 Venini 1992; Brugnoli 1994: 338–40; Antoniadis 2018.
48 For the *fabula praetexta* in general, see Manuwald 2001. Ennius' *Scipio*: Bettini 1977; Scholz 1984; Morelli 2016.
49 Young 1939 and Wacht 1989 remain useful tools despite the advent of the Internet.
50 Occioni 1869: 77–115 ≈ Occioni 1871: 61–90; Mendell 1924; Santini 1982–4; von Albrecht 2006 ≈ von Albrecht 2011.
51 Duff 1934: 1.xiii–xiv; von Albrecht 1964: 177; Küppers 1986: 53–4; Villalba Álvarez 2005: 96 n. 138.
52 Fincher 1979: 151; McGuire 1985: 81 n. 5; Ahl, Davis, and Pomeroy 1986: 2501, 2515; Boyle and Sullivan 1991: 301–3; von Albrecht 1991: 3.1180–1, 1182–4, 1187–8; Cowan 2007b: 2–7.
53 This myth first appears in the *Iliad* (5.648–51, 7.451–3, 21.441–57), while Hesiod refers to the horses of Laomedon twice in the extant fragments (*frr.* 43a.64, 165.10–13 M-W). Apart from scattered references elsewhere in Latin literature (Cic. *Tusc.* 1.65; Prop. 2.14.2; Ov. *Fast.* 6.429–30; Plin. *Nat.* 35.40.139; Mart. 8.6.5–6, 11.4.1–2; Juv. 6.324–6), Ovid relates a shorter version in his *Metamorphoses* (11.194–220), while Valerius Flaccus relates a longer version in his *Argonautica* (2.445–578). The first fall of Troy also appears in the mythographers, including Apollodorus (*Bibliotheca* 2.5.9, 2.6.4) and Hyginus (*Fabulae* 31.4, 89), as well as in all three of the so-called Vatican Mythographers (Myth. Vat. I 1.24, 2.135–7; II 193, 199; III 3.8, 5.7). See Scammell 1934; van der Kolf 1954; Andrews 1965; Griffin 1986; Erskine 2001, esp. 63.
54 The Vergilian commentator Servius remarks on how, throughout the epic, Vergil selects just the right learned epithet to capture just the right nuance, glossing *Laomedontiadae* with *periuri* at *A.* 1.273 and *perfidi* at *A.* 1.468 (see also Serv. *A.* 2.540, 3.248, 4.542). Elsewhere in his notes on the *Aeneid*, Servius makes frequent reference to Laomedon and the myth of the first fall of Troy: see also Serv. *A.* 1.2, 28, 550, 2.13, 201, 241, 312, 318, 610, 643, 3.2, 3, 351, 5.30, 8.157, 291.

3 A Reading of *Punica* 1–10: From Saguntum to Cannae

1 Marso 1483 *ad loc.*; Costanzi 1508: ch. XCII. For Costanzi in general, see Tomani Amiani 1850.
2 Major scholarship for and against the authenticity of the *additamentum Aldinum* includes Heitland 1896; Sabbadini 1905: 1.180–2; Goold 1956: 9–12; von Albrecht 1973: 182; Bassett, Delz, and Dunston 1976: 348; Reeve 1983: 390; Santini 1983: 62–3

≈ Santini 1991: 54–6, as well as 115–16; Ahl, Davis, and Pomeroy 1986: 2497; Delz 1987: lxiv–lxviii; Courtney 1989: 326–7; Brugnoli 1992; Bandiera 1993; Brugnoli and Santini 1995; Brugnoli and Santini 1998; Ariemma 2000b: 581, 581–3; Fröhlich 2000: 38; Dominik 2006: 118 n. 5.

3 Fabius falls ill and dies between Hannibal's return to Italy and Scipio's victory at Zama. If there is a lacuna here, then, in all likelihood, Silius will have recounted the death in the missing verses; if there is no lacuna, however, then Silius will have made the conscious choice to omit a pivotal event in the war and the narrative with significant historical and literary implications.

4 Major scholarship for and against a lacuna, whether after 17.290 or else after 17.291, includes Buchwald 1886: 19–20; Wallace 1958: 101–2; Beaty 1960: 87 n. 5; von Albrecht 1964: 133 n. 34; Fincher 1979: 144; Kißel 1979: 134–6; Delz 1987 *ad loc.*; Matier 1989a: 3; Braun 1993: 175, 180–1; Delz 1995: 148; von Albrecht 1999: 315–16; Marks 2003: 139–40; Tipping 2004: 362–3; Villalba Álvarez 2004: 368 n. 7, 379; Stocks 2014: 36 n. 7, 207 n. 55.

5 Beginnings: Dunn and Cole 1992. Ends: Kermode 1966; Smith 1968; Torgovnick 1981; Fowler 1989; Roberts, Dunn, and Fowler 1997, esp. Fowler 1997b; Grewing, Acosta-Hughes, and Kirichenko 2013; with Hardie 1997, Tipping 2007, and Roumpou 2019 on the *Punica*. Middles: Conte 1992; Kyriakidis and De Martino 2004; with Tipping 2004 on the *Punica*. See also Schmitz, Telg genannt Kortmann, and Jöne 2017; with Marks 2017 on middles in the *Punica*.

6 Book 10: Buchwald 1886: 14–15; Wallace 1958: 100–1; Beaty 1960: 53–4, 62; Niemann 1975: 3–36; Ahl, Davis, and Pomeroy 1986: 2505–11; Braun 1993: 179–80; Marks 1999: 426–35. Book 12: Martin 1946: 146; von Albrecht 1964: 24, 32–9; Burck 1979: 261–3; Kißel 1979: 213–14; Laudizi 1989: 29–30; Fincher 1979: 90; Küppers 1986: 15 n. 60, 60, 178–9; Tipping 2004, esp. 351–67; Dominik 2006: 116–17; Tipping 2010a: 38–9.

7 Fröhlich 2000: 18–58 (cf. 397–401) offers an in-depth analysis of the existing scholarship: see also Häußler 1976–8: 2.259; Küppers 1986: 14–21; von Albrecht 1999: 294–5; Delarue 1992; Fucecchi 2006: 311–15 ≈ Fucecchi 2011: 299–303; von Albrecht 2006: 114–19 ≈ von Albrecht 2011: 102–7; Augoustakis 2010c: 8–10; Gärtner 2010: 77–83; Schubert 2010: 22–6; Wenskus 2010; Stürner 2011. On the structure of historical epic in general, see Häußler 1978.

8 Bickel 1911, esp. 508–12. I thank Ben Harris for the reminder that Tacitus may have composed his *Annals* in eighteen books consisting of three hexads: if so, then he may have composed his *Historiae* in twelve books consisting of two hexads, as well.

9 Martin 1946, esp. 146.
10 Wallace 1958.
11 Burck 1979: 260–70, esp. 263–4: for this observation about the distribution of the narrative material, see also Mendell 1924: 100; Nicol 1936 *passim*; Wallace 1968;

Kißel 1979: 213; Ahl, Davis, and Pomeroy 1986: 2505, 2507; Küppers 1986: 190–2; Marks 2005c: 531–2.
12 Kißel 1979: 211–18, esp. 216: see also Toohey 1992: 205–10.
13 Delarue 1992.
14 Niemann 1975: 3–36, esp. 36: see also Fincher 1979: 6–8.
15 Ahl, Davis, and Pomeroy 1986: 2505–11, esp. 2507–8.
16 Küppers 1986: 15–19, 54–60, 176–92.
17 Braun 1993, esp. 183.
18 Fröhlich 2000: 18–58 (cf. 397–401).
19 Kißel 1979: 216–17; Delarue 1992: 149–50, 160–1.
20 The four Roman generals are grouped together at 13.716–20, 17.160–5, 295–9.
21 Cornell 1986, esp. 249–50.
22 Major discussions include von Albrecht 1964: 16–24; Fincher 1979: 9–13; Kißel 1979: 30–1; Feeney 1982 *ad loc.*; Ahl, Davis, and Pomeroy 1986: 2495; Küppers 1986: 22–60, esp. 22–33; Laudizi 1989: 55–70; Pomeroy 1989: 124–6; Keith 2000: 90–1; Tipping 2004: 347–51; Marks 2005a: 67–72; Tipping 2010a: 1–7. See also Landrey 2014; Hay 2019.
23 The enjambment of *Aeneadum* in *Pun.* 1.2 supports this interpretive translation of *ordior arma* and accordingly transforms every (Roman) hero of the *Punica* into both a historical (or perhaps merely a mythical) descendant of Aeneas and a literary descendant of the Aeneas of the *Aeneid*.
24 There are, of course, many other constructions in Latin which convey the same range of meanings, both literal and figurative: for more on the figurative use of these various collocations to describe a catasterism, see Bartalucci 1989. Throughout the epic, Silius uses the general imagery of heaps (of gold and silver, of corpses, of walls, etc.) and the destruction of the heap by fire and the sword to contrast the ascent to Heaven with the descent to Hell, as well as to contrast victory in foreign war with defeat in civil war: for the heaps motif in Lucan, see Masters 1992: 32, 34, 145. (This imagery of heaps evokes Gigantomachy and, in particular, the Aloadae, Otus and Ephialtes, piling Mt. Pelion on top of Mt. Ossa in their attempt to reach Mt. Olympus.)
25 In addition to the passages discussed in what follows, see also *Pun.* 1.508 (Murrus raising his eyes up to heaven in prayer), 6.466 (Regulus raising his hands and eyes up to heaven in prayer), and 9.168 (Solymus raising his face up to heaven in prayer), quite an interesting set of episodes thematically, as well as 16.319 (a shout raised up to heaven; cf. 9.304).
26 Cures was an ancient Sabine town, home of the Flavians, as well as Numa Pompilius: the Romans identified the divinized Romulus with the Sabine god Quirinus and called themselves "Quirites" (perhaps, "the people of Cures").
27 See Conte 1974: 35–7 ≈ Conte 1986: 57–9 ≈ Conte 2012: 64–7; Hardie 1993a: 6; Miller 1993: 153, 163–4; Hinds 1998: 14–16; Edmunds 2001: 136–7; Barchiesi

2006–9: 56–8; Elliot 2013: 45–6, 144–6, 257–9, 304, 327, 354–5; Fisher 2014: 144; Pelttari 2014: 118–21; as well as Gosling 2002.

28 For the Ennian shape of *Punica* 1.1–2 and 12.410–11, see Pomeroy 2000: 152 n. 26 (on p. 164), who also adds 13.635, as well as Hardie 1993a: 113–15; for *Punica* 12.387–419 in general, see Pinto 1953; Bettini 1976–7; Bettini 1977: 428–32; Casali 2006; Manuwald 2007: 74–82, 87–90; Dorfbauer 2008; Risi 2008; Tipping 2010a: 195–7.

29 Tipping 2004: 370. In general, see Hardie 1993a: 3–10, 27–32.

30 Major discussions include Sechi 1951: 295–6; Kornhardt 1954: 106–23; Beaty 1960: 170–1; Fincher 1979: 96–7; McGuire 1985: 8–10; Matier 1989a: 7; McGuire 1989: 22–3; Boyle and Sullivan 1991: 298–9; McGuire 1997: 56–7; Fucecchi 1999: 338–9; Effe 2004: 95; Tipping 2004: 363–4, 369–70; Schrijvers 2005: 83; Tipping 2007; Gibson 2010: 41; Jacobs 2010: 136–7; Stocks 2014: 11–12, 18–19, 29, 69–70, 80, 132.

31 Silius underscores the structural and thematic importance of *Punica* 10.657–8 for the epic as a whole through a deft intertextual gesture. The closing couplet here recalls, but also significantly alters, the formulation which Aeneas uses to lament the fall of Troy when he claims that, if the Trojans had been able to see the Trojan Horse for what it was before they decided to bring it into their city, "Troy would now stand, and you would remain, lofty citadel of Priam" (*Troiaque nunc staret, Priamique arx alta maneres*, Verg. *Aen.* 2.56, esp. *staret . . . maneres* ~ *stabat . . . maneres*).

32 For a similar example of this specific type of wordplay in the *Punica*, see the description of the bull of Phalaris in book 14: *mutabat gemitus mugitibus* ("it changed moans into moos," 214).

33 See Reed 2016, especially on the relationship between *mora* ("delay") and *Roma*: for more on wordplay in general, see Ahl 1985; O'Hara 1996; Keith 2008; Kwapisz, Petrain, and Szymański 2013; Mitsis and Ziogas 2016.

4 A Reading of *Punica* 11–17: From Cannae to Zama

1 Marks 2017; as well as Fincher 1979: 99–100; Matier 1981: 143; McGuire 1997: 226–9; Stocks 2014: 134–6.

2 Livy includes his similar catalog of Italian defectors at the end of book 22, at 22.61.10–15.

3 Major discussions include Nicol 1936: 121; von Albrecht 1964: 141–2, 161 n. 45; Bassett 1966: 271, 272–3, 273; Fincher 1979: 148; Kißel 1979: 149, 157–8, 214; Burck 1984a: 170–3; McGuire 1985: 10–11, 148–74, 189; Ahl, Davis, and Pomeroy 1986: 2555; Nesselrath 1986: 229; Laudizi 1989: 138–40; McGuire 1997: 95–103, esp. 97, 98–102; Marks 1999: 278–9, 393–414; Marks 2005: 83, 89, 113–14, 168–9, 201–6; Gärtner 2006: 156–9 ≈ Gärtner 2011: 144–7; Tipping 2007: 231–41; Jacobs 2010:

137–9; Marks 2010: 149–50; Tipping 2010a: 161–3, 182–92, 199–201, 211–15, 215–18; Gibson 2013: 76–9; Penwill 2013: 50–2; Wilson 2013: 18–19; Manuwald 2014: 216; Stocks 2014: 216–17; Roumpou 2019.
4 McGuire 1985: 152–63; McGuire 1997: 95–103, esp. 97, 98–102; Marks 1999: 278–9, 408–14; Marks 2005: 201–6; Tipping 2007: 231–5; Tipping 2010a: 182–5.
5 Some MSS read *victa*, while others read *vincta*: Delz prints *victa*, but perhaps *vincta* is correct.
6 In general, see Hardie 1993a: 37–9.
7 Bassett 1966: 273. See also Kißel 1979: 157–8; Laudizi 1989: 139; Hardie 1993a: 38–9, 59–60; Hardie 1997: 158–60; Marks 1999: 401 n. 80; Ripoll 2000c: 497 n. 105; Tipping 2007: 238, 239–41; Tipping 2010a: 161–3, 189–92.
8 Wezel 1873: 40; Woodruff 1910: 380–1; von Albrecht 1964: 161 n. 45; Bettini 1977: 444 n. 2 ≈ Bettini 1979: 000 n. 0; Tipping 2007: 238.
9 Hardie 1997.
10 See, e.g., Bouquet 2001; Bettenworth 2004; Romano Martín 2009; Nasse 2012; Jöne 2017.
11 Vessey 1982b, esp. 335, traces the rise and fall of Hannibal as the "dupe of destiny" across book 3 and argues that book 3 can be read as a synecdoche for the epic as a whole.
12 For the role of the Alps in the *Punica*, see Šubrt 1991.

5 Carthage and Rome in the *Punica*, Part 1

1 On this *alter* theme in general, see Hardie 1993a: 35–40.
2 For the *devotio*, see Versnel 1976; Janssen 1981; Versnel 1981; Pascal 1990; Barton 1993: 40–6; Hardie 1993a: 28–32; Leigh 1993; Ripoll 1998: 373–531; Nicoll 2001; Hill 2004: 189–90; Edwards 2007: 19–45; O'Gorman 2010; Cowan 2011. For the *devotio* in the *Punica*, see Marks 2005b; Marks 2005c: 533–4; Cowan 2007a: 25–6; Cowan 2011: 58–62, 78–93.
3 For progressive and regressive repetition in Vergil, see Quint 1989b ≈ Quint 1993: 50–96. For the notion of post-Vergilian epic in general as a repetition of the *Aeneid*, see Hardie 1993a, esp. 14–18. For the interrelated themes of repetition and empire in Livy, see Kraus 1998.
4 For overviews of this historical and literary motif, see Paul 1982; Ziolkowski 1993. For a wide-ranging essay on the general idea of the "city under attack," see Steiner 1973.
5 For the city in literature, see Lehan 1998. For Rome, see Mazzolani 1972; Ceauşescu 1976; Edwards 1996. Ceauşescu does not mention Silius, but the *Punica* is deeply concerned with the idea of an *altera Roma*; Edwards does not, in fact, use Silius

either, apart from two passing mentions (pp. 70 n. 5 and 86). For Carthage in the *Punica*, see Martin 1986; Opelt 1991; Ciocârlie 2006–8; for Rome in the *Punica*, see Cowan 2007b; Pyy 2018; for both, see Jacobs 2009; Gajderowicz 2011. For Capua in Livy, see Kenty 2017; as well as von Ungern-Sternberg 1975; for Capua in the *Punica*, see Burck 1984b; Cowan 2003: 27–143; Cowan 2007a; Augoustakis 2015; Augoustakis and Littlewood 2019. In a different vein, see Calvino 1972 ≈ Calvino 1974 for a creative exploration of the city as a literal and metaphorical locus / topos.

6   O'Connell 2010: 200–1, 260 reads the epic in much the same terms: "From beginning to end Scipio's career betrayed a restlessness with the norms and constraints imposed by Roman politics and senatorial domination. When confronted, he inevitably, if grudgingly, acceded, but in establishing this pattern he set a precedent of personal ambition that led eventually to Caesar and the collapse of the republic. So, it seems that in order to save the state from Hannibal it was necessary to generate the very type of individual who would ultimately destroy it. This was the true Barcid curse upon Rome. [...] In the end, we are thrown back to the point made earlier about Silius Italicus's appearing to argue that in the very act of fighting Hannibal, Rome put itself on the road to civil war by coming to rely on charismatic generals for survival. If this is the case, then Hannibal had the last laugh." I develop this line of argument across Chapters 5 and 6.

7   Litchfield 1914 collects an unparalleled assemblage of evidence for these exempla, including an invaluable chart of the "national *exempla virtutis* cited by Roman writers through Claudian" (28–35); for more recent work, see Chaplin 2000; Roller 2004; Barchiesi 2006–9; Bücher 2006; Roller 2011; Langlands 2018a–b; Roller 2018b; for exemplarity in the *Punica*, see Tipping 2010a; Reitz 2017. Anderson 1928 conducts a similarly thorough study of "Heracles and his successors," including Alexander, Romulus, Scipio Africanus, Pompey, Caesar, Antony, and Augustus, but not, curiously enough, Hannibal; for Hercules in general, see Galinsky 1972; Silk 1985; Feeney 1986; Feeney 1991 *passim*; Ritter 1995; Morgan 1998; Leigh 2000; Blanshard 2005; Morgan 2005; Rawlings and Bowden 2005; Stafford 2012; Bär 2018. For Hercules in Flavian epic, see Hardie 1993a: 36, 65–71; Ripoll 1998: 86–163; for Hercules in the *Punica*, see Bassett 1966; Kißel 1979: 153–60; Ripoll 1998: 112–32; Asso 1999; Asso 2001; Asso 2003; Augoustakis 2003; Spentzou 2008: 143; Asso 2010. Hardie 1993a: 67 understates the sophistication and complexity of Hercules in the *Punica*: "In Silius Hercules is almost monotonously present as a model for the great men of both Rome and Carthage, above all Scipio and Hannibal." For the general process of *aemulatio*, *imitatio*, *comparatio* (using Caesar and Alexander as the representative case study), see Green 1978.

8   In having Hannibal hail the father of Scipio Africanus (in a generalizing plural) as the *fulmina gentis / Scipiadae* (*Pun.* 7.106–7), Silius engages with a rich tradition of references to various Scipiones as "thunderbolt(s)": see Cic. *Balb.* 34; Lucr. 3.1034;

Verg. *Aen.* 6.842–3; Val. Max. 3.5.1; with Skutsch 1968a; for Hannibal and Scipio as *fulmina belli* pitted against each other in the *Punica*, see Stocks 2014: 182–217. At several points in the epic, Silius ascribes the double paternity of Scipio to his mortal father, Publius, on the one hand, and his immortal father, none other than Jupiter, on the other, and so one might assume that Scipio is the obvious choice for an *alter Jupiter*, but Silius skillfully undercuts that assumption in the epic's finale (17.653–4).

9 Von Albrecht 1964: 55. For *fides* and *perfidia* in the *Punica*, see also Kißel 1979: 96–100; Burck 1988; Thomas 2001; Pomeroy 2010a; Littlewood 2014; as well as Augoustakis, Buckley, and Stocks 2019.

10 See Kißel 1979: 101–52; Ahl, Davis, and Pomeroy 1986 *passim*; Laudizi 1989: 93–140; Matier 1989; Fucecchi 1993; Marks 2005a: 61–110; Spentzou 2008; Stürner 2008; Tipping 2010a: 51–192; Maier 2018. See also Åhman 2014.

11 Marcellus: McCall 2012. Fabius: McCall 2018; Roller 2011 ≈ Roller 2018: 163–96. Scipio and the Cornelii Scipiones: Grimal 1953; Torregaray Pagola 1998; Etcheto 2012; Hölkeskamp 2018.

12 See Kißel 1979: 150–2. Zecchini 2006: 47–8 ≈ Zecchini 2011: 35–6 connects a triad of Scipiones (Scipio together with his father and uncle) with a Flavian triad consisting of Vespasian, Flavius Sabinus, and Domitian. Stocks 2014: 167–81 contrasts this same triad of Scipiones with a triad of Barcids (Hannibal, Hasdrubal, and Mago). Littlewood 2016 contrasts this same triad of Barcids with a Flavian triad consisting of Vespasian, Titus, and Domitian. I would connect the general idea of triads and of heroes pitted against these triads with the single combat of Hercules pitted against Geryon (the Tenth Labor) via the metaphor of the three-headed state as a three-bodied or three-headed monster (e.g., Varro's *Trikaranos*, a lost satire about the triumvirate of Caesar, Pompey, and Crassus).

13 For the relationship between the one and the many (including the idea of the synecdochic hero), as well as the relationship between one and two, see Hardie 1993a: 3–11, 27–35, 49–56, esp. 8–10 for the *Punica*.

14 For the two-headed state as a metaphor for civil war, see Wiseman 2010.

15 For single combat in general, see Monestier 1991; Udwin 1999; for single combat in ancient Greece and Rome, see Armstrong 1950; Glück 1964; Fries 1985; Oakley 1985; van Wees 1988; Parks 1990; Wiedemann 1996; Martino 2008; Woodard 2013. See also Devallet 1984.

16 For the *spolia opima*, see Mensching 1967; Daly 1981; Harrison 1989; Rich 1996; Flower 2000; Sailor 2006; Garani 2007; Ingleheart 2007.

17 For the spectacle of death in ancient Rome, see Bartsch 1994; Plass 1995; Futrell 1997; Leigh 1997; Kyle 1998; Edwards 2007; Erasmo 2008; Hope 2009; Bakogianni and Hope 2015.

18 For the triumph in ancient Rome and elsewhere in the Mediterranean world, see Payne 1962; Versnel 1970; Taisne 1973; Künzl 1988; Auliard 2001; Itgenshorst 2005;

Versnel 2006; Bastien 2007; Beard 2007; Krasser, Pausch, and Petrovic 2008; La Rocca and Tortorella 2008; Pelikan Pittenger 2008; Östenberg 2009; Östenberg 2010; Lundgreen 2011: 178–253; Spalinger and Armstrong 2013; Lange and Vervaet 2014; Lange 2016; Popkin 2016; Goldbeck and Wienand 2017.

19 For decapitation in ancient Rome, see Voisin 1984; Kraus and Woodman 1997: 96. For decapitation in the *Punica*, see Kißel 1979: 89–90; Ahl, Davis, and Pomeroy 1986: 2540–2; Marpicati 1999; Augoustakis 2003; Marks 2008; Tipping 2010a: 43–4; McClellan 2019: 67–114. For decapitation in the ancient Near East, see Dolce 2017.

20 For the narrowly averted single combat between Hannibal and Scipio at the battle of Zama both in the *Punica* and elsewhere in the tradition, see Billot 2014, esp. 73, 74, as well as Hardie 1993a: 38–9. For the narrowly averted single combat between Hannibal and Scipio at Cannae, which transforms into a theomachy between Pallas and Mars, see García Amutxastegi 2015b.

21 For the Gigantomachy, including its associations with (Roman) civil war, see Vian 1951; Vian 1952a–b; Innes 1979; Hardie 1983; Romano 1985; Hardie 1986: 85–156; Massa-Pairault and Pouzadoux 2017a–b; Wright 2018; for its later reception, see Vetter 2002. For the Gigantomachy in Flavian epic, including the *Punica*, see von Albrecht 1964: 31, 36, 37–8, 67 n. 59, 72, 76, 83–6, 87, 143, 152; Kißel 1979: 17 n. 22; Laudizi 1989: 123–4; Fucecchi 1990a; Mezzanotte 1995: 380–1 ≈ Mezzanotte 2016: 452; Fucecchi 2013; Littlewood 2013; Connors 2015; Stocks 2019. For theomachy in Imperial Latin poetry, including the *Punica*, see Ripoll 2006; Chaudhuri 2014. In addition to the Titanomachy and the Gigantomachy, the Typhonomachy and Pythonomachy also figure prominently, e.g., Regulus and the Bagrada serpent in *Punica* 6.

22 West 1923, esp. 60–2.

23 Naevius may have cast the First Punic War as a new Gigantomachy: Fraenkel 1954; Faber 2012; Wright 2018: 96–103; later, Lucretius (3.832–7) and Livy (29.17.6, 30.32.1–3) likewise cast the Second Punic War as a new cosmic combat: Feeney 1984: 181; Giusti 2018: 61–3.

24 Juhnke 1972: 187–8; Fincher 1979: 31; Kißel 1979: 25–6; Küppers 1986: 140–1; Stocks 2014: 112–13.

25 Clack 1976 notes that the meter in 554–5 imitates Hannibal's gait as he drags his feet. Silius foreshadows this moment in his description of Hannibal before the siege in 1.252–6.

26 Silius explicitly compares Hannibal's march over the Alps to the Gigantomachy in 3.494–5.

27 Schinkel 1884: 29, 34; Groesst 1887: 12–13; Sechi 1951: 293–5; von Albrecht 1964: 38 n. 43; Burck 1978: 24–6; Kißel 1979: 51–2; Ahl, Davis, and Pomeroy 1986: 2500; Matier 1989a: 14; Fucecchi 1990: 34–5; Santini 1992: 393; Pomeroy 2000: 159–60; Fucecchi 2005: 17–18; Tipping 2010a: 86–7; Stocks 2014: 73–4.

28 For the Trojan War in Greek and Latin literature, see Erskine 2001; Jahn 2007.
29 For Homer and the Epic Cycle, see Kullmann 1960; Davies 1989; Burgess 2001; West 2013; Sammons 2017.
30 Saguntum as an *altera Troia*: von Albrecht 1964: 180–3; Juhnke 1972: 185–93; Küppers 1986; Asso 2003: 232–5. See also Ripoll 2001b. Saguntum as an *altera Roma*: McGuire 1985: 56–63; McGuire 1997: 209–10; Marks 2005c: 533–4.
31 Juhnke 1972: 185–7; Courtney 1993: 331; Hollis 2007: 330–1. Silius includes a number of such "tags," e.g., *solum Decius Capuae decus* ("Decius, the only glory of Capua," 11.158).
32 von Albrecht 1964: 26; Fincher 1979: 30–1; Kißel 1979: 88–9, 155–6; Küppers 1986: 138–40; Asso 1999: 82–3; Spentzou 2008: 143; Asso 2010: 182–5.
33 von Albrecht 1964: 181–2; Küppers 1986: 177 n. 680, 189; Marpicati 1999: 200 n. 23; von Albrecht 1999: 237 n. 2, 294; Ariemma 2007: 18.
34 von Albrecht 1964: 32–9, esp. 37–8; Burck 1978: 24–6; Ahl, Davis, and Pomeroy 1986: 2500–1; Hardie 1989: 15 n. 55 (on p. 19); Boyle and Sullivan 1991: 301–2; Santini 1992: 393; Pomeroy 2000: 160; Tipping 2004: 351–7, esp. 353–7; Tipping 2010a: 86–7; Schrijvers 2005: 79.
35 For the Gallic sack, including its links with the fall of Troy, see Kraus 1994; Richardson 2012. For the Gallic sack in the *Punica*, see von Albrecht 1964: 26, 35, 39, 44–6; Taisne 1994: 92; Mezzanotte 1995: 360 n. 17 ≈ Mezzanotte 2016: 436–7; Tipping 2010a: 65–6, 77–8.
36 Beaty 1960: 112–13, 124, 156, 162; McGuire 1985: 49–50. Cf. *Pun.* 1.624–6.
37 Nicol 1936: 87, 110; Beaty 1960: 35–6; Romano 1969: 65–6.
38 See Pucci 1998: the term originally appears in Michael Drayton's *Poly-Olbion* (1612/22).
39 Other ancient sources include Plb. 10.32.1–33.7; Cic. *Tusc.* 1.37.89, *Sen.* 20.75; Nep. *Han.* 5.3; Liv. 27.25.6–28.2; V. Max. 1.6.9, 5.1.ext.6; Plin. *Nat.* 11.37.73.189; Front. *Str.* 4.7.26, 38; Plut. *Marc.* 28.1–30.4, *Comp. Pel. Marc.* 3.6, *Fab.* 19.5, *Flam.* 1.4; App. *Hann.* 8.50.208; Amp. 28.4; *Perioch.* 27.7–8; Eutr. 3.16.2; Oros. *Hist.* 4.18.6, 8; *De vir. ill.* 45.7–8; Zonar. 9.9.1. Major modern discussions include Caltabiano 1975; Bernard 2002–3; Flower 2003; Levene 2010: 206–8; McCall 2012: 112–24. See also Giarratano 1934; Klotz 1934; Carawan 1984–5. I thank Ben Harris for the reminder that Silius would have had Marcellus' appearance in Verg. *Aen.* 6.855–9 in mind, as well (esp. the theme of fathers and sons which heightens the pathos in both scenes).
40 Wezel 1873: 100–1; Schinkel 1884: 62; Groesst 1887: 26, 36; Klotz 1934: 314–17; Nicol 1936: 77–8, 120–1; Beaty 1960: 69–70; Juhnke 1972: 406; Fincher 1979: 128; Kißel 1979: 12, 19–20, 128–30; Burck 1984a: 60–8; Ahl, Davis, and Pomeroy 1986: 2539–40; Fucecchi 1990: 153; Nesselrath 1992: 119–20; Henderson 2004: 103–4; Ariemma 2010b: 144–9; Cowan 2010: 340–1; Fucecchi 2010: 225 n. 25, 233–6, 239; Stocks 2010: 163–5; Tipping 2010a: 75–6; Stocks 2014: 41, 145, 147, 162–6, 170 n. 13,

176 n. 24, 183 n. 5, 184, 186–7, 200–1, 228–30. See also Burck 1966–81; Marpicati 1999. For Marcellus in the *Punica* in general, see Ariemma 2010b; Fucecchi 2010; Stocks 2010; Tipping 2010a: 7–13, 41–4, 75–6, 181–2.

6 Carthage and Rome in the *Punica*, Part 2

1. von Albrecht 1964: 109. See also Pérez Vilatela 1994.
2. Major discussions include von Albrecht 1964: 27–8; McDermott and Orentzel 1977: 27–30; Fincher 1979: 46–7, 50–2; Kißel 1979: 38–46, 92, 93, 159–60; Schubert 1984: 45–70; McGuire 1985: 175–81; Czypicka 1987; Laudizi 1989: 35–46; Taisne 1992; Marks 1999: 25 n. 5, 450–3; Giroldini 2005: 170–80; Marks 2005: 211–17; Penwill 2010: 221–9; Fucecchi 2012; Penwill 2013: 46–54.
3. For the relationship between linear and cyclical time, see Vassiliades 2018, as well as Gardner 2012, who rightly suggests an even more finely attuned approach to Roman conceptions of time. For more on conceptions of time (and space) in Greece and, especially, Rome, see Feeney 2007.
4. For Stoic cosmology in Latin literature of the Early Empire, see Lapidge 1979; Lapidge 1989.
5. For military defeat in Roman history and Roman culture, see Rosenstein 1990; Rich 2012; Clark 2014; Lentzsch 2019; Stoll 2019.
6. For the sacrificial substitute, see Girard 1972 ≈ Girard 1977; see also Lincoln 1991.
7. For the curse of Dido, see Murgia 1987; O'Hara 1990: 90–102; Hardie 1993a: 40–2.
8. I see two interconnected verbal resonances in *Alpis . . . apertas*, the first between the words *Alpis* and *apertas*, and the second between *apertas* and Hannibal *ad portas*: in acknowledgment of this wordplay, Silius himself uses *aperio* twice to describe Hannibal's crossing of the Alps (*aperit*, 3.530, 644); cf. *portusque . . . apertos* (7.411, describing the harbor of Caieta) and *portis . . . apertis* (16.694, describing the gates not of Rome, but of Carthage).
9. For the curse of Dido in the *Punica*, see Albrecht 1964: 47–55; Picard 1974; Kißel 1979: 15 n. 13, 23, 31–7, 89; Tupet 1980a–b; Santini 1983: 13–80, 86–91 ≈ Santini 1991: 5–62, 67–72; Ahl, Davis, and Pomeroy 1986: 2494–9; Küppers 1986: 22–45, 61–106; Martin 1986: 69–76; Murgia 1987: 58–9; Laudizi 1989: 77–86, 96–107, 145–7; Hardie 1993a: 64–5, 96; Keith 2000: 91–2, 126–7; Dietrich 2004: 1–2, 2–7, 12–13, 16–17, 27–30; Manuwald 2006; Bernstein 2008: 135–9; Cristofoli 2009; Fernandelli 2009; Ganiban 2010; Leigh 2010: 489–92; Chiu 2011; Nasse 2012: 324–51; Marks 2013; Stocks 2014: 39, 84–7, 87–8, 88–9, 96; Kennedy 2016.
10. As we have seen in Chapter 3, there is no consensus about the authenticity of the so-called *additamentum Aldinum*: either way, these lines contribute to the development of the theme.

11 For an earlier version of this stage in the argument, see Jacobs 2010: 123–6.
12 For fear as a political force in general, see Wood 1995; Robin 2004; Evrigenis 2008; Dumitru Oancea, Halichias, and Popa 2016. For the *metus hostilis* theme in particular, see Lintott 1972; Levick 1982; Bellen 1985; Wiedemann 1993; Kneppe 1994; Levene 2000: 178–80; Rosenberger 2003; Quillin 2004; Kapust 2008; Engels 2009; Kapust 2011: 27–52, esp. 38–43; Hammer 2014: 148–55; Biesinger 2016.
13 The problems surrounding the historicity of this debate have long attracted the attention of scholars: for ancient sources and modern discussion, see Gelzer 1931; Little 1934; Adcock 1946; Hoffmann 1960; Thürlemann 1974; Burian 1978; Hackl 1980; Frank 1985; Vogel-Weidemann 1989; Welwei 1989; O'Gorman 2004.
14 See Earl 1961: 13–16, 41–59; Conley 1981; Koutroubas 1988; Dunsch 2006; Vassiliades 2013.
15 For the *metus hostilis* theme in Vergil and Livy, see La Penna 2008; Giusti 2016; for the *metus hostilis* theme in Sallust, Augustine, and Orosius, see Bonamente 1975. For the relationship between Sallust and Velleius Paterculus, see Woodman 1969; more work needs to be done on the relationship between Sallust and Florus, as well as on that between Silius and Florus.
16 For civil war in general, see Kalyvas 2006; Lacina 2006; Jacoby 2006–7; Blattman and Miguel 2010; Armitage 2017.
17 For civil war in ancient Greece and Rome, see Jal 1962a–c; Jal 1963; Lintott 1982; Henderson 1998; Breed, Damon, and Rossi 2010; Ambühl 2015; Börm, Mattheis, and Wienand 2016; Maschek 2018.
18 For suicide in general, see Durkheim 1897; Halbwachs 1930 ≈ Halbwachs 1978; with Travis 1990. For suicide in ancient Greece and Rome, see Bayet 1951; Grisé 1980; Grisé 1982; Griffin 1986; van Hooff 1990; Hill 2004; Rauh 2015.
19 For civil war in Lucan, as well as Flavian epic, see Masters 1992; Hardie 1993b; McGuire 1997; Ginsberg and Krasne 2018; for civil war in the *Punica*, see Ahl, Davis, and Pomeroy 1986; Fucecchi 1999; Dominik 2003: 492–3; Ariemma 2008; Jacobs 2009; Marks 2010; Tipping 2010a: 36–41; Tipping 2010b: 197–9; Wilson 2013: 15–16; Bernstein 2016a; Littlewood 2016; Bartolomé 2018; for suicide in Flavian epic, including the *Punica*, see McGuire 1989; McGuire 1997; Gärtner 2008; Dietrich 2009; Agri 2010.
20 For Romulus and Remus, see Krämer 1965; Puhvel 1975; Alfonsi 1982; Konstan 1986: 199–200; Bremmer 1987; Miles 1995: 137–78; Wiseman 1995; Bannon 1997; Barcaro 2007; Stem 2007; Neel 2014; Vasaly 2015: 36–40.
21 For these two *Epodes*, see Carrubba 1966; Carrubba 1967; Dufallo 2007: 101–5.
22 For the single combat as a fratricide, see Pogorzelski 2009.
23 For an earlier version of this stage in the argument, see Jacobs 2010: 126–39. For the *metus hostilis* theme in Silius, see McGuire 1985: 11–26, 185–7; Ahl, Davis, and Pomeroy 1986: 2501–4; McGuire 1997: 118, 219; Tipping 2004: 370; Schrijvers 2005:

83–4; Dominik 2006, esp. 122–3; Zecchini 2006: 45 ≈ Zecchini 2011: 33; Tipping 2010a: 26–35, esp. 32–5; Fuccechi 2012: 243–7. Laudizi 1989: 158 explicitly claims that Silius does not concern himself with the *metus hostilis* theme, but this claim simply does not stand up to scrutiny.
24 Occioni 1877, esp. 278–83 ≈ Occioni 1891: 141–53, esp. 148–53.
25 Wezel 1873: 44–5, 89; Schinkel 1884: 10; Nicol 1936: 12–13; Bruère 1959: 229–32; Beaty 1960: 12, 59, 104, 112, 118; Romano 1969: 90; Fincher 1979: 89–90; Matier 1989b: 7–8; McGuire 1997: 134–5; Fucecchi 1999, esp. 305–22, 332–6; Tipping 2004: 365–6; Wilson 2004: 243–6; Marks 2005c: 134; Dominik 2006: 124–5; Ariemma 2010a: 247–8, 249, 257, 269–72; Marks 2010: 135, 137–8; Tipping 2010a: 37–8; García Amutxastegi 2015a: 123–73; Zaia 2016: 21–3, 101–51; Syré 2017: 181–8; Siepe 2019: 73–88.
26 Masters 1992: 216–59 offers the canonical treatment of the theme of the endlessness of civil war in Lucan: see also Henderson 1987 *passim*; Tipping 2011: 223; Tracy 2011.
27 For the historical, cultural, and literary significance of the Temple of Jupiter Optimus Maximus and the Capitol, especially under the Flavians, see Skutsch 1953; Skutsch 1978; Fears 1981; Lindsay 2010; Escámez 2012; Escámez 2013; Escámez 2014; Thein 2014; Burgeon 2018. In general, see also Quinn and Wilson 2013.
28 Wiseman 1978; Wellesley 1981; Wellesley 1975: 192–4; Southern 1997: 17–19; Jones 2002: 14; Heinemann 2016; In general, see Tac. *Hist.* 3.72–5, as well as Plu. *Publ.* 14–15, esp. 15.2–5.
29 Briessmann 1955: 69–83; Wellesley 1956: 211–14; Wiseman 1978: 173–5.
30 Braunert 1953; Jones 1973; Evans 1975; Jones 1982; Strobel 1987; Stefan 2005.
31 Leberl 2004: 167–81; Hulls 2007.

Conclusion: Silius Italicus and the *Punica* in Classical Literature

1 Rebeggiani 2018: 77–8.
2 Barzanò 1982; Coleman 1986: 3089–90; Penwill 2000.
3 Canobbio 2011: 114–15; Canobbio 2017: 108.
4 Those ready to embark on a close reading of a given book of the epic have a wide range of editions, translations, and commentaries to choose from: Attia 1955; Bennett 1978; Venini 1978; Matier 1980; Feeney 1982; Reitz 1982; Küppers 1986; Roosjen 1996; Goldman 1997; Ariemma 2000a; Fröhlich 2000; Littlewood 2011; Zaia 2012; Montes Mérida 2015; van der Keur 2015; Zaia 2016; Bernstein 2017; Lee 2017; Littlewood 2017; Roumpou 2018; Telg genannt Kortmann 2018; Augoustakis and Littlewood: forthcoming; Bernstein: forthcoming; Jacobs: forthcoming.

5 Brouwers 1985; Díaz de Bustamante 1985; Bouquet 2001: 130–64.
6 Bouquet 2001: 141–50. See also D'Arco 2002; Foulon 2002–3; Devillers and Krings 2006.
7 On the backward glance in general in Latin poetry, see Heurgon 1931; Gale 2003; Butler 2009.
8 von Albrecht 1964: 38; cf. 55, 107; Burck 1978: 24–6; Matier 1989a: 11.
9 Liv. 21.51.4, 22.3.10, 33.10, 26.26.10; cf. 24.3.2, 31.7.13, 40.36.14; V. Max. 7.3.ext.8; Flor. *Epit.* 1.22; Aug. *C.D.* 3.18, 19, 31; Serv. *A.* 6.845. See also [Quint.] *Decl.* 3.13; Flor. *Epit.* 1.7.
10 Cic. *Catil.* 1.12, 29, 4.2, 13; *Sul.* 33; *Flac.* 1; *Sest.* 12; *Planc.* 87; *Phil.* 2.17; *Fam.* 10.15.4, 33.1; *Att.* 8.16.2, 9.7.4, 10.3; [Cic.] *Oct.* 6; Sal. *Jug.* 5.2, *Hist.* 1.23 (both passages with Serv. *A.* 8.8); [Sal.] *Caes.* 1.8.4–5; Var. *VPR* 109 Pittà (with Pittà 2014: 276–7); Tac. *Hist.* 1.50, 61, 2.12, 32, 4.55; Porph. *Hor. carm.* 3.14.19–20; SHA *Max. et Balb.* 17.2; August. *C.D.* 3.23, 26, 4.5, 5.22.
11 von Albrecht 1964: 23, 36 n. 39, 44, 49 n. 8, 54–5, 75, 151–2, 165, 172 nn. 14, 16; Kißel 1979: 107–12; McGuire 1985: 18, 22–5; Ahl, Davis, and Pomeroy 1986: 2511–13; Laudizi 1989: 95–6, 109–10 with n. 65; Šubrt 1991: 230–1; McGuire 1997: 83–4; Tipping 2004: 365; Gibson 2005: 187–93; Tipping 2010a: 89–91; Stocks 2014: 67–8.
12 Rimell 2015: 247–52.
13 Hardie 1993a: 55–6.
14 Saylor 1978, esp. 250–5; Leigh 1997: 158–90; Hömke 2010.
15 Stocks 2014: 109 n. 17.
16 Tipping 2010a: 61–4, 89–90.
17 Ahl 1976: 83–4; Masters 1992: 1; McGuire 1997: 84–5; Tipping 2010a: 89–90.
18 For the relationship between the epyllion and Lucan's epic on the same topic, see Grimal 1977.
19 Ripoll 2002 explores the possibility of a Flavian date for the epyllion included in the *Satyrica*.
20 Ahl, Davis, and Pomeroy 1986: 2507.
21 For the idea of Silius as an epitomator, see Reitz 2010.
22 Glücklich and Reitzer 1985; Valcárcel 1995; Müller, Müller, and Richter 2000; Anselm 2004: 151–60.
23 Brizzi 1984 considers the broader implications of the idea that the Romans "began to imitate Hannibal" (*imitari coepit Hannibalem*) on the way to victory over the Carthaginians in the war.
24 Fugmann 2000.
25 Bassett, Delz, and Dunston 1976: 345–8 assembles the scanty evidence for the *Punica* during Late Antiquity and the Middle Ages, including a library catalog and some marginal annotations.

26 Festa 1926a–b offers the standard critical edition and a literary study. Bergin and Wilson 1977 offers an English translation. Other scholarship includes Bernardo 1962; Regn 2009.
27 Martellotti 1954.
28 Occioni 1869: 116–48 ≈ Occioni 1871: 91–116 ≈ Occioni 1891: 114–39; Occioni 1889: 1.xvi–xxi ≈ Occioni 1891: 185–90; Develay 1883; Nichi 1909: 7–27; Mustard 1921: 119–20; von Albrecht 1964: 22–3, 90, 118–44; von Albrecht 1973: 188; Martellotti 1981; Brugnoli 1992, esp. 207–14; Santini 1993; Tedeschi 1994; Caputo 1995; Cassata 1997; ter Haar 1997; Cassata 1998; ter Haar 1999; von Albrecht 1999: 298; Harich-Schwarzbauer 2005; Schubert 2005; Bianchi 2015.
29 Lefebvre de Villebrune 1781b: 1.x–xi, 3.36–8.
30 Foscolo 1823: 97–100, 214–17.

Bibliography

A. B. 1727. *The history of Saguntum, and its destruction by Hannibal*. London.
Abdel Baky, M. 2000. *Histoire et mythologie dans l'épopée des* Punica *de Silius Italicus*. Ph.D. diss., Université Sorbonne Nouvelle – Paris 3.
Acimovic, A. 2007. *Scipio Africanus*. New York, Lincoln, and Shanghai.
Adams, J. N. 2003. "*Romanitas* and the Latin language." *CQ* n.s. 53.1: 184–205.
Adcock, F. E. 1946. "'Delenda est Carthago.'" *CHJ* 8.3: 117–28.
Agri, D. 2010. "Madness, *pietas* and suicide in Statius' *Thebaid* and Silius' *Punica*." In *Zero to hero, hero to zero: In search of the Classical hero*, ed. L. Langerwerf and C. Ryan, 141–60. Newcastle upon Tyne.
Agri, D. 2020. "Allegorical bodies: (Trans)gendering Virtus in Statius' *Thebaid* 10 and Silius Italicus' *Punica* 15." In *Exploring gender diversity in the ancient world*, ed. A. Surtees and J. Dyer, 131–42. Edinburgh.
Ahl, F. M. 1976. *Lucan: An introduction*. Ithaca.
Ahl, F. M. 1985. *Metaformations: Soundplay and wordplay in Ovid and other Classical poets*. Ithaca.
Ahl, F., M. A. Davis, and A. Pomeroy. 1986. "Silius Italicus." *ANRW* 2.32.4: 2492–561.
Åhman, H. B. 2014. *The hero and the law: A study of Silius Italicus' Punica*. Uppsala.
Alfonsi, L. 1982. "La figura di Romolo all'inizio delle Storie di Livio." In *Livius, Werk und Rezeption: Festschrift für Erich Burck zum 80. Geburtstag*, ed. E. Lefèvre and E. Olshausen, 99–106. Munich.
Alston, R. 2015. *Rome's revolution: Death of the Republic and birth of the Empire*. Oxford.
Ambühl, A. 2015. *Krieg und Bürgerkrieg bei Lucan und in der griechischen Literatur: Studien zur Rezeption der attischen Tragödie und der hellenistischen Dichtung im Bellum civile*. Frankfurt am Main.
Ameling, W. 1993. *Karthago: Studien zu Militär, Staat und Gesellschaft*. Munich.
Anderson, A. R. 1928. "Heracles and his successors: A study of a heroic ideal and the recurrence of a heroic type." *HSPh* 39: 7–58.
Anderson, G. 1993. *The Second Sophistic: A cultural phenomenon in the Roman Empire*. London.
Andrews, P. B. S. 1965. "The falls of Troy in Greek tradition." *G&R* 2nd ser. 12.1: 28–37.
Anselm, S. 2004. *Struktur und Transparenz: Eine literaturwissenschaftliche Analyse der Feldherrnviten des Cornelius Nepos*. Wiesbaden.
Antoniadis, T. 2018. "Intratextuality via philosophy: Contextualizing *ira* in Silius Italicus' *Punica* 1–2." In Harrison, Frangoulidis, and Papanghelis 2018, 377–96.

Ariemma, E. M. 2000a. *Alla vigilia di Canne: Commentario al libro VIII dei* Punica *di Silio Italico*. Naples.

Ariemma, E. M. 2000b. "Tendenze degli studi su Silio Italico: Una panoramica sugli ultimi quindici anni (1984–1999)." *BStudLat* 30.2: 577–640.

Ariemma, E. 2007. "Visitare i templi: Ripensamenti virgiliani (e lucanei) nei *Punica* di Silio Italico." *CentroPagine* 1: 18–29.

Ariemma, E. M. 2008. "*Odia fraterna, fraternae acies*: I gemelli gladiatori in Silio Italico (*Pun.* 16. 527–48)." *Lexis* 26: 325–69.

Ariemma, E. M. 2010a. "*Fons cuncti Varro mali*: The demagogue Varro in *Punica* 8–10." In Augoustakis 2010a, 241–76.

Ariemma, E. M. 2010b. "*New trends* del dopo-Canne: Considerazioni su Marcello nei *Punica*." In Schaffenrath 2010, 127–50.

Armitage, D. 2017. *Civil wars: A history in ideas*. New Haven.

Armstrong, A. MacC. 1950. "Trial by combat among the Greeks." *G&R* 19.56: 73–9.

Asdal, K. and H. Jordheim. 2018. "Texts on the move: Textuality and historicity revisited." *H&T* 57.1: 56–74.

Assmann, J. 1992. *Das kulturelle Gedächtnis: Schrift, Erinnerung und politische Identität in frühen Hochkulturen*. Munich.

Asso, P. 1999. "Passione eziologica nei *Punica* di Silio Italico: Trasimeno, Sagunto, Ercole e i Fabii." *Vichiana* 4th ser. 1.2: 75–87.

Asso, P. 2001. "Passione eziologica nei *Punica* di Silio Italico: La morte di Pirene." *AION(filol)* 23: 215–32.

Asso, P. 2003. "Human divinity: Hercules in the *Punica*." *Vichiana* 4th ser. 5.2: 229–48.

Asso, P. 2010. "Hercules as a paradigm of Roman heroism." In Augoustakis 2010a, 179–92.

Asso, P., ed. 2011. *Brill's companion to Lucan*. Leiden.

Astin, A. E. 1967. *Scipio Aemilianus*. Oxford.

Attia, L. D. 1955. *The sixth book of Silius Italicus: A critical commentary*. Ph.D. diss., University of London.

Augoustakis, A. 2001. Facta virum sileo: *Re-constructing female action in Silius Italicus' Punica*. Ph.D. diss., Brown University.

Augoustakis, A. 2003. "*Lugendam formae sine uirginitate reliquit*: Reading Pyrene and the transformation of landscape in Silius' *Punica* 3." *AJPh* 124.2: 235–57. Reprint, in Augoustakis 2016, 388–407.

Augoustakis, A., ed. 2010a. *Brill's companion to Silius Italicus*. Leiden.

Augoustakis, A. 2010b. *Motherhood and the Other: Fashioning female power in Flavian epic*. Oxford.

Augoustakis, A. 2010c. "Silius Italicus, a Flavian poet." In Augoustakis 2010a, 3–23.

Augoustakis, A. 2012. "*Per hunc utero quem linquis nostro*: Mothers in Flavian epic." In *Mothering and motherhood in ancient Greece and Rome*, ed. L. H. Petersen and P. Salzman-Mitchell, 205–23. Austin.

Augoustakis, A., ed. 2013. *Ritual and religion in Flavian epic*. Oxford.

Augoustakis, A., ed. 2014a. *Flavian poetry and its Greek past*. Leiden.
Augoustakis, A. 2014b. "Plautinisches im Silius? Two episodes from Silius Italicus' *Punica*." In *Plautine trends: Studies in Plautine comedy and its reception*, ed. I. Perysinakis and E. Karakasis, 257–74. Berlin.
Augoustakis, A. 2014c. "Valerius Flaccus in Silius Italicus." In *Brill's companion to Valerius Flaccus*, ed. M. Heerink and G. Manuwald, 340–58. Leiden.
Augoustakis, A. 2015. "Campanian politics and poetics in Silius Italicus' *Punica*." *ICS* 40.1: 155–69.
Augoustakis, A., ed. 2016. *Flavian epic*. Oxford.
Augoustakis, A. 2018. "Thomas Ross' translation and continuation of Silius Italicus' *Punica* in the English Restoration." In *Brill's companion to prequels, sequels, and retellings of Classical epic*, ed. R. C. Simms, 335–56. Leiden.
Augoustakis, A. and N. Bernstein, trans. forthcoming. *Silius Italicus'* Punica. London.
Augoustakis, A. and R. J. Littlewood, eds. 2019. *Campania in the Flavian poetic imagination*. Oxford.
Augoustakis, A. and R. J. Littlewood, eds. and trans. forthcoming. *Silius Italicus, Punica 3*. Oxford.
Augoustakis, A., E. Buckley, and C. Stocks, eds. 2019. Fides *in Flavian literature*. Toronto.
Auhagen, U. 2006. "Stoisches bei Silius: Decius und Hannibal (*Punica* XI 155–258)." *Aevum(ant)* 6: 85–97. Reprint, in Castagna, Galimberti Biffino, and Riboldi 2011, 73–85.
Auhagen, U., S. Faller, and F. Hurka, eds. 2005. *Petrarca und die römische Literatur*. Tübingen.
Auliard, C. 2001. *Victoires et triomphes à Rome: droit et réalités sous la République*. Paris.
Badian, E. 1966. "The early historians." In *Latin historians*, ed. T. A. Dorey, 1–38. New York.
Baertschi, A. M. 2013. Nekyiai: *Totenbeschwörung und Unterweltsbegegnung im neronisch-flavischen epos*. Berlin.
Bagnall, N. 1990. *The Punic Wars*. London. Reprint, *The Punic Wars: Rome, Carthage, and the struggle for the Mediterranean*. New York, 2005.
Baier, T. 2006. "Der Götterapparat bei Silius Italicus." *Aevum(ant)* 6: 293–308. Reprint, in Castagna, Galimberti Biffino, and Riboldi 2011, 281–96.
Baier, T., ed. 2012. *Götter und menschliche Willensfreiheit: Von Lucan bis Silius Italicus*. Munich.
Bakhtin, M. 1981. *The dialogic imagination*. Trans. C. Emerson and M. Holquist. Austin.
Bakogianni, A. and V. M. Hope, eds. 2015. *War as spectacle: Ancient and modern perspectives on the display of armed conflict*. London.
Bandiera, E. 1993. "La conformazione prosodico-metrica dell'« Additamentum Aldinum » di Silio Italico." *GIF* 45.2: 195–230.
Bannon, C. J. 1997. *The brothers of Romulus: Fraternal* pietas *in Roman law, literature, and society*. Princeton.
Bär, S. 2018. *Herakles im griechischen Epos: Studien zur Narrativität und Poetizität eines Helden*. Stuttgart.

Barash, J. A. 2016. *Collective memory and the historical past.* Chicago.

Barcaro, A. 2007. "La morte di Remo in età augustea." *RCCM* 49.1: 29–48.

Barchiesi, A. 2006-9. "Exemplarity: Between practice and text." In *Latinitas perennis*, ed. W. Verbaal, Y. Maes, and J. Papy, 2.41–62. Leiden.

Barlow, Joel. 1807. *Columbiad.* Philadelphia.

Barnes, W. R. 1995. "Virgil: The literary impact." In *A companion to the study of Virgil*, ed. N. Horsfall, 257–92. Leiden. 2nd ed., 2000.

Bartalucci, A. 1989. "Il lessico dei catasterismi nel *De astronomia* di Igino e nei testi omologhi." *SCO* 38: 353–72.

Bartolomé, J. 2018. "El combate de los trillizos y la imagen de la guerra civil en las *Púnicas* de Silio Itálico." *Emerita* 86.1: 109–32.

Barton, C. A. 1993. *The sorrows of the Romans: The gladiator and the monster.* Princeton.

Bartsch, S. 1994. *Actors in the audience: Theatricality and doublespeak from Nero to Hadrian.* Cambridge, MA.

Bartsch, S., K. Freudenburg, and C. Littlewood, eds. 2017. *The Cambridge companion to the age of Nero.* Cambridge.

Barzanò, A. 1982. "Domiziano e il *bellum Capitolinum*." *RIL* 116: 11–20.

Bassett, E. L. 1963. "Scipio and the ghost of Appius." *CPh* 58.2: 73–92.

Bassett, E. L. 1966. "Hercules and the hero of the *Punica*." In *The Classical tradition: Literary and historical studies in honor of Harry Caplan*, ed. L. Wallach, 258–73. Ithaca.

Bassett, E. L., J. Delz, and A. J. Dunston. 1976. "Silius Italicus, Tiberius Catius Asconius." In *CTC* 3, ed. F. E. Cranz and P. O. Kristeller, 341–98. Washington, DC.

Bastien, J.-L. 2007. *Le triomphe romain et son utilisation politique à Rome aux trois derniers siècles de la République.* Rome.

Baudnik, Z. 1906. *Die epische Technik des Silius Italicus im Verhältnisse zu seinen Vorbildern.* Krumau.

Bauer, L. 1881. "Das Verhältnis der *Punica* des C. Silius Italicus zur dritten Dekade des Livius." *BBG* 17.4: 145–59 and 17.5: 201–13.

Bauer, L. 1883. *Das Verhältnis der* Punica *des C. Silius Italicus zur dritten Dekade des T. Livius.* Erlangen. Reprint, *ASPE* 3 (1884): 103–60.

Bauer, L., ed. 1890–2. *Sili Italici* Punica. 2 vols. Lipsiae [Leipzig].

Bayet, J. 1951. "Le suicide mutuel dans la mentalité des Romains." *L'année sociologique* 3rd ser. 5[4]: 35–89.

Beard, M. 2007. *The Roman triumph.* Cambridge, MA.

Beaty, M. D. 1960. *Foreshadowing and suspense in the* Punica *of Silius Italicus.* Ph.D. diss., The University of North Carolina at Chapel Hill.

Begbie, C. M. 1967. "The epitome of Livy." *CQ* n.s. 17.2: 332–8.

Bellen, H. 1985. Metus Gallicus–metus Punicus: *Zum Furchtmotiv in der römischen Republik.* Stuttgart.

Bengtson, H. 1979. *Die Flavier: Vespasian, Titus, Domitian; Geschichte eines römischen Kaiserhauses.* Munich.

Bennett, T. C. 1978. *A commentary on Silius Italicus,* Punica *13, 381–895, with special reference to language, meter and rhetorical tropes.* M.A. thesis, University of Victoria.
Berger, S. and B. Niven, eds. 2014. *Writing the history of memory.* London.
Bergin, T. G. and A. S. Wilson, trans. 1977. *Petrarch's Africa.* New Haven.
Bernard, J.-E. 2002–3. "*Historia magistra mortis*: Tite-Live, Plutarque e la fin de Marcellus." In *Hommages à Carl Deroux*, ed. P. Defosse, 2.30–9. Brussels.
Bernardo, A. 1962. *Petrarch, Scipio, and the* Africa: *The birth of humanism's dream.* Baltimore.
Bernstein, N. W. 2008. *In the image of the ancestors: Narratives of kinship in Flavian epic.* Toronto.
Bernstein, N. W. 2016a. "Epic poetry: Historicizing the Flavian epics." In Zissos 2016, 395–411.
Bernstein, N. W. 2016b. "Revisiting Ovidian Silius, along with Lucretian, Vergilian, and Lucanian Silius." In *Repeat performances: Ovidian repetition and the* Metamorphoses, ed. L. Fulkerson and T. Stover, 225–48. Madison.
Bernstein, N. W., ed. and trans. 2017. *Silius Italicus,* Punica *2*. Oxford.
Bernstein, N. W., ed. and trans. forthcoming. *Silius Italicus,* Punica *9*. Oxford.
Bessone, F. and M. Fucecchi, eds. 2017. *The literary genres in the Flavian age: Canons, transformations, reception.* Berlin.
Bettenworth, A. 2004. *Gastmahlszenen in der antiken Epik von Homer bis Claudian: Diachrone Untersuchungen zur Szenentypik.* Göttingen.
Bettini, M. 1976–7. "L'epitaffio di Virgilio, Silio Italico, e un modo di intendere la letteratura." *DArch* 9–10.1–2: 439–48.
Bettini, M. 1977. "Ennio in Silio Italico: A proposito dei proemi al I e al VII degli *Annales* e del proemio allo *Scipio*." *RFIC* 105.4 = n.s. 83.4: 425–47. Reprint, in *Studi e note su Ennio*, 143–71. Pisa, 1979.
Bianchi, N. 2015. "*Per atra silentia noctis*: Nota su Petrarca lettore di Silio Italico." *Myrtia* 30: 207–14.
Bickel, E. 1911. "De Silii *Punicorum* libris VII ss. post Domitianum abolitum editis." *RhM* n.F. 66: 500–12.
Biesinger, B. 2016. *Römische Dekadenzdiskurse: Untersuchungen zur römischen Geschichtsschreibung und ihren Kontexten (2. Jahrhundert v. Chr. bis 2. Jahrhundert n. Chr.).* Stuttgart.
Biliński, B. 1937. *De Catone Silii in Italiae descriptione (Pun. VIII 356–616) uno solo fonte.* Leopoli Polonorum [Lwow].
Billerbeck, M. 1985. "Aspects of Stoicism in Flavian epic." *PLLS* 5: 341–56.
Billerbeck, M. 1986. "Stoizismus in der römischen Epik neronischer und flavischer Zeit." *ANRW* 2.32.5: 3116–51.
Billot, F. 2014. "Representing the battle of Zama to create an iconic event." *Antichthon* 48: 55–76.
Blakemore, S. 2007. *Joel Barlow's* Columbiad: *A bicentennial reading.* Knoxville.
Blanshard, A. 2005. *Hercules: A heroic life.* London.

Blasco Ibáñez, V. 1901. *Sónnica la cortesana*. Ed. F. Sempere. Valencia.
Blass, H. 1876. "Zu Vibius Sequester und Silius Italicus." *RhM* n.F. 31: 133–6.
Blattman, C. and E. Miguel. 2010. "Civil war." *JEL* 48.1: 3–57.
Blumenröder, D. 1694. *De C. Silio Italico, poeta consulari, dissertatio academica*. Halae Magd. [Halle]. Reprint, in *Christophori Cellarii Dissertationes academicae varii argumenti, in summam redactae*, ed. J. G. Walch, 1.71–89. Lipsiae [Leipzig], 1712.
Bolaffi, E. 1959. "L'epica del I secolo dell'impero." *GIF* 12.3: 218–30.
Bolaffi, E. 1960. "Appunti di storia della medicina." *GIF* 13.2: 156–61.
Bona, I. 1996. "Dalla Spagna all'Italia: Il passaggio delle Alpi nei *Punica* di Silio Italico." In *Un incontro con la storia nel centenario della nascita di Luca de Regibus, 1895–1995*, ed. A. F. Bellezza, 181–94. Genoa.
Bona, I. 1998. *La visione geografica nei* Punica *di Silio Italico*. Genoa.
Bonadeo, A. and E. Romano, eds. 2007. *Dialogando con il passato: Permanenze e innovazioni nella cultura latina di età flavia*. Florence.
Bonadeo, A., A. Canobbio, and F. Gasti, eds. 2011. *Filellenismo e identità romana in età flavia*. Pavia.
Bonamente, G. 1975. "Il *metus Punicus* e la decadenza di Roma in Sallustio, Agostino ed Orosio." *GIF* 27.2 = n.s. 6.2: 137–69.
Bond, C. 2009. "The phœnix and the prince: The poetry of Thomas Ross and literary culture in the court of Charles II." *RES* n.s. 60.246: 588–604.
Bönisch-Meyer, S., L. Cordes, V. Schulz, A. Wolsfeld, and M. Ziegert, eds. 2014. *Nero und Domitian: Mediale Diskurse der Herrscherrepräsentation im Vergleich*. Tübingen.
Bonnet, C. 2005. "Carthage, l'« autre nation » dans l'historiographie ancienne et moderne." *Anabases* 1: 139–160.
Börm, H., M. Mattheis, and J. Wienand, eds. 2016. *Civil war in ancient Greece and Rome: Contexts of disintegration and reintegration*. Stuttgart.
Bothe, F. H., trans. 1855-7. *Des Cajus Silius Italicus* Punischer Krieg *oder* Hannibal. 5 vols. in 1. Stuttgart.
Bouquet, J. 2001. *Le songe dans l'épopée latine d'Ennius à Claudien*. Brussels.
Boyle, A. J., ed. 1988. *The Imperial Muse:* Ramus *essays on Roman literature of the Empire; To Juvenal through Ovid*. Berwick.
Boyle, A. J., ed. 1990. *The Imperial Muse:* Ramus *essays on Roman literature of the Empire; Flavian epicist to Claudian*. Bendigo.
Boyle, A. J. and W. J. Dominik, eds. 2003. *Flavian Rome: Culture, image, text*. Leiden.
Boyle, A. J. and J. P. Sullivan, eds. 1991. *Roman poets of the Early Empire*. London.
Brannigan, J. 1998. *New Historicism and Cultural Materialism*. Basingstoke.
Braun, L. 1993. "Der Aufbau der *Punica* des Silius Italicus." *WJA* n.F. 19: 173–83.
Braunert, H. 1953. "Zum Chattenkriege Domitians." *BJ* 153: 97–101.
Breed, B. W., C. Damon, and A. Rossi, eds. 2010. *Citizens of discord: Rome and its civil wars*. Oxford.
Bremmer, J. N. 1987. "Romulus, Remus and the foundation of Rome." In *Roman myth and mythography*, ed. J. N. Bremmer and N. M. Horsfall, 25–48. London.

Bridges, E. 2015. *Imagining Xerxes: Ancient perspectives on a Persian king.* London.
Briessmann, A. 1955. *Tacitus und das flavische Geschichtsbild.* Wiesbaden.
Brizzi, G. 1984. "*Imitari coepit Annibalem* (Flor., I, XXII, 55): Apporti catoniani alla concezione storiografica di Floro?" *Latomus* 43.2: 424–31.
Brizzi, G. 2016. *Canne: La sconfitta che fece vincere Roma.* Bologna.
Brolli, T. 2004. "Silio in Sidonio: Maggioriano e il passaggio delle Alpi." In *ITFC* 3, ed. L. Cristante and A. Tessier, 297–314. Trieste.
Brouwers, J. H. 1982. "Zur Lucan-Imitation bei Silius Italicus." In *Actus: Studies in honour of H. L. W. Nelson,* ed. J. den Boeft and A. H. M. Kessels, 73–87. Utrecht.
Brouwers, J. H. 1985. "Hannibals dromen in Silius' *Punica.*" In *Noctes Noviomagenses J. C. F. Nuchelmans XIII lustris pr. Kal. Sept. anno Domini MCMLXXXV feliciter peractis rude donato ab amicis oblatae,* ed. G. J. M. Bartelink and J. H. Brouwers, 61–73. Weesp.
Bruère, R. T. 1958. "*Color Ovidianus* in Silius *Punica* 1-7." In *Ovidiana: Recherches sur Ovide, publiées à l'occasion du bimillénaire de la naissance du poète,* ed. N. I. Herescu, 475–499. Paris. Reprint, in Augoustakis 2016, 345–87.
Bruère, R. T. 1959. "*Color Ovidianus* in Silius *Punica* 8-17." *CPh* 54.4: 228–45. Reprint, in Augoustakis 2016, 345–87.
Brugnoli, G. 1992. "L'« Additamentum Aldinum » di Sil. 8, 144–223 è di Silio!" *GIF* 44.2: 203–14.
Brugnoli, G. 1994. "Seneca tragico e Silio Italico." *Aevum(ant)* 7: 333–40.
Brugnoli, G. and C. Santini. 1995. *L'Additamentum Aldinum di Silio Italico.* Rome.
Brugnoli, G. and C. Santini. 1998. "Un'occasione mancata." *GIF* 50.2: 261–4.
Brunt, P. A. 1975. "Stoicism and the principate." *PBSR* 43: 7–35.
Bücher, F. 2006. *Verargumentierte Geschichte:* Exempla Romana *im politischen Diskurs der späten römischen Republik.* Stuttgart.
Buchwald, F. 1886. *Quaestiones Silianae.* Gorlicii [Görlitz].
Buckingham, W. T. 1996. *Aspects of Silius Italicus' relation to Virgil in the* Aeneid. M.A. thesis, University of Auckland.
Buckley, Emma. 2018. "Flavian epic and Trajanic historiography: Speaking into the silence." In König and Whitton 2018, 86–107.
Buckley, E. and M. T. Dinter, eds. 2013. *A companion to the Neronian Age.* Malden.
Buecheler, F. 1880. "Coniectanea de Silio Iuvenale Plauto aliis poetis lat." *RhM* n.F. 35: 390–407.
Burck, E. 1943. "Das Bild der Karthager in der römischen Literatur." In Vogt 1943, 297–345.
Burck, E. 1950. *Einführung in die dritte Dekade des Livius.* Heidelberg. 2nd ed., 1962.
Burck, E. 1966–81. "Epische Bestattungsszenen: Ein literar-historischer Versuch." In *Vom Menschenbild in der römischen Literatur,* 2.429–87. Heidelberg.
Burck, E. 1978. *Unwetterszenen bei den flavischen Epikern.* Wiesbaden.
Burck, E. 1979. "Die › Punica ‹ des Silius Italicus." In *Das römische Epos,* 254–99. Darmstadt.

Burck, E. 1984a. *Historische und epische Tradition bei Silius Italicus.* Munich.

Burck, E. 1984b. *Silius Italicus: Hannibal in Capua und die Rückeroberung der Stadt durch die Römer.* Stuttgart.

Burck, E. 1988. "*Fides* in den "Punica" des Silius Italicus." In *Munera philologica et historica Mariano Plezia oblata,* ed. J. Safarewicz, 49–60. Wrocław.

Burgeon, C. 2018. "Domitien et son ascendance herculéo-jupitérienne dans les *Punica* de Silius Italicus." *Interférences.*

Burgess, J. S. 2001. *The tradition of the Trojan War in Homer and the Epic Cycle.* Baltimore.

Burian, J. 1978. "Ceterum autem censeo Carthaginem esse delendam." *Klio* 60: 169–75.

Burnett, A., M. Amandry, and I. Carradice. 1999. *RPC 2, From Vespasian to Domitian (AD 69–96).* 2 parts. London; Paris.

Burnyeat, M. F. 1997. "Postscript on silent reading." *CQ* n.s. 47.1: 74–6.

Bursian, C., ed. 1867. *Vibi Sequestris* De fluminibus etc. libellus. Turici [Zürich].

Bussi, G. A., ed. 1471. *Silii Italici* Punicorum *libri XVII.* Romae [Rome].

Butler, S. 2009. "The backward glance." *Arion* 3rd ser. 17.2: 59–78.

Buzio, M., ed. and trans. 1765. *Libri Caji Silii Italici De bello Punico secundo* = *Libri di Cajo Silio Italico Della seconda guerra cartaginese, tradotti dal Padre Don Massimiliano Buzio, Cherico regolare di S. Paolo.* 3 vols. Mediolani = Milan.

Calder, W. M. 1935. "Silius Italicus in Asia." *CR* 49.6: 216–17.

Calder, W. M. and J. M. R. Cormack, eds. 1962. *MAMA 8, Monuments from Lycaonia, the Pisido-Phrygian borderland, Aphrodisias.* Manchester.

Caltabiano, M. 1975. "Le morte del console Marcello nella tradizione storiografica." In *Storiografia e propaganda,* ed. M. Sordi, 65–81. Milan.

Calvino, I. 1972. *Le città invisibili.* Turin.

Calvino, I. 1974. *Invisibile cities.* Trans. W. Weaver. Boston and New York.

Campbell, D. J. 1936. "The birthplace of Silius Italicus." *CR* 50.2: 56–8.

Canobbio, A. 2011. "Parole greche in Marziale: tipologie di utilizzo e tre problemi filologici (3,20,5; 3,77,10; 9,44,6)." In Bonadeo, Canobbio, and Gasti 2011, 59–89.

Canobbio, A. 2017. "Bipartition and non-distinction of poetical genres in Martial: *magnum* vs *parvum*." In Bessone and Fucecchi 2017, 103–16.

Caputo, R. 1995. "Versi di Silio e rime di Petrarca (contributo all'ipotesi di un 'confronto impossibile')." In *Da una riva e dall'altra: Studi in onore di Antonio D'Andrea,* ed. D. Della Terza, 141–61. Florence.

Carawan, E. M. 1984–5. "The tragic history of Marcellus and Livy's characterization." *CJ* 80.2: 131–41.

Carrio, L. 1583. *Emendationum et observationum libri duo.* Lutetiae [Paris].

Carrubba, R. W. 1966. "The curse on the Romans." *TAPhA* 97: 29–34.

Carrubba, R. W. 1967. "Structural symmetry in Horace, *Epodes* 16.41–66." *RhM* n.F. 110.3: 201–9.

Cartault, A. 1887. "Est-il possible de fixer exactement la date de la composition des « Puniques » de Silius Italicus?" *RPh* 13 = n.s. 11: 11–14.

Casale, F. G. 1954. *Silio Italico*. Salerno.
Casali, S. 2006. "The poet at war: Ennius on the field in Silius's *Punica*." *Arethusa* 39.3: 569–93.
Cassata, L. 1997. "Possibili rapporti intertestuali tra Silio Italico e Petrarca?" In *Munuscula minuscula*, ed. G. Brugnoli, 23–30. Rome.
Cassata, L. 1998. "Silio Italico in Petrarca." *FAM* 15: 55–98.
Castagna, L., G. Galimberti Biffino, and C. Riboldi, eds. 2011. *Studi su Silio Italico*. Milan.
Caven, B. 1980. *The Punic Wars*. London.
Ceauşescu, P. 1976. "*Altera Roma*: Histoire d'une folie politique." *Historia* 25.1: 79–108.
Champlin, E. 2003. *Nero*. Cambridge, MA.
Chaplin, J. 2000. *Livy's exemplary history*. Oxford.
Chaudhuri, P. 2014. *The war with god: Theomachy in Roman Imperial poetry*. Oxford.
Chhana, J. 2005. *Epic visions of Roman rule: Concepts of empire in Silius Italicus' Punica*. Ph.D. diss., The University of North Carolina at Chapel Hill.
Chilver, G. E. F. 1941. *Cisalpine Gaul: Social and economic history from 49 B.C. to the death of Trajan*. Oxford.
Chiu, A. C. 2011. "*Generata e sanguine*: The motivations of Anna Perenna in Silius Italicus, *Punica* 8." *NECJ* 38.1: 3–23.
Christensen, H. 1905. *Das* Alexanderlied *Walters von Châtillon*. Halle a. S.
Ciocârlie, A. 2006–8. "Imaginea Cartaginei la Silius Italicus." *StudClas* 52–54: 127–38.
Ciocarlie, A. 2008. "Carthage et les carthaginois dans l'épopée latine." *REA* 110.2: 541–68.
Clack, J. 1976. "Hannibal's gait." *CW* 70.3: 181.
Clark, J. H. 2014. *Triumph in defeat: Military loss and the Roman Republic*. Oxford.
Clinard, J. B. 1967. *A study of the historical epic at Rome from the Early Republic to the Neronian period*. Ph.D. diss., The University of North Carolina at Chapel Hill.
Coffey, M. 1953–4. *A study of imagery in Latin verse of the Silver age in the genres of epic, tragedy, didactic verse and satire*. Ph.D. diss., Cambridge University.
Coffee, N., C. Forstall, L. Galli Milić, and D. P. Nelis, eds. 2020. *Intertextuality in Flavian epic*. Berlin and Boston.
Coleman, K. M. 1986. "The emperor Domitian and literature." *ANRW* 2.32.5: 3087–115.
Colish, M. L. 1985. *The Stoic tradition from Antiquity to the early Middle Ages*. 2 vols. Leiden. 2nd ed., 1990.
Collington, T. 2001. "Space, time and narrative: Bakhtin and Ricoeur." *Space and Culture* 7–9: 221–31.
Conley, D. F. 1981. "The stages of Rome's decline in Sallust's historical theory." *Hermes* 109.3: 379–82.
Conner, D. A. 2018. Mille simul leti facies: *The allusive battlefield of* Punica *4*. Ph.D. diss., University of Washington.
Connerton, P. 1989. *How societies remember*. Cambridge.
Connerton, P. 2009. *How modernity forgets*. Cambridge.
Connolly, S. 2010. "Lucan's Punic War in the *Disticha Catonis*." *C&M* 61: 193–202.

Connors, C. 2015. "In the land of the Giants: Greek and Roman discourses on Vesuvius and the Phlegraean Fields." *ICS* 40.1: 121–37.

Conte, G. B. 1974. *Memoria dei poeti e sistema letterario: Catullo, Virgilio, Ovidio, Lucano.* Turin. 2nd ed., 1985. Reprint, Palermo, 2012.

Conte, G. B. 1986. *The rhetoric of imitation: Genre and poetic memory in Virgil and other Latin poets.* Ed. and trans. C. Segal. Ithaca.

Conte, G. B. 1992. "Proems in the middle." In Dunn and Cole 1992, 147–59.

Conte, G. B. 2014. *Dell'imitazione: Furto e originalità.* Pisa.

Conte, G. B. 2017. *Stealing the club from Hercules: On imitation in Latin poetry.* Berlin.

Conte, S. 2012. *La Seconda Guerra Tritonide.* Vignate.

Cordes, L. 2017. *Kaiser und Tyrann: Die Kodierung und Umkodierung der Herrscherrepräsentation Neros und Domitians.* Berlin.

Cornell, T. J. 1986. "The *Annals* of Quintus Ennius." *JRS* 76: 244–50.

Cornell, T., B. Rankov, and P. Sabin. 1996. *The Second Punic War: A reappraisal.* London.

Corning, A. and H. Schuman. 2015. *Generations and collective memory.* Chicago.

Cosack, W. 1844. *Quaestiones Silianae.* Halis [Halle].

Costanzi, G. 1508. *Collectaneorum hecatostys prima Hadriano Cardinali dicata.* Fani [Fano].

Cotta Ramosino, L. 1999. "Il supplizio della croce in Silio Italico: *Pun.* I 169–181 e VI 539–544." *Aevum* 73.1: 93–105.

Courtney, E. 1989. "Some problems in the text of Silius Italicus." *RFIC* 117.3 = n.s. 95.3: 325–8.

Courtney, E., ed. 1993. *The fragmentary Latin poets.* Oxford.

Cousin, J. 1939. "Valérius Flaccus, Silius Italicus, Stace." *RCC* 40.2: 375–84. Reprint, in *Études sur la poésie latine: Nature et mission du poète*, 000–000. Paris, 1945; New York, 1978.

Cowan, R. W. 2003. *"In my beginning is my end": Origins, cities and foundations in Flavian epic.* D.Phil. diss., Oxford University.

Cowan, R. 2006. "Absurdly Scythian Spaniards: Silius, Horace and the Concani." *Mnemosyne* 4th ser. 59.2: 260–7.

Cowan, R. 2007a. "The headless city: The decline and fall of Capua in Silius Italicus' *Punica*." Unpublished manuscript.

Cowan, R. 2007b. "Reading Trojan Rome: Illegitimate epithets, avatars, and the limits of analogy in Silius Italicus' *Punica*." Unpublished manuscript.

Cowan, R. 2010. "Virtual epic: Counterfactuals, sideshowing, and the poetics of contingency in the *Punica*." In Augoustakis 2010a, 323–51.

Cowan, B. 2011. "Hopefully surviving: The limits of *devotio* in Virgil and others." *PVS* 27: 56–98.

Cowherd, C. 1972. *Latin poetic sources of the Fabian book of the* Punica *of Silius Italicus.* Ph.D. diss., The University of Chicago.

Cristóbal, V. 1988. "Tempestades épicas." *CIF* 14: 125–48.

Cristofoli, R. 2009. "Il giuramento di Annibale nei *Punica* di Silio Italico: Aspetti storici, ideologici e politici." *BStudLat* 39.2: 474–94.

Czypicka, T. 1987. "Funzionalità del dialogo tra Venere e Giove nel libro III delle "Puniche" di Silio Italico." *Eos* 75.1: 87–93.

D'Arco, I. 2002. "Il sogno premonitore di Annibale e il pericolo delle Alpi." *QS* 28.55: 145–62.

Daemen-de Gelder, K. and J.-P. Vander Motten. 2008. "Thomas Ross's *Second Punick War* (London 1661 and 1672): Royalist panegyric and artistic collaboration in the southern Netherlands." *Quaerendo* 38: 32–48.

Daly, G. 2002. *Cannae: The experience of battle in the Second Punic War*. New York.

Daly, L. J. 1981. "Livy's *veritas* and the *spolia opima*: Politics and the heroics of A. Cornelius Cossus (4.19–20)." *AncW* 4: 49–63.

Damon, C. 2010. "Déjà vu or déjà lu? History as intertext." *PLLS* 14: 375–88.

Danesi Marioni, G. 1989. "Un martirio stoico: Silio Italico, *Pun.* 1.169 sgg." *Prometheus* 15.3: 245–53.

Darwall-Smith, R. 1996. *Emperors and architecture: A study of Flavian Rome*. Brussels.

Dausque, C., ed. 1615/18. *In C. Silii Italici viri consularis* Punica, *seu De bello Punico secundo libros XVII*. Parisiis [Paris].

Davies, M. 1989. *The Epic Cycle*. Bristol. 2nd ed., 2003.

de Jong, I. J. F. and J. P. Sullivan, eds. 1994. *Modern critical theory and Classical literature*. Leiden.

de Rossi, G. B. 1882. "La villa di Silio Italico ed il collegio salutare nel Tuscolo." *BCAR* 2nd ser. 10: 141–8. Reprint, translated into French, *BEG* 2.5: 205–11.

Deane, S. N. 1921. "Archaeological news." *AJA* 25.1: 83–109.

Degrassi, A., ed. 1947. *IIt* 13, *Fasti et elogia*, Fasc. 1, *Fasti consulares et triumphales*. Rome.

Degrassi, A. 1952. *I fasti consolari dell'Impero dal 30 avanti Cristo al 613 dopo Cristo*. Rome.

Delarue, F. 1992. "Sur l'architecture des *Punica* de Silius Italicus." *REL* 70: 149–65.

Delarue, F. 1995. "Les enfers chez Silius Italicus et Stace." *L'école des lettres* 2nd ser. 87.4: 73–86.

Delattre, A. 2011. "Les *Punica* de Silius Italicus et la *Johannide* de Corippe: Quelques éléments rapprochement entre deux épopées africaines." *MH* 68.1: 68–85.

Della Corte, M. 1919. "Pompei: Continuazione degli scavi sulla via dell'Abbondanza." *NSA* 5th ser. 16: 232–42.

Delz, J. 1966. *Die Überlieferung des Silius Italicus: Ein Beitrag zur Geschichte der Philologie im 15. Jahrhundert*. Basel Habilitationsschrift.

Delz, J., ed. 1987. *Sili Italici* Punica. Stutgardiae [Stuttgart].

Delz, J. 1995. "Zur Neubewertung der lateinischen Epik flavischer Zeit." In *Aspetti della poesia epica latina*, ed. G. Reggi, 143–72. Lugano.

Dessau, H. 1916. "Über die Quellen unseres Wissens vom zweiten punischen Kriege." *Hermes* 51.3: 355–85.

Devallet, G. 1984. "Un thème guerrier de l'épopée antique: La bataille des remparts." *Pallas* 31: 5–28.

Develay, V. 1883. "Pétrarque et Silius Italicus." *BBB* 1883, 505–8.
Devillers, O. and V. Krings. 2006. "Le songe d'Hannibal: Quelques réflexions sur la tradition littéraire." In *L'Hellénisation en Méditerranée occidentale au temps des guerres puniques (260–180 av. J.C.), Pallas 70*, ed. P. François, P. Moret, and S. Péré-Noguès, 337–46.
Díaz de Bustamante, J. M. 1985. "El sueño como motivo genérico y como motivo tradicional en Silio Itálico." *Euphrosyne* n.s. 13: 27–50.
Dibbern, C. H. 2017. *A Eneida de Sílio Itálico: A aemulatio e os heróis de Punica*. Ph.D. diss., Universidade de São Paulo.
Dickey, E., ed. 2012–15. *The Colloquia of the Hermeneumata Pseudodositheana*. 2 vols. Cambridge.
Dietrich, J. S. 2004. "Rewriting Dido: Flavian responses to *Aeneid* 4." *Prudentia* 36.1: 1–30.
Dietrich, J. 2009. "Death becomes her: Female suicide in Flavian epic." *Ramus* 38.2: 187–202.
Dionisotti, A. C. 1982. "From Ausonius' schooldays? A schoolbook and its relatives." *JRS* 72: 83–125.
Dixon, S. M. 1973. *Stoic opposition from Nero to Domitian*. M.A. thesis, Australian National University.
Dolce, R. 2017. *"Losing one's head" in the ancient Near East: Interpretation and meaning of decapitation*. London.
Dominik, W. J. 2003. "Hannibal at the gates: Programmatising Rome and *Romanitas* in Silius Italicus' *Punica* 1 and 2." In Boyle and Dominik 2003, 469–97.
Dominik, W. J. 2006. "Rome then and now: Linking the Saguntum and Cannae episodes in Silius Italicus' *Punica*." In Nauta, van Dam, and Smolenaars 2006, 113–27.
Dominik, W. J. 2010. "The reception of Silius Italicus in modern scholarship." In Augoustakis 2010a, 425–47.
Dorfbauer, L. J. 2008. "Hannibal, Ennius und Silius Italicus: Beobachtungen zum 12. Buch der *Punica*." *RhM* n.F. 151.1: 83–108.
Drakenborch, A., ed. 1717. *Caji Silii Italici* Punicorum *libri septemdecim*. Trajecti ad Rhenum [Utrecht].
Drinkwater, J. F. 2019. *Nero: Emperor and court*. Cambridge.
Dudley, D. R., ed. 1972. *Neronians and Flavians: Silver Latin I*. London.
Duff, J. D., ed. and trans. 1934. *Silius Italicus:* Punica. 2 vols. London; Cambridge, MA.
Dufallo, B. 2007. *The ghosts of the past: Latin literature, the dead, and Rome's transition to a Principate*. Columbus.
Dumitru Oancea, M.-L., A.-C. Halichias, and N.-A. Popa, eds. 2016. *Expressions of fear from Antiquity to the contemporary world*. Newcastle upon Tyne.
Dunsch, B. 2006. "Variationen des *metus-hostilis*-Gedankens bei Sallust (*Cat.* 10; *Iug.* 41; *Hist.* 1, fr. 11 und 12 M.)." *GB* 25: 201–17.
Dunn, F. M. and T. Cole, eds. 1992. *Beginnings in Classical literature*. *YClS* 29.
Durkheim, É. 1897. *Le suicide: Étude de sociologie*. Paris.

Dykmans, M., S.J. 1988. *L'humanisme de Pierre Marso*. Vatican City.
Earl, D. C. 1961. *The political thought of Sallust*. Cambridge. Reprint, Amsterdam, 1966.
Eck, W. 1974. "Silius." *RE Suppl.* 14.678-9.
Eckstein, A. M. 2010. "Polybius, 'The treaty of Philinus', and Roman accusations against Carthage." *CQ* n.s. 60.2: 406-26.
Edmunds, L. 2001. *Intertextuality and the reading of Roman poetry*. Baltimore.
Edmunds, L. 2004. "Intratextuality: The parts, the wholes, and the holes." *Vergilius* 50: 158-69.
Edwards, C. 1996. *Writing Rome: Textual approaches to the city*. Cambridge.
Edwards, C. 2007. *Death in ancient Rome*. New Haven.
Effe, B. 2004. *Epische Objektivität und subjektives Erzählen: 'Auktoriale' Narrativik von Homer bis zum römischen Epos der Flavierzeit*. Trier.
Elliott, J. 2013. *Ennius and the architecture of the* Annales. Cambridge.
Engels, D. 2009. "Déterminisme historique et perceptions de déchéance sous la république tardive et le principat." *Latomus* 68.4: 859-94.
Erasmo, M. 2008. *Reading death in ancient Rome*. Columbus.
Erll, A. 2005. *Kollektives Gedächtnis und Erinnerungskulturen: Eine Einführung*. Stuttgart. 2nd ed., 2011.
Erll, A. 2011. *Memory in culture*. Trans. S. B. Young. Basingstoke.
Ernesti, J. C. G., ed. 1791-2. *Caii Silii Italici* Punicorum *libri septemdecim*. 2 vols. Lipsiae [Leipzig].
Erskine, A. 2001. *Troy between Greece and Rome: Local tradition and imperial power*. Oxford.
Escámez, D. M. 2012. "El templo de Júpiter Óptimo Máximo y su identificación con la supervivencia del Imperio: Justificación religiosa de la dinastía Flavia en Roma." In *Historia, identidad y alteridad*, ed. J. M. Aldea Celada, P. Ortega Martínez, I. Pérez Miranda, and Mª de los Reyes de Soto García, 763-84. Salamanca.
Escámez, D. M. 2013. "El templo de Júpiter Óptimo Máximo en la propaganda augústea." In *Los lugares de la historia*, ed. J. M. Aldea Celada, C. López San Segundo, P. Ortega Martínez, Mª de los Reyes de Soto García, and F. J. Vicente Santos, 951-72. Salamanca.
Escámez, D. M. 2014. "Júpiter Óptimo Máximo en la propaganda de Augusto y Vespasiano: Justificación religiosa de dos fundadores dinásticos." *Antesteria* 3: 189-207.
Esposito, P. 2012. "Su alcuni miti tragici in Lucano e nell'epica flavia." In Baier 2012, 99-126.
Etcheto, H. 2012. *Les Scipions: Famille et pouvoir à Rome à l'époque républicaine*. Bordeaux.
Evans, J. K. 1974. *Senatorial history and the principate of Domitian*. Ph.D. diss., McMaster University.
Evans, J. K. 1975. "The dating of Domitian's war against the Chatti again." *Historia* 24.1: 121-4.

Evrigenis, I. D. 2008. *Fear of enemies and collective action*. Cambridge.
Faber, R. 2012. "The ekphrasis in Naevius' *Bellum Punicum* and Hellenistic literary aesthetics." *Hermes* 140.4: 417–26.
Farrell, J. 2017. *The varieties of authorial intention: Literary theory beyond the intentional fallacy*. Cham.
Fears, J. R. 1981. "Jupiter and Roman imperial ideology: The role of Domitian." *ANRW* 2.17.1: 3–141.
Feeney, D. C. 1982. *A commentary on Silius Italicus Book I*. D.Phil. diss., Oxford University.
Feeney, D. C. 1984. "The reconciliations of Juno." *CQ* n.s. 34.1: 179–94.
Feeney, D. C. 1986. "Following after Hercules, in Virgil and Apollonius." *PVS* 18: 47–83.
Feeney, D. C. 1991. *The gods in epic: Poets and critics of the Classical tradition*. Oxford.
Feeney, D. 2007. *Caesar's calendar: Ancient time and the beginnings of history*. Berkeley, Los Angeles, and London.
Feeney, D. 2017. "Carthage and Rome: Introduction." *CPh* 112.3: 301–11.
Feldherr, A., ed. 2009. *The Cambridge companion to the Roman historians*. Cambridge.
Felperin, H. 1992. *The uses of the canon: Elizabethan literature and contemporary theory*. Oxford.
Ferenczi, A. and A. Zissos, eds. forthcoming. *Unity and inconsistency in Flavian epic*. Newcastle upon Tyne.
Fernandelli, M. 2009. "Anna Perenna in Ovidio e in Silio Italico." *GIF* 61.1-2: 139–72.
Festa, N., ed. 1926a. *Francesco Petrarca: Africa*. Florence.
Festa, N. 1926b. *Saggio sull'Africa del Petrarca*. Palermo.
Fincher, H. McC., III. 1979. *A thematic study of Silius Italicus's "Punica"*. Ph.D. diss., The Florida State University.
Fisher, J. 2014. *The Annals of Quintus Ennius and the Italic tradition*. Baltimore.
Flower, H. I. 1996. *Ancestor masks and aristocratic power in Roman culture*. Oxford.
Flower, H. I. 2000. "The tradition of the *spolia opima*: M. Claudius Marcellus and Augustus." *ClAnt* 19.1: 34–64.
Flower, H. I. 2003. "'Memories' of Marcellus: History and memory in Roman Republican culture." In *Formen römischer Geschichtsschreibung von den Anfängen bis Livius: Gattungen, Autoren, Kontexte*, ed. U. Eigler, U. Gotter, N. Luraghi, and U. Walter, 39–52. Darmstadt.
Flower, H. I. 2006. *The art of forgetting: Disgrace and oblivion in Roman political culture*. Chapel Hill.
Flower, H. I. 2010. *Roman republics*. Princeton.
Foscolo, U. 1823. *Essays on Petrarch*. London.
Foucher, A. 2000. *Historia proxima poetis: L'influence de la poésie épique sur le style des historiens latins de Salluste à Ammien Marcellin*. Brussels.
Foulon, É. 2002-3. "Mercure Alètès apparaît en songe à Hannibal." In *Hommages à Carl Deroux*, ed. P. Defosse, 4.366–77. Brussels.

Fowler, D. P. 1989. "First thoughts on closure: Problems and prospects." *MD* 22: 75–122. Reprint, in Fowler 2000, 239–83.

Fowler, D. 1997a. "On the shoulders of giants: Intertextuality and Classical studies." *MD* 39: 13–34. Reprint, in Fowler 2000, 115–37.

Fowler, D. 1997b. "Second thoughts on closure." In Roberts, Dunn, and Fowler 1997, 3–22. Reprint, in Fowler 2000, 284–308.

Fowler, D. 2000. *Roman constructions: Readings in postmodern Latin*. Oxford.

Franchet d'Espèrey, S. 1986. "Vespasien, Titus et la littérature." *ANRW* 2.32.5: 3048–86.

Franchet d'Espèrey, S. 2006. "Réception et transmission des modèles: L'*Énéide* comme modèle aux époques néronienne et flavienne." In *Réceptions antiques: Lecture, transmission, appropriation intellectuelle*, L. Ciccolini, C. Guérin, S. Itic, and S. Morlet, 73–86. Paris.

Fraenkel, E. 1954. "The giants in the poem of Naevius." *JRS* 44: 14–17.

Frank, E. 1974. "Works of art in the epics of Valerius Flaccus and Silius Italicus." *RIL* 108.3: 837–44.

Frank, R. 1985. "The bridle of fear." *Prudentia* 17.1: 19–25.

Franko, G. F. 1994. "The use of *Poenus* and *Carthaginiensis* in early Latin literature." *CPh* 89.2: 153–8.

Fratantuono, L. and C. Stark, eds. forthcoming. *A companion to Latin epic, 14–96 CE*. Malden.

Fries, J. 1985. *Der Zweikampf: Historische und literarische Aspekte seiner Darstellung bei T. Livius*. Meisenheim.

Fröhlich, U., ed. and trans. 2000. *Regulus, Archetyp römischer* Fides: *Das sechste Buch als Schlüssel zu den* Punica *des Silius Italicus; Interpretation, Kommentar und Übersetzung*. Tübingen.

Fronda, M. P. 2010. *Between Rome and Carthage: Southern Italy during the Second Punic War*. Cambridge.

Frowde, P. 1727. *The fall of Saguntum: A tragedy*. London. 2nd ed., 1729; 3rd ed., 1735.

Fucecchi, M. 1990a. "Empietà e titanismo nella rappresentazione siliana di Annibale." *Orpheus* n.s. 11.1: 21–42.

Fucecchi, M. 1990b. "Il declino di Annibale nei *Punica*." *Maia* n.s. 42.2: 151–66.

Fucecchi, M. 1993. "Lo spettacolo delle virtù nel giovane eroe predestinato: Analisi della figura di Scipione in Silio Italico." *Maia* n.s. 45.1: 17–48.

Fucecchi, M. 1999. "La vigilia di Canne nei *Punica* e un contributo allo studio dei rapporti fra Silio Italico e Lucano." In *Interpretare Lucano: Miscellanea di studi*, ed. P. Esposito and L. Nicastri, 305–42. Naples.

Fucecchi, M. 2005. "Il passato come nemico: Annibale e la velleitaria lotta contro una storia esemplare." *Dictynna* 2.

Fucecchi, M. 2006. "*Ad finem ventum*: Considerazioni sull'ultimo libro dei *Punica*." *Aevum(ant)* 6: 311–45. Reprint, in Castagna, Galimberti Biffino, and Riboldi 2011, 299–333.

Fucecchi, M. 2010. "The shield and the sword: Q. Fabius Maximus and M. Claudius Marcellus as models of heroism in Silius' *Punica*." In Augoustakis 2010a, 219–39.

Fucecchi, M. 2012. "Epica, filosofia della storia e legittimazione del potere imperiale: La profezia di Giove nel libro III dei *Punica* (e un'indicazione di percorso per l'epos storico)." In Baier 2012, 235–54.

Fucecchi, M. 2013. "Looking for the Giants: Mythological imagery and discourse on power in Flavian epic." In Manuwald and Voigt, 107–22.

Fucecchi, M. 2014. "The philosophy of power: Greek literary tradition and Silius' *On kingship*." In Augoustakis 2014, 305–24.

Fugmann, J. 2000. "Hannibal als « vir illustris »: Zur Hannibal-Biographie in der Schrift « De viris illustribus urbis Romae »." *MH* 57.2: 141–50.

Fürstenau, G. 1916. *De Sili Italici imitatione quae fertur Enniana*. Berolini [Berlin].

Futrell, A. 1997. *Blood in the arena: The spectacle of Roman power*. Austin.

Gabba, E. 1981. "True history and false history in Classical Antiquity." *JRS* 71: 50–62.

Gabriel, R. A. 2008. *Scipio Africanus: Rome's greatest general*. Washington, DC.

Gabriel, R. A. 2011. *Hannibal: The military biography of Rome's greatest enemy*. Washington, DC.

Gagliardi, D. 1990. "Il giudizio di Plinio Jr. su Silio Italico." *CCC* 11.3: 289–93.

Gajderowicz, J. 2011. *Silius' dual epic: Carthaginian and Roman perspectives in the Punica*. Ph.D. diss., Columbia University.

Galdi, M. 1934. "Gli epitomatori di Livio." In *Studi liviani*, 237–72. Rome.

Gale, M. R. 2003. "Poetry and the backward glance in Virgil's *Georgics* and *Aeneid*." *TAPhA* 133.2: 323–52.

Galinsky, G. K. 1972. *The Herakles theme: The adaptations of the hero in literature from Homer to the twentieth century*. Totowa.

Galinsky, K. 1996. *Augustan culture: An interpretive introduction*. Princeton.

Galinsky, K. 2012. *Augustus: Introduction to the life of an emperor*. Cambridge.

Galinsky, K., ed. 2014. Memoria Romana: *Memory in Rome and Rome in memory*. Ann Arbor.

Galinsky, K., ed. 2016. *Memory in ancient Rome and early Christianity*. Oxford.

Galinsky, K. and K. Lapatin, eds. 2016. *Cultural memories in the Roman Empire*. Los Angeles.

Gallagher, C. 2018. *Telling it like it wasn't: The counterfactual imagination in history and fiction*. Chicago.

Gallia, A. B. 2012. *Remembering the Roman Republic: Culture, politics and history under the Principate*. Cambridge.

Gallivan, P. A. 1974. "Some comments on the *fasti* for the reign of Nero." *CQ* n.s. 24.2: 290–311.

Gallivan, P. 1981. "The fasti for A.D. 70–96." *CQ* n.s. 31.1: 186–220.

Ganiban, R. T. 2010. "Virgil's Dido and the heroism of Hannibal in Silius' *Punica*." In Augoustakis 2010a, 73–98.

Garani, M. 2007. "Propertius' temple of Jupiter Feretrius and the *spolia opima* (4.10): A poem not to be read?" *AC* 76: 99–117.

García Amutxastegi, I. 2009. "Las figuras femeninas en *Púnica* de Silio Itálico: El caso de Sofonisba y de Asbite." *ARENAL* 16.2: 331–51.

García Amutxastegi, I. 2010. "La figura de Sofonisba en Silio Itálico." *EClás* 137: 41–56.

García Amutxastegi, I. 2015a. *Comentario y estudio literario de los relatos de derrota en la épica romana: El libro IX de los* Punica *de Silio Itálico*. Ph.D. diss., Universidad del País Vasco / Euskal Herriko Unibertsitatea.

García Amutxastegi, I. 2015b. "Monomaquia de Escipion y Aníbal en el relato siliano de la batalla de Cannas (9.419–485)." In Ianua Classicorum: *Temas y formas del mundo clásico*, ed. J. de la Villa Polo, P. Cañizares Ferriz, E. Falque Rey, J. F. González Castro, and J. Siles Ruiz, 2.441–8. Madrid.

Gardner, A. 2012. "Time and empire in the Roman world." *JSA* 12.2: 145–66.

Gärtner, T. 2008. "Selbstmord in der römischen Epik der nachaugusteischen Zeit." *AAntHung* 48.3: 365–85.

Gärtner, T. 2010. "Überlegungen zur Makrostruktur der *Punica*." In Schaffenrath 2010, 77–96.

Gärtner, U. 2006. "*Cedat tibi in gloria lausque magnorum heroum celebrataque carmine virtus*: Zu mythologischen Vergleichen und ihrem poetologischem Gehalt bei Silius Italicus." *Aevum(ant)* 6: 147–69. Reprint, in Castagna, Galimberti Biffino, and Riboldi 2011, 135–57.

Gasti, F. and G. Mazzoli, eds. 2005. *Modelli letterari e ideologia nell'età flavia*. Pavia.

Gavrilov, A. K. 1997. "Techniques of reading in Antiquity." *CQ* n.s. 47.1: 56–73.

Geisthardt, J. M. 2015. Zwischen princeps *und* res publica: *Tacitus, Plinius und die senatorische Selbstdarstellung in der Hohen Kaiserzeit*. Stuttgart.

Gelsomino, R., ed. 1967. *Vibius Sequester*. Lipsiae [Leipzig].

Gelzer, M. 1931. "Nasicas Widerspruch gegen die Zerstörung Karthagos." *Philologus* 86 = n.F. 40: 261–99. Reprint, in *Kleine Schriften*, ed. H. Strasburger and C. Meier, 2.39–72. Wiesbaden, 1963.

Genette, G. 1982. *Palimpsestes: La littérature au second degré*. Paris.

Genette, G. 1997. *Palimpsests: Literature in the second degree*. Trans. C. Newmann and C. Doubinsky. Lincoln, and London.

Gentile, A. 1962. "Onorato Occioni (1830–1896) e le „Puniche" di Silio Italico." *La porta orientale* 32.7–8: 287–90.

Gerhold, M. 2002. *Rom und Karthago zwischen Krieg und Frieden: Rechtshistorische Untersuchung zu den römisch-karthagischen Beziehungen zwischen 241 v. Chr. und 149 v. Chr.* Frankfurt am Main.

Gering, J. 2012. *Domitian,* dominus et deus*? Herrschafts- und Machtstrukturen im römischen Reich zur Zeit des letzten Flaviers*. Rahden.

Giarratano, C. 1934. "Fabio, Marcello e Scipione secondo Livio." In *Studi liviani*, 159–82. Rome.

Gibson, B. J. 2005. "Hannibal at Gades: Silius Italicus 3.1–60." *PLLS* 12: 177–95.

Gibson, B. 2010. "Silius Italicus: A consular historian?" In Augoustakis 2010a, 47–72.
Gibson, B. 2013. "Praise in Flavian epic." In Manuwald and Voigt 2013, 67–86.
Gibson, R. K. and R. Morello. 2012. *Reading the Letters of Pliny the Younger: An introduction*. Cambridge.
Gilliard, F. D. 1993. "More silent reading in Antiquity: *Non omne verbum sonabat*." *JBL* 112.4: 689–94.
Ginsberg, L. D. and D. A. Krasne, eds. 2018. *After 69 C.E. – Writing civil war in Flavian Rome*. Berlin.
Girard, R. 1972. *La violence et le sacré*. Paris.
Girard, R. 1977. *Violence and the sacred*. Trans. P. Gregory. Baltimore.
Giroldini, R. 2005. "*Et puer hoc dignus nomine eras*: Un motivo encomiastico per Domiziano in Marziale e Silio Italico." In Gasti and Mazzoli 2005, 163–84.
Giusti, E. 2016. "My enemy's enemy is my enemy: Virgil's illogical use of *metus hostilis*." In *Augustan poetry and the irrational*, ed. P. Hardie, 37–55. Oxford.
Giusti, E. 2018. *Carthage in Virgil's* Aeneid: *Staging the enemy under Augustus*. Cambridge.
Glück, J. J. 1964. "Reviling and monomachy as battle-preludes in ancient warfare." *AClass* 7: 25–31.
Glücklich, H. J. and S. Reitzer. 1985. *Die Hannibalbiographie des Nepos im Unterricht*. Göttingen. 2nd ed., 2011.
Goldbeck, F. and J. Wienand, eds. 2017. *Der römische Triumph in Prinzipat und Spätantike: Probleme—Paradigmen—Perspektiven*. Berlin.
Goldman, M. J. 1997. *A commentary on Silius Italicus' Punica 8.25–241*. M.A. thesis, University of Kansas.
Goldschmidt, N. and B. Graziosi, eds. 2018. *Tombs of the ancient poets: Between literary reception and material culture*. Oxford.
Goldsworthy, A. 2000. *The Punic Wars*. London.
Goldsworthy, A. 2001. *Cannae*. Fields of Battle. London. Reprint, *Cannae: Hannibal's greatest victory*, London, 2007.
Goodhart Gordan, P. W. 1974. *Two Renaissance book hunters: The letters of Poggius Bracciolini to Nicolaus de Niccolis*. New York.
Goold, G. P. 1956. "Observationes in codicem Matritensem M. 31: De Silii et Statii Silvarum scripta memoria." *RhM* n.F. 99.1: 9–17.
Gosling, A. 2002. "Sending up the founder: Ovid and the apotheosis of Romulus." *AClass* 45: 51–69.
Gossage, A. J. 1969. "Virgil and the Flavian epic." In *Virgil*, ed. D. R. Dudley, 67–93. New York.
Gowing, A. M. 2005. *Empire and memory: The representation of the Roman Republic in Imperial culture*. Cambridge.
Grainger, J. D. 2003. *Nerva and the Roman succession crisis of AD 96–99*. London.
Grandazzi, A. and A. Queyrel-Bottineau, eds. 2018. *Antiques uchronies: Quand les Grecs et Romains imaginent des histoires alternatives*. Dijon.

Grassl, H. 1973. *Untersuchungen zum Vierkaiserjahr 68/69 n. Chr.: Ein Beitrag zur Ideologie und Sozialstruktur des frühen Prinzipats*. Vienna.
Green, P. 1978. "Caesar and Alexander: *Aemulatio, imitatio, comparatio*." *AJAH* 3.1: 1–26.
Green, R. P. H. 2006. *Latin epics of the New Testament: Juvencus, Sedulius, Arator*. Oxford.
Greenblatt, S. 1980. *Renaissance self-fashioning: From More to Shakespeare*. Chicago.
Greenblatt, S. 2011. *The swerve: How the world became modern*. New York.
Greenhalgh, P. A. L. 1975. *The year of the Four Emperors*. London.
Grewing, F. F., B. Acosta-Hughes, and A. Kirichenko, eds. 2013. *The door ajar: False closure in Greek and Roman literature and art*. Heidelberg.
Griffin, A. H. F. 1986. "Hyginus, *Fabulae* 89 (Laomedon)." *CQ* n.s. 36.2: 541.
Griffin, M. T. 1984. *Nero: The end of a dynasty*. London.
Griffin, M. 1986. "Philosophy, Cato, and Roman suicide." *G&R* 2nd ser. 33: 64–77, 192–202.
Grimal, P. 1953. *Le siècle des Scipions: Rome et l'hellénisme au temps des guerres puniques*. Paris. 2nd ed., 1975.
Grimal, P. 1977. *La Guerre civile de Pétrone dans ses rapports avec la Pharsale*. Paris.
Grisé, Y. 1980. "De la frequence du suicide chez les Romains." *Latomus* 39.1: 17–46.
Grisé, Y. 1982. *Le suicide dans la Rome antique*. Paris.
Groag, E. 1927a. "14) L. Silius Decianus." *RE* 2.3A.5.77–9.
Groag, E. 1927b. "24) (Silius) Severus." *RE* 2.3A.5.95.
Groesst, J. 1887. *Qua tenus Silius Italicus a Vergilio pendere videatur*. Aquis Mattiacis [Wiesbaden].
Gsell, S. 1913–28. *Histoire ancienne de l'Afrique du Nord*. 8 vols. Paris. Reprint, Osnabrück, 1972.
Hackl, U. 1980. "Poseidonios und das Jahr 146 v. Chr. als Epochendatum in der antiken Historiographie." *Gymnasium* 87: 151–66.
Hadas, M. 1936. "Later Latin epic and Lucan." *CW* 29.20: 153–7.
Hagen, J. 2017. *Die Tränen der Mächtigen und die Macht der Tränen: Eine emotionsgeschichtliche Untersuchung des Weinens in der kaiserzeitlichen Historiographie*. Stuttgart.
Halbwachs, M. 1925. *Les cadres sociaux de la mémoire*. Paris. Reprint, 1952.
Halbwachs, M. 1930. *Les causes du suicide*. Paris.
Halbwachs, M. 1950. *La mémoire collective*. Paris.
Halbwachs, M. 1978. *The causes of suicide*. Trans. H. Goldblatt. London.
Halbwachs, M. 1980. *The collective memory*. Trans. F. J. Ditter, Jr. and V. Yazdi Ditter. New York.
Halbwachs, M. 1992. *On collective memory*. Ed. and trans. L. A. Coser. Chicago.
Hammer, D. 2014. *Roman political thought: From Cicero to Augustine*. Cambridge.
Hamvas, G. 2016. *Ekphraseis in Silver Latin epic*. Ph.D. diss., Pázmány Péter Catholic University.

Hardie, P. R. 1983. "Some themes from Gigantomachy in the 'Aeneid.'" *Hermes* 111.3: 311–26.
Hardie, P. R. 1986. *Virgil's Aeneid: Cosmos and imperium*. Oxford.
Hardie, P. 1989. "Flavian epicists on Virgil's epic technique." *Ramus* 18.1–2: 3–20. Reprint, in Boyle 1990, 3–20.
Hardie, P. 1993a. *The epic successors of Virgil: A study in the dynamics of a tradition*. Cambridge.
Hardie, P. 1993b. "Tales of unity and division in Imperial Latin epic." In *Literary responses to civil discord*, ed. J. H. Molyneux, 57–71. Nottingham.
Hardie, P. 1997. "Closure in Latin epic." In Roberts, Dunn, and Fowler 1997, 139–62.
Harich-Schwarzbauer, H. 2005. "Literarisches Spiel? Petrarcas Schweigen zu Silius Italicus und sein Brief an Homer (*Famil*. 24, 12)." In Auhagen, Faller, and Hurka 2005, 103–19.
Harrison, S. J. 1989. "Augustus, the poets, and the *spolia opima*." *CQ* n.s. 39.2: 408–14.
Harrison, S. J., ed. 2001. *Texts, ideas, and the Classics: Scholarship, theory, and Classical literature*. Oxford.
Harrison, S., S. Frangoulidis, and T. D. Papanghelis, eds. 2018. *Intratextuality and Latin literature*. Berlin.
Harth, H., ed. 1984–7. *Poggio Bracciolini: Lettere*. 3 vols. Florence.
Hartmann, J. M. 2004. *Flavische Epik im Spannungsfeld von generischer Tradition und zeitgenössischer Gesellschaft*. Frankfurt am Main.
Haselmann, H. 2018. *Gewässer als Schauplätze und Akteure in den Punica des Silius Italicus*. Münster.
Häußler, R. 1976–8. *Studien zum historischen Epos der Antike*. 2 vols. Heidelberg.
Häußler, R. 1978. "Strukturfragen historischer Epik in der Antike." *A&A* 24: 125–45.
Hawthorn, G. 1991. *Plausible worlds: Possibility and understanding in history and the social sciences*. Cambridge.
Hay, P. 2019. "The programmatic 'ordior' of Silius Italicus." *SyllClass* 30: 49–71.
Heath, M. 2002. *Interpreting Classical texts*. London.
Heck, E. 1970. "Scipio am Scheideweg: Die *Punica* des Silius Italicus und Ciceros Schrift *De re publica*." *WS* 83 = n.F. 4: 156–80. Originally published in *Lemmata: Donum natalicium Guilelmo Ehlers sexagenario a sodalibus Thesauri linguae Latinae oblatum*, 66–95. Monaci [Munich], 1968.
Heinemann, A. 2016. "Jupiter, die Flavier und das Kapitol; oder: Wie man einen Bürgerkrieg gewinnt." In Börm, Mattheis, and Wienand 2016, 187–235.
Heins, D., ed. 1600–1. *Silius Italicus de secundo bello Punico*. Lugd. Bat. [Leiden].
Heins, D. 1646. *Crepundia Siliana*. Cantabrigiae [Cambridge].
Heister, L. 1734. *Epistola de morte Silii Italici celebris poetae et oratoris ex clavo insanabili*. Helmstadii Saxonum [Helmstedt].
Heitland, W. E. 1896. "The 'great lacuna' in the eighth book of Silius Italicus." *JPh* 24: 188–211.

Hellekson, K. 2001. *The alternate history: Refiguring historical time.* Kent and London.
Helm, R. 1892. *De P. Papinii Statii Thebaide.* Berolini [Berlin].
Henderson, B. W. 1908. *Civil war and rebellion in the Roman Empire, A.D. 69–70.* London.
Henderson, J. 1987. "Lucan/The word at war." *Ramus* 16: 122–64. Reprint, in Boyle 1988, 122–64.
Henderson, J. 1998. *Fighting for Rome: Poets and Caesars, history and civil war.* Cambridge.
Henderson, J. 2002. *Pliny's statue: The Letters, self-portraiture and Classical art.* Exeter.
Henderson, J. 2004. *Morals and villas in Seneca's Letters: Places to dwell.* Cambridge.
Hendrix, H. 2018. "Virgil's tomb in scholarly and popular culture." In Goldschmidt and Graziosi 2018, 281–98.
Hershkowitz, D. 1995. "Pliny the poet." *G&R* 2nd ser. 42.2: 168–81.
Heurgon, J. 1931. "Un exemple peu connu de la *retractatio* virgilienne." *REL* 9: 258–68.
Hexter, R. and D. Selden, eds. 1992. *Innovations of Antiquity.* New York and Abingdon.
Heynacher, M. 1874. *Ueber die Quellen des Silius Italicus.* Ilfeld.
Heynacher, M. 1877. *Ueber die Stellung des Silius Italicus unter den Quellen zum zweiten punischen Kriege.* Nordhausen. Reprint, *Die Stellung des Silius Italicus unter den Quellen zum zweiten punischen Kriege.* Berlin, 1877.
Hill, T. D. 2004. *Ambitiosa mors: Suicide and self in Roman thought and literature.* London.
Hinds, S. 1998. *Allusion and intertext: Dynamics of appropriation in Roman poetry.* Cambridge.
Hitchcock, L. 2008. *Theory for Classics: A student's guide.* Abingdon.
Hoffmann, W. 1942. *Livius und der zweite Punische Krieg.* Berlin.
Hoffmann, W. 1960. "Die römische Politik des 2. Jahrhunderts und das Ende Karthagos." *Historia* 9.3: 309–44. Reprint, in *Das Staatsdenken der Römer*, ed. R. Klein, 178–230. Darmstadt, 1966, 1980.
Hölkeskamp, K.-J. 1987. *Die Entstehung der Nobilität: Studien zur sozialen und politischen Geschichte der römischen Republik im 4. Jhdt. v. Chr.* Stuttgart. 2nd ed., 2011.
Hölkeskamp, K.-J. 2004. *Senatus populusque Romanus: Die politische Kultur der Republik—Dimensionen und Deutungen.* Stuttgart.
Hölkeskamp, K.-J. 2018. "*Memoria* by multiplication: The Cornelii Scipiones in monumental memory." In *Omnium annalium monumenta: Historical writing and historical evidence in Republican Rome*, ed. K. Sandberg and C. Smith, 422–76. Leiden.
Hollis, A., ed. and trans. 2007. *Fragments of Roman poetry, c. 60 BC–AD 20.* Oxford.
Hömke, N. 2010. "Bit by bit towards death – Lucan's Scaeva and the aesthetisization of dying." In *Lucan's Bellum civile: Between epic tradition and aesthetic innovation*, ed. N. Hömka and C. Reitz, 91–104. Berlin.

Hope, V. M. 2009. *Roman death*. London.
Howley, J. A. 2018. *Aulus Gellius and Roman reading culture: Text, presence, and imperial knowledge in the* Noctes Atticae. Cambridge.
Hoyos, B. D. 1998. *Unplanned wars: The origins of the First and Second Punic Wars*. Berlin.
Hoyos, D. 2003. *Hannibal's dynasty: Power and politics in the western Mediterranean, 247–183 BC*. London.
Hoyos, D. 2007. *Truceless war: Carthage's fight for survival, 241 to 237 BC*. Leiden.
Hoyos, D. 2008. *Hannibal: Rome's greatest enemy*. Bristol.
Hoyos, D. 2010. *The Carthaginians*. London.
Hoyos, D., ed. 2011. *A companion to the Punic Wars*. Malden.
Hoyos, D. 2015. *Mastering the West: Rome and Carthage at war*. Oxford.
Hübner, E. 1875. "Quaestiones onomatologicae Latinae." *EphEp* 2: 25–92.
Hulls, J.-M. 2007. "Lowering one's standards—On Statius, *Silvae* 4.2.43." *CQ* n.s. 57.1: 198–206.
Hulls, J.-M. 2018. "A last act of love? Suicide and civil war as tropes in Silius Italicus's *Punica* and Josephus's *Bellum Judaicum*." In Ginsberg and Krasne 2018, 321–38.
Hunt, L., ed. 1989. *The new cultural history*. Berkeley, Los Angeles, and London.
Hunt, P. N. 2017. *Hannibal*. New York.
Huß, W. 1985. *Geschichte der Karthager*. Munich.
Huxley, H. H. 1954. "Silver Latin poetry." In *Fifty years of Classical scholarship*, ed. M. Platnauer, 413–31. Oxford.
Huxley, H. H. 1968. "Silver Latin poetry." In *Fifty years (and twelve) of Classical scholarship, being* Fifty years of Classical scholarship *revised with Appendices*, ed. M. Platnauer, 496–523. Oxford.
Ingleheart, J. 2007. "Propertius 4.10 and the end of the *Aeneid*: Augustus, the *spolia opima* and the right to remain silent." *G&R* 2nd ser. 54.1: 61–81.
Innes, D. C. 1979. "Gigantomachy and natural philosophy." *CQ* n.s. 29.1: 165–71.
Iser, W. 1972. *Der implizite Leser: Kommunikationsformen des Romans von Bunyan bis Beckett*. Munich.
Iser, W. 1974. *The implied reader: Patterns of communication in prose fiction from Bunyan to Beckett*. Baltimore.
Iser, W. 1976. *Der Akt des Lesens: Theorie ästhetischer Wirkung*. Munich.
Iser, W. 1978. *The act of reading: A theory of aesthetic response*. Baltimore.
Iser, W. 1989. *Prospecting: From reader response to literary anthropology*. Baltimore.
Itgenshorst, T. 2005. Tota illa pompa: *Der Triumph in der römischen Republik*. Göttingen.
Jacobs, J. 2009. Anne iterum capta repetentur Pergama Roma? *The fall of Rome in the* Punica. Ph.D. diss., Yale University.
Jacobs, J. 2010. "From Sallust to Silius Italicus: *metus hostilis* and the fall of Rome in the *Punica*." In Miller and Woodman 2010, 123–39.
Jacobs, J., ed. and trans. forthcoming. *Silius Italicus,* Punica 15. Oxford.

Jacoby, R. 2006-7. "Our craving for kindred blood: Why most wars are civil." *WPJ* 23.4: 103-9.

Jahn, S. 2007. *Der Troia-Mythos: Rezeption und Transformation in epischen Geschichtsdarstellungen der Antike*. Cologne.

Jal, P. 1962a. "*Bellum civile . . . bellum externum*." *LEC* 30: 257-67, 384-90.

Jal, P. 1962b. "Le rôle des barbares dans les guerres civiles de Rome, de Sylla à Vespasien." *Latomus* 21.1: 8-48.

Jal, P. 1962c. "Les dieux et les guerres civiles dans la Rome de la fin de la République." *REL* 40: 170-200.

Jal, P. 1963. *La guerre civile à Rome: Étude littéraire et morale*. Paris.

Janssen, L. F. 1981. "Some unexplored aspects of *devotio Deciana*." *Mnemosyne* 4th ser. 34.3-4: 357-81.

Jauß, H. R. 1970. *Literaturgeschichte als Provokation*. Frankfurt am Main.

Jauss, H. R. 1982a. *Aesthetic experience and literary hermeneutics*. Trans. M. Shaw. Minneapolis.

Jauss, H. R. 1982b. *Toward an aesthetic of reception*. Trans. T. Bahti. Minneapolis.

Johnson, W. A. 2000. "Toward a sociology of reading in Classical Antiquity." *AJPh* 121.4: 593-627.

Johnson, W. A. 2010. *Readers and reading culture in the High Roman Empire: A study of elite communities*. Oxford.

Johnson, W. A. and H. N. Parker, eds. 2009. *Ancient literacies: The culture of reading in Greece and Rome*. Oxford.

Jöne, A. 2017. *Abschiedsszenen Liebender im lateinischen Epos*. Münster.

Jones, B. W. 1973. "The dating of Domitian's war against the Chatti." *Historia* 22.1: 79-90.

Jones, B. W. 1982. "Domitian's advance into Germany and Moesia." *Latomus* 41.2: 329-35.

Jones, B. W. 1992. *The emperor Domitian*. London.

Jourdan, F. 2008. "Vertus iréniques et civilisatrices du chant sur le chant: « L'association poétique des citharèdes légendaires (Amphion, Arion et Orphée) chez Horace et Silius Italicus »." *REA* 110.1: 103-16.

Juhnke, H. 1972. *Homerisches in römischer Epik flavischer Zeit: Untersuchungen zu Szenennachbildungen und Strukturentsprechungen in Statius' Thebais und Achilleis und in Silius' Punica*. Munich.

Kahrstedt, U. and O. Meltzer. 1879-1913. *Geschichte der Karthager*. 3 vols. Berlin.

Kajanto, I. 1965. *The Latin cognomina*. Rome.

Kalyvas, S. N. 2006. *The logic of violence in civil war*. Cambridge.

Kapust, D. 2008. "On the ancient uses of political fear and its modern implications." *JHI* 69.3: 353-73.

Kapust, D. J. 2011. *Republicanism, rhetoric, and Roman political thought: Sallust, Livy, and Tacitus*. Cambridge.

Karakasis, E. 2014. "Homeric receptions in Flavian epic: Intertextual characterization in *Punica* 7." In Augoustakis 2014, 251-66.

Karakasis, E. 2018. "Silius Italicus and Polybius: *Quellenforschung* and Silian poetics." In *Polybius and his legacy*, ed. N. Miltsios and M. Tamiolaki, 401–15. Berlin.

Kay, N. M., ed. and trans. 2020. *Venantius Fortunatus:* Vita Sancti Martini; *Prologue and Books I–II*. Cambridge.

Keeline, T. J. 2018. *The reception of Cicero in the Early Roman Empire: The rhetorical schoolroom and the creation of a cultural legend*. Cambridge.

Keith, A. M. 2000. *Engendering Rome: Women in Latin epic*. Cambridge.

Keith, A. M. 2008. "Etymological wordplay in Flavian epic." *PLLS* 13: 231–54.

Keith, A. 2013. "*Sexus muliebris* in Flavian epic." *EuGeStA* 3: 282–302.

Keller, C., ed. 1695. *C. Silii Italici, viri consularis,* De bello Punico secundo *libri XVII*. Lipsiae [Leipzig].

Kennedy, E. 2016. "Reading Aeneas through Hannibal: The poetics of revenge and the repetitions of history." In *Roman literary cultures: Domestic politics, revolutionary poetics, civic spectacle*, ed. A. Keith and J. Edmondson, 185–99. Toronto.

Kenty, J. 2017. "*Altera Roma*: Livy's variations on a Ciceronian theme." *ICS* 42.1: 61–81.

Kerer, A. 1881. *Ueber die Abhängigkeit des C. Silius Italicus von Livius*. Bozen.

Kermode, F. 1966. *The sense of an ending: Studies in the theory of fiction*. London.

Kiernan, B. 2004. "The first genocide: Carthage, 146 BC." *Diogenes* 51.3: 27–39.

Kißel, W. 1979. *Das Geschichtsbild des Silius Italicus*. Frankfurt am Main.

Klaassen Kennedy, E. M. 2005. *Ethnicity and empire: Vergilian imitation in Silius Italicus'* Punica. Ph.D. diss., Bryn Mawr College.

Kline, A. S., trans. 2018. *Silius Italicus:* Punica *(The Second Carthaginian War)*.

Klotz, A. 1927. "17) Ti. Catius Silius Italicus." *RE* 2.3A.5.79–91.

Klotz, A. 1933. "Die Stellung des Silius Italicus unter den Quellen zur Geschichte des zweiten punischen Krieges." *RhM* n.F. 82.1: 1–34.

Klotz, A. 1934. "Die Quellen der plutarchischen Lebensbeschreibung des Marcellus." *RhM* n.F. 83: 289–318.

Kneale, M. 2017. *Rome: A history in seven sackings*. New York.

Kneppe, A. 1994. Metus temporum: *Zur Bedeutung von Angst in Politik und Gesellschaft der römischen Kaiserzeit des 1. und 2. Jhdts. n. Chr*. Stuttgart.

Knox, B. M. W. 1968. "Silent reading in Antiquity." *GRBS* 9.4: 421–35.

König, A. 2018. "Reading civil war in Frontinus' *Strategemata*: A case-study for Flavian literary studies." In Ginsberg and Krasne 2018, 145–78.

König, A. and C. Whitton, eds. 2018. *Roman literature under Nerva, Trajan and Hadrian: Literary interactions, AD 96–138*. Cambridge.

Konstan, D. 1986. "Narrative and ideology in Livy Book I." *ClAnt* 5.2: 198–215.

Konstan, D. and K. A. Raaflaub, eds. 2010. *Epic and history*. Malden.

Koortbojian, M. 2013. *The divinization of Caesar and Augustus: Precedents, consequences, implications*. Cambridge.

Kornhardt, H. 1954. "Regulus und die Cannaegefangenen." *Hermes* 82.1: 85–123.

Koutroubas, D. E. 1988. "*Metus hostilis* as a factor of Roman history according to Sallust." *Ariadne* 4: 81–90. [in Greek]

Krämer, H.-J. 1965. "Die Sage von Romulus und Remus in der lateinischen Literatur." In *Synusia: Festgabe für Wolfgang Schadewaldt zum 15. März 1965*, ed. H. Flashar and K. Gaiser, 355–402. Pfullingen.
Kramer, N. and C. Reitz, eds. 2010. *Tradition und Erneuerung: Mediale Strategien in der Zeit der Flavier*. Berlin.
Krasser, H., D. Pausch, and I. Petrovic, eds. 2008. *Triplici invectus triumpho: Der römische Triumph in augusteischer Zeit*. Stuttgart.
Kraus, C. S. 1994. "'No second Troy': Topoi and refoundation in Livy, book V." *TAPhA* 124: 267–89.
Kraus, C. S. 1998. "Repetition and empire in the *Ab urbe condita*." In *Style and tradition: Studies in honor of Wendell Clausen*, ed. P. Knox and C. Foss, 264–83. Stuttgart.
Kraus, C. S., ed. 1999. *The limits of historiography: Genre and narrative in ancient historical texts*. Leiden.
Kraus, C. S. and A. J. Woodman. 1997. *Latin historians*. Oxford.
Kristeva, J. 1969. Σημειωτική: *Recherches pour une sémanalyse*. Paris.
Kroll, W. 1916. "Das historische Epos." *Sokrates* 70.1–2 = n.F. 4.1–2: 1–14.
Kubler, A. 2018. *La mémoire culturelle de la deuxième guerre punique: Approche historique d'une construction mémorielle à travers les textes de l'Antiquité romaine*. Basel.
Kuhle, M. and S. Kuhle. 2012. "Hannibal gone astray? A critical comment on W. C. Mahaney *et al.*: 'The Traversette (Italia) rockfall: Geomorphological indicator of the Hannibalic invasion route' (*Archaeometry*, 52, 1 [2010] 156–72)." *Archaeometry* 54.3: 591–601.
Kuhle, M. and S. Kuhle. 2015. "Lost in translation *or* Can we still understand what Polybius says about Hannibal's crossing of the Alps?—A reply to Mahaney [*Archaeometry*, 55 (2013), 1196–204]." *Archaeometry* 57.4: 759–71.
Kullmann, W. 1960. *Die Quellen der* Ilias. Wiesbaden.
Künzl, E. 1988. *Der römische Triumph: Siegesfeiern im antiken Rom*. Munich.
Küppers, J. 1986. *Tantarum causas irarum: Untersuchungen zur einleitenden Bücherdyade der* Punica *des Silius Italicus*. Berlin.
Kwapisz, J., D. Petrain, and M. Szymański, eds. 2013. *The Muse at play: Riddles and wordplay in Greek and Latin poetry*. Berlin.
Kyle, D. G. 1998. *Spectacles of death in ancient Rome*. London.
Kyriakidis, S. and F. De Martino, eds. 2004. *Middles in Latin poetry*. Bari.
La Penna, A. 1981. "Tipi e modelli femminili nella poesia dell'epoca dei flavi (Stazio, Silio Italico, Valerio Flacco)." In *Atti del congresso internazionale di studi vespasianei, Rieti, settembre 1979*, ed. B. Riposati, 1.223–51. Rieti. Reprint, in A. La Penna, *Eros dai cento volti: Modelli etici ed estetici nell'età dei Flavi*, 37–65. Venice, 2000.
La Penna, A. 2008. "I danni della pace e il *metus hostilis* secondo Virgilio e Livio." In *Studi offerti ad Alessandro Perutelli*, ed. P. Arduini, S. Audano, A. Borghini, A. Cavarzere, G. Mazzoli, G. Paduano, and A. Russo, 2.85–9. Rome.
La Rocca, E. and S. Tortorella, eds. 2008. *Trionfi romani*. Milan.

Lacina, B. 2006. "Explaining the severity of civil wars." *JCR* 50.2: 276–89.
Laird, A. 2018. "Dead letters and buried meaning: Approaching the tomb of Virgil." In Goldschmidt and Graziosi 2018, 253–64.
Lana, I. 1980. *Scienza, politica, cultura a Roma sotto i Flavi*. Turin.
Lancel, S. 1992. *Carthage*. Paris.
Lancel, S. 1995. *Carthage: A history*. Trans. A. Nevill. Oxford.
Landrey, L. 2014. "Skeletons in armor: Silius Italicus' *Punica* and the *Aeneid*'s proem." *AJPh* 135.4: 599–635.
Lange, C. H. 2016. *Triumphs in the age of civil war: The Late Republic and the adaptability of triumphal tradition*. London.
Lange, C. H. and F. J. Vervaet, eds. 2014. *The Roman Republican triumph: Beyond the spectacle*. Rome.
Langlands, R. 2018a. *Exemplary ethics in ancient Rome*. Cambridge.
Langlands, R. 2018b. "Extratextuality: Literary interactions with oral culture and exemplary ethics." In König and Whitton 2018, 330–46.
Lapidge, M. 1979. "Lucan's imagery of cosmic dissolution." *Hermes* 107.3: 344–70.
Lapidge, M. 1989. "Stoic cosmology and Roman literature, first to third centuries A.D." *ANRW* 2.36.3: 1379–429.
Laudizi, G. 1989. *Silio Italico: Il passato tra mito e restaurazione etica*. Galatina.
Lazenby, J. F. 1978. *Hannibal's war: A military history of the Second Punic War*. Warminster.
Lazenby, J. F. 1996. *The First Punic War: A military history*. London.
Leberl, J. 2004. *Domitian und die Dichter: Poesie als Medium der Herrschaftdarstellung*. Göttingen.
Lee, J. M. 2017. *Silius Italicus' Punica 8. 1–241: A commentary*. M.A. thesis, University of Adelaide.
Lefebvre de Villebrune, J.-B., ed. 1781a. *C. Silii Italici de bello Punico secundo Poema ad fidem veterum monimentorum castigatum, fragmento auctum. Operis integri editio princeps. Curante I. B. Lefebvre de Villebrune*. Parisiis [Paris].
Lefebvre de Villebrune, J.-B., ed. and trans. 1781b. *Second guerre punique, poëme de Silius Italicus, corrigé sur quatre manuscrits, et sur la précieuse édition de Pomponius, donnée en 1471, inconnue de tous les editeurs; complétté par un long fragment trouvé dans la Bibliothèque du Roi; et traduit par M. Lefebvre de Villebrune*. 3 vols. Paris.
Lefèvre, E. 1989. "Plinius-Studien, V: Von Römertum zum Ästhetizismus; Die Würdigungen des älteren Plinius (3, 5), Silius Italicus (3, 7) und Martial (3, 21)." *Gymnasium* 96.2: 113–28.
Lefèvre, E. 2009. *Vom Römertum zum Ästhetizismus: Studien zu den Briefen des jüngeren Plinius*. Berlin.
Legras, L. 1905. "Les « Puniques » et la « Thébaïde »." *REA* 7.2: 131–46 and 7.4: 357–71.
Lehan, R. 1998. *The city in literature: An intellectual and cultural history*. Berkeley, Los Angeles, and London.
Leigh, M. 1993. "Hopelessly devoted to you: Traces of the Decii in Vergil's *Aeneid*." *PVS* 21: 89–110.

Leigh, M. 1997. *Lucan: Spectacle and engagement*. Oxford.

Leigh, M. 2000. "Founts of identity: The thirst of Hercules and the greater Greek world." *JMS* 10.1: 125–38.

Leigh, M. 2010. "Epic and historiography at Rome." In *A companion to Greek and Roman historiography*, ed. J. Marincola, 483–92. Malden.

Lemaire, N.-E., ed. 1823. *Caius Silius Italicus:* Punicorum libri septemdecim ad optimas editiones collati, cum varietate lectionum perpetuis commentariis praefationibus argumentis et indicibus curante N. E. Lemaire. 2 vols. Parisiis [Paris].

Lentzsch, S. 2019. *Roma victa: Von Roms Umgang mit Niederlagen*. Stuttgart.

Leto, G. P., ed. 1471. *Silii Italici* Punicorum libri XVII. Romae [Rome].

Levene, D. S. 2000. "Sallust's *Catiline* and Cato the Censor." *CQ* n.s. 50.1: 170–91.

Levene, D. S. 2010. *Livy on the Hannibalic War*. Oxford.

Levene, D. S. and D. P. Nelis, eds. 2002. *Clio and the poets: Augustan poetry and the traditions of ancient historiography*. Leiden.

Levick, B. 1982. "Morals, politics, and the fall of the Roman Republic." *G&R* 2nd ser. 29.1: 53–62.

Lincoln, B. 1991. *Death, war, and sacrifice: Studies in ideology and practice*. Chicago.

Lindsay, H. 2010. "Vespasian and the city of Rome: The centrality of the Capitolium." *AClass* 53: 165–80.

Lintott, A. W. 1972. "Imperial expansion and moral decline in the Roman Republic." *Historia* 21.4: 626–38.

Lintott, A. W. 1982. *Violence, civil strife and revolution in the Classical city, 750–330 BC*. London. Reprint, 2014.

Lippincott, K. 1989. "The neo-Latin historical epics of the north Italian courts." *RS* 3–4: 415–28.

Litchfield, H. W. 1914. "National *exempla virtutis* in Roman literature." *HSPh* 25: 1–71.

Little, C. E. 1934. "The authenticity and form of Cato's saying 'Carthago delenda est'." *CJ* 29.6: 429–35.

Littlewood, R. J., ed. 2011. *A commentary on Silius Italicus'* Punica 7. Oxford.

Littlewood, R. J. 2013. "Patterns of darkness: Chthonic illusion, Gigantomachy, and sacrificial ritual in the *Punica*." In Augoustakis 2013, 199–216.

Littlewood, R. J. 2014. "Loyalty and the lyre: Constructions of *fides* in Hannibal's Capuan banquets." In Augoustakis 2014, 267–85.

Littlewood, J. 2016. "Dynastic triads: Flavian resonances and structural antithesis in Silius' sons of Hamilcar." In Manioti 2016, 209–27.

Littlewood, R. J., ed. and trans. 2017. *A commentary on Silius Italicus'* Punica 10. Oxford.

López López, R. 2015. *Lorenzo de Zamora: Vida y obra*. Ph.D. diss., Universidad de León.

Lorenz, G. 1968. *Vergleichende Interpretationen zu Silius Italicus und Statius*. Ph.D. diss., Christian-Albrechts-Universität zu Kiel.

Lorenzo, J. 1978. "Técnica descriptiva en Virgilio y Silio Itálico." *CFC* 15: 201–15.

Lovatt, H. 2010. "Interplay: Silius and Statius in the games of *Punica* 16." In Augoustakis 2010a, 155–76.

Lucarini, C. M. 2004. "Le fonti storiche di Silio Italico." *Athenaeum* 102.1 = n.s. 92.1: 103-26.

Lundgreen, C. 2011. *Regelkonflikte in der römischen Republik: Geltung und Gewichtung von Normen in politischen Entscheidungsprozessen*. Stuttgart.

MacDonald, E. 2015. *Hannibal: A Hellenistic life*. New Haven.

Mackay, C. S. 2009. *The breakdown of the Roman Republic: From oligarchy to empire*. Cambridge.

Mahaney, W. C. 2008a. *Hannibal's odyssey: Environmental background to the Alpine invasion of Italia*. Piscataway.

Mahaney, W. C. 2008b. "Hannibal's trek across the Alps: Geomorphological analysis of sites of geoarchaeological interest." *MAA* 8.2: 39-54.

Mahaney, W. C., B. Kapran, and P. Tricart. 2008. "Hannibal and the Alps: Unravelling the invasion route." *Geology Today* 24.6: 223-30.

Mahaney, W. C. et al. 2010. "The Traversette (Italia) rockfall: Geomorphological indicator of the Hannibalic invasion route." *Archaeometry* 52.1: 156-72.

Mahaney, W. C. 2013. "Comments on M. Kuhle and S. Kuhle (2012): 'Hannibal gone astray? A critical comment on W. C. Mahaney *et al*.: "The Traversette (Italia) rockfall: Geomorphological indicator of the Hannibalic invasion route" (*Archaeometry*, 52, 1 [2010] 156-72)." *Archaeometry* 55.6: 1196-204.

Mahaney, W. C. 2016. "The Hannibal route controversy and future historical archaeological exploration in the Western Alps." *MAA* 16.2: 97-105.

Maier, F. K. 2018. "Kein Held im Zögern sein – Die Glorifizierung des Fabius Cunctator bei Silius Italicus." *helden. heroes. héros.* 6.1: 5-13.

Malitz, J. 1985. "Helvidius Priscus und Vespasian: Zur Geschichte der 'stoischen' Senatsopposition." *Hermes* 113.2: 231-46.

Malitz, J. 1999. *Nero*. Munich.

Malitz, J. 2005. *Nero*. Trans. A. Brown. Malden.

Manioti, N., ed. 2016. *Family in Flavian epic*. Leiden.

Manolaraki, E. and A. Augoustakis. 2012. "Silius Italicus and Tacitus on the tragic hero: The case of Germanicus." In *A companion to Tacitus*, ed. V. E. Pagán, 386-402. Malden.

Mantel, N. 1991. Poeni foedifragi: *Untersuchungen zur Darstellung römisch-karthagischer Vertrage zwischen 241 und 201 v. Chr. durch die römische Historiographie*. Munich.

Manuwald, G. 2001. Fabulae praetextae: *Spuren einer literarischen Gattung der Römer*. Munich.

Manuwald, G. 2006. "The Trojans, Dido and the Punic War: Silius Italicus on the causes of the conflict between Romans and Carthaginians." *Aevum(ant)* 6: 65-84. Reprint, in Castagna, Galimberti Biffino, and Riboldi 2011, 53-71.

Manuwald, G. 2007. "Epic poets as characters: On poetics and multiple intertextuality in Silius Italicus' *Punica*." *RFIC* 135.1 = n.s. 113.1: 71-90.

Manuwald, G. 2014. "'Fact' and 'fiction' in Roman historical epic." *G&R* 2nd ser. 61.2: 204-21.

Manuwald, G. and A. Voigt, eds. 2013. *Flavian epic interactions*. Berlin.
Manz, G. 2017. *Roms Aufstieg zur Weltmacht: Das Zeitalter der Punischen Kriege*. Wiesbaden.
María Pemán, J. and F. Sánchez-Castañer, eds. 1954. *La destrucción de Sagunto: Tragedia en verso, en un prólogo y dos partes*. Madrid.
Marks, R. D. 1999. *Scipio Africanus in the* Punica *of Silius Italicus*. Ph.D. diss., Brown University.
Marks, R. 2003. "Hannibal in Liternum." In *Being there together: Essays in honor of Michael C. J. Putnam on the occasion of his seventieth birthday*, ed. P. Thibodeau and H. Haskell, 128–44. Afton.
Marks, R. 2005a. *From Republic to Empire: Scipio Africanus in the* Punica *of Silius Italicus*. Frankfurt am Main.
Marks, R. D. 2005b. "*Per vulnera regnum*: Self-destruction, self-sacrifice and *devotio* in Punica 4–10." *Ramus* 34.2: 127–51. Reprint, in Augoustakis 2016, 408–33.
Marks, R. D. 2005c. "Silius Italicus." In *A companion to ancient epic*, ed. J. M. Foley, 528–37. Malden.
Marks, R. 2008. "Getting ahead: Decapitation as political metaphor in Silius Italicus' *Punica*." *Mnemosyne* 4th ser. 61.1: 66–88.
Marks, R. 2010. "Silius and Lucan." In Augoustakis 2010a, 127–53.
Marks, R. 2013a. "Reconcilable differences: Anna Perenna and the battle of Cannae in the *Punica*." In Augoustakis 2013, 287–301.
Marks, R. 2013b. "The *Thebaid* and the fall of Saguntum in *Punica* 2." In Manuwald and Voigt 2013, 297–310.
Marks, R. D. 2014. "Statio-Silian relations in the *Thebaid* and *Punica* 1–2." *CPh* 109.2: 130–9.
Marks, R. 2017. "A medial proem and the macrostructures of the *Punica*." In Schmitz, Telg gennant Kortmann, and Jöne 2017, 277–91.
Markus, D. D. 2000. "Performing the book: The recital of epic in first-century C.E. Rome." *ClAnt* 19.1: 138–79.
Marpicati, P. 1999. "Silio 'delatore' di Pompeo (*Pun*. 5, 328 ss.; 10, 305 ss.)." *MD* 43: 191–202.
Marso, P., ed. 1483. *Silius Italicus, cum commentariis*. Venetiis [Venice]. Reprint, 1490, 1492, 1493, 1512 [Paris].
Martellotti, G., ed. 1954. *Francesco Petrarca: La vita di Scipione l'Africano*. Milan and Naples.
Martellotti, G. 1981. "Petrarca e Silio Italico: Un confronto impossibile." In *Miscellanea Augusto Campana*, ed. R. Avesani, M. Ferrari, and G. Pozzi, 2.489–503. Padua. Reprint, in *Scritti petrarcheschi*, ed. M. Feo and S. Rizzo, 563–78. Padua, 1983.
Martin, J. 1946. "Die *Punica* des Silius." *WJA* 1: 163–5.
Martin, M. 1986. "Carthage vue de Rome; ou, 'Le rivage des Syrtes' chez Silius Italicus." *Eidôlon* 28: 59–77.
Martin, M. 1990. "Silius lecteur d'Horace." *Orphea voce* 3: 135–58.

Martin, M. and G. Devallet, eds. and trans. 1992. *Silius Italicus:* La guerre punique. Tome IV: Livres XIV–XVII. Paris.

Martino, J. 2008. "Single combat and the *Aeneid*." *Arethusa* 41.3: 411–44.

Maschek, D. 2018. *Die römischen Bürgerkriege: Archäologie und Geschichte einer Krisenzeit*. Mainz.

Mason, S. 2016. *A history of the Jewish War, AD 66–74*. Cambridge.

Massa-Pairault, F.-H. and C. Pouzadoux, eds. 2017a. *Géants et gigantomachies entre Orient et Occident*. Naples.

Massa-Pairault, F.-H. and C. Pouzadoux, eds. 2017b. *Giganti e gigantomachie tra Oriente e Occidente*. Naples.

Masters, J. 1992. *Poetry and civil war in Lucan's* Bellum civile. Cambridge.

Matier, K. O., trans. 1980. *A commentary on the eleventh book of the* Punica *of Silius Italicus*. Ph.D. diss., Rhodes University.

Matier, K. O. 1981. "Prejudice and the *Punica*: Silius Italicus—A reassessment." *AClass* 24: 141–51.

Matier, K. O. 1989a. "Hannibal: The real hero of the *Punica*?" *AClass* 32: 3–17.

Matier, K. O. 1989b. *Silius Italicus at bay: Pliny, prejudice, and the* Punica. Inaugural address delivered at the University of Durban-Westville on 5 October 1989.

Matier, K. O. 1990. "Stoic philosophy in Silius Italicus." *Akroterion* 35: 68–72.

Matier, K. O. 1991. "The influence of Ennius on Silius Italicus." *Akroterion* 36: 153–8.

Maza, S. 2004. "Stephen Greenblatt, New Historicism, and cultural history, *or*, What we talk about when we talk about interdisciplinarity." *MIH* 1.2: 249–65.

Mazzolani, L. 1972. *The idea of the city in Roman thought*. Bloomington.

McCall, J. 2012. *The sword of Rome: A biography of Marcus Claudius Marcellus*. Barnsley.

McCall, J. 2018. *Clan Fabius, defenders of Rome: A history of the Republic's most illustrious family*. Barnsley.

McClellan, A. M. 2019. *Abused bodies in Roman epic*. Cambridge.

McDermott, W. C. and A. E. Orentzel. 1977. "Silius Italicus and Domitian." *AJPh* 98.1: 24–34.

McDermott, W. C. and A. Orentzel. 1979. *Roman portraits: The Flavian-Trajanic period*. Columbia.

McDonald, I. R. 1971. *The Flavian epic poets as political and social critics*. Ph.D. diss., The University of North Carolina at Chapel Hill.

McGuire, D. T. Jr., 1985. *History as epic: Silius Italicus and the Second Punic War*. Ph.D. diss., Cornell University.

McGuire, D. T. Jr., 1989. "Textual strategies and political suicide in Flavian epic." *Ramus* 18.1–2: 21–45. Reprint, in Boyle 1990, 21–45.

McGuire, D. T. Jr., 1995. "History compressed: The Roman names of Silius' Cannae episode." *Latomus* 54.1: 110–18.

McGuire, D. T. 1997. *Acts of silence: Civil war, tyranny, and suicide in the Flavian epics*. Hildesheim.

McGushin, P. 1985. *The transmission of the* Punica *of Silius Italicus*. Amsterdam.

Mendell, C. W. 1924. "Silius the reactionary." *PhQ* 3: 92–106.
Mensching, E. 1967. "Livius, Cossus und Augustus." *MH* 24.1: 12–32.
Meyer, K. 1924. *Silius und Lucan*. Würzburg.
Mezzanotte, A. 1995. "Echi del mondo contemporaneo in Silio Italico." *RIL* 129.2: 357–88. Reprint, translated into English, in Augoustakis 2016, 434–58.
Michel, J. 1912–13. "Die Quellen zur *Raeteis* des Simon Lemnius." *JHAGG* 42 (1912): 97–222 and 43 (1913) 1–112. Reprint, Chur, 1914.
Miething, A. 2011. *Cannae: Vorbereitung und Verlauf der Schlacht von Cannae*. Munich.
Miles, G. B. 1995. *Livy: Reconstructing early Rome*. Ithaca.
Miles, R. 2010. *Carthage must be destroyed: The rise and fall of an ancient civilization*. London.
Miller, J. F. 1993. "Ovidian allusion and the vocabulary of memory." *MD* 30: 153–64.
Miller, J. F. and A. J. Woodman, eds. 2010. *Latin historiography and poetry in the Early Empire: Generic interactions*. Leiden.
Millón Villena, J. A., ed. 2015. *Enrique Palos y Navarro: La destrucción de Sagunto, tragedia nueva*. Sagunto.
Mineo, B. 2011. "Principal literary sources for the Punic Wars (apart from Polybius)." In Hoyos 2011, 111–27.
Miniconi, P. and G. Devallet, eds. and trans. 1979. *Silius Italicus: La guerre punique*. Tome I: Livres I–IV. Paris.
Mitsis, P. and I. Ziogas, eds. 2016. *Wordplay and powerplay in Latin poetry*. Berlin.
Modius, F. 1584. *Novantiquae lectiones*. Francofurti [Frankfurt].
Moles, J. 1998. "Cry freedom: Tacitus *Annals* 4.32–35." *Histos* 2: 95–184.
Momigliano, A. 1990. *The Classical foundations of modern historiography*. Berkeley, Los Angeles, and London.
Monestier, M. 1991. *Duels: Les combats singuliers des origines à nos jours*. Paris. 2nd ed., 2005.
Montes Mérida, J., ed. and trans. 2015. Punica *de Silio Itálico: Introducción, edición crítica y comentario filológico*. Ph.D. diss., Universidad Nacional de Educación a Distancia.
Montrose, L. A. 1989. "Professing the Renaissance: The poetics and politics of culture." In Veeser 1989, 15–36.
Morelli, A. M. 2016. "Lo *Scipio* e la poesia celebrativa enniana per Scipione." In Si verba tenerem: *Studi sulla poesia latina in frammenti*, ed. B. Pieri and D. Pellacani, 53–77. Berlin.
Morelli, U. 2014. *Domiziano: Fine di una dinastia*. Wiesbaden.
Morgan, G. 2006. *69 A.D.: The year of the Four Emperors*. Oxford.
Morgan, L. 1998. "Assimilation and civil war: Hercules and Cacus (*Aen.* 8.185–267)." In Vergil's Aeneid: *Augustan epic and political context*, ed. H.-P. Stahl, 175–98. London.
Morgan, L. 2005. "A yoke connecting baskets: *Odes* 3.14, Hercules, and Italian unity." *CQ* n.s. 55.1: 190–203.
Morzadec, F. 2009. *Les images du monde: Structure, écriture et esthétique du paysage dans les oeuvres de Stace et Silius Italicus*. Brussels.

Most, G. W. 1989. "Cornutus and Stoic allegoresis: A preliminary report." *ANRW* 2.36.3: 2014–65.

Mozley, J. H. 1963-4. "Virgil and the Silver Latin epic." *PVS* 3: 12–26.

Muecke, F. 2005a. "Domizio Calderini's lost « edition » of Silius Italicus." *RPL* n.s. 28: 51–67.

Muecke, F. 2005b. "Pomponio Leto's later work on Silius Italicus: The evidence of BAV, Vat. Inc. I 4." *RCCM* 47.1: 139–56.

Muecke, F. 2010. "Silius Italicus in the Italian Renaissance." In Augoustakis 2010a, 401–24.

Muecke, F. 2011. "Silius Italicus, Tiberius Catius Asconius, Addenda." In *CTC* 9, ed. V. Brown, 256–8. Washington, DC.

Muecke, F. and †J. Dunston, eds. 2011. *Domizio Calderini: Commentary on Silius Italicus*. Geneva.

Müller, J.-F., S. Müller, and T. Richter. 2000. "Die Hannibal-Tragödie des Cornelius Nepos." *AU* 43.6: 49–60.

Murgia, C. E. 1987. "Dido's puns." *CPh* 82.1: 50–9.

Murison, C. L. 1993. *Galba, Otho and Vitellius: Careers and controversies*. Hildesheim.

Mustard, W. P. 1921. "Petrarch's *Africa*." *AJPh* 42.2: 97–121.

Nasse, C. 2012. *Erdichtete Rituale: Die Eingeweideschau in der lateinischen Epik und Tragödie*. Stuttgart.

Nauta, R. R. 2002. *Poetry for patrons: Literary communication in the age of Domitian*. Leiden.

Nauta, R. R., H.-J. van Dam, and J. J. L. Smolenaars, eds. 2006. *Flavian poetry*. Leiden.

Neel, J. 2014. *Legendary rivals: Collegiality and ambition in the tales of early Rome*. Leiden.

Neri, V. 1986. "Dei, Fato e divinazione nella letteratura latina del I sec. d. C." *ANRW* 2.16.3: 1974–2051.

Nesselrath, H.-G. 1986. "Zu den Quellen des Silius Italicus." *Hermes* 114.2: 203–30.

Nesselrath, H.-G. 1992. *Ungeschehenes Geschehen: 'Beinahe-Episoden' im griechischen und römischen Epos von Homer bis zur Spätantike*. Stuttgart.

Neumann, K. J. 1897. "Zu den *Historien* des Sallust." *Hermes* 32.1: 313–17.

Nichi, L. 1909. *Ismerte-e Petrarca Silius „Punica"-ját?* Budapest.

Nicol, J. 1936. *The historical and geographical sources used by Silius Italicus*. Oxford.

Nicoll, W. S. M. 2001. "The death of Turnus." *CQ* n.s. 51.1: 190–200.

Nicols, J. 1978. *Vespasian and the* partes Flavianae. Wiesbaden.

Niemann, K.-H. 1975. *Die Darstellung der römischen Niederlagen in den* Punica *des Silius Italicus*. Bonn.

Noè, E. 1984. *Storiografia imperiale pretacitana*. Florence.

O'Connell, R. 2010. *The ghosts of Cannae: Hannibal and the darkest hour of the Roman Republic*. New York.

O'Gorman, E. 2004. "Cato the Elder and the destruction of Carthage." *Helios* 31.1-2: 99–125.

O'Gorman, E. 2010. "History as group fantasy." *CultCrit* 74: 117–30.
O'Hara, J. J. 1990. *Death and optimistic prophecy in Vergil's Aeneid*. Princeton.
O'Hara, J. J. 1996. *True names: Vergil and the Alexandrian tradition of etymological wordplay*. Ann Arbor. 2nd ed., 2017.
Oakley, S. P. 1985. "Single combat in the Roman Republic." *CQ* n.s. 35.2: 392–410.
Occioni, O. 1869. *Cajo Silio Italico e il suo poema*. Padua. 2nd ed., 1871. Reprint, in Occioni 1891, 29–139.
Occioni, O. 1877. "L'arte in Silio Italico." *NAnt* 34.2 = 2nd ser. 4.2: 275–83. Reprint, in Occioni 1891, 141–53.
Occioni, O., trans. 1878. Le puniche *di C. Silio Italico*. Milan.
Occioni, O., ed. and trans. 1889. *Ti. Catii Silii Italici* Punicorum *libri septemdecim* = Le puniche *di Tiberio Cazio Silio Italico*. 2nd ed. 2 vols. Augustae Taurinorum = Turin.
Occioni, O. 1891. *Scritti di letteratura latina*. Turin.
Önnerfors, A. 1979. *Die Verfasserschaft des Waltharius-Epos aus sprachlicher Sicht*. Opladen.
Önnerfors, A. 1988. *Das Waltharius-Epos: Probleme und Hypothesen*. Stockholm.
Opelt, I. 1991. "Das Stadtbild Karthagos in den «Punica» des Silius Italicus." *Orpheus* n.s. 12.2: 542–8.
Osgood, J. 2006. *Caesar's legacy: Civil war and the emergence of the Roman Empire*. Cambridge.
Osgood, J. 2018. *Rome and the making of a world state, 150 BCE–20 CE*. Cambridge.
Östenberg, I. 2009. *Staging the world: Spoils, captives, and representations in the Roman triumphal procession*. Oxford.
Östenberg, I. 2010. "*Circum metas fertur*: An alternative reading of the triumphal route." *Historia* 59.3: 303–20.
Palmer, R. E. A. 1997. *Rome and Carthage at peace*. Stuttgart.
Papaioannou, S. and A. Marinis, eds. forthcoming. *Tragedy in Flavian epic*. Berlin and Boston.
Paratore, E. 1970. *La II guerra punica nella terza deca di T. Livio*. Rome.
Parks, W. 1990. *Verbal dueling in heroic narrative: The Homeric and Old English traditions*. Princeton.
Pascal, C. B. 1990. "The dubious devotion of Turnus." *TAPhA* 120: 251–68.
Paschalis, M., ed. 2005. *Roman and Greek Imperial epic*. Herakleion.
Pasco, A. H. 1994. *Allusion: A literary graft*. Toronto.
Paul, G. M. 1982. "*Urbs capta*: Sketch of an ancient literary motif." *Phoenix* 36.2: 144–55.
Payne, R. 1962. *The Roman triumph*. London. Reprint, 1963.
Peirano Garrison, I. 2018. "The tomb of Virgil between text, memory, and site." In Goldschmidt and Graziosi 2018, 265–80.
Pelikan Pittenger, M. R. 2008. *Contested triumphs: Politics, pageantry, and performance in Livy's Republican Rome*. Berkeley, Los Angeles, and London.
Pelling, C. 2000. *Literary texts and the Greek historian*. London.
Pelling, C. 2013. "Intertextuality, plausibility, and interpretation." *Histos* 7: 1–20.

Pelttari, A. 2014. *The space that remains: Reading of Latin poetry in Late Antiquity*. Ithaca.
Penwill, J. L. 2000. "Quintilian, Statius, and the lost epic of Domitian." *Ramus* 29.1: 60–83.
Penwill, J. 2010. "Damn with great praise? The imperial encomia of Lucan and Silius." In *Private and public lies: The discourse of despotism and deceit in the Graeco-Roman world*, ed. A. J. Turner, J. H. Kim On Chong-Gossard, and F. J. Vervaet, 211–29. Leiden.
Penwill, J. 2013. "Imperial encomia in Flavian epic." In Manuwald and Voigt 2013, 29–54.
Pérez i Durà, F. J. 1993. "Un nuevo poema épico en los albores del s. XVIII: La *Saguntineida* de J. M. Miñana." In *Humanismo y pervivencia del mundo clásico*, ed. J. M. Maestre Maestre and J. Pascual Borea, 2.775–84. Cadiz.
Pérez i Durà, F. J. and J. M.a Estellés i González, eds. 1991. *Sagunt: Antigüedad e ilustración*. Valencia.
Pérez Mostazo, J. 2017. "*Cantaber ante omnis*: Silio Itálico en el discurso político y cultural vasco del siglo XIX." *Sancho el Sabio* 40: 9–34.
Pérez Mostazo, J. 2018. "Ecos de Silio Itálico en el imaginario vasco." In *Opera selecta: Estudios sobre el mundo clásico*, ed. A. Balda Baranda and E. Redondo Moyano, 151–8. Vitoria-Gasteiz.
Pérez Vilatela, L. 1994. "Alusiones a la guerra dácica de Domiciano en Silio Itálico." In *Actas del VIII congreso español de estudios clásicos, Madrid, 23–28 de septiembre de 1991*, 3.263–6. Madrid.
Pérez Vilatela, L. 2002. "La *Saguntineida* de Miñana: Ponderando la influencia de Silio Itálico." In *Humanismo y pervivencia del mundo clásico: Homenaje al profesor Antonio Fontán*, ed. J. M. Maestre Maestre, L. Charlo Barea, J. Pascual Barea, and A. Fontán Pérez, 3.1097–106. Madrid.
Pfanner, M. 1983. *Der Titusbogen*. 2 vols. Mainz.
Pfeiffer, S. 2009. *Die Zeit der Flavier: Vespasian, Titus, Domitian*. Darmstadt.
Picard, G.-C. 1974. "Le tophet de Carthage dans Silius Italicus." In *Mélanges de philosophie, de littérature et d'histoire ancienne offerts à Pierre Boyané*, ed. P. Gros and J.-P. Morel, 569–77. Rome.
Pinto, M. 1953. "Il medaglione enniano nelle *Puniche* di Silio Italico." *Maia* n.s. 6.3: 224–9.
Piras, G. 2013. "Occioni, Onorato." *DBI* 79: 84–96.
Pittà, A. 2014. "Varro on civil war." *Hermathena* 196–7: 251–90.
Plass, P. 1988. *Wit and the writing of history: The rhetoric of historiography in Imperial Rome*. Madison.
Plass, P. 1995. *The game of death in ancient Rome: Arena sport and political suicide*. Madison.
Plattner, P., ed. 1874. *Die Raeteis von Simon Lemnius*. Chur.
Plattner, P., trans. 1882. Raeteis: *Heldengedicht in acht Gesängen von Simon Lemnius*. Chur.

Pogorzelski, R. J. 2009. "The 'reassurance of fratricide' in the *Aeneid*." *AJPh* 130.2: 261–89.
Pomeroy, A. J. 1989. "Silius Italicus as 'doctus poeta.'" *Ramus* 18.1–2: 119–39. Reprint, in Boyle 1990, 119–39.
Pomeroy, A. J. 2000. "Silius' Rome: The rewriting of Vergil's vision." *Ramus* 29.2: 149–68. Reprint, in Augoustakis 2016, 321–44.
Pomeroy, A. J. 2010a. "*Fides* in Silius Italicus' *Punica*." In Schaffenrath 2010, 59–76.
Pomeroy, A. 2010b. "To Silius through Livy and his predecessors." In Augoustakis 2010a, 27–45.
Pomeroy, A. J. 2016. "Silius Italicus and Greek epic: Imperial culture wars." In Mitsis and Ziogas 2016, 413–36.
Popkin, M. L. 2016. *The architecture of the Roman triumph: Monuments, memory, and identity.* Cambridge.
Potter, D. S. 1999. *Literary texts and the Roman historian.* London.
Prag, J. R. W. 2006. "*Poenus plane est* – but who were the 'Punickes'?" *PBSR* 74: 1–37.
Prenner, A. 2002. "Riecheggiamenti virgiliani e siliani in una metamorfosi dell'« In Rufinum » di Claudiano." *BStudLat* 32.1: 82–96.
Prevas, J. 1998. *Hannibal crosses the Alps: The invasion of Italy and the Punic Wars.* Cambridge MA.
Pucci, J. 1998. *The full-knowing reader: Allusion and the power of the reader in the Western literary tradition.* New Haven.
Pueschel, A. 1907. *De Vibii Sequestris libelli geographici fontibus et compositione.* Halis Saxonum [Halle].
Puhvel, J. 1975. "Remus et frater." *HR* 15.2: 146–57.
Pyy, E. 2018. "In search of *Romanitas*: Literary constructions of Roman identity in Silius Italicus' *Punica*." In *Reflections of Roman imperialisms*, ed. M. A. Janković and V. D. Mihajlović, 128–47. Newcastle upon Tyne.
Quillin, J. M. 2004. "Information and empire: Domestic fear propaganda in Republican Rome, 200–149 BCE." *JITE* 160.4: 765–85.
Quinn, J. C. and A. Wilson. 2013. "Capitolia." *JRS* 103: 117–73.
Quint, D. 1989a. "Epic and empire." *ClAnt* 41: 1–32. Reprint, in Quint 1993, 21–49.
Quint, D. 1989b. "Repetition and ideology in the *Aeneid*." *MD* 23: 9–54. Reprint, in Quint 1993, 50–96.
Quint, D. 1993. *Epic and empire: Politics and generic form from Virgil to Milton.* Princeton.
Raaflaub, K. A. and M. Toher, eds. 1990. *Between Republic and Empire: Interpretations of Augustus and his principate.* Berkeley, Los Angeles, and Oxford.
Rauh, S. H. 2015. "The tradition of suicide in Rome's foreign wars." *TAPhA* 145.2: 383–410.
Rawlings, L. and H. Bowden, eds. 2005. *Herakles and Hercules: Exploring a Graeco-Roman divinity.* Swansea.
Rebeggiani, S. 2018. "Buried treasure, hidden verses: (Re)appropriating the Gauls of Pergamon in Flavian culture." In *Rome, empire of plunder: The dynamics of cultural*

appropriation, ed. M. P. Loar, C. MacDonald, and D.-E. Padilla Peralta, 69–81. Cambridge.
Reed, J. 2016. "*Mora* in the *Aeneid*." In Mitsis and Ziogas 2016, 87–106.
Reeve, M. D. 1983. "Silius Italicus." In *Texts and transmission: A survey of the Latin Classics*, ed. L. D. Reynolds, 389–91. Oxford.
Regn, G. 2009. "Petrarch's Rome: The history of the *Africa* and the Renaissance project." *MLN* 124.1: 86–102.
Reiff, D. 2016. *In praise of forgetting: Historical memory and its ironies*. New Haven.
Reitz, C. 1982. *Die nekyia in den* Punica *des Silius Italicus*. Frankfurt am Main.
Reitz, C. 1993. "Quomodo Silius Italicus clararum mulierum enumeratione carmen suum exornaverit." *VoxLat* 29: 310–19.
Reitz, C. 2010. "Silius als Epitomator?" In Schaffenrath 2010, 99–109.
Reitz, C. 2017. "Political allusion and exemplary thinking in Silius Italicus' *Punica*." *Shagi* [*Steps*] 3.4: 202–12. [in Russian]
Reynolds, J. 1982. *Aphrodisias and Rome*. London.
Rich, J. W. 1996. "Augustus and the *spolia opima*." *Chiron* 26: 85–127.
Rich, J. 2012. "Roman attitudes to defeat in battle under the Republic." In *Vae victis! Perdedores en el mundo antiguo*, ed. F. Marco Simón, F. Pina Polo, and J. Remesal Rodríguez, 82–111. Barcelona.
Richardson, J. H. 2012. *The Fabii and the Gauls: Studies in historical thought and historiography in Republican Rome*. Stuttgart.
Richter, D. S. and W. A. Johnson, eds. 2017. *The Oxford handbook of the Second Sophistic*. Oxford.
Ricoeur, P. 1980. "Narrative time." *CI* 7.1: 169–90.
Ricoeur, P. 1983–5. *Temps et récit*. 3 vols. Paris.
Ricoeur, P. 1984–8. *Time and narrative*. 3 vols. Trans. K. McLaughlin and D. Pellauer. Chicago.
Ricoeur, P. 2000. *La mémoire, l'histoire, l'oubli*. Paris.
Ricoeur, P. 2004. *Memory, history, forgetting*. Trans. K. Blamey and D. Pellauer. Chicago.
Ridley, R. T. 1986. "To be taken with a pinch of salt: The destruction of Carthage." *CPh* 81.2: 140–6.
Ridley, R. T. 2000. "Livy and the Hannibalic War." In *The Roman Middle Republic: Politics, religion and historiography, c. 400–133 BC*, ed. C. Bruun, 13–40. Rome.
Rimell, V. 2015. *The closure of space in Roman poetics: Empire's inward turn*. Cambridge.
Ripoll, F. 1998. *La morale héroïque dans les épopées latines d'époque flavienne: Tradition et innovation*. Louvain and Paris.
Ripoll, F. 1999. "Silius Italicus et Valérius Flaccus." *REA* 4th ser. 101.3–4: 499–521.
Ripoll, F. 2000a. "Réécritures d'un mythe homérique à travers le temps: Le personnage de Pâris dans l'épopée latine de Virgile à Stace." *Euphrosyne* n.s. 28: 83–112.
Ripoll, F. 2000b. "Silius Italicus et Cicéron." *LEC* 68.2–3: 147–73.
Ripoll, F. 2000c. "Variations épiques sur un motif d'*ecphrasis*: L'enlèvement de Ganymède." *REA* 4th ser. 102.3–4: 479–500.

Ripoll, F. 2001. "Le monde homérique dans les *Punica* de Silius Italicus." *Latomus* 60.1: 87–107.

Ripoll, F. 2002. "Le « Bellum ciuile » de Pétrone: Une épopée flavienne?" *REA* 4th ser. 104.1–2: 163–84.

Ripoll, F. 2003. "Vieillesse et héroïsme dans les épopées flaviennes: Silius Italicus et Valérius Flaccus." In *L'ancienneté chez les anciens*, ed. B. Bakhouche, 2.653–75. Montpellier.

Ripoll, F. 2006. "Adaptations latines d'un thème homérique: La théomachie." *Phoenix* 60.3–4: 236–58.

Ripoll, F. 2015. "Statius and Silius Italicus." In *Brill's companion to Statius*, ed. W. J. Dominik, C. E. Newlands, and K. Gervais, 425–43. Leiden.

Ripoll, F. 2017. "Les « interactions » entre Stace et Silius Italicus." *REA* 117.2: 621–37.

Risi, A. 2008. "L'aristeia di Quinto Ennio." *Latomus* 67.1: 56–71.

Ritter, S. 1995. *Hercules in der römischen Kunst von den Anfängen bis Augustus*. Heidelberg.

Roberts, D. H., F. M. Dunn, and D. Fowler, eds. 1997. *Classical closure: Reading the end in Greek and Latin literature*. Princeton.

Robin, C. 2004. *Fear: The history of a political idea*. Oxford.

Rocca-Serra, G. 1990. "*Imitatio Alexandri* et stoïcisme: Manilius et Silius Italicus." In Neronia IV: *Alejandro Magno, modelo de los emperadores romanos*, ed. J. M. Croisille, 379–87. Brussels.

Rodríguez, E. and J. Martín, eds. 1988. *Lorenzo de Zamora:* La Saguntina, o Primera parte de la Historia de Sagunto, Numancia y Cartago *(Alcalá de Henares, 1589)*. Sagunt / Sagunto.

Rodríguez, E. and J. Martín, trans. 1992. *Historia de Sagunto para ilustrar una tragedia llamada* La caida de Sagunto. Sagunto.

Rodríguez, E. and J. Martín, trans. 1995. *Philip Frowde:* La caida de Sagunto; Tragedia. Sagunto.

Rodríguez Cuadros, E., ed. 1996. *Gaspar Zavala y Zamora:* La destrucción de Sagunto; Comedia nueva. Sagunto.

Rogers, B. M. and B. E. Stevens, eds. 2015. *Classical traditions in science fiction*. Oxford.

Rogers, B. M. and B. E. Stevens, eds. 2017. *Classical traditions in modern fantasy*. Oxford.

Rogers, B. M. and B. E. Stevens, eds. 2018. *Once and future antiquities in science fiction and fantasy*. London.

Roller, M. B. 2004. "Exemplarity in Roman culture: The cases of Horatius Cocles and Cloelia." *CPh* 99.1: 1–56.

Roller, M. B. 2011. "The consul(ar) as *exemplum*: Fabius Cunctator's paradoxical glory." In *Consuls and* res publica: *Holding high office in the Roman Republic*, ed. H. Beck, A. Duplá, M. Jehne, and F. Pina Polo, 182–210. Cambridge.

Roller, M. 2018a. "Amicable and hostile exchange in the culture of recitation." In König and Whitton 2018, 183–207.

Roller, M. 2018b. *Models from the past in Roman culture: A world of exempla*. Cambridge.

Romano, D. 1969. *Silio Italico: Uomo, poeta, artista, attraverso una moderna interpretazione filologica e psicologica.* Naples.

Romano, D. 1985. "La Gigantomachia come metafora della lotta per il potere da Orazio a Claudiano." *La Memoria. AFLP* 4: 75–84.

Romano Martín, S. 2009. *El tópico grecolatino del concilio de los dioses.* Hildesheim.

Ronet, P. 2008. *La poésie historique sous le regard de l'histoire: Hannibal chez Silius Italicus et Tite-Live.* Ph.D. diss., Université Paris-Sorbonne – Paris 4.

Roosjen, P. P. K. 1996. *Silius Italicus* Punica *liber XIV: Een commentaar.* Maastricht.

Rosenberger, V. 2003. "The Gallic disaster." *CW* 96.4: 365–73.

Rosenstein, N. 1990. Imperatores victi: *Military defeat and aristocratic competition in the Middle and Late Republic.* Berkeley, Los Angeles, and Oxford.

Ross, T., trans. 1661/72. *The Second Punick War, between Hannibal, and the Romanes: The whole seventeen books, Englished from the Latine of Silius Italicus: With a continuation from the triumph of Scipio, to the death of Hannibal.* London.

Roumpou, A. N. 2018. *Silius Italicus'* Punica *17.341–654: A literary commentary.* Ph.D. diss., University of Nottingham.

Roumpou, A. N. 2019. "Triumph, closure, and the power of the individual in Silius Italicus's *Punica* 17." *ICS* 44.2: 385–407.

Rudich, V. 1993. *Political dissidence under Nero: The price of dissimulation.* London.

Rudich, V. 1997. *Dissidence and literature under Nero: The price of rhetoricization.* London.

Rudich, V. 2015. *Religious dissent in the Roman Empire: Violence in Judaea at the time of Nero.* London.

Runchina, G. 1982. "Da Ennio a Silio Italico." *AFMC* 6: 11–43.

Ruperti, G. A., ed. 1795–8. *Caii Silii Italici* Punicorum *libri septemdecim.* 2 vols. Goettingae [Göttingen].

Rupprecht, H., ed. and trans. 1991. *Titus Catius Silius Italicus:* Punica; *Das Epos vom zweiten punischen Krieg.* 2 vols. Mitterfels.

Rupprecht, H. 1995. "Flavius Josephus, eine bisher nicht beachtete Vorlage für Silius Italicus." *Gymnasium* 102.6: 497–500.

Russell, D. A., ed. 1990. *Antonine literature.* Oxford.

Rutledge, S. H. 2001. *Imperial inquisitions: Prosecutors and informants from Tiberius to Domitian.* London.

Ryan, K., ed. 1996. *New Historicism and Cultural Materialism: A reader.* London.

Sabbadini, R. 1905. *Le scoperte dei codici latini e greci ne' secoli XIV et XV.* 2 vols. Florence.

Sacerdoti, A. 2011. "Madri, paesaggi, poesia: A margine de tre recenti studi su Papinio Stazio e Silio Italico." *BStudLat* 41.2: 611–23.

Sacerdoti, A. 2014. "«La nazione brama d'essere istruita»: Onorato Occioni (1830–1895) e i *Punica* di Silio." In *La tradizione classica e l'unità d'Italia,* ed. S. Cerasuolo, M. L. Chirico, S. Cannavale, C. Pepe, and N. Rampazzo, 2.307–23. Naples.

Saenger, P. 1997. *Space between words: The origins of silent reading.* Stanford.

Sailor, D. 2006. "Dirty linen, fabrication, and the authorities of Livy and Augustus." *TAPhA* 136.2: 329–88.

Salomies, O. 1992. *Adoptive and polyonymous nomenclature in the Roman Empire.* Helsinki.

Salomies, O. 2014. "Adoptive and polyonymous nomenclature in the Roman Empire – Some addenda." In *Epigrafia e ordine senatorio, 30 anni dopo*, ed. M. L. Caldelli and G. L. Gregori, 511–36. Rome.

Sammons, B. 2017. *Device and composition in the Greek Epic Cycle.* Oxford.

Santini, C. 1982–4. "Per una tipologia del concetto di antichità nei *Punica*." *QLF* 2: 163–70.

Santini, C. 1983. *La cognizione del passato in Silio Italico.* Rome.

Santini, C. 1991. *Silius Italicus and his view of the past.* Amsterdam.

Santini, C. 1992. "Personaggi divini (e umani) nella *Tebaide* di Stazio e nei *Punica* di Silio Italico." In *La storia, la letteratura e l'arte a Roma da Tiberio a Domiziano*, 383–96. Mantua.

Santini, C. 1993. "Nuovi accertamenti sull'ipotesi di raffronto tra Silio e Petrarca." In *Preveggenze umanistiche di Petrarca*, ed. G. Brugnoli and G. Paduano, 111–39. Pisa.

Saylor, C. F. 1978. "*Belli spes inproba*: The theme of walls in Lucan, *Pharsalia* VI." *TAPhA* 108: 243–57.

Scammell, J. M. 1934. "The capture of Troy by Heracles." *CJ* 29.6: 418–28.

Schaffenrath, F., ed. 2010. *Silius Italicus: Akten der Innsbrucker Tagung vom 19.–21. Juni 2008.* Frankfurt am Main.

Schieffer, R. 1975. "Silius Italicus in St. Gallen: Ein Hinweis zur Lokalisierung des »Waltharius«." *MLatJb* 10: 7–19.

Schinkel, J. 1884. *Quaestiones Silianae.* Lipsiae [Leipzig].

Schlichteisen, J. 1881. *De fide historica Silii Italici quaestiones historicae et philologicae.* Regimontii Prussorum [Königsberg].

Schmitz, T. A. 2002. *Moderne Literaturtheorie und antike Texte: Eine Einführung.* Darmstadt.

Schmitz, T. A. 2007. *Modern literary theory and ancient texts: An introduction.* Malden.

Schmitz, C., J. Telg genannt Kortmann, and A. Jöne, eds. 2017. *Anfänge und Enden: Narrative Potentiale des antiken und nachantiken Epos.* Heidelberg.

Scholz, Udo W. 1984. "Der 'Scipio' des Ennius." *Hermes* 112.2: 183–99.

Schönberger, Otto. 1965. "Zum Weltbild der drei Epiker nach Lukan." *Helikon* 5.1: 123–45.

Schrijvers, P. 2005. "Omzien in bewondering: Silius Italicus in zijn tijd." *Hermeneus* 77.2: 76–86.

Schubert, W. 1984. *Jupiter in den Epen der Flavierzeit.* Frankfurt am Main.

Schubert, W. 2005. "Silius-Reminiszenen in Petrarcas *Africa*?" In Auhagen, Faller, and Hurka 2005, 89–101.

Schubert, W. 2010. "Silius Italicus – ein Dichter zwischen Klassizismus und Modernität?" In Schaffenrath 2010, 15–28. Originally published in *AAASzeged* 30 (2007): 156–69.

Schulze, W. 1904. *Zur Geschichte lateinischer Eigennamen*. Berlin.
Scott, T. 2017. *The Swiss and their neighbours, 1460–1560: Between accommodation and aggression*. Oxford.
Scullard, H. H. 1959. *From the Gracchi to Nero: A history of Rome from 133 B.C. to A.D. 68*. London. 2nd ed., 1963; 3rd ed., 1970; 4th ed., 1976; 5th ed., 1982.
Sebastian, M. 2017. *Vom punischen zum römischen Karthago: Konfliktreflexionen und die Konstruktion römischer Identität*. Heidelberg.
Sechi, M. 1951. "Silio Italico e Livio." *Maia* 4.3: 280–97.
Serrati, J. 2006. "Neptune's altars: The treaties between Rome and Carthage (509–226 B.C.)." *CQ* n.s. 56.1: 113–34.
Sharrock, A. R. 2015. "Warrior women in Roman epic." In *Women and war in Antiquity*, ed. J. Fabre-Serris and A. Keith, 157–78. Baltimore.
Sharrock, A. and H. Morales, eds. 2000. *Intratextuality: Greek and Roman textual relations*. Oxford.
Sherwin-White, A. N. 1966. *The* Letters *of Pliny: A historical and social commentary*. Oxford.
Siepe, N. 2019. *Die Erzähltechnik des Silius Italicus: Eine narratologisch-intertextuelle Analyse am Beispiel der Schlacht von Cannae (8,622–10,577)*. Ph.D. diss., Rheinischen Friedrich-Wilhelms-Universität zu Bonn.
Silk, M. S. 1985. "Heracles and Greek tragedy." *G&R* 2nd ser. 32.1: 1–22.
Singles, K. 2013. *Alternate history: Playing with contingency and necessity*. Berlin.
Skutsch, O. 1953. "The fall of the Capitol." *JRS* 43: 77–8. Reprint, in Skutsch 1968b, 138–42.
Skutsch, O. 1968a. "De fulminum appellatione Scipionibus indita." In Skutsch 1968b, 145–50.
Skutsch, O. 1968b. *Studia Enniana*. London.
Skutsch, O. 1978. "The fall of the Capitol again: Tacitus, *Ann*. II. 23." *JRS* 68: 93–4.
Smallwood, E. M., ed. 1967. *Documents illustrating the principates of Gaius, Claudius and Nero*. Cambridge.
Smiles, S. 2018. "Ruins and reputations: The tomb of the poet in visual art." In Goldschmidt and Graziosi 2018, 299–316.
Smith, B. H. 1968. *A study of how poems end*. Chicago.
Śnieżewski, S. 2018. *Analiza stylometryczna* Punica *Syliusza Italika*. Cracow.
Solin, H. and O. Salomies, eds. 1988. *Repertorium nominum gentilium et cognominum Latinorum*. Hildesheim. New ed., 1994.
Southern, P. 1997. *Domitian: Tragic tyrant*. London.
Spalinger, A. and J. Armstrong, eds. 2013. *Rituals of triumph in the Mediterranean world*. Leiden.
Spaltenstein, F. 1986. "Le traitement des sources historiques chez Silius Italicus." *REL* 64: 15–16.
Spaltenstein, F. 1986–90. *Commentaire des* Punica *de Silius Italicus*. 2 vols. Geneva.
Spaltenstein, F. 2006. "À propos des sources historiques de Silius Italicus: Une réponse à Lucarini." *Athenaeum* 104.2 = n.s. 94.2: 717–18.

Spawforth, A. J. S. 2012. *Greece and the Augustan cultural revolution*. Cambridge.
Spentzou, E. 2008. "Eluding *Romanitas*: Heroes and antiheroes in Silius Italicus' Roman history." In *Role models in the Roman world: Identity and assimilation*, ed. S. Bell and I. L. Hansen, 133–45. Ann Arbor.
Stafford, E. 2012. *Herakles*. London.
Starr, R., Jr. 1991. "Reading aloud: *Lectores* and Roman reading." *CJ* 86.4: 337–43.
Steele, R. B. 1922. "The method of Silius Italicus." *CPh* 17.4: 319–33.
Steele, R. B. 1930. "Interrelation of the Latin poets under Domitian." *CPh* 25.4: 328–42.
Stefan, A. S. 2005. *Les guerres daciques de Domitien et de Trajan: Architecture militaire, topographie, images et histoire*. Rome.
Stefani, L. E. 1893. *Vita di Caio Silio Italico*. Lecce.
Steiner, G. 1973. "The city under attack." *Salmagundi* 24: 3–18.
Stem, R. 2007. "The exemplary lessons of Livy's Romulus." *TAPhA* 137.2: 435–71.
Stevens, S. T. 1988. "A legend of the destruction of Carthage." *CPh* 83.1: 39–41.
Stocks, C. A. 2010. "[Re]constructing epic: Sicily and the *Punica* in miniature." In Schaffenrath 2010, 151–66.
Stocks, C. 2014. *The Roman Hannibal: Remembering the enemy in Silius Italicus' Punica*. Liverpool.
Stocks, C. 2019. "In a land of gods and monsters: Silius Italicus' Capua." In Augoustakis and Littlewood 2019, 233–48.
Stoffel, C. 2017. "*Otium Campanum* – Silius im Ruhestand (Plin. *epist*. 3,7), Hannibal in Capua (Sil. 11)." *Hermes* 145.4: 375–85.
Stoll, O. 2019. Vestigia cladis: *Roms Umgang mit militärischem Misserfolg; Niederlagen verdrängen, Siege betonen, Resilienz beweisen*. Berlin.
Strobel, K. 1987. "Der Chattenkrieg Domitians: Historische und politische Aspekte." *Germania* 65: 423–52.
Stürner, F. 2008. "Silius Italicus und die Herrschaft des Einzelnen: Zur Darstellung Hannibals und Scipios in den *Punica*." In *Die Legitimation der Einzelherrschaft im Kontext der Generationenthematik*, ed. T. Baier, 221–41. Berlin.
Stürner, F. 2011. "Zwischen Tradition und Innovation: Zur Struktur der *Punica* des Silius Italicus." *WJA* n.F. 35: 147–66.
Stürner, F., trans. forthcoming. *Der Punische Krieg*. Darmstadt.
Sturt, N. J. H. 1977. *Tradition and innovation in the Silver Latin epic simile: A thematic study*. Ph.D. diss., University of London.
Šubrt, J. 1991. "The motif of the Alps in the work of Silius Italicus." *LF* 114.4: 224–31.
Suess, J. 2011. *Divine justification: Flavian Imperial cult*. Oxford.
Sullivan, J. P. 1985. *Literature and politics in the age of Nero*. Ithaca.
Swain, S. 1996. *Hellenism and empire: Language, Classicism, and power in the Greek world, AD 50–250*. Oxford.
Syme, R. S. 1939. *The Roman revolution*. Oxford.
Syme, R. 1958. *Tacitus*. 2 vols. Oxford.

Syme, R. S. 1983. "Eight consuls from Patavium." *PBSR* 51: 102–24.
Syré, E. 2017. *Gewalt und soziale Bindung in Silius Italicus' Punica*. Rahden/Westf.
Szelest, H. 1959. "Martial und Silius Italicus." In *Aus der altertumswissenschaftlichen Arbeit Volkspolens*, ed. J. Irmscher and K. Kumaniecki, 73–80. Berlin.
Taisne, A.-M. 1973. "Le thème du triomphe dans la poésie et l'art sous les Flaviens." *Latomus* 32.3: 485–504.
Taisne, A.-M. 1992. "L'éloge des Flaviens chez Silius Italicus (*Punica*, III, 594–629)." *VL* 125: 21–8.
Taisne, A.-M. 1994. "Stylisation épique de l'*Histoire romaine* de Tite-Live aux chants III et IV de la *Guerre punique* de Silius Italicus." In *Actes du colloque Présence de Tite-Live (Tours, Université, 1992): Hommage au Professeur P. Jal*, ed. R. Chevallier and R. Poignault, 89–99. Tours.
Takács, L. 1998. "Az Aetna leírása Vergilius és Silius Italicus eposzában." *AntTan* 42.1-2: 129–36.
Takács, L. 2002. "L. Annaeus Cornutus egyik töredékének története." *AntTan* 46.1-2: 127–39.
Takács, L. 2004. "The story of a fragment of L. Annaeus Cornutus." *AAntHung* 44.1: 35–46.
Takács, L. 2018. "(The reconstruction of) Lucius Annaeus Cornutus' commentary on Vergil." *Aitia* 8.2.
Tandoi, V. 1985. "Gli epici di fine I secolo dopo Cristo, o Il crepuscolo degli dei." *A&R* n.s. 30.3-4: 154–69. Reprint, in *Scritti di filologia e di storia della cultura classica*, ed. F. E. Consolino, G. Lotito, M.-P. Pieri, G. Sommariva, S. Timpanaro, and M. A. Vinchesi, 2.755–70. Pisa, 1992.
Tedeschi, A. 1994. "La partenza di Scipione per la Spagna: Fra problemi di coscienza e problemi di tradizione letteraria (Livio, Silio Italico e Petrarca a confronto)." *Aufidus* 14: 7–24.
Telg genannt Kortmann, J. R., ed. and trans. 2018. *Hannibal ad portas: Silius Italicus, Punica, 12,507–752: Einleitung, Übersetzung und Kommentar*. Heidelberg.
ter Haar, L. G. J. 1997. "Sporen van Silius' « Punica » in boek 1 en 2 van Petrarca's « Africa »." *Lampas* 30.3: 154–62.
ter Haar, L. G. J. 1999. *Petrarca's Africa: Boek I en II; Een commentaar*. Nijmegen.
Tetlock, P. E., R. N. Lebow, and G. Parker, eds. 2006. *Unmaking the West: "What-if?" scenarios that rewrite world history*. Ann Arbor.
Thein, A. 2014. "Capitoline Jupiter and the historiography of Roman world rule." *Histos* 8: 284–319.
Thomas, B. 1991. *The New Historicism and other old-fashioned topics*. Princeton.
Thomas, J.-F. 2001. "Le theme de la perfidie carthaginoise dans l'oeuvre de Silius Italicus." *VL* 161: 2–14.
Thuile, W. 1980. *Furiae in der nachklassischen Epik: Untersuchungen zu Valerius Flaccus' Argonautica, Papinius Statius' Thebais und Silius Italicus' Punica*. Ph.D. Diss., Leopold-Franzens-Universität zu Innsbruck.

Thürlemann, S. 1974. "*Ceterum censeo Carthaginem esse delendam.*" *Gymnasium* 81.6: 465–76.
Timpe, D. 1972. "Fabius Pictor und die Anfänge der römischen Historiographie." *ANRW* 1.2: 928–69.
Tipping, B. 2004. "Middling epic? Silius Italicus' *Punica*." In Kyriakidis and De Martino 2004, 345–70.
Tipping, B. 2007. "*Haec tum Roma fuit*: Past, present, and closure in Silius Italicus' *Punica*." In *Classical constructions: Papers in memory of Don Fowler, Classicist and Epicurean*, ed. S. J. Heyworth, P. G. Fowler, and S. J. Harrison, 221–41. Oxford.
Tipping, B. 2010a. *Exemplary epic: Silius Italicus'* Punica. Oxford.
Tipping, B. 2010b. "Virtue and narrative in Silius Italicus' *Punica*." In Augoustakis 2010a, 193–218.
Tipping, B. 2011. "Terrible manliness? Lucan's Cato." In Asso 2011, 223–36.
Tomani Amiani, S. 1850. *Memorie biografiche di Giacomo Costanzi da Fano, poeta del secolo XV*. Fano.
Toohey, P. 1992. *Reading epic: An introduction to the ancient narratives*. London.
Torgovnick, M. 1981. *Closure in the novel*. Princeton.
Torregaray Pagola, E. 1998. *La elaboración de la tradición sobre los* Cornelii Scipiones: *Pasado histórico y conformación simbólica*. Zaragoza.
Tracy, J. 2011. "Internal evidence for the completeness of the *Bellum civile*." In Asso 2011, 33–53.
Trapp, J. B. 1984. "The grave of Vergil." *JWI* 47: 1–31.
Trapp, J. B. 1987. "Virgil and the monuments." *PVS* 18: 1–17.
Travis, R. 1990. "Halbwachs and Durkheim: A test of two theories of suicide." *BJS* 41.2: 225–43.
Tucci, P. L. 2017. *The Temple of Peace in Rome*. 2 vols. Cambridge.
Tupet, A.-M. 1980a. "Le serment d'Hannibal chez Silius Italicus." In *Actes du Xe congrès de l'Association Guillaume Budé, Toulouse 8–12 avril 1978*, ed. J. Sirinelli, 181–3. Paris.
Tupet, A.-M. 1980b. "Le serment d'Hannibal chez Silius Italicus." *BAGB* 1980.2, 186–93.
Uccellini, R. 2006. "Soggetti eccentrici: Asbyte in Silio Italico (e altre donne pericolose del mito)." *GIF* 58.2: 229–53.
Udwin, V. M. 1999. *Between two armies: The place of the duel in epic culture*. Leiden.
Ussani, V. 1918. "Per Lucano "De bellis Punicis„ e la critica dei "Dicta Catonis„." *RLC* 1.1: 11–16.
Valcárcel, V. 1995. "La *vita Hannibalis* de C. Nepote." *Veleia* 12: 267–86.
van der Keur, M. 2014. "*Meruit deus esse uideri*: Silius' Homer in Homer's *Punica* 13." In Augoustakis 2014, 287–304.
van der Keur, C. M. 2015. *A commentary on Silius Italicus'* Punica *13: Intertextuality and narrative structure*. Ph.D. diss., Vrije Universiteit Amsterdam.
van der Kolf, M. C. 1954. "Priam and Laomedon from a historical point of view." *Mnemosyne* 4th ser. 7.1: 1–18.

van Hooff, A. J. L. 1990. *Zelfdoding in de antieke wereld: Van autothanasia tot suicide.* Nijmegen: SUN. Simultaneously published in English as *From autothanasia to suicide: Self-killing in Classical Antiquity.* London, 1990.

van Wees, H. 1988. "Kings in combat: Battles and heroes in the *Iliad.*" *CQ* n.s. 38.1: 1–24.

Vander Motten, J. P. and K. Daemen-de Gelder. 2004. "A 'copy as immortal, as its original': Thomas Ross' *Second Punick War* (London, 1661 and 1672)." In *Living in posterity: Essays in honour of Bart Westerweel,* ed. J. F. van Dijkhuizen, P. Hoftijzer, J. Roding, and P. Smith, 185–90. Hilversum.

Vasaly, A. 2015. *Livy's political philosophy: Power and personality in early Rome.* Cambridge.

Vassiliades, G. 2013. "Les sources et la fonction du *metus hostilis* chez Salluste." *BAGB* 2013.1: 127–68.

Vassiliades, G. 2018. "Temps cyclique et temps linéaire à la fin de la République." *VL* 197–8: 51–76.

Veeser, H. Aram, ed. 1989. *The New Historicism.* London.

Veeser, H. Aram, ed. 1994. *The New Historicism reader.* London.

Vekselius, J. 2018. *Weeping for the* res publica: *Tears in Roman political culture.* Lund.

Venini, P. 1969. "Silio Italico e il mito tebano." *RIL* 103.3: 778–83.

Venini, P. 1972a. "Cronologia e composizione nei *Punica* di Silio Italico." *RIL* 106.3: 518–31.

Venini, P. 1972b. "Tecnica allusiva in Silio Italico." *RIL* 106.3: 532–42.

Venini, P. 1978. *La visione dell'Italia nel catalogo di Silio Italico* (Pun. 8, 356–616). *MIL* 36.3: 123–227.

Venini, P. 1992. "La coda di Cerbero: Da Seneca a Silio Italico." *QCTC* 10: 245–7.

Versnel, H. S. 1970. Triumphus: *An inquiry into the origin, development and meaning of the Roman triumph.* Leiden.

Versnel, H. S. 1976. "Two types of Roman *devotio.*" *Mnemosyne* 4th ser. 29.4: 365–410.

Versnel, H. S. 1981. "Self-sacrifice, compensation, and the anonymous gods." In *Le sacrifice dans l'Antiquité,* ed. J. Rudhardt and O. Reverdin, 135–94. Geneva.

Versnel, H. S. 2006. "Red (herring?): Comments on a new theory concerning the origin of the triumph." *Numen* 53: 290–326.

Vessey, D. W. T. C. 1974. "Pliny, Martial and Silius Italicus." *Hermes* 102.1: 109–16.

Vessey, D. W. T. 1982a. "Flavian epic." In *The Cambridge history of Classical literature II: Latin literature,* ed. E. J. Kenney, 580–90. Cambridge.

Vessey, D. W. T. 1982b. "The dupe of destiny: Hannibal in Silius, *Punica* III." *CJ* 77.4: 320–35.

Vessey, D. W. T. 1984. "The origin of Ti. Catius Asconius Silius Italicus." *CB* 60.1: 9–10.

Vetter, A. W. 2002. *Gigantensturz-Darstellungen in der italienischen Kunst: Zur Instrumentalisierung eines mythologischen Bildsujets im historisch-politischen Kontext.* Weimar.

Vian, F. 1951. *Répertoire des gigantomachies figurées dans l'art grec et romain.* Paris.

Vian, F. 1952a. "La guerre des Géants devant les penseurs de l'Antiquité." *REG* 65: 1–39.

Vian, F. 1952b. *La guerre des géants: Le mythe avant l'époque hellénistique.* Paris.

Vidal, J. L. 2010. "*Nec tu diuinam* Aeneida *tempta*: La sombra de la *Eneida* (y otras sombras) en la épica flavia." In *Perfiles de Grecia y Roma: Actas del XII congreso español de estudios clásicos, Valencia, 22 al 26 de octubre de 2007*, ed. M. A. Almela Lumbreras, J. F. González Castro, J. Siles Ruiz, J. de la Villa Polo, G. Hinojo Andrés, and P. Cañizares Ferriz, 747–87. Madrid.

Vidman, L., ed. 1982. *Fasti Ostienses.* Pragae [Prague].

Villalba Álvarez, J. 2004. "Ecos virgilianos en una tempestad épica de Silio Itálico (*Punica* XVII 236–290)." *Humanitas(Coimbra)* 56: 365–82.

Villalba Álvarez, J., trans. 2005. *Silio Itálico: La guerra púnica.* Madrid.

Villalba Álvarez, J. 2008. "Épica e historiografía: La arenga militar en los *Punica* de Silio Itálico y su relación con Tito Livio." In *Retórica e historiografía: El discurso militar en la historiografía desde la Antigüedad hasta el Renacimiento*, ed. J. C. Iglesias Zoido, 341–66. Madrid.

Villarroya, I. 1845. *Las ruinas de Sagunto.* Teruel.

Vinchesi, M. A. 1999. "Imilce e Deidamia, due figure femminili dell'epica flavia (e una probabile ripresa da Silio Italico nell'*Achilleide* di Stazio)." *InvLuc* 21: 445–52.

Vinchesi, M. A., ed. and trans. 2001. *Silio Italico: Le guerre puniche.* 2 vols. Milan. Reprint, 2004.

Vinchesi, M. A. 2005. "Tipologie femminili nei *Punica* di Silio Italico: La *fida coniunx* e la *virgo belligera*." In Gasti and Mazzoli 2005, 97–126.

Visonà, P. 1988. "Passing the salt: On the destruction of Carthage again." *CPh* 83.1: 41–2.

Vogel-Weidemann, U. 1989. "*Carthago delenda est: Aitia* and *prophasis*." *AClass* 32: 79–95.

Vogt, J., ed. 1943. *Rom und Karthago: Ein Gemeinschaftswerk.* Leipzig.

Voisin, J.-L. 1984. "Les Romains, chasseurs de têtes." In *Du châtiment dans la cité: Supplices corporels et peine de mort dans le monde ancien*, 241–93. Paris.

Volpilhac, J., P. Miniconi, and G. Devallet, eds. and trans. 1981. *Silius Italicus: La guerre punique. Tome II: Livres V–VIII.* Paris.

Volpilhac-Lenthéric, J., M. Martin, P. Miniconi, and G. Devallet, eds. and trans. 1984. *Silius Italicus: La guerre punique. Tome III: Livres IX–XIII.* Paris.

von Albrecht, M. 1964. *Silius Italicus: Freiheit und Gebundenheit römischer Epik.* Amsterdam.

von Albrecht, M. 1973. "Silius Italicus: Ein vergessenes Kapitel Literaturgeschichte." In *Argentea aetas: In memoriam Entii V. Marmorale*, ed. F. Della Corte, 181–8. Genoa.

von Albrecht, M. 1991. "L'Italia in Silio Italico." In *Studi di filologia classica in onore di Giusto Monaco*, ed. S. Mariotti, 3.1179–90. Palermo.

von Albrecht, M. 1999. *Roman epic: An interpretative introduction.* Leiden.

von Albrecht, M. 2006. "Tradition und Originalität bei Silius Italicus." *Aevum(ant)* 6: 101–21. Reprint, in Castagna, Galimberti Biffino, and Riboldi 2011, 89–109.

von Contzen, E. 2013. "'I still retain the Empire of my Minde': Thomas Ross's *Continuation* of Silius Italicus (1661, 1672)." *M&H* n.s. 39: 25–46.

von Ungern-Sternberg, J. 1975. *Capua im zweiten punischen Krieg: Untersuchungen zur römischen Annalistik*. Munich.
Wacht, M. 1989. *Concordantia in Silii Italici Punica*. 2 vols. Hildesheim.
Wallace, M. V. T. 1955. *The epic technique of Silius Italicus*. Ph.D. diss., Harvard University.
Wallace, M. V. T. 1957. "The epic technique of Silius Italicus." *HSPh* 62: 159–62.
Wallace, M. V. T. 1958. "The architecture of the *Punica*: A hypothesis." *CPh* 53.2: 99–103.
Wallace, M. T. V. 1968. "Some aspects of time in the *Punica* of Silius Italicus." *CW* 62.3: 83–93.
Wallace-Hadrill, A. 2008. *Rome's cultural revolution*. Cambridge.
Walser, E. 1914. *Poggius Florentinus: Leben und Werke*. Leipzig and Berlin. Reprint, Hildesheim, 1974.
Walsh, P. G. 1982. "Livy and the aims of 'historia': An analysis of the third decade." *ANRW* 2.30.2: 1058–74.
Walter, A. 2014. *Erzählen und Gesang im flavischen Epos*. Berlin.
Walter, U. 2004. *Memoria und res publica: Zur Geschichtskultur im republikanischen Rom*. Frankfurt am Main.
Warmington, B. H. 1988. "The destruction of Carthage: A *retractatio*." *CPh* 83.4: 308–10.
Watts, W. J. 1971. "The birthplaces of Latin writers." *G&R* 2nd ser. 18.1: 91–101.
Weinstock, S. 1971. *Divus Julius*. Oxford.
Wellesley, K. 1956. "Three historical puzzles in *Histories* 3." *CQ* 6.3–4: 207–14.
Wellesley, K. 1975. *The long year A.D. 69*. London: Paul Elek. Reprint, Boulder, 1976. 2nd ed., 1989; 3rd ed., 2000.
Wellesley, K. 1981. "What happened on the Capitol in December A.D. 69?" *AJAH* 6: 166–90.
Welwei, K.-W. 1989. "Zum *metus Punicus* in Rom um 150 v. Chr." *Hermes* 117.3: 314–20.
Wenskus, O. 2010. "Diskussionsbeitrag: Die Siebzehn als kritische Zahl." In Schaffenrath 2010, 97–8.
West, A. B. 1923. "Notes on the multiplication of cities in ancient geography." *CPh* 18.1: 48–67.
West, M. L. 2013. *The Epic Cycle: A commentary on the lost Troy epics*. Oxford.
Wezel, E. 1873. *De C. Silii Italici cum fontibus tum exemplis*. Lipsiae [Leipzig].
White, H. 1973. *Metahistory: The historical imagination in nineteenth-century Europe*. Baltimore.
White, H. 1978. *Tropics of discourse: Essays in cultural criticism*. Baltimore.
White, H. 1987. *The content of the form: Narrative discourse and historical representation*. Baltimore.
Whitmarsh, T. 2001. *Greek literature and the Roman Empire: The politics of imitation*. Oxford.
Whitmarsh, T. 2005. *The Second Sophistic*. Oxford.
Wiedemann, T. 1993. "Sallust's *Jugurtha*: Concord, discord, and the digressions." *G&R* 2nd ser. 40.1: 48–57.

Wiedemann, T. 1996. "Single combat and being Roman." *AncSoc* 27: 91–103.
Wilkinson, S. 2012. *Republicanism during the early Roman Empire*. London.
Wilson, M. 2004. "Ovidian Silius." *Arethusa* 37.2: 225–49.
Wilson, M. 2013. "The Flavian *Punica*?" In Manuwald and Voigt 2013, 13–27.
Winsbury, R. 2009. *The Roman book: Books, publishing and performance in Classical Rome*. London.
Wiseman, T. P. 1978. "Flavians on the Capitol." *AJAH* 3.2: 163–78.
Wiseman, T. P. 1979. *Clio's cosmetics: Three studies in Greco-Roman literature*. Leicester. Reprint, Bristol, 2004.
Wiseman, T. P. 1994. *Historiography and imagination: Eight essays on Roman culture*. Exeter.
Wiseman, T. P. 1995. *Remus: A Roman myth*. Cambridge.
Wiseman, T. P. 2010. "The two-headed state: How Romans explained civil war." In Breed, Damon, and Rossi 2010, 25–44.
Wistrand, E. 1956. *Die Chronologie der* Punica *des Silius Italicus: Beiträge zur Interpretation der flavischen Literatur*. Göteborg.
Wood, K. A. 1933. *A study of the influence of Vergil upon the works of Silius Italicus*. M.A. thesis, University of Maine.
Wood, N. 1995. "Sallust's theorem: A comment on 'fear' in Western political thought." *HPT* 16.2: 174–89.
Woodard, R. D. 2013. *Myth, ritual, and the warrior in Roman and Indo-European antiquity*. Cambridge.
Woodman, A. J. 1969. "Sallustian influence on Velleius Paterculus." In *Hommages à Marcel Renard*, ed. J. Bibauw, 1.785–99. Brussels.
Woodman, A. J. 1989. *Rhetoric in Classical historiography: Four studies*. London.
Woodman, A. J. 2009. "Tacitus and the contemporary scene." In *The Cambridge companion to Tacitus*, ed. A. J. Woodman, 31–44. Cambridge.
Woodman, A. J., ed. 2018. *The* Annals *of Tacitus: Book 4*. Cambridge.
Woodruff, L. B. 1906. *Reminiscences of Ennius in Silius Italicus*. Ph.D. diss., University of Michigan. Reprint, in *Roman history and mythology*, ed. H. A. Sanders, 355–424. New York.
Wright, D. J. 2018. *Giants, Titans, and civil strife in the Greek and Roman world down through the age of Augustus*. Ph.D. diss., Rutgers University.
Yates, F. A. 1966. *The art of memory*. London.
Young, N. D. 1939. *Index verborum Silianus*. Iowa City. Reprint, Hildesheim, 1964.
Yue, K. K. 2011. *The treatment of virtue in Silius Italicus'* Punica. Ph.D. diss., University of Exeter.
Zaia, S. 2012. Fuge proelia Varro: *Commento a Silio Italico,* Punica *9,1–177*. M.A. thesis, Università degli Studi di Padova.
Zaia, S. 2016. Sili Italici Punicorum *liber nonus: Introduzione e commento*. Ph.D. diss., Università degli Studi di Padova.
Zanker, P. 1987. *Augustus und die Macht der Bilder*. Munich.

Zanker, P. 1988. *The power of images in the age of Augustus.* Trans. A. Shapiro. Ann Arbor.

Zecchini, G. 2006. "Silio Italico e Domiziano." *Aevum(ant)* 6: 41–52. Reprint, in Castagna, Galimberti Biffino, and Riboldi 2011, 29–39.

Ziolkowski, A. 1993. "*Urbs direpta*, or how the Romans sacked cities." In *War and society in the Roman world*, ed. J. Rich and G. Shipley, 69–91. London.

Zissos, A., ed. 2016. *A companion to the Flavian age of Imperial Rome.* Malden.

Zwierlein, O. 1970. "Das Waltharius-Epos und seine lateinischen Vorbilder." *A&A* 16: 153–84. Reprint, in *Lucubrationes philologicae*, ed. R. Jakobi, R. Junge, and C. Schmitz, 2.519–64. Berlin.

Index

Aeneas 41, 56–7, 61, 72–3, 93–4, 125–6, 128–30, 130, 146–7, 152, 169–70
Alexander the Great 56, 97
Alexandreis 58
Alps 43, 47, 51, 74, 77, 99, 110–11, 123, 132, 133, 143, 147, 167–70, 173, 174–5
Ampelius 175–81
Anna (Perenna), sister of Dido 48, 82–3, 146–7, 148
Apennines 47, 78, 79
Appian 54–5, 150–1
Appius 47, 79
Arator 58
Archimedes 51, 98
Aris 99, 106
Asbyte 46, 75–6
Asilus 98, 160
Aulus Gellius 55, 149–50
Augustine 54–5
Augustus 17, 18, 74, 119, 141

Bacchus 82, 107, 174–5
Baecula, battle of 43, 51, 99
Barlow, Joel 186 n. 53
Beryas 98, 160
Boethius 169–70
Bostar 46, 47, 76, 77
Bruttii 51, 93–4, 101

Camillus 82, 107, 131–2, 134–5
Campi Magni, battle of 52, 102
Cannae, battle of 6, 43, 44–5, 48–9, 52–3, 56, 57, 59, 62, 63–4, 74, 74–5, 77, 82–5, 86–9, 92–4, 103, 106, 111, 117, 117–18, 121–3, 132, 133, 138, 144–6, 148, 151, 152, 153–61, 172, 175–81
Canusium 49, 85
Capitol, Capitoline Hill 19, 74, 106–7, 115, 116, 118, 119–26, 128–30, 131, 133, 133–5, 147, 162–3, 165–7, 167–70
Capua, fall of 39, 43, 49–50, 92–3, 94–5, 96, 96–7, 106, 123, 130, 160

Carthago Nova (New Carthage), fall of 43, 51, 98–9, 106
Cassius Dio 54–5, 163
Catius Caesius Fronto, Ti. 189 n. 30
Cato the Elder 44, 54, 82, 84, 149–50, 150–1
Catullus 26–8, 58, 58–9
Centenius Paenula 96
Cerrinus Vibellius Taurea 97
Charisius 23–4, 38
Cicero 28–9, 31–2, 56, 169–70
Cilnius 48, 81, 106
Cinna 85
Cinyps 95–6
Claudia Quinta 102
Claudian 58
Claudius Asellus 97
Claudius Nero 51, 99–100, 117, 138
Cloelia 85
Coelius Antipater 54
Colloquium Celtis 24
Corbulo 98
Corippus 58
Cornelius Nepos 55, 176
Cornutus 23–4, 38
Corvinus 47, 79
Council of Constance 1
Crista 49, 84
Crixus 78, 133
Curtius Rufus 56
Cymodoce 152–3

Dasius Altinius 50, 96
De viris illustribus 55, 175–81
Decius Magius 49–50, 94–5, 95
La destrucción de Sagunto (Enrique Palos y Navarro) 8–9
La destrucción de Sagunto (Francisco Sánchez-Castañer and José Maria Pemán) 8–9
La destrucción de Sagunto (Gaspar Zavala y Zamora) 8–9

Dido 41, 46, 48, 56–7, 61, 74, 76, 82–3, 113, 146–9, 169–70
Diodorus Siculus 54
Dionysius of Halicarnassus 54
Disticha Catonis 24
Domitian 4, 20, 58, 74, 77, 162–3, 166
　See also Flavian emperors
Dracontius 58
Ducarius 47, 79, 133

Ennius 57, 58, 59, 64, 67, 72–3
Epictetus 23
Eumolpus 174–5
Eutropius 54–5

Fabius Maximus 43, 46, 48, 49, 51, 52, 57, 75, 76, 81–2, 84–5, 85, 87, 94, 99, 101–2, 116, 117, 119, 134–5, 137, 143–4
Fabius Pictor 54
fabula praetexta 59
Falernus 82
Festus 54–5
Fides 46, 50, 76, 97, 116
First Punic War 42, 74, 80–1, 83–4, 87–8, 153–4
　See also Punic Wars
Flaminius 47, 78, 79, 87, 102, 117, 133
Flavian emperors 4, 5, 5–6, 11–12, 19–20, 35–6, 47, 52–3, 72, 74, 77, 117, 141–6, 152–3, 162–3, 165–6
　See also Vespasian, Titus, *and* Domitian
Florus 54–5, 150, 166–7, 175–81
Frontinus 192 n. 28
Fulvius Flaccus, Cn. 96
Fulvius Flaccus, Q. 50, 94, 96–7

Gades 46, 76, 167–70, 172
Gereonium, battle of 48, 82
Gergenus 79
Geryon 200 n. 12
Gestar 76

Hamilcar, father of Hannibal 42, 42–3, 46, 74–5, 76, 97, 106, 116, 146
Hampsagoras 96
Hannibalic War *see* Second Punic War
Hanno 51, 76, 95, 101, 116

Hasdrubal, brother of Hannibal 43, 51, 99, 99–100, 106, 116
Hasdrubal, son-in-law of Hamilcar and brother-in-law of Hannibal 46, 75, 116
Hasdrubal Gisgo 51, 51–2, 99, 101, 102, 116
Hercules 37–8, 38, 46, 76, 77, 81, 107, 113–14, 115–16, 117–18, 122, 126–8, 174–5
Herodotus 55
Hiero III 97–8
Hieronymus, grandson of Hiero III 97–8
Himilco 98
Homer 57, 97, 126
Horace 58, 58–9, 152
Hostus, son of Hampsagoras 96

Ilias Latina 188 n. 15
Ilipa, battle of 43, 51, 101
Imilce 46–7, 76–7, 167–70
Iris 84
Isalcas, prospective son-in-law of Mago 47, 79
Italia 51, 99, 106

Josephus 55, 163
Julius Caesar 11–12, 17, 17–18, 18, 55, 73, 74, 170–5
Julius Valerius 56
Juno 46, 47, 48, 49, 52, 74–5, 76, 78, 79, 82–3, 84, 85, 95, 96, 102, 102–3, 106, 119–21, 122, 122–3, 123–6, 139, 147, 148, 167
Jupiter 46, 47, 48, 50, 52, 72, 73, 75, 77, 78, 81, 84, 87, 89, 96, 97, 98, 102, 107, 107–8, 110–11, 114, 116, 117–18, 119–26, 128, 141–6, 147, 152–3, 163, 166, 167–70, 174–5
Jupiter Ammon 46, 47, 76, 77, 122–3
Juvenal 58
Juvencus 58

Laelius 98–9, 99, 101
Laomedon 60–2, 114, 131
Larus 101
Lefebvre de Villebrune, Jean-Baptiste 2, 181–2
Lentulus 84–5

Leontini 51, 98, 160
Livius Andronicus 57–8
Livius Salinator 51, 99–100, 117, 138
Livy 5, 12–13, 23, 52–3, 53–6, 64, 65, 67, 69, 69–71, 87–8, 92–3, 110–11, 131, 151–2, 152, 160, 167–70, 176, 181–2
Lucan 5, 5–6, 11–12, 24, 52–3, 58, 59–60, 65, 107–8, 117, 126, 144–5, 151, 170–5, 175–6
Lucilius 58
Lucretius 58, 137

Magna Mater 52, 102, 130–1
Mago, brother of Hannibal 47, 47–8, 50, 51, 77, 78, 80, 85, 95, 99, 101, 116, 133
Maharbal 78, 133
Mancinus, son of Satricus 49, 83–4, 153–61
Marcellus 50, 50–1, 51, 57, 94, 95–6, 97–8, 99, 116, 117, 131, 135–9, 143–4
Marcia, wife of Regulus 81
Mars 49, 73, 78, 79, 84, 89, 107, 122, 123, 125, 169
Martial 4, 21, 22, 24–5, 26–32, 32, 35, 36–7, 53, 163, 166
Marus 48, 57, 80–1
Masinissa 51, 101, 116
Mercury 46–7, 77, 167–70, 172
Metaurus River, battle of 43, 51, 99–100, 117, 138, 152–3
Metellus 49, 84, 85, 150
Minerva *see* Pallas (Minerva)
Minucius Rufus 43, 48, 81–2, 84
Mopsus 75–6
Murrus 38, 46, 75, 113, 121, 126–8, 139, 173

Naevius 57–8, 59
Nero 4, 5, 18, 35, 36, 37, 165–6
Nerva 4, 20–1, 35–6
Nola 50, 95–6, 136, 139

Octavia 59
Octavian *see* Augustus
Orosius 54–5
Orpheus 30–1, 95, 169–70
Othrys 79
Ovid 58, 59, 73, 131, 169–70

Pacuvius Calavius, father of Perolla 50, 94, 95, 160
Palladium 50, 96, 130–1
Pallas (Minerva) 49, 50, 84, 96, 122–3, 123, 125, 130–1
Pan 97
Paullus 48–9, 50, 83, 84–5, 87, 95–6, 97, 102, 117, 138, 143–4
Pausanias 55
Pedianus 95–6
Periochae 54–5
Perolla, son of Pacuvius 50, 95, 160
Petrarch 181–2
Petronius 170–5
Phorcys 84
Plautus 59
Pliny the Elder 32, 55
Pliny the Younger 4, 21, 22, 23, 26, 32–6, 36–9
Plutarch 55
Poggio Bracciolini 1, 181
Polyaenus 192 n. 28
Polybius 54, 110–11, 149, 160, 176
Pompey 11–12, 17, 107–8, 170–5
Pomponia, mother of Scipio Africanus 50, 73, 97
Pomponius Mela 55
Porcius Licinus 191 n. 13
Priam 61, 114
Propertius 59
Proteus 48, 82, 152–3
Prudentius 58
Punic Wars 5, 17, 41–2, 44–5, 54–5, 73–4
    See also First Punic War, Second Punic War, *and* Third Punic War
Punica
    17 or 18 books 5, 45, 63
    lacunae 5, 45, 63–4
    structure 63–7, 108–11, 175–81
    summary 5, 45–53
    title 45
Pyrenees 47, 77

Regulus 42, 48, 73, 76, 80–1, 87–8, 106, 116–17
Remus 41, 89, 151–2
R(h)aeteis (Simon Lemm) 7–8
Romulus 41, 72–3, 89, 107, 122, 125, 134–5, 151–2

Las ruinas de Sagunto (Isidoro Villarroya) 8–9

La Saguntina (Lorenzo de Zamora) 8–9
Saguntineida (José Manuel Miñana) 8–9
Saguntum, fall of 6, 38, 39, 43, 46, 75, 75–6, 83, 106, 107, 115, 116, 119–21, 126–8, 132–3, 139, 141, 143, 147–8, 160, 167, 173
Sallust 55, 117, 150
Sardinia 50, 96
Satricus, father of Mancinus and Solymus 49, 83–4, 153–61
Scaeva 172, 172–3
Scipio, father of Scipio Africanus 47, 50, 52, 57, 77–8, 97, 98, 101, 117, 133
Scipio Aemilianus 37–8, 44, 56, 73, 103, 117, 152–3
Scipio Africanus 43, 43–4, 47, 49, 50, 51, 51–2, 52, 72–3, 73, 78, 89, 97, 98–9, 101–2, 102–3, 104–8, 115, 116, 117, 134–5, 137, 138, 139, 143–4, 150–1, 163, 181–2
Scipio Asiaticus, brother of Scipio Africanus 101
Scipio Nasica, cousin of Scipio Africanus 52, 102
Second Punic War 5, 5–6, 42–3, 44–5, 52–3, 152–3
    See also Punic Wars
La Seconda Guerra Tritonide (Salvatore Conte) 9
Sedulius 58
Sempronius Gracchus 95, 102, 138
Sempronius Longus 47, 78
Seneca the Younger 59, 169–70
Serranus, son of Regulus 48, 80–1
Servilius Geminus 79
Sibyl of Cumae 50, 97
Sidonius Apollinaris 24–5, 58
Silius Decianus, L. 29–30
Silius Italicus, Ti. Catius Asconius
    birth 4, 17, 25–6
    death 4, 4–5, 17, 21, 35–6, 38–9
    name 4, 21–2, 25–6
Silius Severus 29–30, 30–1
Solinus 55
Solymus, son of Satricus 49, 83–4, 153–61

Sónnica la cortesana (Vicente Blasco Ibáñez) 8–9
Sophonisba 102
Statius 24, 58, 163, 165–6
Strabo 55
Suetonius 55, 163, 166
Sychaeus, son of Hasdrubal and nephew of Hannibal 47, 77, 79
Syphax 51–2, 52, 101, 102, 105, 116
Syracuse 50–1, 97–8, 136

Tacitus 4, 21, 22–3, 32, 36, 36–7, 55, 154, 160–1, 162–3, 166
Tagus 75
Tarentum 50, 51, 96, 99
Teuthras 95
Theron 46, 75–6
Third Punic War 43–4, 56, 103, 141, 145–6, 149, 152–3
    See also Punic Wars
Thucydides 55
Tibullus 59, 170
Tiburna, wife of Murrus 76, 113
Ticinus River, battle of 43, 47, 77–8, 133
Tisiphone 46, 76, 116
Titus 4, 20
    See also Flavian emperors
Torquatus 94, 96
Trajan 4, 20–1, 35–6
Lake Trasimene, battle of 43, 47, 78, 79, 80–1, 87, 88, 98, 122, 123, 132, 133, 160
Trebia River, battle of 43, 47, 78, 133, 160
Turnus 56–7, 93–4, 152

Valerius Flaccus 58
Valerius Maximus 55, 150, 169–70
Varro 48–9, 55, 62, 83, 85, 87, 106, 117, 138
Velleius Paterculus 54, 150
Venantius Fortunatus 193 n. 42
Venus 47, 72, 77, 78, 79, 89, 95, 102, 110–11, 122, 125–6, 141–6, 152–3
Vergil 5, 5–6, 11–12, 12–13, 26–8, 28–9, 31–2, 52–3, 56–9, 59–60, 64, 69, 71–2, 89, 93–4, 123–6, 126, 128–30, 133, 144, 144–5, 146–7, 152, 166, 167–70, 174, 181–2
Vespasian 4, 19, 19–20, 37–8
    See also Flavian emperors
Vibius Sequester 25, 55

Vibius Virrius 94, 97
Vulcan 78
Vulturnus 84

Waltharius 58
Wright, Joseph, of Derby 189 n. 41

Xanthippus 76, 81, 83–4, 153–4
Xerxes 37–8

Year of the Four Emperors 4, 5, 11–12, 19, 52–3, 74, 141, 152, 152–3, 154, 160–1, 162–3, 174–5

Zama, battle of 6, 43, 44–5, 88–9, 102–3, 107, 117–18, 138, 139, 148–9, 152–3, 175–81
Zosimus 176

Lightning Source UK Ltd.
Milton Keynes UK
UKHW022345170722
405998UK00003B/82